Cyber Law in Bangladesh

Cyber Law in Bangladesh

Second Edition

Mohammad Ershadul Karim

This book was originally published as a monograph in the International Encyclopaedia of Laws/Cyber Law.

Founding Editor: Roger Blanpain
General Editor: Frank Hendrickx
Volume Editors: Jos Dumortier, Pieter Gryffroy, Ruben Roex & Yung Shin Van Der Sype

Wolters Kluwer

Published by:
Kluwer Law International B.V.
PO Box 316
2400 AH Alphen aan den Rijn
The Netherlands
E-mail: lrs-sales@wolterskluwer.com
Website: www.wolterskluwer.com/en/solutions/kluwerlawinternational

Sold and distributed by:
Wolters Kluwer Legal & Regulatory U.S.
7201 McKinney Circle
Frederick, MD 21704
United States of America
E-mail: customer.service@wolterskluwer.com

ISBN 978-94-035-4540-0

e-Book: ISBN 978-94-035-4550-9
web-PDF: ISBN 978-94-035-4560-8

The Author

Mohammad Ershadul Karim, LLB (Hons.), LLM (University of Dhaka), PhD in Nanotechnology Law and Policy (University of Malaya) is a Senior Lecturer at the Faculty of Law, Universiti Malaya, Malaysia and is the Director of Centre for Law and Ethics in Science and Technology and also a Research Fellow of the Universiti Malaya Malaysian Centre of Regulatory Studies of the same Faculty. Dr Karim has been teaching Research Methodology, ICT Law, and Privacy and Personal Data Protection Law and has widely published in peer-reviewed journals and presented papers in a number of national and international conferences in his areas of interest, i.e., 'legal and regulatory aspects of nanotechnology', 'emerging technological applications and relevant legal issues', 'privacy and data protection law', 'human right to health', 'legal research' and 'renewable energy law', etc.

The second edition of his co-authored book on 'Personal Data Protection Law in Asia' published by Thomson and Reuters, Hong Kong was released in December 2017. He has written chapters on the legal system of Afghanistan, Bangladesh, Bhutan, Iran, Nepal, Maldives and Myanmar in GlobaLex, New York University, United States (US). He has also developed the Research Guide on Nanotechnology Law and Policy and South Asian Association for Regional Cooperation (SAARC) for the same database. His contribution on 'Nanotechnology and International Environmental Law' was included in a book as a chapter published by the Royal Society of Chemistry, the United Kingdom (UK) in November 2016. His contributions on 'Legal Issues in Polymer Nanocomposite', 'Functionalised Nanomaterials: Selected Legal and Regulatory Issues' and 'Functionalised Nanomaterials: Selected Occupational Health and Safety Concerns' were published as book chapters by Elsevier Inc, and 'Biosensors: Ethical, Regulatory, and Legal Issues' was published as a part of Springer Nature's Handbook of Cell Biosensors.

Dr Karim has been managing the National Chapter on Bangladesh for the Yearbook of International Environmental Law published by Oxford University, UK, since 2013. As an enlisted lawyer with Bangladesh Bar Council, having the qualifications to practice before Bangladesh Supreme Court, Dr Karim was instrumental in developing the Bangladesh Code, a collection of thirty-eight volumes containing all existing Acts of Parliament, Ordinances and President's Orders in force in Bangladesh between 1836–2006. He was also a member of the translation team of the Bangladesh Code.

The Author

Besides, Dr Karim served as the Web Administrator and Editor of the first-ever online case law database of Bangladesh, Chancery Law Chronicles (www.clcbd.org) for six years.

Dr Karim has been consulted by different national and international organizations including Japan Government's Patent Office through Kyoto Comparative Law Center, United Nations Development Program, United Nations Women, World Intellectual Property Organization, World Bank Group, European Union, Canadian International Development Agency, Japan International Cooperative Agency, Consumer International, Prime Minister's Office of the Government of Malaysia and Ministry of Justice, Abu Dhabi.

Table of Contents

Table of Contents

List of Abbreviations

3G	Global Growth Generation
A2I	Access to Information
AD	Appellate Division
ADNDRC	Asian Domain Name Dispute Resolution Centre
ADR	Alternative Dispute Resolution
AmEx	American Express
AMTOB	Association of Mobile Telecom Operators of Bangladesh
ANS	Access Network Service
APEC	Asia-Pacific Economic Cooperation
ASEAN	Association of Southeast Asian Nations
ATM	Automated Teller Machines
B2B	Business-to-Business
B2C	Business-to-Consumer
B2G	Business-to-Government
BACCO	Bangladesh Association of Call Center and Outsourcing
BACH	Bangladesh Automated Clearing House
BACPS	Bangladesh Automated Cheque Processing System
BASIS	Bangladesh Association of Software Industries and Services
BB	Bangladesh Bank
BBS	Bangladesh Bureau of Statistics
BCC	Bangladesh Computer Council
BCoC	Bangladesh Competition Commission
BCS	Bangladesh Computer Samity
BdOSN	Bangladesh Open Source Network
BEFTN	Bangladesh Electronic Funds Transfer Network
BGD e-GOV CIRT	Bangladesh e-Government Computer Incident Response Team
BIAC	Bangladesh International Arbitration Centre
BIDA	Bangladesh Investment Development Authority
BLC	Bangladesh Law Chronicles

List of Abbreviations

BLD	Bangladesh Legal Decisions
BNP	Bangladesh Nationalist Party
BPO	Bangladesh Post Office
BPSSR	Bangladesh Payment and Settlement Systems Regulations
BSCCL	Bangladesh Submarine Cable Company Limited
BSEC	Bangladesh Securities and Exchange Commission
BSTI	Bangladesh Standards and Testing Institution
BTCL	Bangladesh Telecommunications Company Limited
BTL	Bangladesh Telecom (Pvt) Ltd.
BTRC	Bangladesh Telecommunication Regulatory Commission
BTS	Base Transceiver Station
BTTB	Bangladesh Telegraph and Telephone Board
BTV	Bangladesh Television
BUET	Bangladesh University of Engineering and Technology
BWA	Broadband Wireless Access
C2C	Consumer-to-Consumer
CA	Certifying Authority
CCA	Controller of Certifying Authorities
CCDS	Citizen Core Data Structure
CCTV	Closed-Circuit Television
CDMA	Code Division Multiple Access
CERT	Computer Emergency Response Team
CID	Criminal Investigation Department
CII	Critical Information Infrastructures
CIRT	Computer Incident Response Team
CLC	Chancery Law Chronicles
CPS	Certificate of Practice Statement
CR	Coordination Request
CRC	Convention on the Rights of the Child
CRPD	Convention on the Rights of Persons with Disabilities
CTC	Cyber Training Center
DDoS	Distributed Denial of Service
DLR	Dhaka Law Reports
DNS	Domain Name System
EAGLE	Emerging and Growth Leading Economies
e-CAB	Electronic Commerce Association of Bangladesh
EFT	Electronic Fund Transfer
e-GP	Electronic Government Procurement

eIDAS	Electronic Identification and Trust Services for Electronic Transactions
EPB	Export Promotion Bureau of Bangladesh
EU	European Union
FBCCI	Federation of Bangladesh Chambers of Commerce and Industries
FDI	Foreign Direct Investment
FICSD	Financial Integrity & Customer Services Department
FIR	First Information Report
FY	Financial Year
GCA	Global Cybersecurity Agenda
GCSCC	Global Cyber Security Capacity Centre
GDP	Gross Domestic Product
GDPR	General Data Protection Regulation
GMPCS	Global Mobile Personal Communication by Satellite
GNI	Gross National Income
GoBISM	Government of Bangladesh Information Security Manual
GPO	General Post Office
GSM	Global System for Mobile Communications
gTLDs	Generic Top-Level Domains
HCD	High Court Division
IANA	Internet Assigned Numbers Authority
IBFT	Internet Banking Fund Transfer
ICANN	Internet Corporation for Assigned Names and Numbers
ICCPR	International Covenant on Civil and Political Rights
ICESCR	International Covenant on Economic Social and Cultural Rights
ICT	Information and Communication Technology
ICX	Interconnection Exchange
IDN	International Domain Name
IEC	International Electrotechnical Commission
IEX	Internet Exchange Services
IGW	International Gateway
IIG	International Internet Gateway
ILDTS	International Long Distance Telecommunication Services
IMEI	International Mobile Equipment Identity
IoT	Internet of Things
IP	Internet Protocol
IPRs	Intellectual Property Rights
ISO	International Organization for Standardization

List of Abbreviations

ISP	Internet Service Provider
ISPAB	Internet Service Providers Association Bangladesh
IT	Information Technology
ITC	International Terrestrial Cable
ITES	IT Enabled Service
ITU	International Telecommunication Union
JPO	Japan Patent Office
KOICA	Korean International Cooperation Agency
LAN	Local Area Network
LDC	Least Developed Country
MAN	Metropolitan Area Network
MFA	Microcredit Regulatory Authority
MFS	Mobile Financial Services
MLR	Mainstream Law Reports
MNOs	Mobile Network Operators
MNP	Mobile Number Portability
MoA	Memorandum of Association
MoI	Ministry of Industries
MoPT	Ministry of Post and Telecommunication
MoU	Memorandum of Understanding
MRP	Maximum Retail Price
NBFI	Non-Bank Financial Institution
NBR	National Board of Revenue
NDC	National Data Center
NEA	National Enterprise Architecture
NEIR	National Equipment Identity Register
NGO	Non-Governmental Organization
NID	National Identity Card
NIX	National Internet Exchange
NMC	National Monitoring Center
NPSB	National Payment Switch Bangladesh
NTMC	National Telecommunication Monitoring Center
NTTN	Nationwide Telecommunication Transmission Network
OECD	Organisation for Economic Co-operation and Development
OIC-CERT	Organisation of Islamic Cooperation- Computer Emergency Response Team
OISF	Office Information and Service Framework
PCSIR	Pakistan Council of Scientific and Industrial Research
PKI	Public Key Infrastructure

POS	Point of Sales
PRA	Personal Retail Account
PSO	Payment System Operator
PSP	Payment Service Provider
PSTN	Public Switched Telephone Network
QoS	Quality of Service
R&D	Research and Development
RMG	Readymade Garments
SCOB	Supreme Court Online Bulletin
SEA-ME-WE-4	Southeast Asia-Middle East-Western Europe International Consortium Submarine Cable
SID	Statistics and Informatics Division
SingTel	Singapore Telecommunications Limited
SME	Small and Medium Enterprises
SMP	Significant Market Power
SPARRSO	Space Research and Remote Sensing Organization
SPI	Space Partnership International
sq	Square
SSL	Secure Sockets Layer
SVRS	Sample Vital Registration System
TLS	Transport Layer Security
TRIPS	Trade-Related Aspects of Intellectual Property Rights
UBID	Unique Business Identification Number
UDCs	Union Digital Centers
UDHR	Universal Declaration of Human Rights
UDRP	Uniform Domain Name Dispute Resolution Policy
UN	United Nations
UNCITRAL	United Nations Commission on International Trade Law
UNCTAD	United Nations Conference on Trade and Development
UNDP	United Nations Development Program
UNESCO	United Nations Educational, Scientific and Cultural Organization
UNGCP	United Nations Guidelines for Consumer Protection
UNODC	United Nations Office on Drugs and Crime
URS	Uniform Rapid Suspension System
USD	United States Dollar
VAS	Value Added Services
VAT	Value Added Tax
VoIP	Voice over Internet Protocol

List of Abbreviations

VPN	Virtual Private Network
VSAT	Very Small Aperture Terminal
WAN	Wide Area Network
WEF	World Economic Forum
WiMAX	Worldwide Interoperability for Microwave Access
WIPO	World Intellectual Property Organization
WSIS	World Summit on Information Society
WTO	World Trade Organization

General Introduction

Chapter 1. General Background of the Country

§1. Geography

1. Bangladesh, literally the land of Bangla language speaking people and officially the People's Republic of Bangladesh,[1] is situated in the north-eastern part of South Asia and covers an area of 147,570 sq. km or 56,977 sq. mi. The country is located between 20° 34' and 26° 38' north latitudes and between 88° 01' and 92° 41' east longitudes. The Bengal Delta, consisting of two Himalayan rivers, i.e., the Ganges and the Brahmaputra and one non-Himalayan river, i.e., the Meghna, is one of the largest deltas in the world.

2. Being the youngest nation-state of South Asia, it is almost entirely surrounded by India, except for a short south-eastern frontier with Myanmar and a southern coastline on the Bay of Bengal. Even before 2015, Bangladesh used to have some of the most perplexing territories on the planet due to the presence of first-order as well as even second-order enclaves and exclaves with India in the northern region. Bangladesh and India used to share the most enclaves in the entire world, and Dahala Khagrabari was the only third-order enclave in the world. However, on 31 July 2015, the governments of these two countries, on the basis of the Land Boundary Agreement, 1974 and Protocol of 2011, physically exchanged 51 former Bangladeshi enclaves in India and 111 former Indian enclaves in Bangladesh.[2]

3. Even though the share of manufacturing and service industries have been growing in recent years in the economy of the country, Bangladesh is mainly known as an agricultural country. Bangladesh is a riverine country with 310 rivers, including tributaries crisscrossing, and these rivers have been playing an influential role in the economic development and progress of the country. The country shares fifty-seven transboundary rivers where fifty-four rivers enter the country from India and three from Myanmar.

1. Article 1, the Constitution of the People's Republic of Bangladesh, 1972.
2. Ministry of External Affairs, Government of India, Exchange of enclaves between India and Bangladesh, 20 Nov. 2015, https://www.mea.gov.in/press-releases.htm?dtl/26048/Exchange_of_enclaves_between_India_and_Bangladesh.

4. Though the country faces natural disasters, e.g., floods and cyclones very frequently, there are some positive sides of the floods since they carry forward silt to make the soil of the country very fertile. The country is a plain land except for some hilly areas in the Myanmar border area. The Padma is the longest river in the country whereas the Meghna is the widest river, where at one point, the river is 12 km wide. Other principal rivers are the Jamuna, the Brahmaputra, the Surma, and the Karnaphuli. Only around 11% area of land is covered by forest. With only 1,052 m (3,451 feet), Saka Haphong in the south-eastern Mowdok Range is the highest peak in the country. On a sunny day with a clear sky just before the winter season (in November), people can enjoy the splendour of the world's third-highest mountain peak of Himalaya, Kanchenjunga from the northern district of Thakurgaon and Panchagarh.

§2. Climate

5. The geographic location of the country has impacts on its climate. Bangladesh has a subtropical monsoon climate characterized by wide seasonal variations in rainfall, high temperatures, and humidity. The country used to have six seasons in a year, i.e., summer, rainy, autumn, late autumn, winter, and spring. That is why the country was known as the 'country of six seasons'. As a result, the inhabitants could experience a new season every two months. Unfortunately, with the passage of time, Bangladesh has become one of the worst victims of global warming and climate change. Because of the effects and consequences of climate change, one may now notice only three distinct seasons, i.e., summer (March to June); rainy season (June to October); and winter (October to March).

6. Between February and March, the weather is like that of spring. During the summer, one may experience scorching heat. On 23 April 2018, the temperature in Dhaka was recorded at 40.2°C, the highest in five decades. The highest temperature ever recorded in Bangladesh was in Rajshahi on 18 May 1972, when the temperature was 45.1°C. During the rainy season in 2017, nearly 8,904 mm of rain was recorded in the first three weeks. Winter is usually treated by the countrymen as the most favourite season due to the availability of abundant fresh vegetables, freshwater fishes and traditional foods. In January 2018, the lowest temperature in the history of the country, i.e., 2.6°C was recorded in Tetulia, Panchagarh. Whilst the inhabitants of Dhaka, the capital of the country, are generally spared from the shivering cold of winter, marginalized and poverty-stricken people of the northern side of the country would suffer severe causalities alongside agricultural and infrastructural damages.

§3. HISTORY

7. The written history of present Bangladesh can be traced back to the fourth century AD when the then Bengal came under the control of the Gupta Empire.[3] The Moguls ruled the country between the thirteenth to the eighteenth century, and then the British took over the rule in 1757 AD. During that time, the present Indian states of Bihar and Orissa were also a part of the Bengal Presidency and were governed from Kolkata. During this period, due to the geographic location, the territory comprising of present-day Bangladesh and Assam was known as East Bengal, and the area comprising of the present Indian states of West Bengal, Bihar and Orissa was known as West Bengal. It was difficult for the British administrators to govern such a huge territory properly. Moreover, East Bengal was dominated by the Muslims, whereas the Hindus were a majority in West Bengal. The British administrators realized that the independence and nationalist movement had started in this part, and so, they applied the 'divide and rule' policy. As a consequence, the then Viceroy of India, Lord Curzon announced the decision of the partition of Bengal in July 1905. Masses of people, irrespective of class and religion, protested against this decision of partition and started movements to motivate people to use locally produced products and boycott British goods. Even with such protests, though mostly isolated and unorganized, the British rulers administered the Indo-Pak subcontinent until 1947 AD.

8. In 1947 AD, the independent states of Pakistan and India were created on the basis of religion: the Muslim majority people decided to form their country as Pakistan, while the Hindu majority people formed their country as India. The present territory of Bangladesh then became a part of Pakistan and was known as the province of 'East Pakistan' in united Pakistan. Since during the British rule, present Bangladesh was a part of India, and subsequently, it was part of Pakistan till 1971; therefore, many events of historical importance which are covered in this monograph, e.g., the introduction of telegraph and telephone, etc. will be identical with that of the history of India and Pakistan. Bangladesh emerged on 26 March 1971 as an independent country on the world's map following a war of liberation for nine months with victory achieved on 16 December 1971.[4]

9. In *Anwar Hossain Manju v. Govt. of Bangladesh & Ors* 16 BLT (HCD) 86, the birth of Bangladesh was consciously depicted in the following manner:

> The people of undivided India, after a very long arduous and tortuous political movements, got their independence from the British yoke in 1947 by the Indian Independence Act, 1947 and the dominions of India and Pakistan emerged. India got its Constitution in 1949 and became a Republic in 1950. The political history of Pakistan was not that happy. It got its first Constitution in 1956,

3. History, Banglapedia, http://en.banglapedia.org/index.php?title=History.
4. For authoritative discussions on the history of the country, *see*, Riaz, A., *Bangladesh: A Political History since Independence* (2016); Srinath, R., *A Global History of the Creation of Bangladesh* (2013).

only to be ditched unceremoniously in 1958. Another Constitution was made in 1962 but again Field Martial (self appointed) Ayub Khan, in violation of the Constitution, handed over the office of President to General Yahia Khan in 1969. A general election was held in 1970, the first as well as the last in the erstwhile Pakistan but when the army President refused to convene the Constituent Assembly, rather, let loose a genocide in the then East Pakistan, independence of Bangladesh was proclaimed on the night following 25th March, 1971, and the people of Bangladesh was proclaimed through a historic war of liberation against the Pakistan army and its murderous local vassals, achieved its independence at a cost of three million martyrs on the 16th day of December, 1971.

10. Being an agro-based region, the nation's formal scientific research lineage may be traced back to 1921 with the establishment of the University of Dhaka. Later on, the then British administrators established the 'Council of Scientific and Industrial Research' in India under the Societies Registration Act, 1860 (Act No. XXI of 1860) in 1942. Subsequently, after the partition in 1947, the 'Pakistan Council of Scientific and Industrial Research (PCSIR)' was created in 1953. The PCSIR established its first eastern regional laboratories in the then Dhaka, Chittagong and Rajshahi in 1955, 1965 and 1967 respectively. During this time, the principal science and technology initiatives were mainly directed towards agriculture production and water management to address various immediate needs of this agro-centric region.

11. At the time of independence in 1971, the country inherited six policymaking and executing agencies for scientific research and development (R&D). These were: (a) Bangladesh Agricultural Research Council, (b) Bangladesh Atomic Energy Commission, (c) Bangladesh Council of Scientific and Industrial Research, (d) Bangladesh Medical Research Council, (e) Council for Works and Housing, and (f) Irrigation, Drainage and Flood Control Research Council.[5] After independence, the country faced a serious financial crisis, political turmoil and various other challenges to develop infrastructure and in nation-building. As a result, science and technology research did not get enough and desirable attention as it should have received. A high-profile National Committee on Science and Technology, now known as National Council on Science and Technology, was only formed on 16 May 1983, as the sole advisory body on science and technology. This Committee drafted a National Science and Technology Policy which was formally approved by the government in 1986.[6]

---

5. Science and Technology, Banglapedia, http://en.banglapedia.org/index.php?title=Science_and_Technology.
6. The National Science and Technology Policy, 2011 was subsequently reviewed and adopted in 2011.

§4. Demographic and Cultural Composition

12. The country is densely populated, and more than 1,000 persons live in Bangladesh per square kilometre. Dhaka (formally spelt as 'Dacca' till 1982) is the capital of the country, and Chattogram (previously 'Chittagong') is dubbed as the commercial capital of the country. With a glorious history of more than four centuries, Dhaka is one of the most densely populated megacities in the world.

13. Bangladesh has come a long way by making remarkable strides in reducing poverty. This is thanks to its diversified and strong growth of the economy, which helps to alleviate poverty in a slow but sustainable manner. According to the Household Income Expenditure Survey (2016–2017), the poverty reduction pace has slowed down and still, almost 25% of the population lives below the poverty line.

14. The overall national poverty rate has fallen for both the urban and rural areas, although the pace is different. In urban areas, the rate is slower than that of rural areas. It is important to share here that 90% of poverty reduction transpires in rural areas, and most of this reduction in poverty is contributed by the employment in manufacturing industries or service sectors. The manufacturing sector, to be specific, the RMG industry itself, caters to reducing 85% of the poverty in the urban areas. It is obvious that in urban areas, poverty reduction is led by welfare gains from employment opportunities in different industries. The demographic and social indicators of the country are projected in Table 1.

Table 1 Demographic and Social Indicators

Indicators	*Data*
Total Population	158.9 million
Male	79.6 million
Female	74.5 million
Growth rate	1.37
Total fertility rate (15–49 years)	2.10
Life expectancy at birth	70.9 years
Male	69.4 years
Female	72.0 years
Literacy rate of population (7+ years)	63.6

Source: Bangladesh Bureau of Statistics, 2017.[7]

15. Bangladesh is the seventh most populous country in the world. Islam is the state religion of the Republic; nevertheless, it is the constitutional responsibility of

7. *Ibid.*

the State to ensure equal status and right in the practice of religious rituals of other religions such as Hindu, Buddhist, Christian.[8] According to the latest Bangladesh Demographic and Health Survey, 2014, Bangladesh is primarily an Islamic country where almost 90% of people are Muslims, whereas 9% are Hindus and other religions constitute the remaining 1%.[9]

16. Bangladesh has the highest number of youths, and in the recent report published by the WEF, based on key areas, i.e., education, economic participation, health, and political empowerment, Bangladesh ranked second as the most gender-equal country in Asia and the top country among the South Asian nations. The demography of the country is diversified with the presence of a good number of indigenous communities.

17. The official language of the country is Bangla,[10] and with a significant number of speakers from the Indian state of West Bengal and Assam, this is the sixth most-spoken language in the world. It is the only language in the world for which some students sacrificed their lives in 1952 when the then Pakistan leaders wanted to declare and impose Urdu as the only state language of the country. In 1999, the United Nations Educational, Scientific and Cultural Organization (UNESCO) recognized the tragic event and declared 21 February every year as the 'International Mother Language Day' to commemorate the 'language martyr'.

18. Adoption of measures to conserve the cultural traditions and heritage of the people, so as to foster and improve the national language, literature and the arts that all sections of the people are offered the opportunity to contribute towards and to participate in the enrichment of the national culture, is an obligation of the state.[11]

19. Baul songs, the traditional art of Jamdani (cloth) and Shital Pati (mat) weaving, Mangal Shobhajatra, a festival to celebrate Pahela Baishakh (the first day of Baishakh, the first month of Bangla new year) on 14 April every year, organized by the students and teachers of Dhaka University's Faculty of Fine Art since 1989 are listed on the UNESCO Representative List of the Intangible Cultural Heritage of Humanity. Historic Sixty Dome Mosque of Bagerhat, ruins of the Buddhist Vihara at Paharpur, and the Sundarbans, one of the largest mangrove forests in the world, are on the list of UNESCO World Heritage. Mahasthangarh and its environs,

---

8. Article 2A, the Constitution of the People's Republic of Bangladesh, 1972. This Article 2A was substituted by s. 4 of the Constitution (Fifteenth Amendment) Act, 2011 (Act XIV of 2011).

   It may be relevant to share here that the issue of state religion was first inserted in the Constitution through the Eighth Amendment in 1988. The Eighth Amendment to the Constitution introduced Islam as the state religion of the country. It is claimed that this 'has caused substantial damage to the secular character of the Constitution of Bangladesh putting the members of the minority communities i.e., Hindus, Christians and Buddhists, in an unequal position in relation to the Muslim' and has tampered the basic structure of the Constitution. *See*, Shah Alam, *The State-Religion Amendment to the Constitution of Bangladesh: A Critique*, *Verfassung und Recht in Übersee*/Law and Politics in Africa, Asia and Latin America, 209–225(1991).
9. Bangladesh Demographic and Health Survey, 2014, March 2016, p. 1.
10. Article 3, the Constitution of the People's Republic of Bangladesh, 1972.
11. Article 23, the Constitution of the People's Republic of Bangladesh, 1972.

Lalmai-Mainamati Group of monuments, Lalbagh Fort, Holud Vihara, Jaggadala Vihara, are the sites on the tentative list of UNESCO World Heritage. The second longest and the longest unbroken sea beach in the World is situated in Cox's Bazar, in the south of the country. Another 18 km long and 3 km wide beach at Kuakata, Patuakhali, is famous for enjoying an unobstructed view of both the sunrise and the sunset every day over the Bay of Bengal.

§5. Population and Vital Statistics

20. As of January 2018, there are a total of 104.1 million voters that were listed in the electoral roll. Of them, 50.42% are male, and 49.58% are female voters. With an area of 147,570 sq. km and a population of about 166,280,712 (July 2014 est., The World Fact Book, CIA), the country has a very high population density at 1,033 persons per sq. km. The population data as per Sample Vital Registration System (SVRS), 2015 Report and the project population of the country are shared in Tables 2 and 3 respectively.

Table 2 Population Data as per SVRS, 2015 Report (in Million)

	1 July 2013	*1 July 2014*	*1 July 2015*
Total	154.7	156.8	158.9
Male	78.3	78.6	79.6
Female	76.4	78.2	79.3
Urban	42.6	44.1	–
Rural	112.1	112.7	–
Annual Growth Rate	1.37	1.37	1.37
Sex ratio (males per 100 females)	102.6	100.5	100.3
Density (per sq. km)	1,049	1,063	1,077
Life expectancy at birth: Both sex	70.4	70.7	70.9
Male	68.8	69.1	69.4
Female	71.2	71.6	72.0

Source: Statistical Pocket Book, Bangladesh, 2016.[12]

12. Bangladesh Bureau of Statistics, SID, Ministry of Planning.

Table 3 Projected Population (Million)

	July 2011	*July 2015*	*July 2019*
Total	151.41	158.96	167.37
Male	77.85	81.63	85.86
Female	73.56	77.33	81.51
Sex ratio: (males per 100 females)	106.00	106.00	105.34

Source: Statistical Pocket Book, Bangladesh, 2016.[13]

§6. Economy

21. During the Pakistan period, in the present Bangladesh, which was known as East Pakistan, 64% of the province could be cultivated, and about 82% of the workforce was employed in the agriculture sector. This part used to produce 76% of the raw jute of the world and being a fish-producing area due to the presence of a huge number of water bodies, this part used to export fish to India. Dacca, as it was spelt then, was the home of famous Dacca muslins[14] and a land of cottage industries, e.g., handloom, conch shell, brass, and bell-metal industries, mat making and bamboo and cane works. In 1962, there were twenty-two textile mills, seven sugar factories, eighteen match factories, seven glassworks, 178 hosiery factories, a paper mill, fourteen jute mills, twenty-eight aluminium works, a cement factory, a newsprint factory, a fertilizer factory, a shipyard and a dockyard.[15]

22. At the time of independence in 1971, the country was portrayed as the 'bottomless basket' or 'international basket case' by some group of people who were sceptical about the consequences of independence of the country. After a mere five decades, the country can be seen as a 'basket full of opportunities, achievements and success stories'. The country has attained tremendous progress and success in various socio-economic sectors.

23. Since the 1990s, with the functioning of the country through the democratically elected government, the country has started to witness economic progress, which in the long run assisted the country to achieve four targets of the Millennium

13. *Ibid.*
14. For a concise history of Muslin of Dhaka, *see* Mohammad Ataul Karim & Mohammad Ershadul Karim, *Protection of 'Handicraft' as Geographical Indications under Municipal Law, TRIPS and BTAs vis-à-vis CETA: 'Bangladeshi Jamdani' as Case Study*, 7 Queen Mary J. Intell. Prop., 49–73 (2017). It is a matter of great pride that in 2016, Jamdani, a modern deviated version of Dhaka Muslin received the recognition by WIPO as the first-ever Geographic Indication product of Bangladesh.
15. Steinberg, S.H. (ed.), *The Statesman's Year-Book: Statistical and Historical Annual of the States of the World for the Year 1962*, 487 (1962).

Development Goals well ahead of time.[16] The country has set global examples in reducing early deaths of infants and child mortality, and women empowerment. Being a moderate Muslim country, Bangladesh has done much work to improve the status of women. Successive governments have invested heavily in education, especially for women and girls. Primary education is free and compulsory for everyone where the government provides free textbooks, both online and offline. The government also provides stipends and scholarships to the girls until the twelfth grade.

24. It is a matter of fact that even a few months ago, the country was considered as the largest least developed country (LDC) in the world in terms of skilled human resources, economic size and a high share of manufactures in total export, which reached 90.5% in 2013 when it was about only 26.2% for LDCs.[17] Even after being an LDC, the country reduced the extreme poverty level from 31.5% in 2010 to 24.3% in 2017. It is likely to be the first LDC ever to graduate to a lower-middle-income country based on all three criteria, i.e., per capita Gross National Income (GNI), Human Assets Index and Economic Vulnerability Index.[18]

25. Bangladesh has one of the fastest economic growth rates in the world in recent years, maintaining an economic growth rate of more than 6% for the previous seven consecutive years and more than 7% in 2018. The World Bank Group, in its latest report published in April 2019, predicted that Bangladesh would be one of the top five fastest-growing economies in the world with a 7.3% Gross Domestic Product (GDP) growth projection.

26. Undoubtedly, the telecommunication and information and communication technology (ICT) sector has been playing an instrumental role in the economic success of the country. From an agro-based and densely populated country having suffered the severe effects and consequences of the Liberation War in 1971, the economic progress of the country in recent times has made it a success story globally. Bangladesh joined the lower-middle-income country category on 1 July 2015 and will receive the status in 2024.[19] Already, the country has successfully fulfilled

---

16. In September 2000, the global leaders signed the United Nations Millennium Development Declaration at the United Nations Millennium Summit. The Declaration set eight ambitious but clear goals measurable targets to combat poverty, hunger, disease, illiteracy, environmental degradation and discrimination against women by 2015.
17. Kathuria, S. & Malouche, M.M., *Toward New Sources of Competitiveness in Bangladesh: Key Findings of the Diagnostic Trade Integration Study, Directions in Development,* xix (2016).
18. Md Jahurul Haque, Chairman of BTRC, Speech delivered at the ITU-BTRC Asia-Pacific Regulators' Roundtable 2018, 6–7 Aug. 2018, Dhaka, Bangladesh, https://www.itu.int/en/ITU-D/Regional-Presence/AsiaPacific/Pages/Events/2018/rr2018/home.aspx.
19. Based on per capita GNI, the World Bank classifies the world's economies into four income groups: (a) Low Income, (b) Lower-Middle Income, (c) Upper-Middle Income, and (d) High Income. Accordingly, the countries with less than USD 1,025 GNI is placed in the group of low income countries, the countries between USD 1,026–USD 3,995 GNI is placed in the category of lower-middle-income countries, the countries between USD 3,996–USD 12,375 GNI is placed in the category of upper-middle-income countries and countries with above USD 12,375 GNI are known as high-income countries.

all the criteria. The country is now working towards achieving its vision to become a middle-income country by its 50th Birthday, i.e., by the year 2021.

27. The recent economic success of Bangladesh has been recognized by various international bodies. Bangladesh was highlighted as the 'Next Eleven',[20] as a prospective country to join the Emerging and Growth Leading Economies (EAGLE)[21] and one of the Global Growth Generation (3G) countries.[22] Recently, in the platform of the World Economic Forum (WEF), the words 'aspiring "tiger" economy' and 'one of Asia's most remarkable and unexpected success stories in recent years' were used to highlight the economic success of the country.[23] HSBC Global Research predicted that the country would be the twenty-sixth largest economy in the world in 2030.[24]

28. In the recent Human Development Index of the United Nations Development Program (UNDP), Bangladesh ranked 133rd out of 189 countries. The position of Bangladesh in the competitiveness ranking has recently shown improvement too. Bangladesh's ranking in the WEF Global Competitiveness Index for 2017–2018 has improved by seven places to 99th among 137 countries. However, there are challenges too. The country has the second most pro-capitalist population, and as a result, it was placed at the bottom of the list of innovative countries in the Global Innovation Index, 2018 developed by the World Intellectual Property Organization (WIPO). As the country is being governed by democratic governments since 1991, it can be anticipated that the success of economic developments in recent times will reflect positively in these indexes in the future.

29. It is evident that the economy is gradually transforming from an agrarian to a strong industrial or resource-based economy. After Financial Year (FY) 2010, the industrial growth became faster; meanwhile, the growth in agriculture started to

---

20. Jim O'Neil, the Chairman of Goldman Sachs Asset Management, listed Bangladesh as one of the 'Next 11' with Egypt, Indonesia, Iran, South Korea, Mexico, Nigeria, Pakistan, the Philippines, Turkey, and Vietnam. These countries could potentially have a BRIC-like impact in rivalling the G7. *See* Sachs, Goldman, 2007. Brazil, Russia, India, China and South Africa (BRICs) and beyond. The Goldman Sachs Group/Global Economics Department, London; Sachs, Goldman, 2007. Global Economics Paper No: 153. The N-11m: More Than an Acronym, 28 Mar. 2007.
21. Spanish bank Banco Bilbao Vizcaya Argentaria introduced this idea in 2010 to describe the ten (EAGLE) countries that can generate 50% of the global economic growth between 2010–2020. Bangladesh was listed as one of the Nest countries with eleven other countries, i.e., Thailand, Nigeria, Poland, Colombia, South Africa, Malaysia, Vietnam, Pakistan, Argentina, Peru and Philippines who were expected to deliver 8% for world's incremental GDP in same time.
22. Citi Investment Research and Analysis in their Policy Insight published in 2011 has listed Bangladesh as one of the global growth generators, i.e., 3Gs. with China, Egypt, India, Indonesia, Iraq, Mongolia, Nigeria, Philippines, Sri Lanka and Vietnam due to their average real per capita GDP growth over the period 2010–2050 – 5% or higher at Purchasing Power Parity exchange rates. *See*, Buiter, W.H., & Rahbari, E., *Global Growth Generators: Moving Beyond Emerging Markets and BRICs, Centre for Economic Policy Research*, Policy Insight No. 55, April 2011.
23. Basu, K., *This Is What You Need to Know about Bangladesh's Remarkable Economic Rise* (24 Apr. 2018), https://www.weforum.org/agenda/2018/04/why-is-bangladesh-booming.
24. Henry, J., *The World in 2030* (28 Sep. 2018), https://enterprise.press/wp-content/uploads/2018/10/HSBC-The-World-in-2030-Report.pdf.

slow down. During 2011–2016, industry and agriculture output correspondingly increased annually by 9.5% and 3.4%. Because of this shift, both the economic growth from agriculture and the impact on reducing poverty from agriculture has lessened. At the same time, the service sector has shown a steady 6% growth from FY 2000 to 2016. This again exhibits that even the economy is no more sticking to agriculture rather shifting towards a more resource and knowledge-based economy, bit by bit.

30. According to the Quantum Index of Industrial Production data in FY17, a substantial growth contribution came from several large-scale industries which include the manufacture of other non-metallic mineral products (32.3%), pharmaceuticals (32.1%), textiles (21.2%) and leather, and related products (53.4%). The overall growth cracked double digits (10.2%) in FY17, which shows impressive sustainable growth in the industrial sector.[25]

31. It is also stipulated that FY18 and onwards, the pharmaceuticals, leather products and textiles sector will lead the economy forward. Another two key factors to the robust economic growth of Bangladesh are export and remittance; the former one has rebounded (raised by 7.4%), and the latter is on an impressive recovery stage (16.5% growth) in FY18. During the first two quarters of FY18, the ready-made garments (RMG) has contributed to export growth by 8.7%, and 56% of remittance income came from the Gulf region.[26]

32. It has already been shared that Bangladesh was primary and historically an agricultural country blessed with very fertile land. Utilization of the fertile land coupled with the dedication of the peasants enables the country to take pride in being the fourth-largest rice producer, the second-largest jute producer, the fourth-largest inland freshwater fish producer, the second-largest jackfruit producer, the seventh-largest mango producer, the eighth-largest guava producer and the tenth-largest tropical fruit producer in the world. However, the economy has been changing with the introduction of industries, manufacturing and service sectors. The country exports RMG, textiles, chemical fertilizers, pharmaceuticals, processed tea, cement, sugar and leather goods, etc. RMG, pharmaceuticals, and software are important export products. Bangladesh is the fifty-fourth largest export economy, the second-largest exporter of RMG since 2009 and the eighth-largest remittance earning country in the world. Even though there are concerns regarding the flawed democracy of the country, the apparent political stability of the country, which started with the resuming of democracy in 1990, has played an obvious instrumental role in the recent development of the country. Some of the economic indicators of Bangladesh are shared in Table 4.

25. The World Bank, Bangladesh Development Update: Building on Resilience, April 2018.
26. *Ibid.*

Table 4 Economic Indicators

Indicators	*Data*
GDP at current market price (in Tk)	17,329 billion
GDP at constant market price (in Tk)	8,835 billion
Per capita GDP in current market prices (in USD)	1,385
Per capita GNI at current market prices (in USD)	1,465
Growth rate at constant prices	7.11
Investment at current prices in Tk)	51.39 billion
Inflation rate (%), General	5.92
Poverty rate for April–June 2016	23.2
Extreme poverty rate for April–June 2016	12.9
Total number of establishments	7,818,565
Total persons engaged	24,500,850
Total export (Million in TK)	3,003,837
Total import (Million in TK)	4,712,495
Share of RMG in national export	89.10
Economically active population (15+)	62.1 million
Employed population (15+)	59.5 million
Unemployed population	2.6 million

Source: Bangladesh Bureau of Statistics, 2017.[27]

§7. Political System

33. There is an elected single-chamber Parliament in Bangladesh, known as Bangladesh Jatiya Sangsad (House of the Nation), which is primarily responsible for making laws.[28] Though Westminster Parliamentary form of government is now followed, after the independence in 1971, in the various junctures of history, the country had a Presidential form of government as well. The country introduced the concept of a non-party caretaker government to run the national election through the

27. Bangladesh Bureau of Statistics (BBS), Statistics and Informatics Division (SID), Ministry of Planning, Government of Bangladesh.
28. Article 65, the Constitution of the People's Republic of Bangladesh, 1972. In *Mofizur Rahman Khan v. Govt. of Bangladesh* (1982) 34 DLR (AD) 321, it was held that the legislature has power of retrospective legislation and retrospective validation of invalid law. Parliament is the supreme legislative authority subject to the constitutional limitations – One of the attributes of legislative supremacy is its power to pass any law on any subject, not prohibited by the Constitution, both prospectively and retrospectively. It can equally validate, subject to Constitution, any earlier law found invalid either prospectively or retrospectively.

Thirteen Amendment to the Constitution and used this system in the national elections held between 1990 to 2008. In 2011, this system of non-party caretaker government was overturned following the decision of the Bangladesh Supreme Court.[29] Since 1991, when the country has restored democratic rule, the President is the head of the State[30] and holds a mere ornamental position, whereas the Prime Minister is the head of the government exercising the real power in running the day-to-day activities in state functioning.

34. There are fifty-eight Ministries and Divisions and 353 Departments under these Ministries. These Ministries and Departments play an important role in implementing their responsibilities within their mandated areas. 'Rules of Business',[31] 'Allocation of Business'[32] and 'Bangladesh Secretariat Instructions' formulated under the 'Rules of Business'[33] are important government policy documents which specify precisely the functions and responsibilities of different Ministries, Divisions and Departments. The 'Warrant of Precedence'[34] sets out the relative precedence or priority in terms of ranks of important officeholders belonging to the three organs of the state, i.e., executive, legislative and judiciary. This warrant or the order is generally used for the invitation of officeholders in important official functions including their seating arrangements, waiting in time to receive and see off, e.g., Very Important Persons such as the President and the Prime Minister when they go abroad and also receive their counterparts within the country.[35]

35. The country is divided into eight administrative divisions in Dhaka, Chattogram, Rajshahi, Khulna, Rangpur, Cumilla (previously 'Comilla'), Barishal, and Sylhet. These Divisions are divided into sixty-four Districts, 492 Upazilas, 4,571 Unions, 19 City Corporations and 330 Pourashavas.[36]

§8. Legal System and Sources of Law

36. In order to understand different legal issues covered under this monograph, it will be beneficial to have some background discussion on the legal system of the country.[37] The legal system of Bangladesh is influenced by the English common law legal system which was instilled during the British colonial regime between

29. *Abdul Mannan Khan v. Bangladesh* (2012) 64 DLR (AD) 169.
30. Article 48(2), the Constitution of the People's Republic of Bangladesh, 1972.
31. The Rules of Business, 1996.
32. The Allocation of Business among the Different Ministries and Divisions, 1996.
33. The first Secretariat Instructions was issued in 1976 under the Rules of Business, 1975 and was translated in Bangla in 1978. It was updated in 2008 and finally in 2014.
34. The Warrant of Precedence, 1986. The AD of the Supreme Court addressed various aspects of the Warrant of Precedence. *See, Bangladesh v. Md. Ataur Rahman & ors.* 9 SCOB [2017] AD 1.
35. Warrant of Precedence, Banglapedia, http://en.banglapedia.org/index.php?title=Warrant_of_Precedence.
36. Bangladesh Bureau of Statistics, Ministry of Planning, Bangladesh Statistics, 2019.
37. For a detail discussion on the historical background of the legal system of Bangladesh, *See, Bangladesh, represented by the Secretary, Ministry of Law, Justice and Parliamentary Affairs and others v. Bangladesh Legal Aid and Services Trust (BLAST)*, 8 SCOB [2016] AD 1.

1757–1947. However, religious laws are followed in case of personal and family disputes. Thus, family matters relating to the believers of different religions as practised in the country such as Islam, Hinduism, Christianity and Buddhism are mainly dealt with personal laws derived from the respective religious texts.

37. The Constitution of the People's Republic of Bangladesh, 1972 is the supreme law of the Republic, and it is not constitutionally possible to enact any law inconsistent with the provisions of the Constitution. If any law is found inconsistent with the provisions of the Constitution that other law shall, to the extent of the inconsistency, be void.[38] Being a country predominantly influenced by the English common law legal system, the Supreme Court of Bangladesh consisting of the Appellate Division (AD) and High Court Division (HCD), performs the duty to interpret the Constitution and other laws of the land.[39]

38. The Constitution of Bangladesh, 1972 was amended in 2012 and through the Constitution (Fifteen Amendment) Act, 2011 (Act No. XIV of 2011) it was included that:

> The historical speech delivered by Bangabandhu Sheikh Mujibur Rahman, the Father of the Nation, in the Racecourse Maidan, Dhaka on the 7th day of March, 1971, the telegram of the Declaration of Independence of Bangladesh made by Bangabandhu Sheikh Mujibur Rahman, the Father of the Nation on the 26th day of March, 1971 and the Proclamation of Independence of the Mujibnagar Government on the 10th day of April, 1971 are the historical speech and instruments of the independence and the struggle of freedom of Bangladesh.[40]

39. Before the discussion on the regulation of the ICT market in Bangladesh and for a better understanding, a discussion on some basic features of the legal system of the country is desirable. Otherwise, for an outsider, some of the words such as 'order' and 'regulation', etc. as frequently used in the domestic legal arena, may create confusion.[41]

40. Article 152 of the Constitution of Bangladesh, 1972, as the Supreme Law of the Land, defines 'law' as any 'Act, ordinance, order, rule, regulation, bye law (by-law), notification or other legal instrument, and any custom or usage, having the force of law in Bangladesh'. In this definition, the word 'Act' means the Act of Parliament,[42] 'Ordinance' denotes the Ordinances promulgated by the President of

38. Articles 7(2) & 26(2), the Constitution of the People's Republic of Bangladesh, 1972.
39. Articles 103(2)(a) & 110, the Constitution of the People's Republic of Bangladesh, 1972.
40. Article 150(2), the Constitution of the People's Republic of Bangladesh, 1972.
41. For an updated overview of Bangladesh legal system, *see*, Karim, E., *UPDATE: The Legal System of the Peoples' Republic of Bangladesh* (July/August 2018), http://www.nyulawglobal.org/globalex/Bangladesh1.html.
42. There are more than 1,000 Acts of Parliament in force in the country. Hardbound copy of Bangladesh Code contains a total of 956 Acts, Ordinances and President's Orders enacted between September 1836 to January 2007. Part V, Ch. II (Arts 80–92) of the Constitution of Bangladesh, 1972

Bangladesh when the Parliament stands dissolved, or the Parliament is not in session,[43] and 'Order' means Presidential Orders made after the independence of the country in 1972 and 1973. Along with these Presidential Orders, there are at least four Acting President's Orders made during and after the liberation war in 1971, which will also be included in the definition of the word 'Order'.[44] These 'Orders' must not be confused with the orders pronounced by the court of laws,[45] statutory orders[46] and 'Orders' as included in the Code of Civil Procedure, where the word 'Order' is apparently used to mean various Chapters of the Schedules.

41. The Ordinances promulgated as per Article 93 of the Constitution of Bangladesh, 1972 deserve special mention in the legal history of Bangladesh as many such Ordinances were promulgated during the two martial law regimes from 15 August 1975 to 9 April 1979 and 24 March 1982 to 11 November 1986. These Ordinances were in force for more than twenty-five years. Subsequently, the Constitution (Fifth Amendment) Act, 1979 (Act No. I of 1979) validating the Martial Law was declared void in the judgment pronounced by the AD of the Supreme Court of Bangladesh (in Civil Petition for Leave to Appeal No. 1044-1045/2009). Similarly, the Constitution (Seventh Amendment) Act, 1986 (Act No. I of 1986) validating the Martial Law was also declared void in the judgment pronounced by the AD of the Supreme Court of Bangladesh (in Civil Appeal No. 48/2011). Since these Martial Laws were declared unconstitutional, all the Ordinances enforced and promulgated by Martial Law Proclamation between the period from 15 August 1975 to 9 April 1979 and from 24 March 1982 to 11 November 1986 respectively have ceased to have effect due to omission of Articles 3A and 18 and 19 respectively of the Fourth Schedule to the Constitution of the People's Republic of Bangladesh regarding ratification and confirmation of the said Ordinances by the Constitution (Fifteenth Amendment) Act, 2011 (Act No. XIV of 2011).

---

deals with the law-making process and financial procedure. The law-making process can be found, http://www.parliament.gov.bd/index.php/en/parliamentary-business/business-of-the-house/bill-and-legislation/legislative-procedure. *See also* Murphy, G., *How Legislation Is Drafted and Enacted in Bangladesh*, 27 Stat. L. Rev., 133–149 (2006).

43. *See*, for reference, Art. 93 of the Constitution of Bangladesh, 1972. It should be noted that an Ordinance so made must be presented before Parliament at its first meeting following the promulgation of the Ordinance. Unless such Ordinance is earlier repealed, it shall cease to have effect at the expiration of thirty days after it is so presented or, if a resolution disapproving of the Ordinance is passed by the Parliament before such expiration, upon the passing of the resolution.
44. The Bangladesh (Collection of Taxes) Order, 1971 (Acting President's Order No. 1 of 1971), The Bangladesh (Administration of Banks) Order, 1971 (Acting President's Order No. 3 of 1971), The Bangladesh (Taking Over of Control and Management of Industrial and Commercial Concerns) Order, 1972 (Acting President's Order No. 1 of 1972), The Bangladesh (Administration of Financial Institutions) Order, 1972 (Acting President's Order No. 3 of 1972).
45. According to ss 2(14) and 2(2) of the Code of Civil Procedure, 1908 (Act No. V of 1908), 'order' means the formal expression of any decision of a Civil Court. An order is not a decree, which is the formal expression of an adjudication which conclusively determines the rights of the parties.
46. A statutory order means an order passed as required by law and if so passed it would have the force of law as if made by the legislature itself. *DCCI v. Secretary, Ministry of Works*, 39 DLR 145.

42. As a result, the government has decided to make new laws in Bangla by way of necessary amendment and modification of such Ordinances as may be considered necessary after reviewing the necessity and relevance of such Ordinances promulgated. Accordingly, the government has been updating some of the Ordinances promulgated during these martial law regimes.[47]

43. However, some Ordinances promulgated during these martial law regimes have been maintained through the provisions of the Implementation of Certain Ordinances promulgated from 15 August 1975 to 9 April 1979 (Special Provisions) Act, 2013 (Act No. VI of 2013) and the Implementation of Certain Ordinances promulgated from 24 March 1982 to 11 November 1986 (Special Provisions) Act, 2013 (Act No. VII of 2013). As a result, one may still find some of these Ordinances available in the Bangladesh Code.

44. These three types of laws, i.e., Acts of Parliament, Ordinance and Presidential Orders, are treated as 'primary legislation' in the Bangladesh context. The Supreme Court, as the guardian of the Constitution, can declare any law void if the provision of the law is found to be inconsistent with the Constitution.[48]

45. Rules and regulations, bye-laws (by-laws), etc. are regarded as delegated and subsidiary legislation. Parliament, by the provisions of an Act of Parliament, can delegate its law-making power to any person or authority to make statutory orders, rules, regulations, bye-laws or other instruments having a legislative effect.[49] Usually, the government Ministry that is in charge of implementing any law, by being empowered by the Parliament through primary legislation, e.g., an Act of Parliament, frames subsidiary legislations such as orders, rules, regulations, bye-laws or other instruments having legislative effect containing detailed provisions in order to assist the stakeholders in the implementation of that law.

46. In *Raghib Rauf Chowdhury v. Bangladesh and others*, 9 SCOB [2017] HCD, 34 at paragraph 37, it was held that the Parliament can delegate its power to any person or authority by an Act of Parliament, to make orders, rules, regulations, bye-laws or other instruments having a legislative effect. From a plain reading of Article 65 of the Constitution, it can be seen that unless and until the parliament delegates its power to any authority or any department within the limit of the country, they cannot make any Rule and thus, the Parliament is the sole authority to enact a rule or law and only the Parliament can delegate its powers to any authority to formulate regulations or any guidelines.

47. The word 'regulation' may cause some confusion as the word is used mostly as subsidiary legislation in the legal arena of Bangladesh. However, there are some

47. For Example, the Bangladesh Sangbad Sangstha Ordinance, 1979 (Ordinance No. XX of 1979) was repealed and updated by the Bangladesh Sangbad Sangstha Act, 2018 (Act No. LXV of 2018). Similarly, the Marine Fisheries Ordinance, 1983 (Ordinance No. XXXV of 1983) was repealed and updated by the Marine Fisheries Act, 2020 (Act No. 19 of 2020).
48. Articles 7(2) and 26, the Constitution of Bangladesh, 1972.
49. Proviso to Art. 65(1), the Constitution of Bangladesh, 1972.

'regulations' which have the status of primary legislation since historically primary laws were known as 'regulations'.[50] According to the Rules of Business and its Schedule I, i.e., Allocation of Business, these 'regulations' are framed by the administrative Departments established under various Ministries of the government.

48. All Bangladeshi existing primary laws are available in the Bangladesh Code containing laws since 1836.[51] Bangladesh Code was updated in 2006 in thirty-eight volumes. Some of the 'Regulations',[52] though they have the status of primary legislation, were not included in the Bangladesh Code as section 6 of the Bangladesh Laws (Revision and Declaration) Act, 1973 provides to include only the Acts of Parliament, Ordinances and President's Orders in the Bangladesh Code.

49. In the definition of 'law' under Article 152 of the Constitution, 1972, 'byelaws (by-laws)' are made by the statutory public authorities, i.e., any public or private body, such as Bangladesh Computer Council (BCC), which is created through the enactment of a statute; 'notification' means the Gazette notifications usually published by Bangladesh Government Press.[53] Generally speaking, 'legal instruments' denote the documents executed between parties such as deeds, contracts and agreements, etc. These instruments have a binding effect between the executing parties if properly made following the proper legal requirements derived from the provisions of different domestic laws. In the case of *AZ Rafique Ahmed v. Bangladesh Council of Scientific and Industrial Research*, 31 DLR (1979) 222, when a body was created by a resolution of a Ministry, a question was raised whether the resolution can be treated as law as it is not made in exercise of any law-making power of the

50. Under the Regulating Act, 1773 of British India, the Governor-General in Council sitting at Fort William in Bengal was empowered to make Regulation for good governance of the East India Company's settlement at Fort William and other subordinate factories and places. Accordingly, the Governor-General passed hundreds of Regulations between 1773 to 1833. Subsequently, the Charter Act, 1833 empowered the Governor-General in Council at Kolkata to make laws for the whole of India, and since then the laws passed by the Governor-General were called Acts. *See*, Bangladesh Law Commission Report No. 116 published in 2012.
51. Section 6 of the Bangladesh Laws (Revision and Declaration) Act 1973 provides that 'All Acts of Parliament, Ordinances and President's Orders in force in Bangladesh shall be printed in chronological order under the name and style of the Bangladesh Code.'
52. The Wills and Intestacy Regulation, 1799 (Regulation V of 1799); The Charitable Endowment, Public Buildings and Escheats Regulation, 1810 (Regulation XIX of 1810); The Government Indemnity Regulation, (Regulation XI of 1822); The Alluvion and Diluvion Regulation 1825 (Regulation XI of 1825); The Revenue Commissioners Regulation, 1829 (Regulation 1 of 1829); The Sati Regulation, 1829 (Regulation XVII of 1829); The Land Revenue (Settlement and Deputy Collectors) Regulation, 1833 (Regulation IX of 1833).
53. It may be relevant to share here that Gazettes are of two types: Weekly Gazettes and Extraordinary Gazettes. Matters of legal nature are normally in Extraordinary Gazettes. *See* Bangladesh Government Press, https://www.dpp.gov.bd/bgpress/index.php/document/gazettes/140.

President or Parliament. The AD held that the resolution is covered by the expression 'other legal instrument'. Finally, customary laws and usages, which are extensively followed, e.g., in the Chittagong hill tracts region of the country, come 'within the ambits of law and as such they cannot be violated'.[54]

50. Bangla is the state language of the Republic.[55] In 1987, the Bangla Bhasha Procholon Ain, 1987 (Act No. 2 of 1987) (The Introduction of Bangla Language Act, 1987) was enacted, and it was provided that after the enactment of the law, everywhere in Bangladesh including in government offices, courts, semi-government and statutory public authorities, except in case of correspondence with foreign countries, examination and cross-examination in the court of laws and all other legal activities shall be written in Bangla.[56] Bangla is widely used as a language of business in subordinate courts. Whereas, in the Supreme Court, English is used as a language of business though it is reported that some members of the Bar and Bench have started using Bangla even in the Supreme Court. One may find that in many instances, honourable Judges of the Supreme Court have delivered judgments in Bengali also and sometimes used the English equivalent of some of the terms which are not easily understandable or do not have equal words or expressions in Bangla.

51. Following the enactment of this law, it can be seen that since 1987, almost all the Acts of Parliaments have been enacted in Bangla. In 1998, the government asked for the opinion of the Law Commission of Bangladesh regarding the making or introduction of authentic texts of authorized translation of the original Bangladesh texts of all such laws.[57] The Law Commission recommended positively by stating that to attract foreign investment and to transact trade and commerce, exports

---

54. *Pruesiau Aug Marma and another v. Aungmra Shang Marma and another*, 14 SCOB [2020] HCD. Usages are also recognized in sections 2 and 3 of the Alluvion and Diluvian Regulation, 1825 (Bengal Regulation XI of 1825), which is apparently one of the oldest laws in force, containing rules for the general information of individuals as well as for the guidance of Courts of Judicature, in the country which provide for how the claims and disputes as to alluvial lands are to be decided when there are clearly recognized and established usage, and when there is no such established usage.
55. Article 3, the Constitution of the People's Republic of Bangladesh, 1972.
56. Section 3, the Bangla Bhasha Procholon Ain, 1987 (Act No. 2 of 1987).
57. The Law Commission of Bangladesh was established through the provisions of the Law Commission Act, 1996 (Act No. XIX of 1996). The Preamble of the Law provides that in the context of the changes in the socioeconomic conditions of the country, introduction of free market economy and huge backlog of cases pending for trial in different courts, and for re-examination of the legal aspects of the fundamental human rights situation, and repeal of the obsolete laws for making provisions in respect of other matters of public importance including upgrading the standards of the legal education, and for making recommendation to the Government for review and timely reform of the existing laws and enactment of new laws, as the case may be, it is expedient and necessary to establish a permanent Law Commission. The Law Commission is empowered, *inter alia*, to identify the causes for delay in the disposal of civil and criminal cases at various tiers of Courts and to expedite disposal of the cases and to ensure justice as speedily as possible, to recommend amendment of the laws or enactment of new laws in appropriate cases after review and research of the relevant laws, to recommend on the legal matters referred by the Government from time to time. *See* s. 6, the Law Commission Act, 1996 (Act No. XIX of 1996).

and imports with foreign countries on a competitive basis, the laws, rules and regulations on trade, commerce, investment, exports, imports, industries, banking etc. which are enacted or framed in Bangla hardly have any use. The Law Commission, by sharing that the availability of unofficial translations has no legal sanction or authenticity, further proposed to include the provision for making or introducing authentic English text.[58] As a result, some laws, having commercial or international implications, though were originally enacted in Bangla, are subsequently translated into English by the drafting wing of the Ministry of Law, Justice and Parliamentary Affairs and only these versions of laws are treated as authentic texts of authorized translation.[59] On the other hand, some Acts of Parliaments which were enacted before 1987 in English were translated into Bangla later on due to their importance and wide use.[60]

52. It may be relevant to share here that according to the rules of interpretation of statutes if there are any general laws and special laws on the same issue, the provisions of the special law will prevail. The same rule is also followed in Bangladesh and therefore, even though one may find legal provisions on some issues in the domestic general law, the provisions of the specially enacted laws shall prevail. Similarly, if any legal remedy is ordinarily available under both general law and special law, the remedy prescribed by the special law must be sought in exclusion of the one available under the general law.[61]

---

58. The Law Commission, Government of the People's Republic of Bangladesh, Report on Necessity of English Translation of Law drafted in Bengali, Report No. 14, date of submission 14 May 1998.
59. For example, the Bangladesh Telecommunication Regulation Act, 2001 (Act No. XVIII of 2001) was originally enacted in Bangla, but it was subsequently translated into English. Similarly, the Companies Act, 1994 (Act No. 18 of 1994), the Copyright Act, 2000 (Act No. 28 of 2000), the Chemical Weapons (Prohibition) Act, 2006 (Act No. 37 of 2000), the Public Procurement Act, 2006 (Act No. 24 of 2006), the Right to Information Act, 2009 (Act No. 20 of 2009), the Trade Mark Act, 2009 (Act No. 19 of 2009), the Money Laundering Prevention Act, 2012 (Act No. 5 of 2012), the Breast-milk Substitutes, Infant Foods, Commercially Manufactured Complementary Foods and the Accessories Thereof (Regulation of Marketing) Act, 2013 (Act No. 35 of 2013), etc. were all enacted originally in Bangla, but later on translated into English. Nevertheless, it may be relevant to share here that, sometimes such authentic translation may not be able to present the content of the law in a clear manner. In the case of *Jamuna Television Limited and another v. Bangladesh and others*, 2005, 34 CLC (HCD) [8911] = 57 DLR (2005) 345, referring to the authentic English translation of the of the Bangladesh Telecommunication Act (Act No. 18 of 2001) shared by the then Attorney-General, Md Abdur Rashid J. mentioned that 'After the commencement of the Act, the Government … published a translation of the Act, which is known to be as Authentic English Text of the Act. However, in case of conflict between the Act and the said translation, the Act shall prevail. Learned Attorney-General read all relevant provisions of the English version. Sometimes, we found the translation led us to nowhere.'
60. For example, the Mines Act, 1923 (Act No. IV of 1923) was originally enacted in English. Later on, on 15 Nov. 2007, the Ministry of Law, Justice and Parliamentary Affairs published the Bangla translated version of the law. Similarly, some other laws which were originally enacted in English were subsequently translated into Bangla. For example, the Bangladesh Small and Cottage Industries Corporation Act, 1957 (East Pakistan Act No. XVII of 1957), the Bangladesh Sangbad Shangtha Ordinance, 1979 (Ordinance No. XX of 1979), the Administrative Tribunal Act, 1980 (Act No. VII of 1981), the Civil Aviation Authority Ordinance, 1985 (Ordinance No. XXXVIII of 1985).
61. *DCCI v. Secretary*, Ministry of Works, 39 DLR 145.

53. In relation to the content of this monograph, various directives, notifications, instructions and guidelines issued by the relevant ministries, administrative departments and regulators will be discussed. All these are crucial and binding on the subjects even though these are not included within the definition of 'law' under Article 152 of the Constitution of Bangladesh, 1972.

54. Bangladesh is a member of most of the leading international and regional, political and economic organizations and has signed most of the relevant international human rights instruments. The country's commitment to international peace and peaceful settlement of international disputes is reflected in the Constitution of the country.[62] Bangladesh is a leading troop-contributing country for the United Nations (UN) peacekeeping mission. The Permanent Mission of Bangladesh in the UN has been leading the Group of LDCs since October 2015.

§9. Legal Status of Policy

55. In various parts of this monograph, various policies such as national policy on telecommunication, ICT and electronic commerce, etc., will be discussed. Though it is difficult to explain the precise role and legal effect and status, these policies framed by the government play a very significant role in guiding various organs in running the state activities. Out of more than a hundred policies available in various sectors, two policies, i.e., the National Fisheries Policy, 1998 and the National Livestock Development Policy, 2007, could be identified which contain a provision on 'Legal status' of these policies. However, a closer look at the language of these provisions on 'Legal status' will reveal that these are merely the provisions on the scope of these policies,[63] and there is no indication about the legal status of these policies.

---

62. *See*, Preamble and Art. 25, the Constitution of the People's Republic of Bangladesh, 1972.
63. 4.Legal status of the National Fisheries Policy.

> 4.1 All the government and autonomous organizations, multi-national institutions, various non-governmental organizations, voluntary organizations, and persons who are working within the geographical territory of Bangladesh for the development of fisheries resources, harvesting and preservation, export-import or other businesses, related to the fisheries sector will be included in the National Fisheries Policy.
>
> 4.2 All the water bodies suitable for fisheries production and their fisheries resources and conservation, development and management will be under this policy.
>
> 3. Legal Status of the National Livestock Development Policy.

All the government and autonomous organizations, multi-national institutions, NGOs, CBOs (community based organizations), and persons who are working within the geographical territory of Bangladesh for the management, development and conservation of livestock resources, import-export or other business related to the livestock sub-sector will be under the purview of National Livestock Development Policy.

56. It will be pertinent to share that these national policies should not be confused with the 'Fundamental Principles of State Policy' as encapsulated in the Constitution of Bangladesh, 1972. The Fundamental Principles of State Policy are fundamental to the governance of Bangladesh. Constitutionally, these Principles are applied by the State in the making of laws. These Principles are also used as a guide to the interpretation of the Constitution and of the other laws of Bangladesh, and they form the basis of the work of the State and of its citizens but are not judicially enforceable.[64]

57. Sometimes, an individual Department or organization can formulate a Policy on any issue containing detailed provisions on that issue and such Policy provisions play an important role in regulating internal matters. For example, an organization can develop the ICT Policy containing provisions that the officers/ staff of all levels, including subsidiary bodies, and all other granted users of ICT assets should follow and define their responsibility for the protection and appropriate use of information, applications, computer system and network.

58. Even though there are various policies, which are like plans or set of ideas the government uses in making decisions, their legal status is somehow uncertain. In *National Board of Revenue v. Abu Saeed Khan and others*, 2012, 41 CLC (AD) [8674] = 18 BLC (AD) (2013) 116, the AD of Bangladesh Supreme Court observed that '[u]nless the policy or action is inconsistent with the Constitution and the laws, or arbitrary or irrational or by exercise of abuse of power, the court will not interfere. If the policy cannot be faulted on the grounds of arbitrariness/or irrationality or perversity or mala fide, judicial interference is impermissible even if it hurts the business interest of a party. The court cannot dictate neither that a certain policy ought to have been adopted nor can it opine that a policy should be changed. An executive policy is not open to impeachment unless it infringes any constitutional or statutory provision. In economic regulation or tax matters, judicial restraint is necessary, and the judgment of the executive should not be interfered with'. Therefore, it is clear that the executives can formulate any policy and implement the provisions thereof as long as they are not inconsistent with the Constitution or any statutory provisions.

---

64. Article 8(2), the Constitution of Bangladesh, 1972. The nature and judicial enforceability of these principles were evaluated in *Kudrat E-Elahi Panir v. Bangladesh*, 44 DLR (AD) 319.

Chapter 2. Telecommunication Infrastructure

§1. Introduction

59. Telecommunication sector plays an increasingly important role in the socio-economic development of any country. In Bangladesh, this sector has contributed to introducing some epoch-making changes in recent years. Bangladesh became a member of the Universal Postal Union on 7 February 1973, of the International Telecommunication Union (ITU) on 5 September 1973, and of the Asia Pacific Telecommunity on 1 July 1979. Besides, Bangladesh is also a member of the Commonwealth Telecommunications Organization, Telecommunication units of Organisation of Islamic Cooperation and South Asian Telecommunications Regulators' Council.

60. A well-developed telecommunication infrastructure works as the backbone in today's information society and in the proper functioning of the internet. In order to know the telecom infrastructure in Bangladesh, it will be relevant to shed some light on the historical development of this sector, even though realizing the diversity of this sector and political history of the country, it seems to be difficult to share a precise chronological history of this sector. Hence, only the most important historical events will be shared, followed by some statistics and regulatory requirements in this regard.

§2. Emergence of Telecommunication System

I. Pre-independence Era

61. After Samuel Morse invented Telegraph in 1837, telecommunication related activities were first established in Kolkata, India by the postal system under the Post and Telegraph Department of British India in the form of the telegraph during 1852–1853.[65] During that time, present Bangladesh was part of undivided India under the British colonial administration. Between 1853 and 1855, telegraph lines were constructed all over India, including Kolkata, and in 1855, telegraph service was made open to the public.

62. The Telegraph Act, 1885 (Act No. XIII of 1885) was the first legislation enacted to regulate this evolving telegraph service. By virtue of the provisions of this law, the telegraph authority was empowered, subject to certain limitations, to place and maintain the line of a telegraph established or maintained by the Government under, over, along or across, and posts in or upon, any immovable property.[66]

65. Two different years, i.e., 1852 and 1853 can be found in the authoritative literature in this regard. *See* Banglapedia entry on Telecommunication, http://en.banglapedia.org/index.php?title=Telecommunication. BTCL, 'Telecom Museum: Chronological Development of Telecommunication in Subcontinent', http://old.btcl.gov.bd/en/189/museum.
66. Section 10 of the Telegraph Act, 1885 (Act No. XIII of 1885).

During that time, telecommunication services were delivered using iron and copper wire. Even though the word 'telegraph' was used in the title of the law for an obvious reason, the definition of the word 'telegraph' as included in the law is very wide and has also included modern telecommunication within its ambit, and therefore, even after 135 years, the definition still remains relevant and timely. As the definition has been serving the purpose well for years, there was no need felt to amend it.[67] Subsequently, wireless telegraphy was introduced, and the Wireless Telegraphy Act, 1933 (Act No. XVII of 1933) was enacted to regulate the possession of wireless telegraphy apparatus in this part of the world.[68]

63. After the historical event of partition in 1947, present Bangladesh became a part of the then Pakistan, where there were 14,000 landlines in the whole of Pakistan. The Pakistan Telegraph and Telephone Department was established in 1962, and regular telecommunication activities were regulated and monitored by this Department. On 30 June 1965, there were 135,000 government-owned telephones, and out of a total of 11,150 post offices, 1,340 had telegraph facilities. Besides, there were 93 independent telegraph offices.[69]

II. Post-Independence Era

64. After the independence of Bangladesh in 1971, the above two laws of 1885 and 1933 were adapted with modification.[70] The Eastern wing of the erstwhile Pakistan Telegraph and Telephone Department was renamed the Bangladesh Telegraph and Telephone (T & T) Department and was placed under the authority of the Ministry of Posts and Telecommunications. Due to the financial constraints and infrastructural limitations resulting from the liberation war damages and immediate subsequent political turmoil, this body could not function well. As a result, till the end of the 1970s, the benefits of this telecommunication service could only be enjoyed by the government offices, business communities of medium and large towns and a few urban elites.[71]

---

67. Section 2 of the Telegraph Act, 1885 (Act No. XIII of 1885) defines 'telegraph' as an electric, galvanic or magnetic telegraph, and includes appliances and apparatus for making, transmitting or receiving telegraphic, telephonic or other communications by means of electricity, galvanism or magnetism.
68. Section 2 of the Wireless Telegraphy Act, 1933 (Act No. XVII of 1933) defines 'wireless telegraphy apparatus' as any apparatus, appliance, instrument or material used or capable of use in wireless communication, and includes any article determined to be wireless telegraphy apparatus, but does not include any such apparatus, appliance, instrument or material commonly used for other electrical purposes unless it has been specially designed or adapted for wireless communication or forms part of some apparatus, appliance, instrument or material specially so designed or adapted.
69. Steinberg, S.H. (ed.), *The Statesman's Year-Book: Statistical and Historical Annual of the States of the World for the Year 1967–1968*, 443 (1967).
70. Relevant laws which were in force during the time of independence were adopted with necessary modification through the provisions of the Bangladesh (Adaptation of Existing Laws) Order, 1972 (President's Order No. 48 of 1972) and the Bangladesh Laws (Revision and Declaration) Act, 1973 (Act No. VIII of 1973).
71. Banerjee, I. & Logan, S. eds, *Asian Communication Handbook 2008,* 113 (2008).

65. This Bangladesh T & T Department was reconstructed as a corporate body and was renamed as Bangladesh Telegraph and Telephone Board (BTTB) in 1975 through the promulgation of the Telegraph and Telephone Board Ordinance, 1975 (Ordinance No. XLVII of 1975). In 1979, this BTTB was reconstructed as a constitutional body through the promulgation of the Bangladesh Telegraph and Telephone Board Ordinance, 1979 (Ordinance No. XII of 1979), which was made for the efficient management, operation and development of the telegraphs and telephones Board in the country. It has already been shared that the country faced political turmoil immediately after the independence and that situation continued till the 1990s. As a result, like most of the sectors, this telephone and telegraph sector was also developing without any proper and right direction. The situation started changing when the democratically elected governments resumed exercising state power and started taking government policies. Some of these policies are shared below.

A. *National Telecommunication Policy, 1998*

66. In 1998, the Ministry of Post and Telecommunication (MoPT) first formulated the Bangladesh National Telecommunication Policy, which is 'a summary statement of the philosophy, objectives, strategies and the methodology to ensure equitable and judicious execution of the business of telecommunications' in Bangladesh.[72] It was formulated 'to ensure the orderly and rapid growth of telecommunication services, both in quality and quantity and the use of telecommunication technology in order to support the socio-economic development, in line with the national aspirations'.[73] It was anticipated that this Policy 'will act as a catalyst towards the growth and development of telecommunication in the country with a view to producing a modern, balanced and dynamic society'.[74]

67. This Policy of 1998 laid the basic design of a liberalized telecommunication sector in Bangladesh and paved the way for the separation of the policy, regulation, and operational functions that were centralized at that time.[75] The higher judiciary of the country has evaluated the background, importance and impact of this National Telecommunication Policy, 1998. In 2005, Honourable Justice Md Abdur Rashid J. of the HCD of the Supreme Court penned the background and impact of this Policy in the following manner:

> 38. In 1998, the government of the day ultimately realised the need of the time and benefits of the information superhighway and came out with the National Telecommunications Policy. Conscious of the low level of the telecommunication sector, limitations to the growing demands, low level of, investment and outdated and outmoded systems and technology, it decided to open up the telecommunication sector for public participation. It introduced the guidelines for

72. Conclusion, the National Telecommunication Policy, 1998.
73. The Policy Objectives, the National Telecommunication Policy, 1998.
74. Strategies, the National Telecommunication Policy, 1998.
75. Preamble, the National Telecommunication Policy, 2015 (Draft).

> development of a national sound telecommunication infrastructure to support the economy and welfare of the country by providing telecommunication facilities, and quality of service to the citizenry. The policy was viewed to ensure orderly development of the telecommunication sector through provision of services in all the areas of the country.
> 39. Such policy decision was earth breaking in the context of this land where nothing does move without much effort in the sense that the government decided to break away from the age-old monopoly in the control of flow and management of all sorts of communication of information. It decided to open up the telecommunication system to the public for participation in the free exchange of ideas, dissemination of information without restraints, dissemination of knowledge, airing of different viewpoints and debating and form in one's own views and expressing them, which are, no doubt, the basic indicia of a free, society. Such decision was definitely in conformity with the mandate of the Constitution to ensure access of the people to information. Such policy is also in line with the declared policy of the government for a free market economy. ...[76]

68. Later on, in *World Tel Bangladesh Ltd. v. Bangladesh represented by the Secretary Ministry of Post and Telecommunications and others*, 2006, 35 CLC (AD) [284] = 11 MLR (2006) (AD) 65, Mr Justice Md Fazlul Karim of the AD of the Supreme Court discussed the background and importance of in the following way:

> 42. Our legislation in the field [of telecommunication system and services] has been made keeping pace with the technological developments in the world. While all other developed countries have enacted laws specially governing the broadcasting media, we have been lagging behind centering round the Telegraph Act, 1885 which has, to some extent, become inadequate to meet the technical eventualities due to latest technological advancement and developments.
> 43. Thus, in the interest of the 'freedom of speech and expression' as guaranteed in the Constitution, the Government has adopted National Telecommunication Policy, 1998 in order to boost up the telecommunication sector which has been characterised by a very low level of penetration, limited capability to meet the growing demand, low level of investment, and old outdated systems and technologies necessitating reactive remedial measures, and to develop a material serene telecommunication infrastructure to support the economy and welfare of the country by providing telecommunication facilities on demand, assuring satisfactory quality of services and ensuring value to the customers.
> 44. The policy objectives designed in upholding the commitment of Government to resolve the short-comings, outline the objectives, strategies and other related aspects of telecommunication and ensure the orderly and rapid growth

---

76. *Jamuna Television Limited and another v. Bangladesh and others*, 2005, 34 CLC (HCD) [8911]=57 DLR (2005) 345.

of telecommunication services, both in quality and quantity and the use of telecommunication technology in order to support the socio-economic development in line with the national aspirations.

69. Six strategies, i.e., targets (telephone penetration and teledensity), role of public and private sector operators, information infrastructure, international network, new services and master plan and eighteen policy objectives, i.e., exchange of information, promotion of national integration, universal access, digitalization, competitive framework, private sector development, resource mobilization, liberalized tariff policy, access to new technology, private sector investment, foreign investment, implementation strategy, human resource development, defence and security, information technology (IT), local manufacturing, regulatory framework, protection of users' interest and service standards were set in the Policy.

70. The Policy recommended establishing a separate statutory autonomous Regulatory Commission under the Ministry of Post & Telecommunications. Accordingly, the Bangladesh Telecommunication Regulation Act, 2001 (Act No. 18 of 2001) was enacted to establish an independent regulatory commission, i.e., the Bangladesh Telecommunication Regulatory Commission (BTRC), the principal telecommunication watchdog of the country. The BTRC started its journey on 31 January 2002. The law was subsequently amended in 2010 to empower the BTRC with more powers and authority including the provision that the permission of the government is required to provide telecommunication services, international calls, import telecommunication equipment, etc.

B. National Telecommunication Policy, 2015 (Draft)

71. In August 2015, the draft of the National Telecommunication Policy was released by the Posts and Telecommunications Division of the Ministry of Posts, Telecommunications and Information Technology. This Policy is a summary statement of the philosophy, mission, objectives, strategies and methodology to ensure equitable and judicious execution of the business of telecommunication in the country.[77] The policymakers realized that with the substantial developments on all fronts in telecommunication services including the internet, mobile and broadband since the adoption of the Policy, i.e., the National Telecommunication Policy, 1998, 'the sector became more interdependent with the global trends of regulation, market structure, and customer needs'. As a result, 'with the prospects of the new technologies, citizens are being exposed to different new threats from the cyberspace' and therefore, 'the 1998 Policy and associated legislations require revision to reflect the demands of the present day and the future'.[78]

72. This draft Policy of 2015 revealed that the broadband services were not expanded in rural areas at the same pace as it was in the urban areas. Therefore, the

77. Conclusion, the National Telecommunication Policy, 2015 (Draft).
78. Preamble, the National Telecommunication Policy, 2015 (Draft).

draft Policy, 2015 set the vision, i.e., to 'provide affordable and universally accessible quality telecommunication services to support the nation's sustainable development goals and to integrate the country with the global knowledge economy'.[79] Moreover, the draft Policy 2015, with the aim to last for at least ten years, set five guiding principles to ensure the development and sustainability of a vibrant telecommunication sector in the country and these are: open and competitive market, universal access, effective governance, appropriate regulation and forward-looking.

73. The draft Policy, 2015 set nine policy objectives, and these are: (a) affordable and universal access, (b) quality of service (QoS) and customer protection, (c) development of telecommunication market and services, (d) management of scarce resources, (e) investment, (f) efficiency and innovation, (g) employment and entrepreneurship, (h) standardization and local hardware and software production, and (i) environment-friendly networks.

74. In order to attain these policy objectives, the draft Policy 2015 has included thirteen strategies, and these are: (a) to provide a customer-friendly telecommunication framework, (b) to facilitate introduction of efficient telecommunication infrastructures and services, (c) effective use of social obligation fund, (d) to improve regulatory certainty, transparency and effectiveness, (e) protection of customer rights and service quality, (f) effective utilization of Spectrum and other telecommunication resources, (g) to coordinate with other policies and strengthen international cooperation, (h) to enable proper management of Cyberspace, (i) to enhance R&D and manufacturing of telecommunication and IT equipment and products, (j) to enhance the competitiveness of State-owned Enterprises, (k) to ensure security, (l) to enable disaster and emergency management, and (m) to encourage environmental protection.

75. Finally, it was claimed that in June 2016, the Policy, with the slogan 'telephone for all', was approved containing the target of 100% teledensity, 65% internet penetration with 40% fixed broadband penetration and connection of every union, the lowest tier of local government administration, with fibre and wireless broadband by 2021.[80] It may be relevant to share here that neither the recently adopted National Telecommunication Policy 2018 nor the official website of BTRC has any reference regarding the adoption of this Policy 2015. Instead, the National Telecommunication Policy 2018 provides that this Policy 2018 will replace the National Telecommunication Policy 1998.

---

79. Vision, the National Telecommunication Policy, 2015 (Draft).
80. Star Business Report, New telecom policy finally gets nod, The Daily Star, 28 Jun. 2016, https://www.thedailystar.net/business/new-telecom-policy-finally-gets-nod-1246846.

C. National Telecommunication Policy, 2018

76. In October 2018, the National Telecommunication Policy 2018 was formulated by the Posts and Telecommunications Division of the Ministry of Posts, Telecommunications and Information Technology. This Policy is a summary statement of the philosophy, mission, objectives, strategies and the methodology to ensure equitable and judicious execution of the business of telecommunication in the country.[81] Like the Policy of 2015, this Policy of 2018 was also adopted with the aim to last for at least ten years, and this Policy of 2018 has also set the same five guiding principles, i.e., open and competitive market, universal access, effective governance, appropriate regulation and forward-looking.

77. Though the Policy of 2015 adopted nine policy objectives, the Policy of 2018 adopted ten policy objectives. While doing so, the Policy of 2018 has adopted all the policy objectives of the Policy of 2015[82] and added a new policy objective, i.e., safety and security from cybercrime. Similarly, the Policy of 2018 has adopted all thirteen strategies as adopted in the Policy of 2015.[83] The Policy of 2018 has laid out goals for short-term (i.e., by 2020), mid-term (i.e., by 2023), and long-term (i.e., by 2027). In the short term, initiatives will be taken to: (a) increase the telepenetration of fixed and mobile telephones up to 95% and the internet penetration up to 60%, (b) extend optical fibre connectivity to all District and Upazila headquarters and Unions, (c) ensure availability of high-speed wireless broadband service up to all Upazila headquarters, and (d) introduce digital broadcasting in the country. In the mid-term, 100% teledensity and internet penetration and 70% broadband penetration will be achieved. In the long term, the policymakers target that 100% population in 100% of villages will enjoy the broadband service. The government has recently formed a Committee to review and assess action plans under the ICT Policy, 2018 through a gazette notification of 2 September 2019. Since the Policy of 2018 was adopted only a couple of months ago, it will be better to wait for a while to evaluate its effectiveness properly and systematically.

81. Conclusion, the National Telecommunication Policy, 2018.

82. The nine policy objectives are: (a) affordable and universal access, (b) QoS and customer protection, (c) development of telecommunication market and services, (d) management of scarce resources, (e) investment, (f) efficiency and innovation, (g) employment and entrepreneurship, (h) standardization and local hardware and software production, and (i) environment-friendly networks.

83. These are: (a) customer-friendly telecommunication framework, (b) facilitate introduction of efficient telecommunication infrastructures and services, (c) effective use of social obligation fund, (d) improve regulatory certainty, transparency and effectiveness, (e) protection of customer rights and service quality, (f) effective utilization of Spectrum and other telecommunication resources, (g) coordinate with other policies and strengthen international cooperation, (h) enable proper management of Cyberspace, (i) enhance R&D and manufacturing of telecommunication and IT equipment and products, (j) enhance the competitiveness of State-Owned Enterprises, (k) ensure security, (l) enable disaster and emergency management, and (m) encourage environment protection.

III. Mobile Network Providers

78. Historically, the government was enjoying the monopoly right over telegraph and telecommunication-related activities,[84] and the BTTB was both a service provider and regulator. The liberalization of the telecommunication sector in the country began in 1989 when the BTTB entered into an agreement on 26 June 1989 with a private limited company named Bangladesh Telecom (Pvt) Ltd. (BTL). Through this Agreement, BTL was permitted to operate several telecommunication systems including Cellular Mobile Telephone Service in the rural areas of 200 Upazilas.[85] Besides, Sheba Telecom (Pvt.) Ltd. was simultaneously given a licence to provide cellular mobile services in the rural areas of 199 Upazilas, and the Pacific Bangladesh Telephone Ltd. received the licence to introduce mobile phone service in the country. In 1993, Pacific Bangladesh Telephone Ltd., with the brand name 'CityCell', introduced cellular phone service by using Code Division Multiple Access (CDMA) technology. Even though this CDMA technology offered many benefits, unfortunately, it was found to be expensive, and so, the price of owning a cellular phone was still very high, and only a few rich people could afford this. This initiative introduced the momentum in the history of socio-economic development of the country.

79. During 1996–1997, telecommunication licences were given to Grameen Phone and Telecom Malaysia International Bangladesh. These companies started their operations with the brand names of 'Grameenphone' and 'AKTEL' respectively. Both these companies and Sheba Telecom started using Global System for Mobile Communications (GSM) technology to provide their services. Use of this GSM technology in providing telecommunication services enabled the paradigm shift on the reduction of mobile tariff and paved the way to make cellular phones available to the reach of the middle-class group in Bangladesh and eventually, to the grassroots people of the country.

80. In 2004, the only state-owned mobile phone operator, Teletalk Bangladesh Ltd., started its operation. In 2005, Abu Dhabi based Warid Telecom International LLC got the GSM licence to provide telecommunication services in the country. In the same year of 2005, Egyptian mobile operator Orascom acquired Sheba Telecom and started the operation in the country in the name of 'Banglalink'. In 2007, Warid launched its service in the Bangladesh market as the sixth mobile phone operator. By the provisions of the Bangladesh Telegraph and Telephone Board (Amendment) Ordinance, 2008 and the Bangladesh Telegraph and Telephone Board (Amendment) Act, 2009, a company namely 'Bangladesh Telecommunications Company Limited (BTCL)' was created and started its journey from 1 July 2008.

---

84. Under s. 4 of the Telegraph Act, 1885 (Act No. XIII of 1885), the Government enjoys the exclusive privilege of establishing, maintaining and working telegraphs, though the government may grant licence with conditions and payment to any person to establish, maintain or work a telegraph within any part of Bangladesh.
85. *Hutchison Telecom Bangladesh Ltd. v. Bangladesh Telegraph and Telephone Board and others*, 48 DLR (AD) (1996) 30; *Bangladesh Telecom (Pvt.) Ltd. v. Bangladesh T & T Board & others*, 1993, 21 CLC (AD) [755] = 48 DLR (AD) (1996) 20.

81. When all the six mobile network operators (MNOs), i.e., (a) CityCell, (b) Grameenphone, (c) AKTEL, (d) Teletalk Bangladesh, (e) Warid, and (f) Banglalink were serving the customers, the local market witnessed the pressure of stiff competition, which compelled the operators to adjust their market shares. Consequently, Japanese NTT DoCoMo bought a 30% share of AKTEL in 2008. Grameenphone was listed in the stock exchange of the country in 2009. In 2010, AKTEL changed its brand name to 'Robi' and transformed into Robi Axiata Ltd. The Indian giant Bharati Airtel acquired a 70% share in Warid Telecom in January 2010. In November 2016, Robi and Airtel Bangladesh merged together, and Axiata Group became the owner of 68.7% of the share, Bharti group owned 25% share, and the remaining share was owned by the Japanese NTT DoCoMo. In 2020, Robi Axiata was listed in the stock exchange and Airtel acquired the 6.3% share of DoCoMo for an undisclosed sum. Singapore Telecommunications Limited (SingTel) purchased most of the share of 'CityCell', the oldest mobile operator of Bangladesh. As a result, presently, only four mobile operators, i.e., Grameen Phone, Robi Axiata, Banglalink, and Teletalk, have been providing mobile telecommunication networking services in the country.

§3. History of Radio

82. Any discussion on telecommunication will remain incomplete without the discussion on the radio. It is evident that in the history of Bangladesh, the radio played extremely important roles during the Partition of India and Pakistan in 1947, the language movement in 1952, the Indo-Pak War in 1965, the mass movement in 1969 and the liberation war in 1971.[86]

83. The then British Raj established six radio stations in the name of 'All India Radio', including one in Dhaka, in 1939 to disseminate the news and information of World War II. The Chief Minister of the then undivided Bengal, AK Fazlul Huq inaugurated the 'All India Radio Dhaka', which was popularly known as the 'Dhaka Dhwani Bistar Kendra' to the locals. After the Partition in 1947, it was named 'Radio Pakistan' in 1960. During the Liberation War in 1971, 'Swadhin Bangla Betar Kendra' literally 'Independent Bangla Radio Center', played a significant role in inspiring and motivating the freedom fighters. This was renamed Bangladesh Betar on 6 December 1971, just ten days before the independence of the country and started broadcasting in Independent Bangladesh on 22 December 1971. It is the only state-owned public broadcaster in the country.

84. Besides this national broadcaster, there are some private radio stations that broadcast their programmes through private-owned FM radio. These radio stations

86. Jahan, N., *Bangladesh Betar: The Story of Glory*, Daily Star, 24 Feb. 2017, https://www.thedailystar.net/star-weekend/heritage/bangladesh-betar-the-story-glory-1365967; Swadhin Bangla Betar Kendra, Banglapedia, http://en.banglapedia.org/index.php?title=Swadhin_Bangla_Betar_Kendra.

need to adhere to the provisions of the Telegraph Act, 1885, the Wireless Telegraphy Act, 1933 and the Bangladesh Telecommunication Regulation Act, 2001 to get the licence of FM radio broadcasting from the Ministry of Information. A policy document entitled 'the Private-Owned FM Radio Station Installation, Broadcast and Operation Policy, 2010' was formulated in this regard. This Policy contains detailed provisions on application, ownership, licence fee, renewal of a licence, security money, conditions of the licence, professional and technical standards, equipment, etc. required to obtain the licence and run the radio station. The Policy of 2010 provides for the establishment of a National Regulatory Committee and a Technical Sub-Committee under the National Regulatory Committee to deal with the regulatory and technical issues. In order to start such radio stations, the entrepreneurs need to follow the provisions of this Policy strictly. After getting a licence from the Ministry of Information, an application is to be made to BTRC to assign frequency and to import Earth Station and satellite news-gathering equipment. The Policy of 2010 contains a detailed list of events or issues which the FM radios cannot broadcast. Most importantly, it is provided that the FM radio stations need to preserve the broadcasted contents for ninety days and cannot broadcast advertisements for more than 20% of the transmission time. Even though the researchers found that there is still a long way to go for these FM radios to become a part of mass media, these FM radio stations have been playing an important role in entertaining the audiences and disseminating information.[87] It is reported that till 2018, a total of twenty-nine organizations, including the state-sponsored Bangladesh Betar, have received FM Radio licences.[88]

85. Besides, some community radios are also broadcasting programmes in the country. The demand for the establishment of community radios started in 1998 with the initiative of 'Community Radio for Grassroots People' based in the southern coastal district of Patuakhali; however, community radios came into formal operation after the framing of the 'Community Radio Installation Broadcast and Operation Policy, 2008'. Though there are some concerns,[89] so far, seventeen Community Radio stations[90] have been broadcasting altogether 120 hours of programmes every day on information, education, local entertainment, and development activities within their coverage areas of 17 km.[91]

86. Moreover, there are many internet-based or online radios which have been playing an important role by broadcasting programmes in Bengali and thus, contribute to spreading the Bengali culture in the world. Nevertheless, the legal status

87. Atiqur Rahman & Habiba Rahman, *Private FM Radio in Bangladesh*, 39 Media Asia, 17–22 (2012).
88. BTRC, Annual Report, 2019–2020 [Bangla], p. 47.
89. Kaberi Gayen, *Community Radio in Bangladesh: The Policy and the Spirit*, 39 Media Asia, 32–39 (2012).
90. Bangladesh National Report, Human Rights Council Working Group on the Universal Periodic Review Thirtieth session, 7–18 May 2018, United Nations General Assembly, A/HRC/WG.6/30/BGD/1.
91. Rabeya Rahaman & Md Rakibul Hoque, *Radio for Education in Bangladesh: Trends and Future Scope*, XXXV J. Bus. Studies, 223–237 (August 2014).

and regulation of these online radios are not very clear, and it seems that they are not regulated by the Ministry of Information and the national telecommunication regulator, BTRC.

§4. History of Television

87. On 25 December 1964, in the then East Pakistan, the first television transmission began experimentally with the help of a 300-watt transmitter as a pilot project in the private sector. During that time, every evening, programmes were broadcast for three hours and that could cover a radius of 16 km. Subsequently, the government of Pakistan took over this to make it a station of Pakistan Television Corporation. After the Independence of Bangladesh in 1971, it was nationalized in 1972 in the name of Bangladesh Television (BTV) and moved to Rampura, Dhaka on 6 March 1975. Subsequently, a total of twelve satellite transmitters were installed in Chittagong, Sylhet, Mymensingh, Brahmanbaria, Rangpur, Natore, Thakurgaon, Jhenaidah, Khulna, Satkhira, Patuakhali and Noakhali to cover almost every corner of the country. In 1980, BTV started colour programme transmission. A project funded by the Spanish government was undertaken to make BTV's programmes available to overseas viewers. BTV, the only channel that has been transmitting programmes using terrestrial television broadcasting technology, transmits private sector package programmes to bring about variety in its programme pattern. BTV world, a satellite-based channel, owned by the government has been airing signals worldwide.[92]

88. The government also approved private TV channels to operate transmission for viewers of both home and abroad. Ekushey Television, with its official transmission since 14 April 2000, became the first private terrestrial TV channel in Bangladesh. Regarding the licence for broadcasting, private-owned television channels need to follow similar provisions like FM radios, i.e., a broadcasting licence is to be obtained from the Ministry of Information and for spectrum allocation, an application is to be made to BTRC.[93] At present, there are thirty-two television channels, including four State-owned channels operating in Bangladesh.[94]

§5. History of Computer

I. Pre-independence Era

89. The first computer, i.e., a computer of IBM Mainframe Computer of 1620 series, was installed in 1964 at the Atomic Energy Center of the then Eastern wing

92. Television, Banglapedia, http://en.banglapedia.org/index.php?title=Television.
93. *Chairman, Bangladesh Telecommunication Regulatory Commission and others v. Ekushey Television Ltd. and others*, 14 MLR (2009) (AD) 369.
94. Bangladesh National Report, Human Rights Council Working Group on the Universal Periodic Review Thirtieth session, 7–18 May 2018, United Nations General Assembly, A/HRC/WG.6/30/BGD/1.

of Pakistan Atomic Energy Commission, Dacca. Thereafter, Habib Bank, which was running its banking activities in the then East Pakistan, Dacca, installed the third generation Mainframe IBM 1401 computer, whereas the United Bank used IBM 1901 in the late sixties for performing accounting works in these banks. Before the independence of Bangladesh in 1971, an IBM 360 computer was set up at the Bureau of Statistics in 1969. A Mainframe computer was also installed at Adamjee Jute Mills during the same period.[95] Before independence, computer hardware and software-related courses were included, though in a limited way, in the curricula of Mathematics, Physics, Applied Physics and Electronics at the university level.[96] Late Mr Md Hanif Uddin Mia is recognized as the first computer programmer of the country who installed a second-generation digital mainframe computer in 1964 at the then East Pakistan Atomic Energy Commission.

II. Post-Independence Era

90. After the independence in 1971, big computers such as IBM 370, IBM 9100 and IBM 4341, etc. were installed in the Bangladesh Bureau of Statistics. In September 1979, an IBM 370 and an IBM 4331 Mainframe Computer were introduced at the Bangladesh University of Engineering and Technology (BUET), and a Computer Centre was also established at BUET. Atomic Energy Research Establishment at Savar installed an IBM 4341 Mainframe Computer in 1981. The Dhaka University Computer Centre began its journey with an IBM 4331 Mainframe Computer in 1985. Subsequently, BUET founded the Computer Science and Engineering Department in 1984, whereas Dhaka University founded the Computer Science Department in 1992. Computer education has been included in the syllabus at the higher secondary level since 1991 and at the secondary level since 1994.[97]

91. It is believed that personal computers were starting to become popular in the country from the mid-nineties and the use of computers by the printing presses in the late 1980s played an important role in this regard.[98] In 1987, writing in Bangla on the computer was first materialized when Mr Mainul Islam, an engineer managed to write Bangla in Apple-Macintosh computer using his self-evolved font 'Mainulipi' on a conventional English keyboard. The difference in the type and form of Bangla and English alphabets was resolved using the four-layer keyboard of Macintosh. Two more Bangla fonts, i.e., 'Shahidlipi' and 'Jabbarlipi' were evolved immediately after Mainulipi.[99]

95. Established in 1950 at Narayangonj, the Adamjee Jute Mills was once the largest jute mill in the world. The Mill was closed on the ground of continuous loss in 2002. *See*, for more, Anu Muhammad, *Closure of Adamjee Jute Mills: Ominous Sign,* 37 Eco. Pol. Wkly., 3895–3897 (21–27 Sep. 2002).
96. Computer, Banglapedia, http://en.banglapedia.org/index.php?title=Computer.
97. *Ibid.*
98. Sadik Hasan, *Introducing E-government in Bangladesh: Problems and Prospects*, 78 Inter'l Soc. Science Rev., 111–125 (2003).
99. Computer, Banglapedia, http://en.banglapedia.org/index.php?title=Computer.

92. The next year, i.e., in 1988, the first interface 'Bijoy', useable in Apple-Macintosh computer, was built by a private organization, 'Anando Computers' and the layout of the first Bangla keyboards such as 'Bijoy' and 'Munir' were also developed. In 1992, a self-sufficient Bangla Disk Operating System based word processing software was developed by another private organization, 'Safeworks'. For IBM computer, they developed the software named 'Barna' where three types of keyboard, i.e., Munir, Bijoy, and Easy, along with a customized keyboard, could be used. This can be considered as a milestone in popularizing the use of personal computers in the country. Some other keyboards such as Rupali, Provat and so on also played an instrumental role in this regard. Following the use of Bangla in the computer, the role of the computer in offices and printing industries in Dhaka rapidly assumed a great dimension. A free, open source and very easy to use and user-friendly Bangla typing software and keyboard 'Avro' developed by Mehdi Hasan Khan and released in 2003 through OmicronLab with the slogan 'let the language be free' has taken the expansion of Bangla language in this field to another level.[100] Exportable software development in Bangladesh commenced in 1995 while exportable multimedia system development began in 1997.[101]

93. While all this progress was happening in almost isolated manners, the policymakers realized the need to do these formally through official institutional arrangements. In 1983, a National Committee was formed to purchase computers as per the government's requirements. In 1988, the Committee was renamed as the National Computer Board, which was further renamed in 1989 as BCC and was made a statutory body under the Ministry of Science and Technology. An Act of Parliament, i.e., the Bangladesh Computer Council Act, 1990 (Act No. 9 of 1990), was enacted to this effect. Since its establishment, BCC has been working as a government advisory body on making computer-related actives popular in the country.[102]

94. Besides BCC, various professional bodies have been set up to foster computer culture in the country. Established in 1979, Bangladesh Computer Society is the leading and the only government-approved professional organization of computer and information systems engineers, scientists and technologists. A list of some other such professional bodies includes Bangladesh Association of Software Industries and Services (BASIS), Electronic Commerce Association of Bangladesh (e-CAB), Internet Service Provider (ISP), Bangladesh Association of Call Center and Outsourcing (BACCO), Association of Mobile Telecom Operators of Bangladesh (AMTOB).

---

100. It may be relevant to share here that even before the 'Avro', there was another open-source Bangla keyboard named 'Ekushey' developed by Dr Robin Upton of Altruists International, UK. *See* The Story of Ekushey Project, https://www.ekushey.org/?page/Story_of_Ekushey_Project.
101. Computer, Banglapedia, http://en.banglapedia.org/index.php?title=Computer.
102. Section 6, the Bangladesh Computer Council Act, 1990 (Act No. 9 of 1990).

§6. HISTORY OF THE INTERNET

95. The political history of Bangladesh played an influential role in the introduction of ICT and the internet in the country. In 1988, the country received the first invitation to link to the Information Highway through a submarine cable, which was rejected by the then military dictator Lieutenant General H.M. Ershad due to the lack of knowledge about the internet and the Information Super Highway and to save the image of his illegitimate government.[103]

96. In 1994, the democratically elected party, Bangladesh Nationalist Party (BNP) (1991–1996) received another offer to connect the country free of cost to the Information Highway through a submarine cable together with neighbouring countries of South Asia. Even though India, Pakistan and Sri Lanka accepted the offer, the then BNP government refused to accept it due to the fear that the classified state information would be lost. But the next government led by Awami League (1996–2001) took the first important steps to connect the country to Information Super Highway through the Bangladesh Submarine Cable Network project. An IT Task Force headed by the Prime Minister was also formed. In the next general election held in October 2001, ICT became a central issue and both the rivals, i.e., BNP and Awami League included this use of ICT with due importance in their election manifesto.[104]

97. The use of the internet in Bangladesh was started first in 1995 on a limited scale through offline email. On 6 June 1996, it was made open for the use of the public through Very Small Aperture Terminal (VSAT). Online internet connection started mushrooming through an ISP by the name Information Services Network Limited. At present, there are more than fifty ISPs in the country, including the government-owned BTTB. Mobile internet was started in 2004 using General Packet Radio Service technology. In 2005, Bangladesh got connected with the submarine cable network. In 2006, mobile phone operator Grameen Phone started a more speedy Edge service.

98. In the Information and Communication Technology Act, 2006 (Act No. 39 of 2006), section 2 has included the definition of 'internet' to mean 'such an international computer network by which users of computer, cellular phone or any other electronic system around the globe can communicate with one another, interchange information and can browse the information presented on the websites'.

99. In 2009, the HCD of the Supreme Court had referred to the definition of the term 'closed-end fund' available in the internet encyclopaedia 'Wikipedia'.[105] In

103. Sadik Hasan, *Introducing E-government in Bangladesh: Problems and Prospects*, 78 Inter'l Soc. Science Rev., 111–125 (2003).

104. *Ibid.*

105. *Ibrahim Akand and others v. Securities and Exchange Commission and others*, 2009, 38 CLC (HCD) [8221]; 30 BLD (HCD) (2010) 49. The Supreme Court also referred Wikipedia in *Bangladesh National Women Lawyers Association (BNWLA) v. Government of Bangladesh*, 2011, 40 CLC (HCD) [4739]; 31 BLD (HCD) (2011) [324] to define 'eve' and 'even teasing'.

2013, the students of the Computer Science and Engineering Department of Shahjalal University of Science and Technology developed 'Pipilika' (www.pipilika-.com), the country's first and only search engine which could search web resources both in Bengali and English, though the search engine is not active now.

§7. History of Submarine Cable

100. Submarine cables, the first one being laid across the English Channel from Dover, England to Calais, France in 1850 and the last between India and the United Arab Emirates in 1986, are considered as the backbone of the internet, international network and global e-commerce. More than 420 submarine cables spanning around 700,000 mi facilitate over 95% of international communications.[106] Joining the submarine cables has a huge impact on the progress and development of internet services in any country. These submarine cables have strategic importance as well, and therefore, the issue of their protection is already well recognized through various international legal instruments.[107] Moreover, in 2010, the UN described submarine communications cables as 'critical information infrastructure' (CII) and recognized that they are 'vitally important to the global economy and national security of all States'.[108] It has already been shared that Bangladesh missed the opportunity to link to the Information Super Highway through submarine cables twice in 1988 and in 1994 due to political reasons and lack of knowledge and expertise of the persons responsible in the decision making.

101. The process to join the submarine cable system formally started with the signing of a Memorandum of Understanding (MoU) with the Southeast Asia-Middle East-Western Europe International Consortium Submarine Cable [(SEA-ME-WE-4) in short (SMW4)] on 4 September 2002. Another agreement on construction and maintenance with the SMW4 consortium was signed on 27 March 2004. In 2006, a submarine cable landing station was inaugurated at Jhilongjha, Cox's Bazaar and about BDT 5 billion was spent for this purpose. With this initiative, Bangladesh joined the SMW4 submarine cable system for the first time, and it was the sole international optic fibre submarine cable landing in Bangladesh.

102. A new government-owned company, i.e., Bangladesh Submarine Cable Company Limited (BSCCL) was incorporated in 2008 with the aim, *inter alia*, to

---

106. For an updated list and map of the existing submarine cable, please *see* Submarine Cable Map, https://www.submarinecablemap.com/#/.
107. A number of international legal instruments have already been adopted containing provisions on the protection of the submarine cables. A list of these instruments includes: The International Convention for the Protection of Submarine Cables (1884), the Convention on the Territorial Sea and the Contiguous Zone (1958), the Convention on the High Seas (1958), and the United Nations Convention on the Law of the Sea (1982). *See*, generally, Tara Davenport, *Submarine Cables, Cybersecurity and International Law: An Intersectional Analysis*, 24(1) Cath. U. J. L. & Tech., 57–109 (2015).
108. United Nations General Assembly Resolution [A/RES/65/37] of 7 Dec. 2010 on 'Oceans and the law of the sea'.

connect Bangladesh to the global information superhighway and strengthen the national ICT sector. This company is now considered as the country's prime telecommunication service provider, though there are three terrestrial cables in the Bangladesh-India borders in Jessore, Sylhet-Cumilla and Kurigram through which Bangladesh may also get connected to the global communication network. After the landing of SMW4, with its nearly 250 Gbps of bandwidth, the internet infrastructure in Bangladesh has significantly improved. This twenty-year lifespan cable is about to expire soon in 2025.

103. Since its capacity cannot be increased and the maintenance fee of the cable is relatively high, BSCCL undertook the second submarine cable project, i.e., SEA-ME-WE-5 (SMW5) with 200 Gbps which will reach 1,500 Gbps eventually. BSCCL joined the SMW5 consortium in 2014. The landing station of this second submarine cable was constructed in Kalapara, Pathuakhali at the cost of around BDT 6.6 billion. Bangladesh has been connected to SMW5 cable since February 2017, and it is expected that it will remain operational for the next 20–25 years.

104. Since early 2018, the government has started the preparation for the third submarine cable, and an MoU was signed with SEA-ME-WE-6 (SMW6) consortium since the internet data consumption rate at the domestic level has been increasing exponentially. In December 2020, the project proposal for this third submarine cable was approved and an agreement was signed with SMW6 in September 2021. It is anticipated that the third submarine cable will be installed by June 2024. The country will get connected with it through the landing station in Cox's Bazar and it is anticipated that the additional bandwidth can also be exported as some neighbouring countries have already expressed their interests in this regard. Besides, the government is actively considering the proposal of one private sector entrepreneur to introduce the first private submarine cable in the country. Moreover, the government has taken a stand to welcome proposed Asia Pacific land-based connectivity to be effective from 2026 through the Asian Highway project.

105. In 2011, BTRC issued Regulatory and Licensing Guidelines for Issuing License to Build, Operate and Maintain International Terrestrial Cable (ITC) Systems and Services in Bangladesh. Based on these Guidelines, apart from the BSCCL, six ITC operators, i.e., Fibre@Home, Summit Communications, Novocom, 1Asia Alliance Communication, BD Link Communication, and Mango Teleservices received licences from BTRC to provide internet access services, and these ITCs have been providing internet access services through terrestrial cables. As a result, it is believed that even if there is an issue with the submarine cable, telecommunication services will not be disrupted in the country.[109]

---

109. It may be relevant to share here that in November 2007, there was an intentional sabotage with two man-made cuts in the first submarine cable at two points near Cox's Bazar and Feni in a week. Bangladesh lost 100% international communications for at least one week and the Bangladesh Telegraph and Telephone Board lost USD 1.05 million in revenue. *See* Michael Sechrist, Cyberspace in Deep Water: Protecting Undersea Communications Cables By Creating an International Public-Private Partnership, Harvard Kennedy School, 23 Mar. 2010, https://www.belfercenter.org/sites/default/files/files/publication/PAE_final_draft_-_043010.pdf.

§8. History of Satellite

106. The journey of satellites started in this part of the world as a response to the management of natural disasters and calamities which had serious consequences on the agro-based socio-economic scenario. During the Pakistan period, in 1968, an Automatic Picture Transmission Ground Station was established in the then Atomic Energy Center for real-time weather images collected directly from meteorological satellites.

107. In a war-ravaged country, the Space and Atmospheric Research Centre was established at the Bangladesh Atomic Energy Commission and subsequently, Bangladesh Landsat Programme was included in the five-year plan in 1975. The first Standard A Satellite Earth Station of the country started its journey in Betbunia under Kawkhali Upazila of Rangamati district on 14 June 1975, to work with INTELSAT to survey natural resources and to monitor and manage environmental disasters. Subsequently, Standard B Satellite stations were established in Talibabad, Gazipur. The third Satellite Earth Station together with an International Trunk Exchange was established for the purpose of smooth communication at Mohakhali, Dhaka in 1994. Since 1995, another direct satellite was established to bridge exclusive communication between Sylhet and London.[110]

108. The Bangladesh Space Research and Remote Sensing Organization (SPARRSO), an affiliated organization of the Ministry of Defence, was established through the provisions of the Bangladesh Space Research and Remote Sensing Organization Act, 1991 (Act No. 29 of 1991). SPARRSO is statutorily responsible to facilitate the peaceful uses of outer space and remote sensing technology in the country, though the organization mainly focuses on remote sensing activities to share weather updates, and space-related activities are monitored by BTRC.

109. In 2017, with the support of Japan under the Joint Global Multi-Nation Birds Satellite project, BRAC Onnesha (which means search or exploration) built the first nano-satellite in Bangladesh. This Satellite, shaped like a cube of 10 cm edge, is capable of passing over Bangladesh four to six times a day.[111] This nano-satellite was launched on a SpaceX Falcon 9 rocket by its CRS-11 mission to the International Space Station from Kennedy Space Centre, Florida, United States (US) on 3 June 2017. The ground station was set up on the rooftop of Building-4 of the BRAC University, Mohakhali, Dhaka.

---

110. Raisinghani, M.S. & Rahman, M., *Barriers to IT Industry Success: A Socio-Technical Case Study of Bangladesh*, in Tan, B.F. (ed.), *Cases on Global IT Applications and Management: Successes and Pitfalls*, 277–302, at 300 (2002).
111. Tasfia Huda, Brac Onnesha: Bangladesh's first nano-satellite, 30 Jul. 2017, https://www.dhakatribune.com/magazine/weekend-tribune/2017/07/30/brac-onnesha-bangladeshs-first-nano-satellite.

110. In April 2008, BTRC formed a Committee to explore the possibility to own a communication satellite for the country. A US-based consultancy firm 'Space Partnership International (SPI)' was appointed to launch a Communication and Broadcasting Satellite. The Committee submitted an electronic filing for 102° East and 69° East and Coordination Request (CR) notification to ITU. However, after objections from different South Asian and Asia Pacific region countries, the request of Bangladesh could not be accepted, and as a result, Bangladesh had to rent an orbital slot from a Russian company 'Intersputnik'. Finally, on 10 May 2018, by launching the satellite using SpaceX & Falcon-9 from the Cape Canaveral launch pad in Florida, US, Bangladesh became the fifty-seventh country in the world that has sent her own satellite, i.e., Bangabandhu Satellite-1, a geostationary communication and broadcasting satellite with the aim to ensure improved communication and broadcasting. While Thales Alenia Space of France in association with local engineers will handle the satellite for the next three years, Betbunia Ground Station, Gazipur was prepared to serve as the secondary control centre for Bangabandhu Satellite-1.[112] This satellite will serve the country for eighteen years i.e., until 2036.

111. The Satellite started its transmission by telecasting the South Asian Football Federation Championship held in August 2018 in Dhaka. The government has made it mandatory for local private TV Channels to use the bandwidth of this satellite, and since October 2019, all thirty-six such channels have been using this satellite for their commercial transmission. The government has been earning BDT 12.5 million annually from these channels though the cost of this satellite's installation and operation is BDT 300 million.[113] Even though it is very unlikely that the government can recoup the installation and operational cost of the Bangabandhu Satellite-1, the satellite has already grabbed ITU's very prestigious 'Recognition of Excellence' award.

112. A state-owned company, i.e., the Bangladesh Satellite Company Limited was established in 2017 to perform post launching activities, such as operation and control from the ground stations, marketing, and sales services, etc. of the Bangabandhu Satellite-1. The government has already taken initiatives to launch the second satellite, i.e., Bangabandhu-II possibly by 2023 and sought four orbital slots for 69° East, 74° East, 102° East, and 133° East from the ITU. A British firm was selected to recommend the suitable type from among the various types of satellites.

113. The absence of a dedicated regulator responsible to explore the ultimate potentials of peaceful uses of outer space-related activities in the Bangladesh context is still an important concern. Recently, a legislation titled the Bangabandhu Sheikh Mujibur Rahman Aviation and Aerospace University Act, 2019 (Act No. 5

112. For more, *see* 3 Mohammad Ershadul Karim, *Bangabandhu Satellite-1: Technological and Legal Development*, in Encyclopedia of Public International Law in Asia, 127–129 (Central and South Asia) (2021).

113. Bilkis Irani, PwC Selected as Consultant for Bangabandhu-2 satellite, 8 Jan. 2021, Dhaka Tribune, https://www.dhakatribune.com/uncategorized/2021/01/04/pwc-selected-as-consultant-for-bangabandhu-2-satellite.

of 2019) was also enacted to promote aviation and aerospace technology for the economic development of the country and it was decided to establish the proposed University at Lalmonirhat.

§9. Telecommunication Infrastructure

114. Due to significant technological advancements in the field of telecommunication, it was realized that the existing domestic laws, especially, i.e., the Telegraph Act, 1885 and the Wireless Telegraphy Act, 1933, the provisions of which give the government exclusive privilege to establish, maintain and work on telegraph and telephone-related activities were not sufficient. Therefore, in order to develop sound telecommunication infrastructure in the country, in 1998, the government formulated the National Telecommunications Policy, which provided for the enactment of a comprehensive law.[114] The Bangladesh Telecommunication Regulation Act, 2001 was consequently enacted. Nevertheless, it was realized that all these legal and policy initiatives were not adequate to address many of the new generation technologies. Therefore, the International Long Distance Telecommunication Services (ILDTS) Policy 2007 was formulated containing detailed provisions regarding telecommunication infrastructure in Bangladesh. This Policy was subsequently revised in May 2010 as the ILDTS Policy 2007 could not be implemented properly even though regulatory moves such as illegal call termination activities were going on. It will be pertinent to share that even though the Policy was revised in 2010, the revised Policy has maintained all the policy objectives of the Policy of 2007 but included the modified ways to achieve these objectives.

115. The BTRC, being the principal national telecommunication regulator, follows the provisions of the ILDTS Policy 2010. In performing its statutory and regulatory responsibilities, BTRC has been issuing licences to entrepreneurs to provide telecommunication services in three different layers, i.e., international layer, national layer, and access layer. These layers, also known as Network Topology, are projected below:

(a) *International layer* (works with satellite backup facilities to provide global internet connectivity):
   (i) International Gateway (IGW)[115] Services (all international voice calls are routed through IGWs).
   (ii) International Internet Gateway (IIG)[116] Services (all international data traffic is routed through IIGs).
(b) *National layer*:

114. It has already been shared that the National Telecommunications Policy, 2015 was revised in 2018, containing identical policy objectives and strategies.
115. Under the ILDTS Policy 2010, IGWs are switching systems through which international voice traffic (VoIP and clear channel) is sent and received. IGW allows physical monitoring of the traffic flow.
116. Under the ILDTS Policy, 2010, IIG refers to switching systems through international data traffic is sent and received. It allows computer-based voice traffic (messenger, etc.).

   (i) Interconnection Exchange (ICX)[117] (all national inter-operator voice calls are routed through ICXs).
   (ii) National Internet Exchange (NIX)[118] (all national inter-operator data traffic is routed through NIXs).

(c) *Access layer*:
   (i) Services provided to the subscribers through Access Network Service (ANS) Operators such as Public Switched Telephone Network (PSTN), Cellular, Cable Service Provider, and ISPs.

116. The entrepreneurs need to obtain licences through auction/bidding in order to provide these services.[119] BTRC, along with the provisions as encapsulated in Chapter five of the Bangladesh Telecommunication Regulation Act, 2001, has framed the Bangladesh Telecommunication Regulatory Commission (Licensing Procedure) Regulations, 2004 (last amended in 2009) to this end. Under these Regulations, licences are required to provide: (a) PSTN, (b) Cellular Mobile Phone Services, (c) Global Mobile Personal Communication by Satellite (GMPCS), (d) National Long Distance Service, (e) Overseas Telecommunication Service, (f) Internet Data Communication Service, (g) Data Communication Service, (h) VSAT Services, (i) Paging Services, (j) Radio Trunking services, (k) Voice over Internet Protocol (VoIP) Technology/Service, (l) Network Service, (m) IGW, (n) ICX, (o) Internet Exchange Services (IEX), (p) Internet Protocol (IP) Telephony Services, (q) 3G Services, (r) Broadband Wireless Access (BWA) Services, (s) Call Centre Services, (t) Telecom Value Added Services (VAS), (u) Submarine Cable Service, (v) Satellite Service, (w) Amateur Radio, and (x) Vehicle Tracking Services.[120] Providing telecommunication services without the permission of the government by obtaining a licence is a punishable offence of serious nature for which the accused can be held liable to pay a fine of up to BDT 3 billion or imprisonment up to ten years or both.[121]

117. On the other hand, licences can be obtained without auction/bidding to provide the services of NIX, Nationwide Telecommunication Transmission Network

---

117. Under the ILDTS Policy, 2010, ICX refers to switching system, which provides interconnections among the existing/future telecommunication network of the operators and allows monitoring, lawful interception facilities and roaming number portability.
118. Under the ILDTS Policy, 2010, NIX refers to switching systems through which all domestic Internet data communication will be routed via NIX to minimize usage of international bandwidth.
119. Schedule I to the Bangladesh Telecommunication Regulatory Commission (Licensing Procedure) Regulations, 2004 (last amended in 2009) provides that for services such as Cellular Mobile Phone Service, GMPCS, Overseas Telecom Service, Paging Service (for commercial purpose), Radio ...ing Service (for commercial purpose), PSTN, NLD, IGW, ICX, IEX, 3G Services, BWA Ser... ...marine Cable Service, Satellite Service, etc competitive bidding and/or auction licensing ... applicable. Whereas, for services such as VoIP Technology/Service, Network ... Service, Data Communication Service, IP Telephony Services, Call Centre Ser... Amateur Radio, and Vehicle Tracking Services, etc. open and/or auction ... all be applicable.
120. ...gladesh Telecommunication Regulatory Commission (Licensing Procedure)
121. ...ladesh Telecommunication Regulation Act, 2001 (Act No. 18 of 2001).

(NTTN) Service Provider, Vehicle Tracking Services, IP Telephony Service Provider (Nationwide, Central, Zone and Zonal), ISP (Nationwide, Central, Zone, Zonal, Category A, Category B and Category C), VSAT User, VSAT Provider, VSAT Provider with HUB, Call Centre, Hosted Call Centre, Hosted Call Centre Service Provider, International Call Centre, Call Centre Registration Certificate. Around 900 entrepreneurs have so far taken licences to provide VoIP services.

118. As of March 2019, there are twenty-five IGW,[122] thirty-seven IIG,[123] twenty-six ICX,[124] three BWA[125] and seven ITC[126] service providers. There are four National PSTN,[127] seven zonal PSTN,[128] and only one rural PSTN, i.e., Integrated Services Limited. There are 146 nationwide ISPs, ninety-six Central zone ISPs, and 211 zonal ISPs: of them, fifty-one are in the south-east zone, fifty-eight in the south-west zone, fifty-seven are in the north-east zone and forty-five are in the north-west zone.

---

122. Bangla Trac Communications Limited, BTCL, Mir Telecom Ltd., Novotel Limited, Global Voice Telecom Limited, BG Tel Limited, HRC Technologies Limited, Roots Communication Ltd. 1Asia Alliance Gateway Ltd., Unique Infoway Limited, Sigma Engineers Limited, DBL Telecom Limited, Apple GlobalTel Communications Ltd., First Communications Limited, Mos5 Tel Limited, Cel Telecom Limited, Ranks Telecom Limited, Bangla Tel Limited, SM Communication Limited, Platinum Communications Limited, Bangladesh IGW Limited, Digicon Telecommunication Limited, Venus Telecom Limited, Hamid Sourcing Limited, Bestec Telecom Limited.
123. BTCL, Mango Teleservices Ltd., Maxnet Online, I-TEL Limited, Global Fair Communications Limited, Level-3 Carrier Limited, Newtex Pacific Limited, BD Hub Limited, 1Asia Alliance Communication Ltd., Fibre@Home Ltd., Bangladesh Submarine Cable Company Ltd., Green land Technologies Ltd., Radiant Communications Limited, Integrated Business Systems & Solutions (Pvt.) Ltd., Rego Communications Ltd., Abir Telecommunications Limited, Peerex Networks Limited, Summit Communications Ltd., Toron Limited, Optimax Communication Ltd., Aamra Technologies Ltd., Intraglobe Communications Limited, Apple Communication, Cybergate Ltd., Delta Infocom Ltd., FM-Spectrum Telecom Limited, Exabyte Ltd., Sky Tel Communication Ltd., BD Link Communication Ltd., Bangla Phone Ltd., Managewell Communication Ltd., Equitel Communication Ltd., Velocity Networks Limited, Earth Telecommunication (PVT) Ltd., NovoCom Limited, Coronet Corporation Ltd., Virgo Communications Ltd.
124. BTCL, Getco Telecommunications Limited, M & H Telecom, Paradise Telecom Ltd. Teleplus Network Limited, Bantel Limited, Cloud Tel Limited, Bangla ICX Ltd., Voicetel Ltd. Imam Network Ltd., Integrated Services Limited, Mother Telecommunication, Agni Systems Limited, New Generation Telecom Limited, Softex Communication Limited, Cross World Telecom Ltd., Jibondhara Solutions Ltd., RingTech (Bangladesh) Ltd., Purple Telecom Limited, Gazi Networks Limited, Micro Trade, Tele Exchange Limited, M. M. Communications Ltd., S R Telecom Limited, Bangla Telecom Limited, Vertex Communications Ltd.
125. Augere Wireless Broadband (Bangladesh) Limited, Banglalion Communications Ltd., Bangladesh Internet Exchange Limited.
126. BTCL, Fibre @ Home Limited, Summit Communications Limited, Novo Communication Ltd., BD Link Communication Ltd., Mango Teleservice
127. BTCL, Tele Barta Ltd., Ranks Telecom Limited, National Telecom Ltd
128. WorldTel Bangladesh Limited (Central Zone) Bangla Phone Limited (com Limited (North-East), Westec Limited (South-East), One Tel Com West), S.A Telecom System Ltd. (South-East), Nextel Telecom Lim

§10. SHARING OF MOBILE TELECOMMUNICATION INFRASTRUCTURE

119. Telecommunication infrastructures are indispensable for ensuring effective telecommunication services. In the absence of adequate operational infrastructures, it is difficult to provide desired services to the consumers. Already the telecom consumers of Bangladesh have been suffering for various reasons apparently due to inadequate telecommunication structure even though the ANS, i.e., broadband access services, cellular mobile phone services and fixed telephony services providers are duty-bound to provide standard QoS as per the provisions of the Bangladesh Telecommunication Regulatory Commission (ANS Operator's Quality of Service) Regulations, 2018. Under this Regulations, 2018, the issue of call drops, which is caused mainly due to technical reasons, e.g., spectrum used by the MNOs and inadequate telecommunication infrastructures, is to be within the statutory limit. Nevertheless, the issue of excessive call drops has turned out to be a real concern for the stakeholders. The result of a very recently conducted drive test in different locations of Dhaka city (between 23 January 2021 to 8 January 2021) revealed that the MNOs were providing desired standard quality services, though in a similar test in Chottogram Division (between 13 February 2021 to 14 March 2021) the result was found negative in terms of desired standard quality services.[129] Pertinent to mention here that the MNOs believe that this is caused due to the very high spectrum fee, frequency price and some other related unfavourable conditions which prevent them from installing a sufficient number of towers.[130]

120. Telecommunication structures are broadly classified into two categories: active and passive infrastructure.[131] Examples of active infrastructure include the sharing of elements of the active layer of a mobile network, e.g., antenna, base station or core network elements, mobile roaming. On the other hand, examples of passive infrastructure include: antenna, feeder, shelter or support cabinet, transmission equipment, real estate and mast.

121. Sharing of telecommunication infrastructure allows the service providers to offer services at a lower or reasonable cost. In Bangladesh, a densely populated

129. Bangladesh Telecommunication Regulatory Commission, QoS DT Results of Dhaka, 24 March, http://www.btrc.gov.bd/notice-board/mobile-operators-quality-services-qos-drive-test-result-dhaka-city-0; Bangladesh Telecommunication Regulatory Commission, QoS DT Results of Chattogram, 29 Mar. 2021, http://www.btrc.gov.bd/notice-board/mobile-operators-qos-quality-service-drive-test-results-chattogram-division.

130. Association of Mobile Telecom Operators of Bangladesh, The trap of call drop, https://www.amtob.org.bd/index.php?/home/newsdetails/192.

131. According to the Guidelines for Infrastructure Sharing, 2008, 'Active Infrastructure Sharing is the sharing of electronic infrastructure & facility. It includes sharing of Base Transceiver Station (BTS)/Node B, spectrum, antenna, feeder cable, Radio Access Network, microwave radio equipment, billing platform, switching centres, router, Base Station Controller (BSC)/Radio Network Controller, optical fibre/wired access and backbone transmission network, database etc.' Whereas, 'Passive Infrastructure Sharing is the sharing of non-electronic infrastructure & facility. It includes sharing of physical sites, buildings, shelters, towers/masts, electric power supply and battery backup, grounding/earthing, air conditioning, security arrangement, poles, ducts, trenches, right of way.'

developing country with frequent incidents of natural calamity and disasters, the regulator in the telecommunication sector, i.e., BTRC has started the infrastructure sharing programmes informally in 2003 followed by the adoption of a formal policy initiative, i.e., the Guidelines for Infrastructure Sharing in 2008.[132] The MNOs of the country mainly own the towers, and the regulators attempted to create two separate industries, i.e., the network business and the infrastructure services to make the telecommunication infrastructure effective and competitive. Therefore, the Guidelines was formulated to encourage telecommunication service providers to remove uncertainty and create a framework for better cooperation in infrastructure sharing by incorporating provisions on the requirement to lease out/rent out/swap infrastructure on a non-discriminatory basis to other service providers.

122. The Guidelines has rightly identified that the sharing of infrastructure assists to minimize the cost of network deployment and protecting the environment by reducing the proliferation of towers and facilities installation. Thus, this will enable the service providers to provide better and efficient service to the subscribers and enhance competition amongst telecommunication operators in more cooperative environments.[133]

123. The Guidelines of 2008 has specified certain conditions, set some requirements and stipulated procedure to allow the infrastructure provider to share the rest of the infrastructure after keeping a maximum of 25% of spare passive infrastructure, i.e., non-electronic infrastructure & facility, sharing of physical sites, buildings, shelters, towers/masts, electric power supply and battery backup, grounding/earthing, air conditioning, security arrangement, poles, ducts, trenches, right of way, optical fibre/wired access and backbone transmission network, etc. in the respective licensing zone/area at a rate based on the directives set by BTRC.

124. The Guidelines was subsequently amended in 2011 to extend, *inter alia*, the definition of 'passive infrastructure' to include 'in-house wiring, sub-loop (Wire/Cable) and local-loop (Wire/Cable)'. Besides, most importantly, the previous mandatory provision to jointly develop, build, maintain and operate optical/wired backbone transmission network by the operators was amended and made the mandated transmission backhaul sharing only via the NTTN Licensee[134] protocol preventing the infrastructure sharing among the MNOs. Simultaneously, the operators were allowed to sell/lease the excess capacity/core/fibre of the transmission network to the NTTN Licensees. Moreover, previously, the Guidelines kept the option to issue a password to the BTRC, licensed operators and anyone permitted by the BTRC so that detailed information as stored on the website of the operators could be accessed. The revised Guidelines has removed such obligations. Furthermore, the

---

132. No. BTRC/LL/INF-SHARING (304)/2008-1108.
133. Introduction, the Guidelines for Infrastructure Sharing, 2008.
134. Licences are given only two entities, i.e., Summit Communications Limited and Fibre@Home Limited.

revised Guidelines amended the procedure for negotiation of an Infrastructure Sharing Agreement. There is no mention of 25% sharing anymore, and as a result, it was found that less than 18% of total passive resources are shared by the operators.[135]

125. In 2013, mobile operators were issued with the spectrum to deploy 3G services nationwide. To expand 3G coverage nationwide, and to provide better 3G services, operators need a robust transmission network. Since the QoS of NTTN was questionable, mobile operators had no choice but to deploy their own transmission backhaul to deliver better communication services. This had been causing an overspend for the operators since they were not able to share their transmission network with others. Tables 5 and 6 show the statistics on tower sharing by the MNOs in 2014 and 2018 respectively.

Table 5 Tower Sharing by MNOs in Bangladesh[136]

Ser	*MNO*	*Own Tower*	*Shared Tower (as Provider)*	*Shared Tower (as Seeker)*
1	Banglalink	8,374	488	1,313
2	Grameenphone	8,454	2,836	233
3	Robi	5,723	1,069	1,279
4	Airtel	3,573	305	1,472
5	CityCell	881	138	15
6	Teletalk	–	–	750 (BTCL)
	Total	27,005		

Source: BTRC, August 2014.

Table 6 Estimated Tower Count and Revenue Market Share of MNO in Bangladesh

Ser	*MNO*	*Own Tower*	*Revenue Market Share (%)*
1	Grameenphone	7,800	45
2	Edotco	8,242	36
3	Banglalink	6,000	12
4	Airtel	3,800	7
5	Teletalk	4,100	–
	Total	29,942	100

135. Md Wahid-Uz-Zaman, *Mobile Infrastructure Sharing in Bangladesh: Bottlenecks and Way Forward*, XXXVI J. Bus. Stud., 77–89 (April 2015).

136. Table slightly modified. Md Wahid-Uz-Zaman, *Mobile Infrastructure Sharing in Bangladesh: Bottlenecks and Way Forward*, XXXVI J. Bus. Stud., 77–89, at 85 (April 2015).

Source: TowerXchange, 2018.[137]

126. In April 2017, the BTRC published the draft of 'Regulatory and Licensing Guidelines for Tower Sharing License' to introduce active sharing in the Infrastructure Sharing Guidelines to allow the implementation of In-Building Solutions including Distributed Antenna System among the telecom operators to enable them to share their certain Active Elements. A fifteen-member Committee was formed to analyse and evaluate the application of the draft guidelines followed by the reporting to BTRC. The draft was subsequently finalized with the title 'Regulatory and Licensing Guidelines for Issuing License for Tower Sharing in Bangladesh' in April 2018 containing relevant information to obtain licences to develop, build, own, acquire, rent, lease, operate and maintain tower for providing telecommunication services in the country.

127. According to the Guidelines of 2018, tower sharing, which 'includes requirement to lease out/rent out/swapping Tower on a non-discriminatory basis to other service providers', 'is an approach to ensuring optimum utilization of telecommunication resources, land, infrastructure and power; to reduce environmental hazards; to reduce the CAPEX and OPEX; to achieve higher economies of scale; to promote healthy competition by reducing the entry-cost for new entrants; and to reduce the wastage of land route to develop telecommunication network and infrastructure'.

128. Till November 2018, four companies, i.e., Edotco Bangladesh Tower Company Limited, TASC Summit Tower, Kirtankhola Tower Bangladesh Limited (previously known as iSON ETC Tower, a subsidiary of Africa-based iSON Groups subsidy iSON Tower) and AB HiTech Consortium Limited (an associate entity of Swedish High Tech AB) received the tower sharing licence after fulfilling the criteria required for mobile network tower sharing company licence. These companies will have to pay BDT 25 crore as a licence acquisition fee and BDT 5 crore as an annual renewal fee. Moreover, they need to share 5.5% of their revenue with the government and 1% as the social obligation fund from the second year of the licences. Few other entities such as State-owned BTCL, BD Tower Business Company Consortium, FTA Bangladesh Limited, and Jamuna Tower have also applied for the licence. Bangladesh is a market of around 30,000 towers, and after these regulatory initiatives, it is evident that infrastructure sharing is well-established in the country with a prevailing tenancy ratio of around 1.25.[138]

---

137. Tower Xchange, *TowerXchange's Analysis of the Independent Tower Market in Asia: Selected Asian Tower Market Size Comparisons, Q1-2018*, 70 (July 2018), available at: https://www.towerxchange.com/publication/towerxchange-23-0718/.

138. *Ibid.*, at p. 67.

§11. Last Few Words

129. The government of Bangladesh has declared 12 December as the 'National Information and Communication Technology day' as on this day, the present government set its election manifesto of 'digital Bangladesh'. In the latest survey and statistics conducted by the Oxford University's Internet Institute, i.e., The Online Labour Index, it is found that Bangladesh is second in terms of IT outsourcing works and 16% of the global online workers are based in Bangladesh.

130. Already, the government has inaugurated several toll-free hotline numbers, and people have been enjoying the benefits of these hotlines. A list of these hotlines includes: official emergency telephone number at the National Command and Control Centre, popularly known as the Police Control Room for police help, fire service, ambulance and commission of any crime ('999'), anti-corruption commission call centre to inform about any kind of corruptions ('106'), information relating to violence against women or child marriage ('109'), issues relating to the protection of child ('1098'), for legal aid ('16430'). Some charge-based dedicated services were introduced too. These are: for government information ('333'), national identification number ('105'), violation of human rights ('16108'), etc. With all these initiatives, there are, unfortunately, parallel negative news and reports also highlighting that the ICT sector of the country is not progressing and flourishing in the same way as it is supposed to be. Yet, the International Trade Administration of the US Department of Commerce hailed the ICT sector as the 'best prospect industry sector' for Bangladesh.[139]

139. International Trade Administration, Information and Communication Technology (ICT), Bangladesh – Country Commercial Guide, https://www.trade.gov/country-commercial-guides/bangladesh-information-and-communication-technology-ict.

Chapter 3. The Information and Communications Technology Market

§1. Introduction

131. After the ICT revolution powered by the internet coupled with the world wide web opened for general and commercial use in the 1990s, like many other developing countries, both Bangladesh and India started concentrating on the exploitation and utilization of this sector for the socio-economic development of the country. Bangladesh enacted the BCC Act, 1990 (Act No. 9 of 1990) to establish a Council responsible for promoting computers and developing the overall IT infrastructure for the socio-economic development of the country.[140] However, due to several factors, mainly political and economic, Bangladesh could not utilize the prospects of this sector as compared to the achievements of India. Politically, this sector received many instabilities coupled with varying importance by different governments guided by their political ideology and understanding. Due to the absence of strong economic strength and primarily agrarian nature of the economy, the public sectors and private entrepreneurs could not invest enough in the R&D of this sector. Nevertheless, this situation has changed in recent years, and Bangladesh has turned out to be an important and reliable destination for ICT investment and outsourcing assignments because of several factors such as very low operating cost, a pool of talented young, and government support to grow the industry, etc.

132. In the previous Industry Policy of Bangladesh 2005, various types of domestic industries were classified into four categories: (1) large (more than 100 workers), (2) medium (between 25–100 workers), (3) small (less than 25), and (4) cottage (where members of a family are engaged). Besides, there are reserved industries[141] and thrust sectors.[142] Computer software and ICT goods were listed as Thrust sectors, and IT-based activities and telecommunication were listed as service industries. This Industry Policy, 2005 was revised in 2016 even though the government released a draft to formulate the Policy in 2010.

---

140. Section 6, the Bangladesh Computer Council Act, 1990 (Act No. 9 of 1990).
Interestingly, the said law has also encapsulated a definition of 'information technology' to mean the processing of information through computer and the transfer of information using tele-electronic communication system. Section 2(c), the Bangladesh Computer Council Act, 1990 (Act No. 9 of 1990).

141. Under the Industry Policy 2005, some Industries are necessary to be kept reserved by the government in the interest of national security and are sensitive. These are: (1) arms and ammunitions and other military equipment and machineries, (2) nuclear power, (3) security printing and minting and (4) afforestation and Mechanized Extraction within the boundary of reserved forest.

142. Under the Industry Policy 2005, the 'thrust sectors' are those industries/industrial sub-sectors which have already been able to successfully contribute to the country's industrialization and poverty alleviation by increasing GDP, creating employment opportunities and increasing export income. Special incentives and financial facilities such as tax exemptions, exemption from dual taxation, tax holiday, and taxation at a reduced rate or accelerated depreciation (if the tax holiday and tax exemption facilities cannot be provided for new industries in the future) can be considered.

133. The Industry Policy 2016 stipulates an increase in the industry sector's share in GDP, i.e., from the present 29% to 35% by 2021, with the proportion of the workforce employed in the sector concurrently rising to 25% of the country's total labour force from the present 18%. The significant feature of this Policy 2016 is that for the first time, a Plan of Action to achieve different issues under the Policy is included at the end of this Policy. In the latest Industry Policy 2016, the criteria of different classes of industries were revised. Industries are classified into large, medium, small, Micro, cottage, handicrafts, high-tech,[143] creative, reserved, thrust sectors, priority sector and controlled sectors.[144] In this Policy, the ICT/Software industry is listed as thrust sector; IT Enabled Service (ITES) and activities such as systems analysis, design, solution system development, information service, call centre service, offshore development centre, business process outsourcing, etc. and telecommunication are listed as the service sector. Telecommunication industry (Mobile/Cellular and fixed-line phone), satellite channel, VoIP and IP telephone are included as a controlled sector. This chapter will highlight the telecommunication and ICT market in Bangladesh.

§2. Mobile Phone Subscribers

134. In terms of mobile network coverage, in 1997, only three districts out of sixty-four districts were covered; in 2000, a total of thirty districts; fifty districts came under the mobile coverage in 2002, and in 2004, the number reached sixty-one districts. Since then, mobile telephone connections have become an important vehicle in the socio-economic development of the country.

135. In 2015, the mobile ecosystem added around USD 13 billion of economic value and generated 6.2% of GDP in the country. This figure includes the direct economic impact of mobile operators and the broader ecosystem and the indirect impact as well as the productivity increase brought about by the use of mobile technologies.[145]

136. With 85 million unique subscribers in 2017, Bangladesh is the fifth largest mobile market in the Asia Pacific. Only one in five Bangladeshis subscribed to mobile internet services in 2017, despite 3G networks covering more than 90% of the population.[146] BTRC has been regularly updating the number of mobile phone subscribers in Bangladesh since January 2012 on its official website. The official statistics of mobile phone subscribers are shared below:

---

143. 'High-tech industry' means knowledge and capital-based, highly technical environment-friendly and IT/ITES/gene technology or R&D dependent technology.
144. Controlled sector industries are those industries for the establishment of which in the private sector, the entrepreneurs need to obtain permission or no objection certificate on the grounds of, *inter alia*, national security and culture.
145. GSM Association, Economic Impact: Bangladesh Mobile Industry, 2017, at p. 2.
146. GSM Association, Country overview: Bangladesh Mobile industry driving growth and enabling digital inclusion, 2018, at p. 3.

Timeline	*Number of Mobile Phone Subscribers*
January 2012	86.559 million
January 2013	97.389 million
January 2014	114.808 million
January 2015	121.860 million
January 2016	131.956 million
January 2017	128.281 million
January 2018	147.000 million
January 2019	157.544 million
January 2020	165.615 million
January 2021	171.854 million
September 2021	180.25 million

Source: Bangladesh Telecommunication Regulatory Commission.[147]

137. As of September 2021, there were 180.25 million mobile phone subscribers in the country. Of them, 83.78 million subscribers have been using the mobile phone services of Grameen Phone Ltd., 53.04 million have been using the services of Robi Axiata Limited, 37.02 million subscribers have been taking the services provided by Banglalink Digital Communications Ltd., and 6.41 million people have been using the services provided by Teletalk Bangladesh Ltd.[148] This gives the indication that, presently, there are only four MNOs providing telecommunication services in Bangladesh.

138. More than 30 million people in the country have been using smartphones.[149] This number has been increasing, though not satisfactorily compared to the neighbours and other countries of the Asia Pacific, and it was found that 41% of the total mobile phone users of the country use smartphones. Even though 95% of the population are now covered by 4G mobile broadband networks, of the smartphone users of the country, 47% use 2G, 25% use 3G and 28% use 4G connections.[150]

139. It is believed that about 30% of the total mobile handsets used in the country have been imported illegally and some of these are used to commit various illegal and criminal activities. Therefore, the government has taken an initiative to develop a National Equipment Identity Register (NEIR) for the imported mobile phones in the country following the International Mobile Equipment Identity (IMEI) number, a fifteen-digit unique identification or a serial number assigned to

147. BTRC, Mobile Phone Subscribers in Bangladesh, http://www.btrc.gov.bd/telco/mobile.
148. *Ibid.*, http://www.btrc.gov.bd/content/mobile-phone-subscribers-bangladesh-february-2021.
149. BTRC, Annual Report, 2019–2020 [Bangla], at p. 7.
150. GSM Association, Achieving mobile-enabled digital inclusion in Bangladesh, 2021.

all mobile handsets. BTRC has published the draft of the Directive in this regard for public consultation. Already over 118 million IMEI numbers have been added to the NEIR.[151]

§3. Internet Subscribers

140. With regard to the official number of internet subscribers from the official statistics available on the website of BTRC, it can be seen that in February 2012, there were 31,140,804 thousand active internet subscribers who subscribed to or connected to the internet within the last ninety days. In January 2013, the number reached 30,480,071 thousand; in January 2014, it was 35,522,889 thousand; in January 2015, the number reached 42.766 million; in January 2016, the number reached 56.167 million; in January 2017, the number was 66.779 million; in January 2018, the number reached to 80.829 million, in January 2019, it was 91.421 million, in January 2020, it was 99.246 million, and as of September 2021, there were 128.78 million internet subscribers in the country. Of them, 118.71 million subscribers were using mobile internet, whereas 10.07 million subscribers have been using the internet through ISPs and PSTN.[152] Apparently, it is evident that the internet subscribers using ISP and PSTN are not increasing rapidly, and the MNOs are the prime contributor in assisting people's access to the Internet.

141. It is evident that Bangladesh has one of the lowest internet penetration levels in the region. While network coverage remains a barrier to access, particularly in rural and remote areas of the country, coverage by itself does not guarantee access. The enablers are critical to creating the right conditions for mobile internet connectivity to flourish in the country even after recent progress. In particular, the country scores below average on infrastructure and affordability enablers relative to its regional peers. The slow transition to mobile broadband technologies in Bangladesh is also, in part, a matter of timing: following similar delays to the 3G auction, the 4G/LTE spectrum auction only took place in February 2018 making Bangladesh one of the last countries in South Asia to award licences for the technologies.[153]

§4. Computer Users

142. In the latest official statistics published in 2015, using ITU's Manual for Measuring ICT Access and Use by Households and Individuals, 2009 edition, it was revealed that the number of people who have been using the computer in Bangladesh is not very encouraging. It can be seen that at the national level, only 3.1%

151. Bilkis Irani, Days of Illegal Mobile Phones to Be Numbered by 2021, 26 Oct. 2021, Dhaka Tribune, https://www.dhakatribune.com/business/2020/10/26/days-of-illegal-mobile-phones-to-be-numbered-by-2021.
152. BTRC, Internet Subscribers in Bangladesh, http://www.btrc.gov.bd/telco/internet.
153. GSM Association, Country overview: Bangladesh Mobile industry driving growth and enabling digital inclusion, 2018, at p. 3.

of the households had a fixed-line telephone connection, 5.7% and 4.8% of households had computers and internet connections at home.[154] It is a matter of fact that in the ITU's ICT Development Index 2017, the number of users had increased. It was found that there were fixed-telephone subscriptions per 100 inhabitants (0.48), mobile-cellular telephone subscriptions per 100 inhabitants (77.88), international internet bandwidth per internet user (bit/s) (915,409), percentage of households with computers (9.59), percentage of households with internet access (14.50), percentage of individuals using the internet (18.25), fixed (wired)-broadband subscriptions per 100 inhabitants (3.77), and active mobile-broadband subscriptions per 100 inhabitants (17.79).[155] Finally, even though it seems that the number of users has increased to some extent as demonstrated in the ITU's ICT Development Index 2017, it will take a lot more comprehensive, coordinated and robust effort from the stakeholders to make the figure satisfactory.

§5. ICT Market: An Overview of Relevant Sectors

143. Being a generic technology, ICT has diversified use and applications. Due to this, there are differences of opinion on the sectors that should be included as ICT sectors. It is believed that to calculate the computer market, services such as data processing, consultancy, and computer hardware installation, operation and maintenance should also be considered. Generally speaking, IT services can be of three types: (1) application (e.g., network and systems integration, information security, consulting, web applications, etc.), (2) engineering (e.g., hardware and software), and (3) ITES. ITES can again be *vertical* (e.g., banking, capital market, insurance, manufacturing, retail, telecommunication, technology, travel, etc.) and *horizontal* (e.g., customer interaction and support, financial and administration, human resources, procurement services, knowledge services).

144. The BASIS used to classify and publish their reports by classifying the market into software and ITES only. On the other hand, Bangladesh Computer Samity (BCS), the leading professional body and association in the computers and information systems in the country, classifies the ICT sector into four areas: (1) Hardware, (2) Software Solution, (3) Network Solutions, and (4) ITES.[156] Whereas, to the Bangladesh Investment Development Authority (BIDA),[157] services such as software development, business process outsourcing, ITES, Hardware Assembling & Trading and Online & Cloud Services are included within the Bangladeshi IT

154. Bangladesh Bureau of Statistics, Report on ICT Use and Access by Individuals and Households Bangladesh, 2013, October 2015, p. 24.
155. ITU, ICT Development Index, 2017, https://www.itu.int/net4/itu-d/idi/2017/index.html#idi2017 economycard-tab&BGD.
156. BCS, IT Scenario of Bangladesh.
157. Bangladesh Investment Development Authority is an agency established under the Prime Minister's Office, through the provisions of the Bangladesh Investment Development Authority Act, 2016 (Act No. 36 of 2016), with the responsibility to encourage and facilitate private investment in the country.

industry.[158] Therefore, while discussing the market in this chapter, the statistics on the market of these sectors/areas will be primarily shared.

145. Telecom & ICT sectors are major contributing sectors to national GDP, which is over 6% consistently over the past decade. Bangladesh ranked 22nd in the Global Service Location Index, formerly known as Offshore Location Attractiveness Index, developed by AT Kearney in 2016 and ranked 21st in the Index of 2017. This Index help companies to understand factors in selecting the potential locations for offshore services.

146. Software development in Bangladesh was started in the early 1980s and started growing after the mid-1990s due to the obvious reason, i.e., the introduction of the internet for public use in the country. According to BIDA, the total investment in the ICT sector is BDT 500 billion (50,000 crores), and it is the largest contributor to Foreign Direct Investment (FDI) in the country. Total estimated IT Industry size is USD 120 Million (including export). Software contributes around 44%, and ITES contributes around 56% to the overall industry revenue. In the next five years, 1% of the country's total GDP will come from the software and IT services sector. Over 800 IT companies are now flourishing in the country and capturing a significant share in the international markets. Approximately 30,000 professionals, most of them being IT and other graduates, are employed in the industry. BASIS members provide or have provided customized software development (55.66%), ITES (16.98%), e-commerce or web services (12.45%), mobile application (4.72%), company product (4.34%), system integration (3.02%), consulting (1.51%), R & D services (0.94%), value-added reseller/Software (0.38%) and product distributor reseller (0.05%).[159]

147. According to BASIS, the national trade body for software and ITES established in 1997, approximately 1 million people have been working directly in the ICT sectors, where 250,000 are professionals. More than 1,500 IT enterprises and 838 member companies, who are members of BASIS, have been exporting their products and services in more than sixty countries (excluding freelancing services) and generating revenue of USD 600 million. 44% of BASIS members provide software-related services, and 56% generate revenue through ITES. North America is the main export destination.[160]

148. The government has taken various initiatives to exploit the benefits of this sector. Since 1996, the government granted zero or very low tariffs on computers and other related goods for the software industry. The government also declared several incentives such as 100% corporate tax exemption till 2024, 60% Value

158. Bangladesh Investment Development Authority, Sector Profile: Information Technology Industry, July 2019.
159. Bangladesh Investment Development Authority, ICT Sector in Bangladesh, http://bida.gov.bd/?page_id=2288.
160. Bangladesh Association of Software & Information Services, Bangladesh Software and IT Service Industry: Recent Trends & Dynamics, https://demo.basis.org.bd/public/files/publication/5e127be40ba48Bangladesh%20Software%20and%20IT%20Service%20Industry%20Overview.pdf.

Added Tax (VAT) exemption on rentals and utilities, 50% personal income tax reduction for foreign employees for three years, up to 10% cashback on total export revenue, full repatriation of capital and dividend without any restrictions on foreign equity holding to harness the benefits of this sector.

§6. Hardware Manufacturing

149. Bangladeshi entrepreneurs and companies usually do not produce computer hardware rather prefer to import these from renowned overseas manufacturers, though some local companies also assemble products in the country.[161] Nevertheless, it is apparent that the scenario has been changing in the last couple of years. In 2010, the Telephone Shilpa Sangstha Limited, an industrial organization under the MoPT having the facilities to produce computer hardware, started to assemble laptops with the name of the country's national bird, 'Doyel' (magpie robin). The price of this Laptop was only USD 120, which caught the attention of the mass media from home and abroad, and the interest of the countrymen. However, the project was not successful due to, *inter alia*, the battery life of the product. Bangladesh Cable Shilpa Industry Limited, another industrial organization under the MoPT, has been producing optical fibre cable since July 2011.

150. In the private sector, since September 2017, Walton Hi-Tech Industries Ltd. has started its full-fledged computer factory in Gazipur, near Dhaka. With the current setup, the factory can produce around 60,000 laptops, 30,000 desktop computers, and 30,000 monitors every month. The company uses Windows operating system under a Memorandum of Agreement signed with Microsoft. It is a matter of great pride that the company has started exporting laptops to Nigeria and Nepal. It has been reported that entrepreneurs in different Hi-Tech Parks have started producing hardware and will produce computer motherboards in the country soon. Bangladeshi IT entrepreneurs have started exporting internet of things (IoT) devices to different countries, including Saudi Arabia.

151. Besides, at least eleven organizations received the 'Mobile Phone Handset Manufacturer and Vendor Enlistment Certificate' and ten organizations, e.g., Walton High-Tech Industries Ltd. and Fair Electronics Ltd., have been assembling and marketing mobile phone handsets of 'Walton, Samsung, Symphony, Itel-Techno, 5 Star, Winstar, Vivo, Lava, DTC & Oppo' brands in the local market. All these ten organizations have received 'A' category licence and manufactured, assembled and marketed 14,522,464 mobile handsets.[162]

---

161. For example, Symphony, with the capability to assemble 500,000 handset per month started the assembling unit in Ashulia, near Dhaka in September 2018.
162. BTRC, Annual Report, 2019–2020 [Bangla], p. 54.

§7. REVENUE GENERATED

152. One may identify that there are differences in statistics produced by the public bodies and industry people on revenue generated from the software and ITES sectors. Nevertheless, software and ITES sectors are very important and emerging export sectors of the country. The statistics generated from the Export Promotion Bureau of Bangladesh (EPB), based on the data collected from the National Board of Revenue (NBR) and Bangladesh Bank (BB), on the export revenue earned from various computer services between 2011 and 2016 are projected below.

Table 7 Export of Computer Services

	2011–2012	*2012–2013*	*2013–2014*	*2014–2015*	*2015–2016*
	(Volume in Thousand USD)				
1. Computer Services	70,331	32,889	125,544	133,921	154,243
1.1 Computer Data Processing	21,973	–	47,564	73,926	106,733
1.2 Computer Consultancy Services	4,852	5,498	8,571	10,844	9,926
1.3 Export of Computer Software	42,753	62,669	68,508	47,895	35,368

Source: Export Statistics Book (2015–2016), EPB.

153. In the recent annual publication of the EPB, Export Statistics 2018–2019, which is the 'authentic picture of the country's export trade' it can be seen that the country earned USD 132.54 million, 152.83 million, 190.94 million, 182.01 million and 225.02 million in the year 2014–2015, 2015–2016, 2016–2017, 2017–2018 and 2018–2019 respectively by exporting computer services. In the same Export Statistics 2018–2019, the service sector is classified in a different way, i.e., computer services and information services and therefore, one may notice a slightly different figure than the preceding paragraph. During this period the country earned 0.94 million, 1.43 million, 0.75 million, 6.46 million and 0.35 million from information services in the year 2014–2015, 2015–2016, 2016–2017, 2017–2018 and 2018–2019 respectively.

154. In 2017, EPB reported that the Bangladesh software industry witnessed a 25.76% jump and earned USD 191 million.[163] However, according to BASIS, the ICT products and services industry in Bangladesh had earned nearly USD 800 million in the same year, whereas USD 500 million was earned from software export,

163. Ibrahim Hossain Ovi, ICT Export Earnings Rise by 25% in FY'17, 8 Aug. 2017, Dhaka Tribune, https://www.dhakatribune.com/business/2017/08/08/ict-export-earnings-rises-25-fy17.

USD 13 million from outsourcing and freelance work, and USD 15–USD 20 million from games and mobile application development.[164]

§8. Conclusion

155. Successive Bangladeshi governments have taken initiatives that ultimately assisted the country to be an important destination in the world for software and ITES development. The prospect of the country to exploit this sector is already acknowledged by various corners. There are still some challenges, and in order to overcome these challenges, the policymakers should consider concentrating on human resource development through proper training, ensuring uninterrupted availability of high-speed internet, electricity and supporting infrastructure, etc.

156. Bangladesh is projected to be one of the worst victims of climate change, and many people will be displaced and face unemployment problems. This will create multi-dimensional problems in the near future. It has already been shared at the beginning of this chapter that the policymakers missed the initial opportunities of the ICT sector in the 1990s, which was exploited by countries such as India and the Philippines. The policymakers should consider the importance of human resource development in the niche areas and thrust sectors such as IoT, blockchain, cloud computing, cyber security, quantum computing, etc. The policymakers can consider the experience of the RMG sector of the country which, though generating a huge amount of foreign currency, is limited in producing a few basic products. The policymakers of the RMG sector have realized the importance of making diversified dressy clothes recently. Some factories have started producing such clothes, and the entrepreneurs have started yielding more profits in turn for the same amount of effort. Bangladeshi IT sector entrepreneurs should consider this approach positively and should explore newer sectors in the market.

157. The present government has taken various programmes including the establishment of IT parks under the Bangladesh Hi-Tech Park Authority, which is establishing Software Technology Park and IT Training & Incubation Centre throughout the country to attract the local and foreign investors for the development of IT/ITES industries. With this, the government's move for the third submarine cable after the successful installation of the second one in Patuakhali and drastic move for uninterrupted electricity will hopefully make Bangladesh one of the top reliable and lucrative IT/ITES investment destinations soon.

---

164. ICT export fetches USD 800 million in 2017, The Daily Star, 17 Nov. 2017, https://www.thedailystar.net/frontpage/ict-export-fetches-800m-2017-1492510.

Chapter 4. e-Commerce: Facts and Figures

§1. INTRODUCTION

158. The use of the internet to promote and facilitate business and commercial activities commenced immediately when the internet was made available for public and general use in the mid-nineties. Globally, e-commerce sales hit an estimated USD 25.6 trillion, with 1.45 billion online shoppers, which grew by 8% from 2017 and the e-commerce sales value in 2018 was equivalent to 30% of the global GDP.[165] The figure will be very high given the fact that the COVID-19 has dramatically changed our daily life and forced us to shop online to facilitate to maintain social distancing and less gathering in the public place in the new normal. Some of the electronic commerce platforms such as Amazon, Taobao, Alibaba, eBay, Rakuten, etc., have been playing such an integral part in our daily life that it will be difficult to think of a day without them.

159. Even with the significant contribution resulting from the transaction of goods and services, there are some serious concerns too. Security and trust are the two most important factors a country needs to ensure a conducive environment for e-commerce. Affordable internet access, payment mechanism for the payment of goods and services transacted online and effective solutions for the delivery of these goods and services are crucial for an effective and successful e-commerce ecosystem.[166]

160. As the importance of electronic commerce has only been increasing in this networked and connected but borderless global village, and since there is no single designated global organization with the mandate to regulate electronic commerce matters exclusively, a number of international organizations have been functioning to shape different aspects of electronic commerce. For example, UNCITRAL has developed the Model Law on Electronic Commerce, 1996 'to enable and facilitate commerce conducted using electronic means by providing national legislators with a set of internationally acceptable rules aimed at removing legal obstacles and increasing legal predictability for electronic commerce'.[167] As of now, at least seventy-six countries in the world are found to be influenced by this Model law while enacting their domestic e-commerce legislation. Even though Bangladesh does not have a specific law on e-commerce, this Model law influenced in shaping the legal regime of the country; though, unfortunately, the provisions of digital and electronic certification and signature are only included in the Information and Communication Technology Act, 2006 (Act No. 39 of 2006).[168]

165. UNCTAD, Global e-commerce hits $25.6 trillion – latest UNCTAD estimates, https://unctad.org/news/global-e-commerce-hits-256-trillion-latest-unctad-estimates.
166. UNCTAD, 'Information Economy Report, 2015: Unlocking the Potential of E-commerce for Developing Countries', p. 34.
167. United Nations Commission on International Trade Law, https://uncitral.un.org/en/texts/ecommerce/modellaw/electronic_commerce.
168. UNCITRAL Model Law on Electronic Commerce (1996) – Status, https://uncitral.un.org/en/texts/ecommerce/modellaw/electronic_commerce/status.

161. The Organisation for Economic Co-operation and Development (OECD), an intergovernmental economic organization of thirty-seven industrialized nations founded to stimulate economic progress and world trade, has been playing pivotal roles in shaping the regulatory framework in the area of internet taxation, e-commerce consumer protection, information security and privacy. International Organization for Standardization (ISO) has been playing significant roles in developing various standards with the aim to make the e-commerce ecosystem more trusted and secured. WIPO deals with intellectual property rights (IPRs), e.g., copyright, trademark and patent, etc. infringements on e-commerce platforms, Internet Corporation for Assigned Names and Numbers (ICANN) is the leading international organization that maintains, monitors and regulates the domain names, which are also crucial for the desirable development of e-commerce. World Trade Organization (WTO) covers trade barrier aspects in the e-commerce ecosystem. In the absence of an internationally binding legal framework, the forum provided by the Hague Conference on Private International Law can be considered to deal with internet jurisdiction, civil procedure and commercial issues. International Chamber of Commerce shapes the business-to-business (B2B) self-regulation and helps to develop best practices. The contribution of regional organizations such as the European Union (EU) in developing the regional legal framework is inevitable. UNESCO has been promoting the campaign to minimize the digital divide and regional organization such as Asia Pacific Economic Co-operation has been assisting the small and medium enterprises (SMEs) by way of developing informative materials. The countries around the world, be a member or not of these international organizations, are free to develop their national legal and regulatory framework by adopting the regulatory tools proposed by these organizations depending on the application of international law doctrine of incorporation and doctrine of transformation in their domestic context.

162. In order to assess the e-commerce legal framework, special attention is to be given to the legal provisions in four areas, i.e., electronic transactions, consumer protection, privacy and personal data protection, and cybercrime.[169] Globally, 79% of the countries have enacted laws on e-transaction, 52% have laws on consumer protection, 58% have laws on privacy, and 72% of the countries have a law on cybercrime. Of the four important areas, Bangladesh does not have a law on privacy and data protection, though a draft of the law in the form of Rules, a subsidiary legislation under the Digital Security Act, 2018 (Act No. 46 of 2018) has been released.[170] Since all these topics, i.e., consumer protection, privacy and personal data protection and cybercrime will be covered in detail in the subsequent chapters of this monograph, this chapter will provide a glimpse.

163. It has been reiterated in different parts of this monograph that Bangladesh is historically known as an agrarian country, though the manufacturing sector has begun contributing significantly to the national GDP for the last couple of decades.

---

169. *Ibid.*, p. 63.
170. UNCTAD, Summary of Adoption of e-Commerce Legislation Worldwide, https://unctad.org/en/Pages/DTL/STI_and_ICTs/ICT4D-Legislation/eCom-Global-Legislation.aspx.

Culturally, the people of this part of the world were not habituated to spending on purchasing luxury goods, and this habit could be identified even after the economic progress of the country in recent times. The cultural and social settings of the country are influenced by extended and joint family values where every member of the family is used to care and share with each other had a role to play in this regard. Moreover, people used to believe in purchasing products after assessing and evaluating them in their presence. Nevertheless, the electronic or online or internet-based commercial activities (hereinafter referred to as 'e-commerce') started in the country almost at the same time in the 1990s along with other countries when the Bangladeshi expatriates mainly used to send gift items for their near and dear ones using e-commerce platforms. Unfortunately, due to various inherent problems and limitations, along with the cultural, political and economic reasons, such as trust and confidence issues, low internet penetration, lack of online payment system, underdeveloped product delivery system, absence of redress mechanisms etc. this sector could not bloom properly and did not get enough success in this densely populated country. Fortunately, the situation has been changing gradually in recent years as the policymakers have taken some pragmatic initiatives to boost up this sector and the country has been experiencing the growth of this sector in recent years. In the recent report of the United Nations Conference on Trade and Development (UNCTAD), it was found that the country has set 'exemplary' foundations for the bridge over the digital divide and can be benefitted from an e-commerce boost after laying this foundation.[171] This Chapter will be an attempt to cover various aspects of e-commerce in Bangladesh.

§2. Definition of e-Commerce and Related Terms

164. There are differences among the stakeholders as to the precise language, definition, and scope of e-commerce. e-Commerce can broadly be defined as the 'production, distribution, marketing, sale or delivery of goods and services by electronic means'.[172] It is also defined as 'digitally enabled commercial transactions between and among organisations and individuals'.[173] Thus, in this kind of commerce, all transactions are mediated by digital technologies over the internet and the Web through the exchange of value. It may be relevant to share here that even though both the issues of 'electronic business' and 'electronic commerce' are used interchangeably in the existing literature, the scope of 'electronic business' is wider than 'electronic commerce' as the idea of electronic business covers all business aspects including compliance and regulatory issues and commercial activities.[174]

165. UNCTAD preferred the definition of e-commerce suggested by the OECD, which has defined 'an e-commerce transaction is the sale or purchase of goods or

171. UNCTAD, Bangladesh: Rapid eTrade Readiness Assessment, 2019.
172. World Trade Organization adopted this definition for the purpose of Work Programme on Electronic Commerce, 30 Sep. 1998 (WT/L/274).
173. 13 Laudon, Kenneth C. & Traver, C.G., *E-commerce: Business, Technology, Society,* 8 (2017).
174. *Ibid.*, at p. 9.

services, conducted over computer networks by methods specifically designed for receiving or placing of orders'.[175] In this definition, the orders made by telephone calls, facsimile or manually typed emails are excluded. Therefore, the existence of an e-commerce platform is needed. Moreover, payment and delivery do not need to be conducted online.

166. Individuals or entities can transact their goods and services online by using a computer, both desktop and laptop, and cellular phone using Mobile Apps or browsers (known as Mobile Commerce or m-Commerce). Transactions using e-commerce platforms can take place within the jurisdiction of one country or can cross the national border (cross-border e-commerce).

167. In Bangladesh, instead of e-commerce, policy documents, e.g., the National Digital Commerce Policy 2018, have used the concept 'digital commerce' and defined it as 'the electronic/digital commerce where the transactions of all kinds of goods and services are conducted using the Internet and other digital network using digital devices'. Thus, this definition has taken a wider approach than the approach of OECD to include all kinds of goods and services, use of the internet and other network services, and use of all digital devices. Therefore, the business activities conducted over telephone calls, facsimile or manually typed emails, etc., will also be included in the definition. It will be pertinent to share here that in the previous Draft of the Policy, which was released in 2016, merely a Facebook page e-commerce without having a trade licence would not be considered as e-commerce.

§3. Types of e-Commerce

168. e-Commerce can take various shapes and forms, such as B2B, Business-to-Consumer (B2C), Consumer-to-Consumer (C2C) and Business-to-Government (B2G). In B2B e-Commerce, two or more business organizations or commercial entities transact products or goods and services, such as exchange of information.[176] B2C e-Commerce is a more popular and common form in the present world where the consumers enjoy the opportunity to select and buy goods and services of their own choice from business entities.[177] In C2C e-Commerce, the consumers enjoy the opportunity to sell and buy used and unused goods which are sometimes not possible to produce on a large or commercial scale.[178] In the present-day world, in order to ensure transparency and accountability, governments use various

175. OECD Guide to Measuring the Information Society 2011, p. 72.
176. In Bangladesh context, examples of B2B e-Commerce sites include BizBangladesh, Bangladesh Garment Manufacturers Employee Association's B2B Web Portal.
177. Example of B2C e-Commerce sites in Bangladesh include online food delivery sites such as HungryNaki, FoodPanda and Pickaboo, etc.
178. Example of C2C e-Commerce sites include Bikroy.com, Ekhanei.com, and ClickBd.com, etc. in Bangladesh.

e-commerce platforms to purchase required goods and services. This type of e commerce is known as B2G e-Commerce.[179]

§4. Emergence of e-Commerce in Bangladesh

169. Coincidentally, the recent democratic history of Bangladesh and the history of making the internet available for public use are almost contemporary. Bangladesh resumed its democratic move in 1991, and the internet was made available for public use in the mid-nineties. Bangladeshi enthusiast entrepreneurs attempted to utilize the benefits of the internet and use this for business and commercial purposes. The government also realized the importance of this sector and included this in the first National ICT Policy formulated in 2002. Even though there were huge prospects, the e-commerce sector in the country could not reach a satisfactory level.

170. The enactment of the Bangladesh Telecommunication Regulation Act, 2001 (Act No. 18 of 2001), the Information and Communication Technology Act, 2006 (Act No. 39 of 2006) (hereinafter 'ICT Act, 2006') and subsequent amendments have a positive impact on the growth of IT and promotion of e-commerce and mobile-commerce activities in the country. After the significant political shift in 2009, with the political commitment of the government through their slogan 'digital Bangladesh' and with the improvement of the economy, electronic or internet-based commercial activities have started evolving. In 2009, BB, the Central Bank of the country, permitted online transactions. In 2010, the Post Office Act 1898 (Act No. VI of 1898) was amended to allow Post Offices to provide the Universal Postal Service all over Bangladesh and beyond.[180] Moreover, the Post Officers were empowered to enter into new business ventures such as e-commerce.[181]

171. In 2013, BB permitted the purchase of goods and services using an international credit card, and finally, in March 2017, permission was given to introduce an online money transfer service, PayPal, through the state-owned Sonali Bank. In 2018, multi-national e-commerce giant Alibaba acquired the leading Bangladeshi e-commerce site, Daraz, and Alibaba's sister concern, Alipay, bought a 20% share in bKash, which is the largest mobile financial service provider in Bangladesh.

172. It is estimated that there are 2,500 e-commerce sites and around 150,000 e-commerce pages on Facebook and every day 15,000–20,000 deliveries are done at the retail level. The size of the e-commerce sector is growing significantly: in 2016, it was a market of BDT 4 billion; in 2017, it crossed the mark of BDT 17 billion, and the market is expected to reach BDT 70 billion by 2021. In 2016, a total of USD 50 million was invested in this sector, where USD 10 million was penetrated by way of FDI. Retail e-commerce is growing at a rate of 72% per month.

---

179. In Bangladesh, examples of B2G e-Commerce sites include national e-Government Procurement portal.
180. The Post Office (Amendment) Act, 2010 (Act No. I of 2010).
181. Section 4A(2)(e), the Post Office Act, 1898 (Act No. VI of 1898).

However, the issue of concern is that 60% of customers are based in Dhaka, and 90% of payments are made at the time of delivery of goods.[182] These give an indication of the inadequate popularity of this sector and also that the customers are not completely sure if they will really receive the right product.

173. Social media platform such as Facebook is a popular method for advertising and selling products since this can save the cost of creation and maintenance of websites but has the prospect of reaching a wider community. The e-CAB, the trade body for e-commerce in the country, was established in 2014 and has been playing a leading role in shaping the e-commerce ecosystem in the country. BASIS also has another platform, i.e., BASIS e-Commerce Alliance, which represents a segment of the e-commerce community of the country.

§5. Challenges of e-Commerce

174. Over the years, different organizations and scholars have attempted to identify some of the major challenges and constraints that the e-commerce industry has been facing in Bangladesh. Some of these challenges include inadequate delivery mechanisms, relatively low internet penetration rate, lack of a robust online transaction system, occurrence of online fraud, undeveloped online marketing practices, absence of robust privacy and personal data protection policy, absence of a strong independent regulatory body for the telecommunication sector, underdeveloped infrastructure such as towers and communication network hubs, e-commerce related limited educational and promotional activities, shortage of uninterrupted electricity supply, absence of robust legal framework, high price on computer and computer equipment, etc.[183] Culture is another important factor as Bangladeshi people prefer to buy goods by checking these personally and from the businessmen's' end also, lack of professionalism and commitments are evident which are again influenced by the agro-centric history of the country where business professionalism was not historically nurtured and practised.

175. An easy and workable procedure to address customers' grievances or disputes between the parties in the e-commerce ecosystem is fundamental for the success of e-commerce activities. This is somehow not very strong in the context of Bangladesh. As a result, there is frequent news that the consumers have been cheated with wrong or sub-standard products on many occasions. Such activities are harmful to the business growth of genuine e-commerce entrepreneurs. These things have already been reflected in various reports published by international organizations. For example, in the recently published UNCTAD B2C e-Commerce Index 2020, which measures an economy's preparedness to support online shopping, it

182. Rahman, S., *E-commerce Business Growing Fast, the Financial Express* (22 Jun. 2018), https://thefinancialexpress.com.bd/trade/e-commerce-business-growing-fast-1529640416.

183. Md Moktar Ali, Rafiuddin Ahmed & Arifur Rahman, *Present Scenarios, Opportunities and Obstacles of E-Business in Bangladesh*, 16 D.U. J. Marketing, 1–22 (June 2013) (Published in April 2016).

was revealed that in 2017, only 6% of the internet users and 1.3% of the total population purchased things online. Though the number of internet users increased recently as shared in Chapter 3 of this monograph, it is unfortunate that the position of the country in the global ranking has dropped significantly, i.e., from 103 in 2019 to 115 in 2020.[184]

§6. Legal and Regulatory Developments

176. Some of the study findings shared above were conducted a few years back and in between, the government has taken several initiatives to overcome many of these identified challenges and constraints. An important development is that the number of mobile phone and internet subscribers have been increasing significantly. The ITU's latest profile on Bangladesh indicates that 88.1% and 30% of inhabitants have a mobile phone and mobile broadband subscription respectively. Industry body, e-CAB's 2017 report states that Bangladesh has 99% geographical coverage in voice and data connectivity.

177. From the definition of 'law' in the Bangladesh context, as shared in Chapter 1 of this monograph, it is apparent that there is no specific and exclusive law on e-commerce in Bangladesh. Examples of exclusive laws on e-commerce can be found in Malaysia and the Philippines.[185] Specific and clear provisions on electronic transactions facilitate commercial activities online by providing legal certainty by recognizing the electronic signature, records, and communications, etc. The ICT Act, 2006 covers these to some extent in the Bangladesh context. The government has taken initiatives to promote electronic fund transfer (EFT) and set a regulatory framework for an online payment system. It is apparent that the government has taken the initiative to amend the ICT Act, 2006 significantly and from the Draft Amendment titled the Information and Communication Technology (Amendment) Act, 2019 available on the website of the ICT Division, it is evident that if the amendments come into force, many provisions will be updated.

178. Recently, in July 2021, the Ministry of Commerce formulated 'the Digital Commerce Operational Guidelines' under the National Digital Commerce (Amended) Policy, 2020 with the aim to (a) ensure transparency, responsibility, accountability, (b) creation of employments by expanding digital business, (c) increase the confidence of the consumers and ensure their rights by way creating discipline in the digital business, (d) create more new entrepreneurs by creating a competitive market. These Operational Guidelines contain only three Chapters and

184. United Nations Conference on Trade and Development, *The UNCTAD B2C E-Commerce Index 2020: Spotlight on Latin America and the Caribbean*, UNCTAD Technical Notes on ICT for Development, No. 17, https://unctad.org/system/files/official-document/tn_unctad_ict4d17_en.pdf.

185. For example, the Electronic Commerce Act, 2006 (Malaysia), the Electronic Commerce Act, 2000 (Republic Act No. 8792) (Philippines).

define various terms, e.g., marketplace, goods, services, warranty, guarantee, counterfeit products, defective products, digital wallet, lottery, multi-level activities, Personal Retail Account (PRA) and Unique Business Identification Number (UBID).

179. Chapter 3 contains provisions on display of information relating to sellable goods and services on the marketplace and sale and purchase, in Chapter 3 of the Guidelines, some important provisions are included. For example, the Guidelines provide what can and cannot be done on Websites, market places or social media. According to the Guidelines, multi-level marketing or network business, online betting or online gambling, unauthorized lottery, drug selling, etc. are prohibited. The market players need to display any of these documents, e.g., trade licence, VAT registration number, Tax Identification Number, UBID, PRA on their online marketplace or social media page. With all these provisions, there are, however, some limitations, both serious and minor, of these Guidelines. Though Clause 3.1.1 of the Guidelines provides in general terms that 'all relevant laws as in force shall be applicable in digital commerce business', one of the main limitations of this Guidelines is that these are mere Guidelines, formulated under the National Digital Commerce (Amended) Policy, 2020, and there is no clear provision as to the legal consequences if anyone fails to follow these. The Guidelines has defined 'authority' as the government, which is very vague and does not many any sense. There are some other limitations.

180. The formulation of such Guidelines is undoubtedly welcoming in the context of Bangladesh, though various countries have introduced similar provisions in their respective legal system by way of primary or secondary/subsidiary legislation to ensure certainty and compliance. While the Guidelines came into force on 4 July 2021, the country has already experienced various e-commerce scams involving millions of dollars leaving the consumers ruined and general citizens shattered when some e-commerce platforms collected a huge amount of money through lucrative and colourful advertisements with the promise to cashback offers and emblazed the lion share of the amount thus collected knowing the existing institutional loopholes and limitations in the laws of the country. Though several criminal cases were filed and the police arrested some of the accused, this is still uncertain how the victim consumers will be able to recover their money. The Ministry of Commerce has already introduced a 'Central Digital Commerce Cell', the HCD has formed a Committee in this regard and the Ministry of Commerce has also taken initiatives to refund the consumers the amount pending in the payment gateway. However, the amount is very small compared to the amount lost and it will take some time to know how the overall situation is tackled. The following segments will highlight some of the relevant issues in the discussion of legal aspects of e-commerce in the Bangladesh context.

§7. Electronic Fund Transfer

181. EFT is fundamental for the success of the e-commerce business. Credit Card service was first started in the country in 1996 by the Standard Chartered Bank followed by National Bank Limited. In 1998, Vanik Bangladesh Limited, now Lanka Bangla Finance Limited, started the service. The Citi Bank introduced the American Express (AmEx) card in 2009 and deserves the credit to make Credit Card services popular in the country.

182. Earlier, the various parties involved in the domestic e-commerce sector were suffering as BB, the Central Bank of Bangladesh, was a little rigid in allowing EFT. In 2009, the BB introduced an online payment system to facilitate fund transfers and payments of utility bills electronically by credit card. In 2010, BB took a significant step when it issued the Bangladesh Electronic Funds Transfer Network (BEFTN) Operating Rules. By using the provisions of the Rules, electronic money transfers between the banks started in the country. BB realized that this BEFTN 'is the most critical component in the development of a modern payments system infrastructure' and it was anticipated that this 'will provide the foundation for providing access to every banked and non-banked consumer as well as every business customer to facilitate electronic commerce'.[186]

183. Subsequently, BB had introduced the electronic platform, National Payment Switch Bangladesh (NPSB), on 27 December 2012 to attain interoperability in retail banking transactions originating from different electronic delivery channels, e.g., Automated Teller Machine (ATM), Point of Sales (POS), the internet and mobile applications etc. Furthermore, the NPSB was initiated to boost up cashless and electronic payments all over the country. Fifty-one banks have been operating interbank ATM transactions, whereas forty-six banks are operating interbank POS transactions through NPSB.[187]

184. In 2014, BB framed the Regulations on Electronic Fund Transfer, 2014 to promote, regulate and ensure a secure and efficient payment system in Bangladesh. Moreover, BB has also revised the Bangladesh Payment and Settlement Systems Regulations (BPSSR) 2009 and replaced it with the BPSSR 2014.

185. The growth of the e-commerce industry has been inhibited by low usage of credit and debit cards (cash remains the main payment method) and the unavailability or restrictions on major online transaction sites, such as PayPal. In March 2017, BB permitted the state-owned Sonali Bank to launch online money transfer services with PayPal. In 2018, IPay Systems Limited introduced the first digital wallet service in the country having the licence on Payment Service Provider (PSP) obtained from BB.

186. Most e-commerce portals in Bangladesh have integrated merchant accounts to facilitate credit card transactions. Besides, almost all e-commerce websites also offer multiple other payment methods. However, the payment in cash after the delivery of the product is still the prominent financial transaction method in the country

186. Foreword, BEFTN Operating Rules, 10 Aug. 2010, BB.
187. BB, NPSB, https://www.bb.org.bd/fnansys/paymentsys/natpayswitch.php.

as more than 90% of e-commerce users prefer this. Very few e-commerce businesses operate on the system of only delivering the product after receiving payment through a wire/bank transfer.

§8. Improved Product Delivery System

187. An advanced product delivery system, a fundamental component of the e-commerce ecosystem, has been a real challenge for the e-commerce entrepreneurs in Bangladesh. To solve this issue, in December 2016, the national postal authority, General Post Office (GPO), had signed an MoU with the e-CAB to run a pilot project. Under this MoU, the e-commerce parcels of the e-CAB member organizations were collected from eleven post offices and delivered through the Tejgaon branch. After the success of the project, in December 2018, GPO with its vast network of 9,886 post offices including 8,460 post offices outside the divisional cities and almost 40,000 staff, started utilizing its e-post service for e-commerce deliveries.[188]

§9. Digital Marketing

188. With strong progress in the number of mobile internet subscribers and digital infrastructure, more local companies are investing in digital marketing, mainly the new generation entrepreneurs. The absence of spam, phishing-related provisions, and personal data protection laws in the existing law influence the growth of digital marketing. Besides, the present system of intellectual property protection lacks a sufficient legal framework to protect IPRs and thus, invites unscrupulous business practices.

189. In Bangladesh, social media is very popular to reach the netizens with goods and services. The social media platform, Facebook, with more than 29 million users in Bangladesh, is the most popular one and is also a major e-commerce platform. There are over 8,000 e-commerce Facebook pages run by local entrepreneurs. Many of such entrepreneurs solely use Facebook to advertise and sell their products, ranging from clothes, beauty products to food. With faster internet connections, YouTube is also gaining popularity in the country.[189] The capital of the country, Dhaka, was listed as the second-largest city after Bangkok, with the most active Facebook users.

---

188. It may be relevant to share here that GPO started the electronic mail service, 'e-Post' from 16 Aug. 2000 to assist the people to send and receive messages or scanned images through email. From the point of view of security and privacy of the sender and receiver, it may seem to be unusual; however, for the very ordinary rural people, this service can be seen as a modern-day telegram system.
189. Bangladesh – e-Commerce, https://www.export.gov/article?id=Bangladesh-ECommerce.

§10. Legal and Regulatory Framework: An Assessment

190. It has already been shared that in the e-commerce ecosystem, the availability of four sectorial laws, i.e., electronic transactions, cybercrime, consumer protection, and privacy and personal data protection, are treated as cornerstones. Of these four categories, domestic legal provisions on electronic transactions are available in the ICT Act, 2006 and provisions on different cybercrimes can be found in the Digital Security Act, 2018 (Act No. 46 of 2018). There is no specific law on the protection of personal information in the country though the Digital Security Act, 2018 (Act No. 46 of 2018) contains a provision, i.e., section 26 which prohibits the collection of personally identifiable information without lawful authority. A Draft of Personal Data Protection Rules is available on the website of the ICT Division since the last few months of 2019. As the Rules is still in the Draft stage, it will be better to wait for a while to comment on the Draft. On the issue of consumer protection, though a law, i.e., the Consumers' Rights Protection Act, 2009 (Act No. 26 of 2009) was enacted, there are many limitations of this law. Moreover, section 3 of this Law provides that the provisions of this law shall be deemed as additional to other provisions as available in the existing laws. One may come across some news in the national news media regarding the enforcement of this consumer protection law, but the effectiveness of this law in the realm of e-commerce is yet to be tested precisely. Since most of the consumer-related disputes are amicably settled, apparently, the Apex court has not received an opportunity to assess the effectiveness of the law so far as no such matter was brought before the court.

191. Looking at the provisions of the Consumers' Rights Protection Act, 2009 (Act No. 26 of 2009), it can be seen that the government has definitely considered the UN Guidelines for Consumer Protection, initially adopted by the General Assembly in 1985 and revised in 1999. However, the Guidelines was recently revised in 2015, and obviously, the recent revisions are not considered in the Consumers' Rights Protection Act, 2009 (Act No. 26 of 2009) as the law was not amended so far after its enactment. UNCTAD had already released a Manual on Consumer Protection in 2017. As the effectiveness of any law depends on its implementation, the policymakers should consider reviewing the existing law in light of the recent international legal developments and this is crucial in the context of e-commerce ecosystem.

192. In this context, it can also be shared that the OECD Council had approved the Guidelines for Consumer Protection in the Context of Electronic Commerce on 9 December 1999 to help ensure that the consumers are equally protected in the same way when they shop online. The Guidelines contained some broad principles on (a) transparency and effective protection, (b) fair business, advertising and marketing practices, (c) online disclosures, i.e., information about the (i) business, (ii) goods or services, and (iii) transaction, (d) confirmation process, (e) payment, (f) dispute resolution and redress, (g) privacy, (h) education and awareness, (i) implementation, and (j) global cooperation. The Guidelines were updated in 2016.

193. The revised OECD Guidelines of 2016 also included more or less all the above principles with revision and modification. For example, with privacy, the issue of 'security' is also included. In the case of education and awareness, 'digital competence' is also included. There are scopes in the Consumers' Rights Protection Act, 2009 (Act No. 26 of 2009) to make rules and regulations under sections 80 and 81, respectively to carry out the purposes of the law. Therefore, the policymakers can consider updating the national law based on the OECD revised Guidelines of 2016 and best practices followed by different countries.

§11. THE NATIONAL DIGITAL COMMERCE POLICY, 2018

194. The government had formulated the e-Commerce Policy titled the 'National Digital Commerce Policy' on 16 July 2018 to restore trust in e-commerce websites by making digital transactions safer. The Policy Goal is to establish a digital commerce system and to digitalize the trading system by creating a local and international market. This Policy has considered UNCTAD's four indicators of B2C e-Commerce Index 2016, i.e., (a) internet use penetration, (b) arrangement of secure server, (c) credit card penetration, and (d) postal reliability score. Besides, the government has identified that for a proper digital commerce policy, there should be eight pillars, i.e., (a) ICT infrastructure, (b) digital transaction, (c) digital commerce platform, (d) efficiency development, (e) awareness campaign programmes, (f) digital security, (g) digital procurement, and (h) inclusion of matters relating to business and logistics.

195. Instead of popular use of the term, 'e-commerce', the government has preferred to use the phrase 'digital commerce' since it was believed that under the existing legal framework mobile commerce is not included within e-commerce. Nevertheless, it seems that this understanding of the inclusion of mobile commerce is not proper as the definition of 'electronic' in the ICT Act, 2006 has already included digital technologies.[190] In the recently framed ICT Policy 2018 also, while including the provisions on e-commerce, the word 'digital' was used.

196. This Policy was formulated to attain fifteen very broad objectives. Some of the objectives are included to: (a) improve the conditions and expansion of business through digital commerce, (b) create a conducive environment to run digital commerce businesses, (c) ensure transparency, accountability and responsibility in the running of digital commerce business, (d) assist in building trust and confidence between the buyer and sellers during the transactions in digital commerce, (e) adopt policy and take legal initiatives to preserve the interest of the entrepreneurs, buyers and sellers, (f) assist in consumer protection, (g) coordinate between relevant bodies to remove various risks in digital transaction, (h) assist in the development of necessary infrastructure, (i) coordinate and provide assistance in product supply and

---

190. According to s. 2(3) of the Information and Communication Technology Act, 2006, 'electronic' means electrical, digital, magnetic, wireless, optical, electromagnetic or any technology having equivalent such capability.

transport, (j) create suitable environment conducive to run cross-border digital commerce, (k) make ease the access to finance for the small and medium entrepreneurs, and (l) preserve intellectual property in digital commerce. The Policy contained elaborate provisions to attain these objectives in different stages; short term (by 2021), mid-term (by 2025), long term (by 2030) and very long term (by 2041).

197. The Policy provides for the establishment of a Central Cell to implement the Policy. It is also provided that the list of digital commerce entities will be published on the website, and every digital commerce entity shall publish their email ID, phone number, registration number, and product descriptions in their website/Apps/marketplace. The Policy has no indication about the regulation or governance of social media platforms, such as Facebook-based e-commerce activities in the country and so, the status of these is not certain. The Policy has imposed responsibilities on the digital commerce entities to take the initiative to protect the consumer in digital commerce by way of sharing clear product specifications and conditions, including conditions on products or price return or replacement.

198. Undoubtedly, the formulation of this Policy is a milestone in the history of digital commerce in Bangladesh and can be seen as the outcome of the constant lobby and demand of the trade bodies such as e-CAB and BASIS e-Commerce Alliance. The Policy has encapsulated some interesting and timely provisions for the expansion of this sector such as the opportunity of foreign investment in a joint venture with Bangladeshi companies with 49:51 equity ownership, introduction and promotion of insurance schemes, the formation of an advisory council, consumers' code of conduct, etc. However, alongside the concerns regarding the legal status of the Policy, the implementation of these Policy provisions will remain a huge challenge for sure and will demand a lot more research work and resource allocations on the part of the policymakers as many provisions are very wide and difficult to measure. It is a matter of great concern as it is reported that the government is working on revising the Policy with provisions through which 100% FDI owned by foreign companies can be considered within a regulatory framework. If such an initiative is taken, the local entrepreneurs will face stiff challenges for sure.

§12. WAY FORWARD

199. In the E-commerce Assessment 2016–2018, Bangladesh ranked 88 out of 151 countries in the UNCTAD B2C e-Commerce Index. It was revealed in the Assessment that only 36.6% of firms use email to interact with clients/suppliers, whereas the global average is 63.8%. Access to financing is equally a major constraint for Bangladeshi firms, and during 2013–2017, when the global average was 20.1, in the Bangladesh context, it was 22.8.[191] Bangladesh is doing well in the postal reliability index. When globally the index was 43.4, in the case of Bangladesh, it was 31.5. Only 5.4 people out of every 100 used a mobile phone or the

191. UNCTAD, Summary of Adoption of E-Commerce Legislation Worldwide, https://unctad.org/en/Pages/DTL/STI_and_ICTs/ICT4D-Legislation/eCom-Global-Legislation.aspx.

internet to access a financial institution account during 2014–2017.[192] Unfortunately, the position of the country in the global ranking, i.e., UNCTAD B2C e-Commerce Index has been dropping, i.e., from 103 in 2019 to 115 in 2020.[193] This indicates that there are some serious problems in the existing e-commerce ecosystem which need to be addressed properly and systematically.

200. Taking into account the best practices, the policymakers can consider initiating some steps to harness the benefits of this sector. The enactment of a dedicated law with an implementation body and involvement of the judicial body through which the stakeholders will get faster remedy is a demand of the time. Since 2000, the UNCTAD e-Commerce and Law Reform Programme has been supporting various countries of Africa, Asia and Latin America to improve their legal regimes that address electronic commerce, provide capacity-building training workshops, etc. A workshop on electronic commerce was organized between 20–21 June 2017 and relevant issues were discussed though these are not clearly reflected in the policy updates.[194]

201. The policymakers, while working on the development of an effective legal framework, can encourage SMEs to create interactive websites and encourage them to make their online presence visible. The government can consider offering some tax incentive in this regard if the websites are hosted within the country.[195] This has the prospect of serving two purposes: it will encourage more electronic business, and the consumers will have additional trust as the websites will be hosted within the country, and therefore, they will be under additional regulatory oversight. Such websites should keep the address and other relevant details of the business entities for a certain period and make the platform liable to ensure the reliability and genuineness of the business organizations and their products.

202. The Ministry of Commerce, Ministry of Information and Communication and Planning Commission are jointly promoting e-commerce in Bangladesh. The government formed an e-commerce Committee headed by the Secretary, Ministry of Commerce. Ministry of Information and Communication is working to enact a law regarding 'Electronic Transaction Act'. Moreover, the Ministry of Industries

---

192. COUNTRY PROFILE: BANGLADESH - eTrade for all, https://etradeforall.org/wp-content/uploads/countryprofiles/2021/BANGLADESH.pdf.
193. United Nations Conference on Trade and Development, *The UNCTAD B2C E-Commerce Index 2020: Spotlight on Latin America and the Caribbean*, UNCTAD Technical Notes on ICT for Development, No. 17, https://unctad.org/system/files/official-document/tn_unctad_ict4d17_en.pdf.
194. The Workshop was organized by the Ministry of Commerce and Bangladesh Foreign Trade Institute in collaboration with WTO and UNCTAD.
195. It may be relevant to share here that Malaysian government used to offer 20% tax incentive to SMEs for five years for creation of website hosted within the national jurisdiction.

(MoI) is currently facilitating e-commerce chat and helping to disseminate information in several industrial sectors, such as RMG, Frozen Goods, Leather & Leather Products, Diamond, etc.[196]

203. The Government of Bangladesh became the first country to sign the Framework Agreement on Facilitation of Cross-border Paperless Trade in Asia and the Pacific in August 2017 and has ratified the Agreement on 30 October 2020. In the fiscal year of 2015–2016, the government wanted to impose 4% VAT on e-commerce transactions. The initiative was dropped after strong opposition from the stakeholders. Recently, on 13 June 2019, NBR issued a notification and introduced a new service code S099.60 in the Value Added Tax and Supplementary Duty Act, 2012 (Act No. 47 of 2012) under the heading of 'Online Product Sale'. Through this, the government has again taken the decision to impose 5% VAT on the commission, fee, revenue and service charges, etc. the e-commerce platforms receive from the manufacturers for the sale of the product. Thus, this provision shall not be applicable on products for which VAT is already paid once when the product was purchased instead this provision is applicable only for the commission and service charges, etc. received by the e-commerce entrepreneurs. A Guideline was also issued on 22 September 2019 in this regard.

204. Trade bodies such as e-CAB and BASIS have a greater role to play in the promotion of this sector by making the consumers aware and helping them in improving their trust and confidence in the e-commerce ecosystem. They can also take industry self-regulation initiatives for their members and strictly implement these for their better future. Already, the computer sector has introduced Maximum Retail Price (MRP) Policy and warranty policy using which the members of the trade association are bound to follow MRP of goods and minimum warranty period. Similar initiatives can be considered by the members of e-CAB and BASIS. Though some e-commerce sites in Bangladesh, such as Pickaboo, allow the customers to return the product within three days, a coordinated move will help to build the trust of the customers which will ultimately help to grow this sector.

---

196. Md Rakibul Hoque, Mohammad Afshar Ali & Mohammad Abdullah Mahfuz, *An Empirical Investigation on the Adoption of E-commerce in Bangladesh*, 25 Asia Pacific J. Inf. Systems, 1–24 (2015).

Chapter 5. e-Government Initiatives

§1. Introduction

205. The Constitution of the People's Republic of Bangladesh, 1972 (hereinafter 'Constitution of Bangladesh, 1972'), being the Supreme Law of the land, has imposed several responsibilities and duties on the government.[197] It is the responsibility of the State to emancipate the peasants, workers and backward sections of the people from all forms of exploitation.[198] The Constitution, in Article 15, has further encapsulated the provision of basic necessities as 'a fundamental responsibility of the State' and this provision of the Constitution has influenced the government to take various development activities.[199] Besides, the raising of the nutrition level and improvement of public health are among the primary duties of the government.[200] Moreover, under Article 19 of the Constitution of Bangladesh, 1972, the government needs to take initiatives to ensure equality of opportunity for all citizens. This provision is referred to be the constitutional mandate when the government formulated the National ICT Policy in 2002, 2009, 2015 and 2018.

206. Undoubtedly, the ICT applications have the potential to assist the government in fulfilling those constitutional obligations and duties. Using ICTs tools and applications, with or without the internet, government services and information can be shared and exchanged between the government and various agencies of the government, between the government and business, the government and citizens, and vice versa. ICTs were recognized by the world leaders as a key development enabler in World Summit on Information Society (WSIS) in Geneva in 2003 and in Tunis in 2005 (Tunis Commitment).

207. It has already been shared that the use of ICTs became part of the election manifesto of the political parties in the country since the general election of 2001. Examples of some of the e-government initiatives were listed in the United Nation's

197. Article 19 of the Constitution of Bangladesh, 1972 stipulates that the government shall take initiatives to ensure equality of opportunity to all citizens and the reference of this Art. 19 was included in the preamble of the National ICT Policy, 2015 since ICTs have the prospects to ensure equality of opportunities.
198. Article 14, the Constitution of Bangladesh, 1972.
199. Article 15 of the Constitution of Bangladesh, 1972 provides that 'It shall be a fundamental responsibility of the State to attain, through planned economic growth, a constant increase of productive forces and a steady improvement in the material and cultural standard of living of the people, with a view to securing to its citizens:
    (a) the provision of the basic necessities of life, including food, clothing, shelter, education and medical care;
    (b) the right to work, that is the right to guaranteed employment at a reasonable wage having regard to the quantity and quality of work;
    (c) the right to reasonable rest, recreation and leisure; and
    (d) the right to social security, that is to say, to public assistance in cases of undeserved want arising from unemployment, illness or disablement, or suffered by widows or orphans or in old age, or in other such cases.'
200. Article 18, the Constitution of Bangladesh, 1972.

E-Government Development Index since 2003. Nevertheless, it cannot be ignored that the present government led by the Bangladesh Awami League which is in power since 2008 deserves special credit for the recent success of the country in the ICT sector. Before the national election in 2008, this political party declared its political manifesto, i.e., Vision 2021, the Golden Jubilee anniversary of independence of the country through the 'Perspective Plan of Bangladesh 2010–2021: Making Vision 2021 A Reality'.[201] The continuous commitment of the government to render various services using ICTs is also reflected in the latest Seventh Five Year Plan (FY 2016–2020).[202] The subsequent election manifesto of the government party in 2014 promised to take Bangladesh much forward and aspired to be a developed country by 2041.

208. In a densely populated country with limited resources and underdeveloped infrastructure, successive governments of Bangladesh have taken various initiatives to employ ICTs to deliver government services as these can be seen in other parts of the world. Initially, due to the lack of adequate supportive infrastructure, the volume of service was very low. Subsequently, with the expansion of the mobile phone industry and telecommunication infrastructure coupled with the economic strength of the country, the government has started executing its various services and activities online and offline using ICTs. Since it is difficult to share here the detailed developments powered by ICTs in the country chronologically, this chapter will mainly highlight the major policy initiatives and events.

§2. E-GOVERNMENT DEVELOPMENT AND E-PARTICIPATION INDEX

209. The concept 'e-government' denotes the use of ICTs to deliver various services of the government to citizens and businesses effectively and efficiently. e-Governance initiatives try to deal with two interrelated and mutually exclusive objectives, i.e., (a) *internal*, which promises to ensure effective and efficient operations of various government organs, and (b) *external*, which promises to fulfil stakeholders' needs and expectations in a simple, effective and efficient manner. e-Governance activities assist the governments in providing cost-effective and efficient service delivery to citizens to improve transparency leading to corruption control and poverty reduction.[203]

201. The General Economic Division of the Planning Commission of Bangladesh published the 'Perspective Plan of Bangladesh 2010–2021: Making Vision 2021 A Reality', which is 'a strategic articulation of the development vision, mission, and goals of the Government in achieving a prosperous Bangladesh grounded in political and economic freedoms a reality in 2021'. This Plan provides the road map for accelerated growth and lays down broad approaches for eradication of poverty, inequality, and human deprivation with the expectation that by 2021 the war against poverty will have been won, the country will have crossed the middle income threshold, with the basic needs of the population ensured, their basic rights respected, when everyone is adequately fed, clothed and housed, and have access to health care.

202. *See*, Part 2: Sector Development Strategies, Sector 12: Digital Bangladesh and Information Communication Technologies.

203. Shahjahan Bhuiyan, *Modernizing Bangladesh Public Administration Through E-governance: Benefits and Challenges*, 28 Gov't Info. Q., 54–65 (2011).

210. Along with the government's participation in the e-Government Development Index of the UN since 2003, the government has also taken various initiatives to include citizens in the process of digitalization by providing them relevant information online in the various decision-making processes. These are also reflected in the e-Participation Index of the UN. It can be seen that due to the active involvement of the government, the ranking of the country has been improving in these Indexes. In the latest ICT Development Index 2017, published by the ITU, Bangladesh ranked 147 out of 173 countries. The country ranked 115th among 193 countries in the UN e-Government Survey 2018, advancing thirty-five steps since 2012 when it ranked 150. The position of Bangladesh in the e-Government Development and e-Participation Index since 2003 is projected below:

Year	*e-Government Development Index*	*e-Participation Index*
2020	119	95
2018	115	51
2016	124	84
2014	148	84
2012	150	109
2010	134	102
2008	142	78
2005	162	151
2004	159	151
2003	159	123

Source: UN E-government Knowledgebase.[204]

§3. National ICT Policies

211. Since 2001, once the utilization of ICTs started receiving importance politically and getting its place in the election manifestos of the major political parties contesting in the national elections, successive governments have formulated national ICT Policies. The first of such policies was formulated in 2002 and subsequently revised and updated in 2009, 2015 and 2018. These Policies have set: (a) vision, i.e., the national aspirations to maximize the use of ICT for national development, (b) objectives, i.e., a set of related goals to be achieved to realize the vision, (c) strategic theme, i.e., a broad recommendation to guide the development and implementation of specific items, and (d) action item, i.e., a particular implementation task under a strategic theme with clearly specified outcomes, time limits and actors. This part will shed light on important aspects of these ICT Policies.

204. United Nations E-government Knowledgebase, https://publicadministration.un.org/egovkb/en-us/Data/Country-Information/id/14-Bangladesh.

The National ICT Policy, 2002

212. In 1999, a Committee was formed to formulate the first national ICT policy. The Committee developed the National ICT Policy in 2002 with one vision, i.e., to build an ICT-driven nation comprising of a knowledge-based society by 2006. The following ten objectives were set in the first National ICT Policy, 2002:

(1) In order to give a thrust to the ICT sector and expeditious development of the software industry and its export, the required infrastructural facilities and legal framework will be created.
(2) To provide effective incentives for the development of the ICT sector to both local and foreign entrepreneurs.
(3) To develop an efficient ICT infrastructure that provides open access to the international and national network.
(4) To promote and facilitate the use of ICT in all sectors of the economy for transparency, good governance, and efficiency improvement.
(5) To establish a legislative and regulatory framework for ICT issues like IPR, data security and protection, digital signature, e-commerce, ICT education, etc. as well as to ensure quality ICT education provided by different private organizations.
(6) To set up national databases that are reliable and easily accessible to all the people of the country.
(7) To promote the use of ICT by providing special allocations for ICT project implementation in the public sector. To train the decision makers in ICT use and promote an ICT culture.
(8) To develop a large pool of world-class ICT professionals to meet the needs of local and global markets.
(9) To set up a very high-quality ICT institution to continuously promote and foster ICT Industry.
(10) To enact Laws and Regulations for uninterrupted growth of ICT, in conformity with WTO stipulations.

213. The Policy included provisions on training and human resource development, ICT infrastructure, R&D, ICT industry (software, hardware, and service), e-commerce, e-Government/e-Governance, healthcare, agriculture and poverty alleviation, social welfare, transportation, tourism, environment, judiciary, regional and international cooperation, etc. In order to implement the Policy, it was stipulated to increase the spending in ICT to at least 2% of the Annual Development Programme by 2006. In the same Policy, some legal issues were also identified, such as the implementation of software copyright-related provisions by establishing appropriate enforcement bodies, enactment of ICT-related law immediately, initiatives to be taken to ensure data security and interoperability through the setting of encryption standards, and the international agreement on interoperability, etc. The Policy stipulated that the '[t]he Government shall use ICT system within the public administration to improve efficiency, reduce wastage of resources, enhance planning and raise the quality of services'. Nevertheless, being the first Policy in this field, the

Policy Objectives set could not be achieved properly as a very short period of the time of only four years, i.e., 2006 was set to meet very ambitious objectives in this regard. As a result, the revision of the Policy was needed.

The National ICT Policy 2009

214. During 2007–2008, there was no elected government in Bangladesh. During this time, the non-party Caretaker Government led by Dr Fakhruddin Ahmed as the Chief Adviser ruled the country. On 4 May 2008, the Ministry of Science and Information and Communication formed the National ICT Policy Review Committee since the ICT Policy, 2002 'could not reach the professed levels of success due to lack of appropriate plans to achieve the goals set in the policy as well as poor implementation of the underlying actions'.[205] The Committee submitted the draft of the revised Policy in September 2008. Later on, the Ninth National Parliamentary Election was held on 29 December 2008, and Bangladesh Awami League formed the government. The new government published the National ICT Policy within a very short time in July 2009 so that the government's pledge to make digital Bangladesh could be made to happen before 2021.

215. This ICT Policy, 2009 was formulated with one vision and several objectives with the hope that the successful implementation of these vision and objectives will 'facilitate materialise Digital Bangladesh which the government pledged to build within 2021'.[206] With the vision to maximize the use of ICTs for national development, the Policy set ten broad objectives covering social equity, productivity, integrity, education and research, employment generation, strengthening exports, healthcare, universal access, development of environment-friendly green technology and development of infrastructure, such as power, regulatory framework for effective adoption of ICTs in Bangladesh. A total of fifty-six strategic themes, 306 action items meant to be implemented in short (eighteen months or less), medium (five years or less) or long (ten years or less) term and actors responsible for the implementation of these were identified. Compared to the previous Policy of 2002, the Objectives included in this Policy were relatively more practical. However, one of the main limitations of this Policy was that though a general time frame was set to achieve these Objectives, strategic themes and action items, no specific time periods were set from when initiatives will be taken to achieve these.

The National ICT Policy 2015

216. In 2015, the government revised the National ICT Policy of 2009 to meet the needs of the time. In this Policy, one vision, i.e., to establish a transparent, responsible and accountable government through the expansion of ICTs and making their multi-dimensional use and to make the country a middle-income country by 2021 and a developed country by 2041 was set. Moreover, 10 Objectives, 54

205. Executive Summery, Proposed National ICT Policy, 2008, September 2008.
206. Preamble, National ICT Policy, 2009.

strategic themes, and 235 actions items were set in a pyramid shape. In this Policy, to achieve all these, the specific timeframe was set, i.e., short (by 2016), medium (by 2018) or long (by 2021) term and actors responsible for the implementation of these were identified. This Policy has included all the 10 Objectives of the Policy of 2009, i.e., social equity, integrity, universal access, education and research, employment generation, strengthening exports, development of infrastructures such as power, the regulatory framework for effective adoption of ICTs, healthcare, development of environment-friendly green technology, and productivity. This time, the order of these Objectives was re-arranged.

The National ICT Policy 2018

217. Just two weeks before the General Election in 2018, the ICT Division of the Ministry of Post, Telecommunication and Informational Technology adopted and published the latest ICT Policy, 2018 by repealing the National ICT Policy of 2015. In this latest version of the ICT Policy, 2018, a set of definitions of concepts such as automation, interoperability, digital government, enterprise resource planning, artificial intelligence, digital commerce, digital divide, device, digital security, digital payment, digital signature, IPRs, and managed service are included. The Policy of 2018 maintains the same Vision as it was in the Policy of 2015, i.e., to establish a transparent, responsible and accountable government through the expansion of ICTs and making their multi-dimensional use so that the country can be upgraded to a middle-income country by 2021 and developed country by 2041. However, the Objectives are revised, and instead of ten Objectives as included in the Policy of 2009 and 2015, only eight Objectives were included in the Policy of 2018 under the heading of: (1) Digital Government, (2) Digital Security, (3) Social Equity and Universal Access, (4) Education, Research and Innovation, (5) Skill Development and Employment Generation, (6) Strengthening Domestic Capability, (7) Environment, Climate & Disaster Management, and (8) Enhancing Productivity. Besides, in this Policy, fifty-five strategic themes were included and to achieve all these, the specific timeframe was set, i.e., short (by 2021), medium (by 2030) or long (by 2041) term, and actors responsible for the implementation of these Objectives were identified. This Policy has included many ambitious goals and targets, and it will take some more time to evaluate the effectiveness of these policy goals.

§4. Digital Bangladesh Initiative

218. The government formed an ICT Task Force in 2000 which was subsequently renamed as Digital Bangladesh Task Force in 2009, the top body towards the technology-driven Bangladesh. Access to Information (A2I) division under the Prime Minister's Office is the focal point regarding e-government activities.

219. Prior to the general elections of 2008, Bangladesh Awami League announced its manifesto, its 'Vision 2021' and 'Digital Bangladesh' action plans to transform Bangladesh into a middle-income country by 2021. The Digital Bangladesh strategy has four broad components, i.e., human resource development, connecting citizens, digital government and ICT in business.[207] It was identified that in order to implement the Digital Bangladesh vision, the following needs are to be addressed:

(1) Ensuring a Networked Society which covers issues that are vital to creating a society where organizations and individuals have equitable access to ICT-enabled resources.
(2) Revitalizing the Key Service Sectors which covers the primary areas of government's service to citizens.
(3) Ensuring Strong Support Framework which covers the main areas necessary for creating a stable foundation for Digital Bangladesh.[208]

220. To create a Digital Bangladesh, the government has taken a programme, such as Bangla Govt Net (between April 2010–June 2014) and Info Sarkar (July 2011–June 2016) under which it can connect around more than eighteen thousand government offices. The Union Digital Centers (UDCs) are being expanded to give public services to remote people. Till last June 2018, a total of 4,149 unions were brought under optical fibre connectivity by installing 120,008 km optical fibre. Rural people have been getting the benefits of these initiatives and the amount of time, cost and visit reduced significantly in the following manner:

Service	*Before UDC*			*After UDC*		
	Time (Hrs)	*Cost (USD)*	*Visit*	*Time (Hrs)*	*Cost (USD)*	*Visit*
Birth Registration	211.52	1.6	2.19	7.58	0.9	1.23
Citizen Certificate	24.9	0.7	1.71	2.97	0.5	1.07
Exam Registration	6.27	1.2	1.07	2.3	0.2	1.03
Death Registration	39.39	1.9	2.5	4.52	0.6	1.09
Photocopy	5.55	0.9	1.14	0.49	0.2	1.01
Computer Compose	16.84	1.5	1.44	0.63	0.5	1.02
Photography	39.7	1.6	1.82	1.36	0.4	1.04

207. A2I Programme Prime Minister's Office, 'Strategic Priorities of Digital Bangladesh', January 2011.
208. *Ibid.*

Service	*Before UDC*			*After UDC*		
	Time (Hrs)	*Cost (USD)*	*Visit*	*Time (Hrs)*	*Cost (USD)*	*Visit*
Internet Browsing	3.02	1.7	1.28	0.53	0.4	1.02
Electricity Bill Payment	4.31	0.9	1.21	0.343	0.2	1
Job Search	12.47	2.6	1.5	0.75	0.7	1

Source: A2I Program, Prime Minister's Office.[209]

§5. IMPORTANT E-GOVERNMENT INITIATIVES

221. The government has taken various ICT-driven initiatives, and many of such initiatives received global recognition. This is neither possible nor desirable to discuss all these initiatives in this monograph. Therefore, from all these initiatives, only some of the significant ones will be discussed here. There are: Bangladesh National Web Portal,[210] database of laws through Bangladesh Code,[211] online income tax filing system,[212] electronic Land Record System,[213] necessary forms, online application for driving licence, e-Tendering for government procurement,

209. Innovation Brief, Union Digital Centres: Reaching the Unreached through an Innovative Public-Private Entrepreneurship Model, A2I Program, Prime Minister's Office, June 2017, a2i.pmo.gov.bd/wp-content/uploads/2017/12/5-Union-Digital-Center.pdf.
210. Bangladesh National Portal, http://www.bangladesh.gov.bd/, launched on 23 Jun. 2014, is the single window containing relevant government information and services in Bangla and English. This Web portal, with more than 25,000 websites, is the world's largest National Content Portal. Bangladesh received the WASIS Award in 2015 for the national web portal. Even though this Portal has received several international recognitions, researchers have identified some drawbacks of the portal such as non-maintenance and non-availability of services, etc. *See* Sultana, I. & Sobhan, M.A., 'On the National Web Portal of Bangladesh for e-Service Delivery'. In 2014 International Conference on Informatics, Electronics & Vision (ICIEV), IEEE, 2014, pp. 1–6.
211. Section 6 of the Bangladesh Laws (Revision and Declaration) Act, 1973 (Act No. VIII of 1973) provides that 'All Acts of Parliament, Ordinances and President's Orders in force in Bangladesh shall be printed in chronological order under the name and style of the Bangladesh Code.' Thus, Bangladesh Code is the compilation of authentic version of primary laws, i.e., Acts of Parliament, Ordinances and President's Orders in chronological order as in force in the country.
212. The government has introduced the Electronic Tax Identification Number (e-TIN) since July 2013. Using the online tax payment system, https://etaxnbr.gov.bd/, taxpayers can submit income tax return and relevant documents electronically.
213. In order to reduce land-related disputes and complexities, the Ministry of Land has introduced the electronic land record system, http://rsk.land.gov.bd/, using which one can get documents on land ownership and possession such as Record of Rights or RS Khatian or Porcha. Out of 35 million ownership or possession related documents, the authority has already uploaded over 14.6 million documents. The service seekers need to provide some information such as name, national ID card number, phone number, etc., and need to pay the fee through online or mobile banking. Once done, he will get the certified copy of the desired document by post.

textbook, Tottho Apa,[214] e-Ticketing and mobile ticketing, exam and admission results using mobile phones, Government Gazette through BG Press, etc. Bangladesh government started the machine-readable passport initiative in 2010.[215] Recently, the government has initiated the electronic passport project, and through the successful implementation of this project, electronic passports will replace machine-readable passports.

222. Access to all benefits and services, including ICT, has been identified as a right under the Rights and Protection of the Persons with Disabilities Act, 2013. It may be very interesting to share here that in the year 2018, various laws enacted used the word 'digital' in relation to the law, which gives an indication about the government policy to make the country digitalized. These are the Hindu Welfare Trust Act, 2018,[216] the Rajshahi Development Authority Act, 2018,[217] the Electricity Act, 2018,[218] the Press Institute Bangladesh Act, 2018,[219] the Digital Security Act, 2018, the Community Clinic Health Aid Trust Act, 2018,[220] the Bangladesh Shishu Academy Act, 2018 and the National Curricula and Textbook Board Act, 2018, etc.

223. The government has taken various initiatives. In order to introduce electronic office management in the government offices, the government formed an inter-ministerial Committee on 22 May 2013. The Secretariat Instructions, 2014 has included important provisions on the introduction of information and communication technologies in the government offices.

224. Bangladesh government has established Tier- IV National Data Centre (NDC), which is one of the largest data centres in the world: one of the first in Asia and tenth 'Uptime certified' NDC in the world. The data centre was established in Kaliakoir Hi-Tech Park in the Gazipur, around 50 km away from Dhaka. Such a data

---

214. Tottho Apa (literally, information sister), http://totthoapa.gov.bd/ is an initiative of Jatiya Mohila Sanghtha, a statutory body under the Ministry of Women and Children Affairs, taken to disseminate information relating to women and children with the aim to empower them through ICTs.
215. The brief history of passport, including machine readable passport, is discussed in *Tariqul Islam v. Bangladesh and Others,* 2016, 45 CLC (HCD) [9712] = 68 DLR (HCD) (2016) 150; *Md. Ruhul Kabir Rizvi v. Government of Bangladesh and others*, 2017 (1) LNJ 23.
216. Section 8, while dealing with the functions of the Trust, provides in clause (o) that the Trust shall develop digital database on Hinduism.
217. Section 6, while dealing with the power and functions of the Authority, provides in clause (16) that the Authority shall perform all services online and shall preserve and monitor all service-related documents digitally beside the existing system. Whereas, s. 6(17) of the Act provides that the Authority shall publish all relevant data and statistics online.
218. In s. 2, the definition of electricity 'meter' includes digital meter.
219. Section 6, while dealing with the power and functions of the Institute, provides in clause (7) that the Institute will develop, *inter alia*, interactive website, digital archive and digital museum.
220. Section 10, while dealing with the responsibility and functions of the Trust, provides in clause (i) that the Trust shall use and ensure, in appropriate cases, the use of digital system in all activities of the Trust and Community Clinics.

centre will assist the data capacity of various government agencies while the government will be running its digitalization process and thus, will help the citizens get better e-government services. Presently, there is a Tier-III data centre based in the BCC.

225. Targeted and intentionally designed e-services developed to be used in Government to Government, Government to Consumer, Government to Business or government-to-employee matters are a critical component for establishing e-government. The government has established National Enterprise Architecture (NEA) named Bangladesh National Digital Architecture, the coordinated framework of national e-services, to assist interoperability and operation of e-government activities. This initiative promises to provide speedy service in the 'whole of government' through which the coordination of the government's different agencies can be ensured to provide the citizen faster services exempting them to do the same thing again. For example, if a citizen provides his fingerprint once for getting the National Identity Card (NID), this same fingerprint can be used, through this process of NEA, to get the driving licence subsequently. All government entities are currently engaged in providing e-services to the citizens and business; and therefore, it is important to follow the identical framework, principles, standards, guidelines, software, tools and infrastructure, etc. In this regard, NEA plays a significant role through the NEA Bus (known as National e-Service Bus). Under this scheme, already various services are introduced such as e-Pension for the Directorate of Primary and Mass Education, Food procurement system for DG Food office, Online Recruitment System for ICT Division, NID verification service, Govt. Employee verification service, Alapon Messenger App and Geospatial Data service, etc.

226. Moreover, the government has framed various supporting documents to implement the Digital Bangladesh strategy. A list of some of these documents include, but is not limited to: (a) Citizen Core Data Structure (CCDS) Guideline, 2012, (b) Proactive Information Disclosure Guideline, 2014 to make the citizens involved in the law-making process, (c) Use of Social Media Policy by the government Office Guidelines, 2016, (d) Strategic Priorities of Digital Bangladesh, (e) Guidelines for Utility Bill Payment, and (f) National e-Governance Architecture.

227. The government has introduced several helplines, and some of these services have started providing quality services to the citizens. One may know government information by dialling 333, can contact the anti-corruption commission by dialling 106, ask for emergency services by calling 999 and inform the law enforcement authority regarding violence against women and children by dialling 109. Besides, most Government Ministries and agencies have formulated Citizen's Charters to better inform citizens about their rights and the services they should receive from these government bodies. These Citizens' Charters are also uploaded on the websites.

228. The BCC, in cooperation with the Korean International Cooperation Agency (KOICA), had developed the e-Government Master Plan for Digital Bangladesh with the vision, i.e., 'e-government for Digital Bangladesh' and goal 'Make

Citizens' Lives Easier, Make Businesses Competitive and Make Government Innovative' in October 2018. While developing the National ICT Policy of 2015, similar initiatives of Korea and India were considered. This Master Plan has rightly pointed out that there is no single authority that is entrusted for monitoring or overseeing the implementation of e-government activities in Bangladesh; instead, there are various bodies such as the Prime Minister's Office, A2I Programme, Cabinet Divisions, Ministry of Planning, Ministry of Post, Telecommunication and ICT, Ministry of Local Government, Rural Development and Co-operatives, Ministry of Public Administration. Of many suggestions, this Master Plan was suggested for enacting an e-Government Act by 2020. It is believed that adherence to such a Master Plan will assist the government in governing and implementing all e-government services and making consistent policies, which will make a significant contribution in implementing the national ICT Policy.

Part I. Regulation of the ICT Market

Chapter 1. Regulatory Framework of the Telecommunication and ICT Sector

§1. Introduction

229. Optical fibre submarine cable, as has already been discussed, works as the backbone of the internet and the satellites play a supporting role in this regard in the global context. However, the telecommunication infrastructures play a decisive role within the national territory of any country in making people connected, get and enjoy ICT goods and services. Therefore, a discussion on the regulation of these sectors demands special attention.

230. Effective and efficient regulation of these sectors is desired for the mutual benefits of the stakeholders involved in these sectors. Effective regulation helps to avoid market failure, foster effective competition, protect consumer interests and increase citizens' access to technology and services. It is believed that in an effective telecommunication regulatory framework, certain critical elements such as the functional aspects of the regulatory authority; decision-making processes; accountability; consumer protection, dispute resolution and enforcement powers should be included. Consideration of regulation and proper implementation of these features are key elements for creating an enabling environment for the development of the telecommunication sector with increased consumer welfare.[221] Since various regulatory matters are covered in different chapters of this monograph, this chapter will primarily shed focus on the regulators and market players.

§2. Regulation: An Overview

231. Regulation is broadly defined as the imposition of rules by the government, backed by the use of penalties that are intended specifically to modify the economic behaviour of individuals and firms in the private sector. Various regulatory instruments or targets such as prices, output, rate of return (in the form of profits,

221. The World Bank, InfoDev and the ITU, Telecommunications Regulation Handbook, Tenth Anniversary Edition, 2011, p. 9.

margins or commissions), disclosure of information, standards and ownership ceilings, etc., are frequently used in this regard for monitoring the behaviour of the market players.[222]

232. Regulations are adopted depending on the needs and conditions of the market. For an effective regulatory framework, certain critical elements such as 'functional aspects of the regulatory authority; decision-making processes; accountability; consumer protection, dispute resolution, and enforcement powers' should be considered.[223] In the telecommunication sector, regulations help to avoid market failure, ensure consumer interest protection, promote effective competition and prevent anti-competitive practices, increase investment, etc.[224]

233. Depending on nature and demand, regulation can be of various types, such as *ex ante* or anticipatory and *ex post* regulation, rules or principle-based and goals or outcome-based regulation, command and control regulation, industry self-regulation and co-regulation, etc. The concept '*ex ante*' literarily means 'before the event', and in *ex ante* regulation, preferred in regulating various aspects of telecommunication sectors, as the sector has been emerging, the regulators try to identify or predict issues before their emergence and thus, attempts to shape the behaviour of the stakeholders through regulatory interventions. On the other hand, the words '*ex post*', as opposed to *ex ante*, mean 'after the event', and *ex post* regulation, preferred in the context of competition law, aiming to ensure a competitive market, fixes problems after their occurrence.

234. In rules or principle-based regulation, some broad and prescriptive principles or rules are drafted to give the market players advance notice about what can and cannot be done. On the other hand, in goals or outcome-based regulation, without any precise prescription, some goals, outcomes or standards are set by the regulators where they do not bother how the market players will achieve these. In *command and control regulation*, the regulators set some conditions and suggest specific technologies to use for meeting those conditions.

235. Finally, in the case of industry self-regulation, market players of a particular industry develop a set of rules or principles of behaviour and decide to adhere to these voluntarily. On the other hand, in co-regulation, the market players enjoy 'considerable flexibility in shaping self regulatory guidelines, consumer advocacy groups have a seat at the table, and government sets default requirements and retains general oversight authority to approve and enforce these guidelines'.[225]

---

222. OECD, Glossary of Industrial Organisation Economics and Competition Law, compiled by Khemani, R.S. & Shapiro, D.M., commissioned by the Directorate for Financial, *Fiscal and Enterprise Affairs* (1993), https://stats.oecd.org/glossary/detail.asp?ID=3295.
223. Blackman, C. & Srivastava, L., *Telecommunications Regulation Handbook*, Tenth Anniversary Edition, 9 (2018).
224. ICT Regulation Toolkit, http://www.ictregulationtoolkit.org/toolkit/6.2.
225. Rubinstein, I., *The Future of Self-Regulation Is Co-regulation the Cambridge Handbook of Consumer Privacy, from Cambridge University Press (Forthcoming)* (2016).

§3. TELECOMMUNICATION REGULATION

236. Telecommunication infrastructures play a decisive role within the national territory of any country in helping people get and enjoy ICT goods and services. The telegraph, the telephone and the internet were all invented as electronic means of communication. The ITU, a specialized agency of the UN founded in 1865, functions as one of the most important global policy forums of ICT matters. Therefore, before the discussion on telecommunication, the internet and ICTs in the Bangladesh context, a discussion on how these sectors are regulated or governed globally demand special attention.

237. According to the ITU, the telecommunication sector is now experiencing the fourth generation of regulation. In the *first generation*, the post and telephone administrations were maintained by the government and such a situation prevailed till the 1990s. The state used to enjoy monopoly during this time until when the wave of liberalization and privatizations began, which propelled the beginning of the *second generation* regulation of the telecommunication sector. During this generation, a culture of balanced and managed competition could be noticed when new services, i.e., mobile phones were introduced 'on a limited competitive basis while preserving the nation's investment in existing infrastructure'.[226] In the *third generation of regulation*, i.e., in the first decade of this century, an inter-modal competition could be observed where mobile service providers started to compete against the state-run services in voice telephony and cable TV system operators started to enter into internet access and voice market. In this generation of regulation, a 'concerted effort to protect competition, often by protecting or subsidizing the new competitors themselves' by way of 'network unbundling, rate rebalancing and universal service funds' could be observed and many of these regulatory innovations are still in place.[227] Diversity and adaptability characterize this present *Fourth generation of regulation.* In this generation, '[t]elephone network operators have upgraded their offerings to include triple-play mobile, Internet access and video services. Voice-over-Internet-Protocol (VoIP) services now transcend national boundaries to bring voice and video to laptop computers at a fraction of standard international direct-dialed telephone rates'.[228] Now, '… regulators may face the need to adapt. Spectrum managers who have been used to assigning spectrum statically, through band plans, may now need to adapt to the future of opportunistic sharing through TV white spaces, which rely on database or (in the future) cognitive-sensing technologies. Banking regulators may have to adapt to the challenges of monitoring monetary flows over mobile networks, while telecommunication regulators learn to detect manipulations of virtual currency or financial fraud on those same networks.

226. International Telecommunication Union, *Trends in Telecommunication Reform Special Edition, 4th Generation Regulation: Driving Digital Communications Ahead,* 175 (2014).
227. *Ibid.*
228. *Ibid.*

Telecommunication regulators may need to redefine the markets they regulate as video content forever changes the economics and business plans of network operators and Internet service providers'.[229]

238. The fourth-generation regulators need to focus on various issues such as coverage network services, universal access to broadband internet, consumer protection, inappropriate content, unwanted communications, privacy, spectrum management, balanced regulation (co-regulation and/or self-regulation), cooperational (regional and inter-regional) role, consultation collaboration, interconnection, licensing authorizations and net neutrality.[230]

239. The ITU, the specialized agency of the UN headquartered in Geneva along with four regional and seven area offices, play the leading role in the regulation and governance of the telecommunication and ICT sector. ITU runs its functions and activities in three main areas, i.e., radio communication, standard and development. ITU's Radio-communication sector manages radio-frequency spectrum, satellite orbits and space services to ensure safety of life on land, sea and in the sky. ITU standards (known as Recommendations) set the foundation in the ICT operations and functioning. Hundreds of ITU standards cover 'everything from core network functionality to next-generation services' such as 'Internet access, transport protocols, voice and video compression, home networking, and myriad other aspects of ICTs' to ensure that the ICT networks and devices speak the same language.

§4. Internet Regulation

240. There is no universally agreed definition of the term 'internet' and therefore, various definitions are available in the existing literature. In simple terms, the term 'internet' or shortly 'net' is used to mean a worldwide large system of computer and communication networks that allows people to share and exchange information and communicate with each other through computers or electronic devices. Various words such as 'online', 'cyberspace', 'infosphere' and 'world wide web', etc., are frequently used in our daily life conversation as synonymous to the internet though all these have context-specific different meanings.

241. World wide web ('www' or 'web' in short) is a collection of web pages found on this network of computers. The HyperText Markup Language (HTML) is used to design web pages capable to be displayed in the web browser. Web browsers such as Google Chrome, Internet Explorer, Mozilla, Opera, Safari, etc. are used to access the web. It is believed that there are three layers of the web: the surface web, the dark web and the deep web. In the surface (also called the Visible Web, Indexed Web, Indexable Web or Lightnet, regular Net) web layer, websites are indexed in the ordinary search engines such as Google, Yahoo, Bing, etc. and can be accessed without the need of any special arrangement. Only 4% of the indexed

229. *Ibid.*
230. *Ibid.*, at p. 27.

web contents are available in this layer. Websites on the deep web are not indexed by popular search engines and require additional action to visit. Dark web or net requires a special type of browser, e.g., The Onion Router and the domain name onion is used for the websites in this layer. Even though the dark web is now very popular among cybercriminals, this layer was invented to avoid surveillance, and activities in this layer may not be always illegal.

242. Due to the magnitude of web cyberspace and the actors involved along with the rapid developments in the sector, the effective or suitable way of 'regulation' of cyberspace is a very complex, perplexing and contentious issue. There are three main theories of cyberspace regulation: liberal institutionalists, cyberlibertarians and statists. *Liberal institutionalists* advocate for an international institution and rule-based multilateralism in managing cyberspace, *libertarians* propose to make cyberspace free from oppressive regulation that may restrict the liberty of people in the infosphere, and *statists* feel that the state, being the most important subject of international law, should take the responsibility to govern cyberspace.[231] However, a close look at the regulatory framework of any country in the world will reveal that a better regulatory framework shares some features of all these three theories and there are combinations of strict state regulations in selected sectors, institutional self-regulation in some sectors, and there are free spaces where the netizens can share ideas freely.

243. There is no single owner of the internet and therefore, it is governed and regulated following multi-stakeholder approaches. The World Summit on the Information Society's Tunis Agenda, 2005, stipulates that 'Internet governance is the development and application by governments, the private sector and civil society, in their respective roles, of shared principles, norms, rules, decision-making procedures, and programmes that shape the evolution and use of the Internet.'[232] Whereas, according to UNESCO, 'Internet governance is the complementary development and application by governments, the private sector, civil society and the technical community, in their respective roles, of shared principles, norms, rules, decision-making procedures, and activities that shape the evolution and use of the Internet.'[233] In the discussion of 'regulation' in the context of the Internet, issues relating to (a) technical, structural or architectural aspects, (b) internet access, (c) content, and (d) user are covered.

244. In the internet ecosystem, some issues are regulated internationally through authoritative bodies and national regulators enjoy the exclusive right to regulate some aspects of the internet by applying different regulatory tools and methods

231. Robert, R. & Choucri, N., *The Role of Cyberspace in International Relations: A View of the Literature* (2012).
232. Tunis Agenda for the Information Society, World Summit on the Information Society, 2005, http://www.itu.int/net/wsis/docs2/tunis/off/6rev1.html.
233. UNESCO, Internet Governance, https://en.unesco.org/themes/internet-governance.

highlighted above. Within the UN, the ITU plays the main role in relation to internet regulation. UNCTAD also has some role to play in relation to consumer protection, electronic commerce, etc. WIPO sets rules for copyrights on the internet. The WTO, the only global international organization dealing with the rules of trade between nations, also have significant contributes. Besides, the Internet Governance Forum, established by the UN Secretary-General and convened annually, is a multi-stakeholder forum for dialogue on public policy issues.

245. Various technical standards relating to the internet are developed and confirmed by ITU, Internet Engineering Task Force; ISO has been playing the leading role in the developments of the security standards, whereas World Wide Web Consortium develops open HTML standards needed to develop web pages. ICANN is mainly responsible to manage the domain names.

§5. Telecommunication Regulation in Bangladesh

246. Telecommunications and ICT sectors have been playing significant roles in the socio-economic development of Bangladesh, and the contributions of these sectors can be seen everywhere. Before 1989, the government agencies used to enjoy the monopoly in the telecom sector, and therefore, the issue of market regulation was not considered seriously. However, after the privatization, with the entry of various players in the local market, the stakeholders started feeling the importance of regulation in the sector and this issue was included in the government policies, including the first National Telecommunication Policy of the country.

247. In Bangladesh, generally, a combination of *ex ante* and *ex post,* and command and control regulations are followed to regulate and govern various aspects of the telecommunication sector. For example, in case of various types of licensing, the principles of *ex ante* regulations are followed; whereas after the licences are obtained and the licensee enters the market, then to ensure the competitive market, the principles of *ex post* regulations are followed. Besides, in some cases, following the command and control regulation principles, the government specifies what kind of technologies and telecommunication equipment can be imported and used to provide services. Moreover, it is also possible to refer to a very few industries specific self-regulatory instruments in this regard, e.g., the Code of Practice of Internet Service Providers Association of Bangladesh (ISPAB), containing provisions on, *inter alia*, customer service, contracts and complaints, Online safety & Security, Best Common Practice Statements, Breaches of the Code and Sanctions, etc.

248. The Telegraph Act, 1885 (Act No. XIII of 1885), the Wireless Telegraphy Act, 1933 (Act No. XVII of 1933) enacted during the British colonial regime and the Bangladesh Telecommunication Regulation Act, 2001 (Act No. 18 of 2001) can be considered as the three main legislations regarding the telecommunication sector in Bangladesh. From the Preambles, it is evident that the Telegraph Act, 1885 was enacted and subsequently adapted to amend the law relating to Telegraphs in Bangladesh, the Wireless Telegraphy Act, 1933 was enacted to regulate the possession of wireless telegraphy apparatus and the Bangladesh Telecommunication Regulation Act, 2001 was enacted to provide for the establishment of an independent Commission for the purpose of development and efficient regulation of telecommunication system and telecommunication services in Bangladesh.

249. It should be appreciated that the intent, purpose and objects of these legislations are different and have not overlapped each other. Section 4 of the Bangladesh Telecommunication Regulation Act, 2001 has also addressed this issue and made it clear that in case of any possible conflict between the legislation, i.e., these two Acts for the sake of development and efficient regulation of telecommunication system and services, the provisions of Act 2001 shall apply.

250. The Telegraph Act, 1885 (Act No. XIII of 1885) contain five chapters, i.e., Preliminary (Part I, sections 1–3), Privileges and Powers of the Government (Part II, sections 4–9), Powers to place telegraph lines and posts (Part III, sections 10–19B), Penalties (Part IV, sections 20–32), and Supplemental Provisions (Part V, section 33). The Law gives the exclusive privilege in respect of telegraphs (section 4), power to grant and revoke licence (sections 4, 8), order to intercept messages (section 5), make rules for the conduct of telegraphs (section 7) and recovery of dues (section 7A). Besides, the law provides that the government shall not be responsible for loss or damage (section 9). The Law has given the government extensive powers to the telegraph and local authority to place and maintain, repair or remove telegraph lines and posts (sections 10, 11, 13 and 17), to alter position of gas or water pipes or drains (section 14), and removable of trees interrupting telegraphic communication (section 18), etc. Moreover, the Law has made a list of activities, e.g., establishing, maintaining or working unauthorized telegraph (section 20), breach of condition of licence (section 20a), use of unauthorized telegraphs (section 21), intrusion into signal room, trespass in telegraph office or obstruction (section 23), unlawful attempt to learn contents of messages (section 24), intentional damage or tampering with telegraphs (section 25), injury to or interference with a telegraph line or post (section 26), telegraph officer or other official making away with or altering or unlawfully intercepting or disclosing messages, or divulging purport of signals (section 26), telegraph officer's fraudulent sending of messages without payment (section 27), misconduct (section 28), sending of fabricated or obscene messages (section 29), retention of a message delivered by mistake (section 30), bribery (section 31) and attempt to commit offences (section 32) and provides punishment for these offences, i.e., imprisonment up to three years and fine up to BDT 1,000 [approximately USD 11].

251. It may be relevant to share here that though this law was enacted when present-day India, Pakistan and Bangladesh were ruled and governed by the British colonial rulers, this law is still in force in these three countries. While in Bangladesh, the country has been following the provisions of the law as these were enacted in 1885 with almost no amendment, India has amended the law several times in 2006 and 2019 to meet the demand of the time. A new part, i.e., Part IIA was inserted in the Law in 2006 to include provisions on Universal Service Obligation Fund, i.e., a fund created to provide access to telegraph services to people in the rural and remote areas at affordable and reasonable prices. Though Bangladesh is almost twenty-five times smaller than India, the insertion of such a provision in Bangladesh law could help assist the people living in remote places to have access to telegraph services.

252. It will be pertinent to share that though the right to privacy is not constitutionally recognized in the country, the Indian Supreme Court, while interpreting section 5(2) of the Telegraph Act, 1885 (Act No. XIII of 1885), has yet declared that the provision on telephone tapping of the politicians' phone by the Central Bureau of Investigation is a serious invasion of individual's privacy.[234] Unfortunately, in the case of Bangladesh, though the right to privacy of every citizen's correspondence and other means of communication, subject to any reasonable restrictions imposed by law in the interests of the security of the State, public order, public morality or public health, is constitutionally recognized under Article 43(b) of the Constitution of Bangladesh, 1972, an HCD bench of Justice M Enayetur Rahim and Md Mostafizur Rahman rejected a writ petition filed to investigate at least twenty high-profile leaked conversations between 2013–2021.[235]

253. The Wireless Telegraphy Act, 1933 (Act No. XVII of 1933) was enacted to regulate the possession of wireless telegraphy apparatus, i.e., any apparatus, appliance, instrument or material used or capable of use in wireless communication, but excluding those used for other electrical purposes, unless it has been specially designed or adapted for wireless communication.[236] The Law prohibits the possession of wireless telegraphy apparatus without a licence issued by the Director-General, Bangladesh Post Office (BPO), or an officer authorized by him on this behalf as per the provisions of this law (sections 3 & 5). Such possession of wireless telegraphy apparatus without having a proper licence is an offence for which someone may be held liable for a fine of up to BDT 250 [approximately USD 3].

254. Like the Telegraph Act, 1885 (Act No. XIII of 1885), the Wireless Telegraphy Act, 1933 (Act No. XVII of 1933) has not been amended so far also, rather the law was adapted as it is with limited cosmetic changes only. This is really unfortunate that the policymakers have not considered the importance of the amendment of these colonial laws considering the rapid technological changes. Countries like Ireland and South Africa having similar colonial history repealed their laws to meet the need of the present time.[237] Accordingly, Ireland repealed the Telegraph Act, 1863 and the Telegraph Act, 1869 and enacted the Communication Regulation Act, 2002.

---

234. *People's Union for Civil Liberties v. Union of India*, AIR 1997 SC 568.
235. High Court dismisses plea for probe into leaked phone conversations, https://www.dhakatribune.com/bangladesh/court/2021/09/29/high-court-dismisses-plea-for-probe-into-leaked-phone-conversations.
236. Long title & s. 2(2), the Wireless Telegraphy Act, 1933 (Act No. XVII of 1933).
237. Matthan, R., *Telecom*, in Kapur, D. & Khosla, M. (eds), *Regulation in India: Design, Capacity, Performance*, 172–173 (2019).

255. The Bangladesh Telecommunication Regulation Act, 2001 is the main law enacted after the independence of Bangladesh to provide for the establishment of an independent Commission for the purpose of development and efficient regulation of telecommunication systems and telecommunication services in Bangladesh. The Law contains fourteen chapters: preliminary matters (Chapter I, sections 1–5), establishment and composition of Commission (Chapter II, sections 6–20), financial matters of Commission (Chapter III, sections 21–28), broad objectives, powers and functions (Chapter IV, sections 29–34), licences for telecommunication, etc. (Chapter V, sections 35–47), tariff, charge, etc. (Chapter VI, sections 48, 49) standard of telecommunication apparatus and service (Chapter VII, sections 50–54), radio communication and spectrum management (Chapter VIII, sections 55–58), receipt and disposal consumer-complains (Chapter IX, section 59), inspection and compulsory enforcement (Chapter X, sections 60–65), offence, penalty, investigation and trial (Chapter XI, sections 66–88) transitional provisions, transfer of rights and liabilities (Chapter XIII, sections 89–93) and miscellaneous (Chapter XIV, pp. 94–103).

256. Taking into account the definition of technical words and the provisions of the Bangladesh Telecommunication Regulation Act, 2001, it is evident that the law of 2001 was enacted for the purpose of development and efficient regulation of telecommunication systems and telecommunication services and to transfer certain power and function regarding telecommunication to BTRC since the provisions of the Telegraph Act, 1885 and the Wireless Telegraphy Act 1933 were inadequate.[238] Moreover, looking at the definitions of the words 'telegraph', 'wireless communication' and 'telecommunication' as used in these three laws of 1885, 1933 and 2001 respectively, 'it appears that the three Acts distinctly and separately detailed about the gradual developments that have taken place through the passage of time in the field of telegraph, wireless communication and telecommunication systems and services'.[239]

257. In *Bangladesh Telecommunication Regulatory Commission v. Ekushey Television Ltd.*, 58 DLR (AD) (2006) 83, the AD of the Supreme Court examined whether the Act, 2001 has an overriding effect over all other legislations in the field vis-à-vis the applicability of the old legislation in respect of the granting of a licence for Broadcasting as contemplated in section 3(2) of the Bangladesh Telecommunication Regulation Act, 2001. When the issue was contested at the HCD, the HCD revealed that '[i]n interpreting the aforesaid preambles of the old Acts after the establishment of the BTRC by the Act of 2001 as an independent commission a person has to fall back upon the provision of section 4 of the Telegraph Act, 1885 and section 5 of the Wireless Telegraphy Act, 1933'. Section 4 of the Telegraph Act, 1885 provides for the issuance of a licence for the purpose of broadcasting its programme. The HCD further revealed held that ' … if even after the enactment of Act of 2001 the provision of section 4 of the Telegraph Act, 1885 and section 5 of the

238. *Bangladesh Telecommunication Regulatory Commission v. Ekushey Television Ltd.*, 58 DLR (AD) (2006) 83.
239. *Ibid.*

Wireless Telegraphy Act, 1933 are to be resorted to by a person for the purpose of issuance of licence in respect of matter mentioned in sub-section (2) of section 3 then the mere purpose of the creation of independent Commission as stated in the Preamble of the Act 2001 will be frustrated'.

258. The HCD, referring to the provisions of section 4 of the Telegraph Act, 1885 and section 5 of the Wireless Telegraphy Act, 1933 held that '... the said two sections clearly show that the legislature knowing fully well about the inapplicability of the said two old laws with the modem telecommunication system and service and matters ancillary thereto have given an overriding clause to the new law, the Act of 2001 and held that the Act of 2001 is applicable in respect of all the matters mentioned in section 3 of the Act and BTRC in the sole and exclusive authority to grant such licence necessary for the purpose in the manner as prescribed in the Act and no licence from the Ministry of Information would be necessary for the matters mentioned in section 3 of the Act'.

259. Finally, the AD found that the HCD was erroneous on its findings that 'the Act 2001 is applicable in respect of all matters as mentioned in section 3 of the Act and BTRC is the sole and exclusive authority to grant such licence necessary for the purpose in the manner as provided in the Act and no separate licence from the Ministry of Information would be necessary for the matters mentioned in section 3(2) of the Act' and held that 'Bangladesh Telecommunication Act, 2001 has not been made applicable to any "broadcasting", a radio broadcasting station or a television broadcasting station or licensing of such station, broadcasting apparatus or an apparatus for receiving any message or other information or a programme transmitted by way of broadcast or the business of such apparatus, which job have been preserved to the Govt. of Bangladesh under the provisions of Telegraph Act, 1885 to provide for the issuance of licence or no-objection for the purposes inasmuch as the Wireless Telegraphy Act, 1933 regulates the possession of Wireless Telegraphy apparatus in Bangladesh by empowering the Director General, Bangladesh Post Office or an officer authorised by him to issue licenses for the purpose'.[240]

§6. Telecommunication and ICT Regulators in Bangladesh

260. There are several bodies, i.e., ministries, departments and regulators, etc., who are entrusted with and empowered to monitor and oversee, directly or indirectly, different sectors and aspects of telecommunication sectors in Bangladesh. The list of these government Ministries includes:

(a) Ministry of Posts, Telecommunications and IT.
(b) Ministry of Science and Technology.
(c) Ministry of Finance.
(d) Planning Division.
(e) Ministry of Information.

240. *Ibid.*

(f) Ministry of Home Affairs.

261. The Ministry of Posts, Telecommunications and IT is the lead Ministry of the government which performs the telecommunication and ICT-related major responsibilities and functions through its two Divisions: (a) Posts and Telecommunications Division, and (b) ICT Division. This chapter will highlight the activities of these two Divisions and selected agencies established under these Divisions.

262. According to the recently amended Allocation of Business,[241] the Posts and Telecommunications Division is responsible for performing the business of the government, *inter alia*, such as (a) postal services, (b) telecommunication services: telegraph and telephones, (c) telephone industries, etc. Various organizations, such as (a) BTRC, (b) BPO, (c) BTCL, (d) Bangladesh Submarine Cable Company Ltd., (e) Teletalk Bangladesh Ltd., (f) Telephone Shilpa Sangstha, (g) Bangladesh Cable Shilpa Ltd., (h) Department of Telecommunications, (i) Mailing operator and courier services licensing authority, and (j) Bangladesh Communications Satellite Company Limited, were established to perform the duties of this Division.

263. Whereas, under the recently amended Allocation of Business,[242] the ICT Division is responsible for dealing with, *inter alia*, (a) policy matters relating to ICT in pursuance of national objectives and plans, (b) Digital Bangladesh Taskforce and other national entities on ICT, (c) commercialization of ICT services and formulation of guidelines for making those easily accessible to the people and monitoring of its implementation, and (d) take initiatives on bridging the Digital Divide. Under the ICT Division, four organizations: (a) Department of ICT, (b) Bangladesh Hi-Tech Park, (c) BCC, (d) Controller of Certifying Authorities (CCA) were established to perform the mandated activities of this Division. This segment will shed light on some of these government bodies.

§7. Bangladesh Telecommunication Regulatory Authority

264. The National Telecommunication Policy, 1998 proposed to establish an independent telecommunication regulatory commission. Accordingly, the BTRC was established as the regulatory body in charge of monitoring and overseeing telecommunication-related activities in the country. The BTRC was established, through the provisions of the Bangladesh Telecommunication Regulation Act, 2001 (Act No. 18 of 2001), which provides for the establishment of an independent Commission for development and efficient regulation of telecommunication systems and telecommunication services in Bangladesh.[243] After the enactment of the law, BTRC was established under section 6 of the law on 31 January 2002, with the vision to facilitate connecting the unconnected through quality Telecommunication services

241. S.R.O. No. 24 & 25-Law/2014, dated 10 Feb. 2014.
242. *Ibid.*
243. Long Title, the Bangladesh Telecommunication Regulation Act, 2001 (Act No. 18 of 2001).

at an affordable price by introducing new technologies. Subsequently, the title of Act No. 18 was amended in 2010 and changed to the Bangladesh Telecommunication Regulation Act, 2001.

265. It will be pertinent to share here that this Act of 2001 is not applicable to any matter relating to any broadcasting, radio broadcasting station, television broadcasting station or licensing of such station. But it is applicable in case of allocation of frequency for such radio station or television station or broadcasting apparatus, or control of the allocated frequency or use of a telecommunication apparatus in combination with broadcasting apparatus or use of telecommunication apparatus for the purpose of broadcasting.[244]

266. After the law was enacted in 2001, in the case of *Jamuna Television Limited and another v. Bangladesh and others*, 2005, 34 CLC (HCD) [8911] = 57 DLR (2005) 345, Md Abdur Rashid J., while commenting on the various aspects in the formation of the BTRC, stated that 'Section 18 of the Act however, provides for appointment by the Government of the secretary to the Commission, which makes the intention of the government very clear not to see the Commission really independent of it. The government by tradition was not prepared to have complete trust and confidence upon the Commission. Keeping the power in the hands of the Government to appoint the secretary and to execute its policy and decision through the vehicle of secretariat is an age-old practice of the bureaucracy of the land.' Moreover, in the same judgment, the Court commented on the conduct and functioning of the Commission. To quote Md Abdur Rashid J., 'Very objective of the Act was to make the Commission independent, meaning independent of all authorities of the Republic including the government. … The Commission was brought into existence with great expectation that they would act fast and independent of any push by and pull from any quarter and only for the benefit and service of the people in this age of information revolution. The law made them independent and their services more secured than any other servants of the Republic. But they love to behave as servants of the government. They appear to have acted at every stage of the proceeding at the cue of the Ministry.

The national media, both print and electronic, hardly miss a day in reporting the failings of such commissions, statutory or constitu-tional. Close scrutiny makes it clear that failing of such commissions is not so much for any dearth of legal provisions as for failing of the members of such commissions in the discharge of their duties and functions. Is it the long association of the members of the commissions with the government which makes them subservient and servitude in their attitude, thought and action, we are not sure. What we are certain about is, if they cannot think and act as independent as the law commands them then, even God cannot make them independent.

244. Section 3, the Bangladesh Telecommunication Regulation Act, 2001 (Act No. 18 of 2001). *See also*, *Bangladesh Telecommunication Regulatory Commission v. Ekushey Television Ltd.*, 58 DLR (AD) (2006) 83.

It may also be noted that none of the commissions till date did complain about any interference of any quarter in the exercise of their duties, statutory or constitutional, nor did they seek even before the apex Court any clarification or interpretation of any law lacking or impeding them, in any way, from acting independently. Sooner they become conscious of the law that created them and the rights, interest and expectation of the people, the better it will be for them and the nation.'

267. Initially, BTRC used to enjoy full regulatory authority including the issuance of all kinds of licences to provide telecommunication services and approval of tariffs, radio communications, spectrum management, issuance of spectrum assignment licence, etc. However, with the subsequent amendment of the law in 2010, a certain power of BTRC was vested with the MoPT. As a result, the MoPT becomes the concerned authority to deal with certain issues, i.e., to give approval in relation to the issuance of the Operator's licence and the matters relating to establishing, maintaining and operating telecommunication systems and providing telecommunication services in the country such as licensing procedure, issuance of Guidelines where necessary and taking necessary decision in these regards. On the other hand, the power of BTRC relating to other matters, i.e., issues relating to spectrum allocation, determination of allocation fees, its management, issuance of the required licence, i.e., Spectrum Agreement Licence, determination of fees and charges and other inclusive affairs, etc., remained unchanged by virtue of sections 55 and 24 of the Act, 2001.[245]

268. In *ETV Ltd and another v. Bangladesh and others* 56 DLR 91, it was held that '[t]he functions of the Ministry and that of the Government have been laid down in sections 33 and 34 of the Act and in none of these two sections any reference has been made reserving the power either by the Ministry or the Government as to issue licence but, in fact, these two sections have reserved the right of the Ministry and the Government to take policy decision in telecommunication sector and to encourage the development of the sector in Bangladesh both nationally and internally'.

269. Chapter IV of Act No. 18 of 2001 (sections 29–34) contains detailed provisions on broad objectives, powers and functions of BTRC. The broad objectives of the Commission are to: (a) encourage the orderly development of a telecommunication system that enhances and strengthens the social and economic welfare of Bangladesh; (b) ensure, in keeping with the prevalent social and economic realities of Bangladesh, access to reliable, reasonably priced and modern telecommunication services and internet-services for the greatest number of people, as far as practicable; (c) ensure the efficiency of the national telecommunication system and its capability to compete in both the national and international spheres; (d) prevent and abolish discrimination in providing telecommunication services, to progressively effect reliance on competitive and market-oriented system, and in keeping with these objectives, to ensure effective control of the Commission; and (e) encourage

---

245. *Orascom Telecom Bangladesh Ltd v. Bangladesh and others*, 2012, 41 CLC (HCD) [8790] = 18 BLC (HCD) (2013) 148.

the introduction of new services and to create a favourable atmosphere for the local and foreign investors who intend to invest in the telecommunication sector in Bangladesh.[246]

270. BTRC is generally responsible to: (a) regulate the establishment, operation and maintenance of telecommunication services in Bangladesh; (b) protect the interests of the local consumers in respect of the charges imposed on them, and their access to telecommunication services and the quality and variety of such services; (c) encourage R&D activities in telecommunication, and innovative activities and investment in providing telecommunication services; (d) protect the social and economic interests of the consumers, to respond to their needs, and to control and abolish the existing and probable oppressive or discriminatory conduct or activities of the telecommunication service providers; (e) maintain and promote competition among the service providers in order to ensure high-quality telecommunication services; (f) ensure protection of the privacy of telecommunication; (g) collect, from within and outside Bangladesh, information on telecommunication and internet and to analyse and assess their impact on Bangladesh and to take necessary action or, as the case may be, to make necessary recommendations to the Government; and (h) frame a national scheme of numbering plan to be followed in telecommunication and to modify it whenever necessary.[247] Besides, in any changed circumstances, BTRC can introduce new changes in the conditions of the licence without any retrospective effect, and the licence holder is bound to follow such changes.[248]

271. It may be relevant to share here that the BTRC, having the sole and exclusive authority to allocate frequency for running television channels, does not need to obtain permissions from any other authority when someone has already managed the no-objection certificate from the Ministry of Information to run a satellite television.[249] In a very recent case, the petitioner, Spice Television Private Limited managed the no-objection certificate of the Ministry of Information to run a satellite television and applied to BTRC that took three years to allocate frequency permanently. BTRC was taking such a long time as it was waiting for the clearance of the Ministry of Home Affairs. From the fact of the case, it can be seen that BTRC also requested and managed the clearances from the other two security agencies of the government. The HCD confirmed that such clearance from another Ministry is not required and BTRC, as per the provisions of sections 55(1), 55(2) & 56(8) of the Bangladesh Telecommunication Regulation Act, 2001 can take this decision alone.[250]

246. Section 29, the Bangladesh Telecommunication Regulation Act, 2001 (Act No. 18 of 2001).
247. Sections 30 & 31, the Bangladesh Telecommunication Regulation Act, 2001 (Act No. 18 of 2001).
248. *Orascom Telecom Bangladesh Ltd v. Bangladesh and others*, 2012, 41 CLC (HCD) [8790] = 18 BLC (HCD) (2013) 148.
249. *Ekushey Television Ltd. and another v. Bangladesh and others*, 2003, 32 CLC (HCD) [4239] = 56 DLR (2004) 91.
250. *Spice Television Private Limited v. Government of Bangladesh and others*, 2020 [Writ Petition No. 3141 of 2019]. *See also*, *Jamuna Television Limited and another v. Bangladesh and others*, 2005, 34 CLC (HCD) [8911] = 57 DLR (2005) 345.

272. Under sections 89 and 90 of the Bangladesh Telecommunication Regulation Act, 2001, the BTRC is empowered to amend any condition of the licence or licence agreement which is inconsistent with the provisions of the Act. However, before cancelling or suspending a licence, the BTRC must follow the procedure mentioned in section 46 of this Act, 2001, which 'ensures due process of law and eliminates every chance of arbitrary exercise of the statutory powers of cancellation'.[251] In *World Tel Bangladesh Ltd. v. Bangladesh represented by the Secretary Ministry of Post and Telecommunications and others 11 MLR (2006) (AD) 65,* BTRC cancelled the licence of World Tel on the grounds of public policy, and the said cancellation order, when challenged in the superior court, was upheld by both the HCD and AD.

273. Based on the authority given under section 90 of the Bangladesh Telecommunication Regulation Act, 2001, the BTRC exercised its power to revoke the exclusivity clause in the licence of World Tel, received before the formation of BTRC, which allowed it to prohibit the entry of other operators for four years in the Dhaka Central Zone indicating that the clause was monopolistic, and thus, against the national law and policy. Once challenged, the HCD upheld the decision of BTRC and held that 'there is no provision in the BT Act, 2001 which provides for any such monopoly to any particular operator and that the right accrued under the previous regulation cannot be taken away by subsequent regulation'.[252]

274. BTRC performs its functions, duties and responsibilities through five departments. These are: (a) administration; (b) systems and services; (c) engineering and operations; (d) legal and licensing; and (e) spectrum management, two directorates, i.e., (a) finance, account & revenue and (b) enforcement & inspection, and one wing, i.e., media & publication.

275. In discharging its functions and responsibilities, BTRC primarily follows the provisions of telecommunication sectorial laws such as (a) Bangladesh Telecommunication Regulation Act, 2001, (b) the Wireless Telegraph Act, 2001 and (c) the Telegraph Act, 1933, and policies such as (a) the National Telecommunication Policy, 2018 (b) the National ICT Policy, 2018, (c) the ILDTS Policy, 2010 and (d) the National Broadband Policy, 2009. Besides, BTRC also follows the Interconnection Regulations, 2004, National Numbering Plan and National Frequency Allocation Plan. Moreover, BTRC has issued various Regulations,[253] Instructions,[254]

---

251. *Jamuna Television Limited and another v. Bangladesh and others*, 2005, 34 CLC (HCD) [8911] = 57 DLR (2005) 345.
252. *World Tel Bangladesh Ltd. v. Government of Bangladesh and others*, 11 MLR (2006) (HC) 201.
253. For example, the BTRC (ANS Operator's QoS) Regulations, 2018. This Regulation is applicable to all ANS operators providing: (i) Broadband Access Services; (ii) Cellular Mobile Phone Services; (iii) Fixed Telephony Services; (iv) Any other service introduced by BTRC through administrative order from time to time. These ANS operators have direct access with the subscribers and they need to provide QoS, i.e., the main indicators of the performance of a telecommunication network and of the degree to which such network conforms to the standards as specified in these Regulations for specified parameters.

Directives[255] and Guidelines.[256] Even though these are not included within the definition of 'law' under Article 152 of the Constitution of Bangladesh, 1972, all these Instructions, Directives and Guidelines will have legal effects and will be binding on the stakeholders.

From its inception till June 2020, BTRC has deposited BDT 600 billion to the government exchequer.[257] Since October 2012, Teletalk Bangladesh has been providing 3G Mobile services, and four Mobile phone operators were given 3G Mobile licences through an auction held on 8 September 2013. Licences were given to Grameenphone, Robi, Banglalink and Teletalk on 19 February 2018 to provide 4G/LTE mobile services. As per the Guidelines framed in this regard, these operators will have to establish 4G/LTE mobile networks in the first stage in all the divisional towns within the first nine months, in the second stage within the next twenty-four months in 30% districts downs, and in the third stage, within thirty-six months in all district towns.

The success of BTRC, since its inception, is projected in a comparative setting in the following table:

No.	*Issue*	*2002–2003*	*June 2018*	*June 2019*	*June 2020*
1.	Teledensity (%)	0.54	92.67	97.46	96.05
2.	Internet Density (%)	0.1	53.65	57.44	61.07
	3G Mobile Subscribers	5.5 million	*	61.66 million	57 million

Another example of Regulations is the BTRC (Interconnection) Regulations, 2004 (amended in 2008), which were framed to: (a) encourage orderly development of the telecommunication systems, (b) prevent and abolish discrimination in the provision of services, ensuring fair competition, (c) encourage the introduction of new services, (d) promote and safeguard the interests of consumers by ensuring reliable and fairly priced modern services with reasonable accessibility. These Regulations were also framed to ensure effective telecommunication services in the territory of Bangladesh through mutual agreements between the operators and/or interconnection access providers. Due to the provisions of these Regulations, the users of one telecommunication network are able to use the same or other network. These Regulations set the rights and obligations of the operators, i.e., anyone who has received licence for establishing or operating a telecommunication system or providing telecommunication service or operating a system.

Besides, there are also Regulations, i.e., the BTRC (Administrative Fine) Regulations, 2007.

254. For example, Instructions for the usage of Satellite Phone in Bangladesh, Instructions for Issuance of Enlistment Certificate for the Operation of BPO/Call Centre (International and Domestic), 2013, Instruction Regarding IIG, 2014 (No. 1749), Instruction Regarding IIG, 2015 (No. 1635), Instruction Regarding ISP, 2015 (No. 1683), Instruction Regarding IIG, 2016 (No. 339), Instruction Regarding ISP, 2016 (No. 402), Instructions for Installing BTS at the Border Region of Bangladesh, 2017, Instructions for Establishment of Mobile Phone Handset Assembling and Manufacturing Plant in Bangladesh, 2018, Instructions on IoT Devices Importation in Bangladesh, April 2018.
255. Directives on SMS-based Premium Rate Services 2010, Directives for airtime uses of Mobile Financial Services (MFS) 2013, Directives on Commercial Toll Free Services 2018, Directives on Virtual Private Network (VPN), 2017.
256. The Guidelines, http://www.btrc.gov.bd/forms-and-guidelines-old-page.
257. BTRC, Annual Report, 2019–2020 [Bangla], p. 10.

No.	*Issue*	*2002–2003*	*June 2018*	*June 2019*	*June 2020*
	4G Mobile Subscribers	–	*	19.13 million	35.2 million
3.	Number of Mobile Phone subscribers	5,050,000	150,900,000	*	*
4.	Number of Internet subscribers	100,000	87,700,000	*	*
5.	Number of various types of licence holders	139	2,647	3212	3482
6.	Internet Bandwidth price (in BDT)	1,027,000	625	625	600
7.	Revenue earned (in Crore)	120.07	6,445.36	3,058.88	4,719.82
8.	Network coverage	50 out of 64 districts	All 64 districts	All 64 districts	All 64 districts
9.	Dealer Possession and Radio Communication Vendor Licence	31	950	634	*
10.	Frequency allocation (organizations)	35	905	1024	*

* No information included in the Report.

Source: Bangladesh Telecommunication Regulatory Commission.[258]

276. The Legal and Licensing Department of BTRC is mainly responsible to monitor the implementation of the provisions of the laws, such as (a) the Telegraph Act, 1885, (b) the Wireless Telegraphy Act, 1933, (c) the Bangladesh Telecommunication Regulation Act, 2001, (d) the Information and Communications Technology Act, 2006, (e) the Cable Television Network Operation Act, 2006, (f) the Terrestrial Television Transmission Benefits Preservation Act, 2009, (g) the Pornography Control Act, 2012, (h) the Competition Act, 2012, and (i) the Digital Security Act, 2018.

277. BTRC initiates legal actions against anyone who provides telecommunication services without permission or a valid licence. Besides the criminal cases, BTRC lodges certificate cases against the defaulters under the Public Demands Recovery Act, 1913 (Bengal Act No. III of 1913) for the recovery of the outstanding amount. Cases filed and disposed against, and on behalf of the Commission in the subordinate courts, sessions Judge courts, HCD and AD of the Supreme Court

258. BTRC, Annual Report, 2017–2018, p. 15; BTRC, Annual Report, 2018–2019, p. 16; BTRC, Annual Report, 2019–2020 [Bangla], p. 14.

from the FY 2010–2011 to 2017–2018 are projected in the Table below:

Sl. No.	*Financial Year*	*Cases Filed*	*Cases Disposed of*
1.	2010–2011	14	12
2.	2011–2012	51	18
3.	2012–2013	20	16
4.	2013–2014	33	5
5.	2014–2015	48	27
6.	2015–2016	30	21
7.	2016–2017	52	15
8.	2017–2018	36	12
9.	2018–2019	28	05
10.	2019–2020	21	19

Source: Bangladesh Telecommunication Regulatory Commission.[259]

278. Though the market players are generally bound to follow any decision of the regulators, there are instances that some of the decisions of BTRC were challenged in the court of law. In *KM Alam & Co. and another v. People's Republic of Bangladesh, and others*, 2011, 40 CLC (HCD) [8802] = 18 BLC (HCD) (2013) 221, the petitioners moved to the HCD with regard to the appointment of Chartered Accountants Firms to conduct Inspection and Special Audit of Telecom Operators in Bangladesh by BTRC. The HCD found irregularities in the procuring process of appointing the Auditors and held that 'BTRC is a statutory body and entrusted with the power of the people by the statute to deal with the State largess and benefits through its regulatory process. Therefore, BTRC cannot act as a private individual and grant benefits or largess in whatever way it likes. Besides, the concerned procurement is relating to the audits to be conducted on telecom operators in Bangladesh which is a booming sector in Bangladesh involving thousands of *crores* of taka. If a minimum irregularity/illegality in the procuring process is allowed, it will encourage corrupt people hiding behind the curtain to get an illegal opportunity in the procuring process and cause huge damage to the public interest.' It was further held that 'From the very beginning to the end, the BTRC not only defied the law but also acted in a very highhanded way as if the concerned officials were dealing with their private properties or benefits. They should not forget that they are the trustees of the people's power and properties and, as such, their steps will be tested on the touchstones of equality and reasonableness as guaranteed under Articles 27 and 31 of our Constitution.' With these observations, the HCD declared the decision of the Review Panel of BTRC regarding the appointment of auditor to be unlawful, having no legal effect.

259. BTRC, Annual Report, 2016–2017, p. 97, BTRC, Annual Report, 2017–2018, pp. 95–96, BTRC, Annual Report, 2018–2019, p. 112 and BTRC, Annual Report, 2019–2020 [Bangla], p. 103.

279. Very recently, the legality of the procedures followed by BTRC under sections 63 and 65 of the Bangladesh Telecommunication Regulation Act, 2001 (Act No. 18 of 2001) dealing with an enforcement order and penalty for its violation, and imposition of administrative fines respectively were challenged.[260] Under section 63 of this Act of 2001, BTRC may direct the licensee or the holder of the permit or certificate to show cause within thirty days as to why an enforcement order shall not be issued or why the licence or permit or certificate shall not be cancelled if a licensee or the holder of a certificate or permit violates any provision of this Act or regulations or any condition of the licence or permit in operating a system or in providing a service. On the other hand, section 65 of this Act of 2001, while empowering the BTRC to make regulations for the imposition of an administrative fine, in addition to those already specified in this Law, for violation of the provisions of this Act or regulations, provides for the process and procedure to be followed in such instances.

280. In the case of *Grameenphone Limited v. Bangladesh Telecommunication Regulatory Commission (BTRC) & ors.*, 14 SCOB [2020] HCD 1, there were allegations against the petitioner, Grameenphone that the petitioner failed to comply with the terms and conditions of the guidelines, licence and the provisions of the Act, 2001 and also failed to justify such failure. A show-cause notice, without expressly mentioning that it is issued under section 63(2) of this Act, 2001, was issued by the BTRC and replied by the petitioner. Yet, even after having the reply, it is claimed that after determining the nature of the offence and the amount of loss, the BTRC took the decision to impose the maximum amount of statutory fine, i.e., BDT 30 million against the petitioner, again without expressly mentioning that the fine was imposed under section 65 of this Act.

281. The petitioner denying the allegations of BTRC as to the violation of law and terms and conditions of the licences, etc., submitted that even if there is any violation by the petitioner (which is denied), BTRC did not follow the due process mentioned in section 65 of this Act, 2001. A combined reading of sections 63 and 65 of this Act, 2001 reveals the process the BTRC should follow in imposing an administrative fine in case of alleged violations of the law or provisions of the licences. Accordingly, BTRC will first have to issue a show-cause notice upon a suspected violator to ascertain the allegation under section 63. Next, the suspected violator will have to reply to the notice and if the BTRC is not satisfied with the reply, then it can impose an administrative fine within the prescribed limit under section 63(3). If the BTRC decides to impose a fine, it will determine the amount based on the 'nature of the offence' and 'amount of loss'. After that, BTRC shall issue a notice under section 65(2) to the violator stating the amount of the fine and will ask the violator to pay such fine within a prescribed time limit. However, in this instant case, the BTRC, instead of imposing a fine under section 65, imposed a fine under section 63 of this Act under the consideration that section 63 is a stand-alone provision using which the BTRC can invoke fine independently of section 65.

---

260. *Grameenphone Limited v. Bangladesh Telecommunication Regulatory Commission (BTRC) & ors.*, 14 SCOB [2020] HCD 1.

282. Honourable Justice Syed Refaat Ahmed examined the necessary co-relationship between the provisions of sections 63 and 63 of this Act and held that 'section 65 in its entirety is the corridor within the statutory scheme through which the sanctity of the section 63 penal sanction must be gauged. Consequentially, any failure to trigger section 65 or any of its components necessarily leads to a statutory infraction resulting in a more fundamental constitutional infraction'. Moreover, the court also considered the huge amount of fine imposed and found that this maximum fine was not imposed based on 'an in-built mechanism of fair play' devised in section 65 of this Act, rather resulting from 'an exercise of unfettered discretion', and finally, declared that these acts of BTRC were done without lawful authority having no legal effect.

§8. Bangladesh Post Office

283. BPO,[261] with its countrywide network through 9,886 post offices, provides a wide range of basic postal services, and financial & ICT-based digital postal services. The Director-General of BPO or any officer authorized by him is the competent authority to issue licenses to possess wireless telegraphy apparatus under the Wireless Telegraphy Act, 1933 (Act No. XVII of 1933).[262] Since 16 August 2000, Bangladesh Postal Department has started the e-post service using which people can send and receive messages and scanned images using emails. This is an important initiative to give electronic mail services to people without internet access. This service is now available in sixteen Head Post Offices. This Department also provides several digital services such as electronic money transfer service (popularly known as mobile money order service), postal cash card, Western Union remittance, Post e-Centre, Post e-Payment, Post Call Centre, International Financial Service, etc. Electronic money transfer service is available in 2,750 post offices, and anyone interested can transfer money electronically following some simple steps.[263] BPO has updated the electronic money transfer system by introducing a digital financial service 'Nagad' in March 2019 and has been working towards becoming a trusted delivery service in the e-commerce ecosystem of the country.

§9. Bangladesh Submarine Cable Company Limited

284. BSCCL,[264] a core telecommunication service provider and international submarine cable operator of Bangladesh and an IIG, assists in providing Long-haul communication between Bangladesh and the rest of the world. The Company emerged as a public limited company in July 2008 and is a party in both SMW-4 and SMW-5 Consortiums. The submarine cable network is expected to be the main

261. Bangladesh Post Office, http://bangladeshpost.gov.bd/.
262. Section 5, the Wireless Telegraphy Act, 1933 (Act No. XVII of 1933).
263. Electronic Money Transfer Service, https://bdpost.portal.gov.bd/site/page/f51a53e6-926b-48a7-a927-8331e2f326ff/-.
264. Bangladesh Submarine Cable Company Limited, http://www.bsccl.com/.

telecommunication infrastructure for 'Digital Bangladesh' by the year 2021. BSCCL-IIG has been helping the people of the country to get broadband internet with a cheaper rate and better QoS, and thus, will play the leading role in the implementation of National ILDTS & ICT policies aiming at developing modern tele-network and high-speed Broadband internet in Bangladesh.[265]

§10. Department of ICT

285. The Prime Minister of Bangladesh leads the activities to promote ICT in the country through the Cabinet Division and A2I Program. The Department of ICT was created on 30 April 2011 and transformed into a Ministry on 4 December 2011. Subsequently, on 10 February 2014, this Ministry of ICT was merged with the MoPTs under the name of MoPT and ICT, where the Ministry of ICT started functioning as the ICT Division. Apparently, this ICT Division is responsible for implementing the provisions of the ICT Act, 2006, the Bangladesh Hi-Tech Park Authority Act, 2010 (Act No. 8 of 2010) and the Digital Security Act, 2018 (Act No. 46 of 2018). Accordingly, four statutory authorities were established, and these are: (a) Department of ICT, (b) Bangladesh Hi-Tech Park, (c) BCC, and (d) CCA. The ICT Division has already established a Digital Security Agency, under section 5 of the Digital Security Act, 2018 (Act No. 46 of 2018) on 5 December 2018.

§11. Bangladesh Hi-Tech Park Authority

286. The Bangladesh Hi-Tech Park Authority was established through the provisions of the Bangladesh Hi-Tech Park Authority Act, 2010 (Act No. 8 of 2010) which was enacted for the setting up and development of hi-tech industries in different places of Bangladesh. The law originally defined 'hi-tech industry' as the knowledge and capital-based, eco-friendly and IT, ITES and R&D-related industry.[266] Subsequently, this definition was amended in 2014, and a few new industries such as software industry, biotechnology, renewable energy, green energy, hardware were included within the definition of 'hi-tech'.[267] So far, Hi-Tech parks are established in Kaliakoir, Gazipur (Bangabandhu Hi-Tech City), Rajshahi (Bangabandhu Sheikh Mujib Hi-Tech Park), Sylhet (Sylhet Electronic City), Jashore (Sheikh Hasina Software Technology Park), Natore (Sheikh Kamal IT Training and Incubation Centre) and Dhaka (Software Technology Park, Janata Tower).

287. The Bangladesh Hi-Tech Park Authority Rules, 2015 were framed containing provisions on the appointment of developers for the development of the parks, conditions to be fulfilled to establish industries in these parks, including foreign investment etc. Very recently, in 2018, Bangladesh Hi-tech Park Authority has been

---

265. Company History, Bangladesh Submarine Cable Company Limited, http://www.bsccl.com/com_history.
266. Section 2(12), the Bangladesh Hi-Tech Park Authority Act, 2010 (Act No. 8 of 2010).
267. Section 2(c), the Bangladesh Hi-Tech Park Authority (Amendment) Act, 2014 (Act No. 9 of 2014).

designated as the central, one-stop service authority along with the BIDA, Bangladesh Economic Zones Authority, Bangladesh Export Processing Zone Authority under the One Stop Service Act, 2018 (Act No. 10 of 2018). This One Stop Service Act, 2018 was enacted to make the local and foreign investment process faster and timely.

§12. BANGLADESH COMPUTER COUNCIL

288. In 1983, a national Committee named National Computer Committee was formed with the aim to purchase computers for catering to the government requirements. In 1988, the Committee was renamed the National Computer Board. This Board was further reformed in 1989 and was made into a statutory body under the Ministry of Science and Technology in the name of BCC. The BCC has now been working as a government advisory body on computers.[268] BCC, a statutory and autonomous body under presently the ICT Division, of the Ministry of Science and ICT, was established by the BCC Act, 1990 (Act No. IX of 1990). The Council is responsible for, *inter alia*, formulating and implementing national strategies and policies in the field of computer and IT; and determining the standards and specifications of computer and IT.[269]

§13. MINISTRY OF INFORMATION

289. The Ministry of Information is responsible for regulating television channels, radio and newspapers in the country. Thus, it has an important role in regulating Fake News or disinformation. Anyone should first apply for a licence or no objection certificate for Broadcasting to the Ministry of Information and after obtaining the same, can approach the BTRC for allocation of frequency and other ancillary matters.[270] Section 3(2) of the Bangladesh Telecommunication Regulation Act, 2001 (Act No. 18 of 2001) excludes the application of the law and authority of BTRC to grant a licence for Radio and Television Broadcasting. However, the BTRC has the power to allocate frequency spectrum to those who are granted a licence or no objection certificate by the Ministry of Information for Radio and Television Broadcasting.[271] BTRC has the exclusive jurisdiction to grant a licence for telecom systems and services under section 36 of the Bangladesh Telecommunication Regulation Act, 2001. But it cannot grant a licence for broadcasting and telecasting programmes through satellite channels.[272]

---

268. Computer, Banglapedia, http://en.banglapedia.org/index.php?title=Computer.
269. Section 6, the Bangladesh Computer Council Act, 1990 (Act No. IX of 1990).
270. *Bangladesh Telecommunication Regulatory Commission v. Ekushey Television Ltd.*, 58 DLR (AD) (2006) 83.
271. *Chairman, Bangladesh Telecommunication Regulatory Commission and others v. Ekushey Television Ltd. and others,* 14 MLR (2009) (AD) 369.
272. Ministry of Information, represented by its Secretary, *Government of Bangladesh and others v. Jamuna Television Limited and others*, 14 MLR (2009) (AD) 114.

§14. Other Relevant National Regulatory Authorities

290. In the area of telecommunication and ICT, there are few other authorities that have been performing regulatory functions and duties. The Planning Division and the Ministry of Finance develop the business and budget plans.[273] All relevant agencies of the government develop their information plans to include them in the Annual Performance Agreements and report to the Prime Minister through the Cabinet Division. Besides, the Bangladesh Police, which works under the Ministry of Home Affairs, plays a significant role in the investigation of various types of cybercrimes and any telecommunication-related crimes. The Ministry of Science and Ministry of Education play crucial roles in popularizing ICT throughout the country. The NBR sets the tax rate and exemption from tax regarding ICT and ITES in the country.

§15. Association of Trade Bodies

291. ICT and Telecommunication sector trade bodies in the country play an important role as a bargaining agent in shaping the legal and policy regime of this section, and in regulating members through industry self-regulation tools. A brief discussion on these trade bodies is shared below.

§16. Association of Mobile Telecom Operators of Bangladesh

292. AMTOB, established in 2001, is a national trade body representing all mobile telecom operators, i.e., Banglalink, GrameenPhone, Citycell, Robi and Teletalk.[274] This body is the official voice for the mobile industry of the country and by providing a forum for discussion it has been interacting with relevant stakeholders, both, national and international. AMTOB facilitates a conducive environment for its members and industry stakeholders to establish an infrastructure required to deliver affordable mobile telephone services in Bangladesh aiming to eliminate the digital divide.[275] Almost every year, after the release and before the approval of the national annual budget, AMTOB shares its views regarding the proposed tax rate in this sector.

§17. Bangladesh Association of Software & Information Services

293. BASIS is the national trade body for the software & ITES industry of Bangladesh. Established in 1998 with only eighteen charter members, the BASIS

273. For example, the Ministry of Finance has issued a gazette notification on 14 Jan. 2019 through which the ITC, IIG and NTTN were given exemption of VAT over 5%.
274. Association of Mobile Telecom Operators of Bangladesh, https://www.amtob.org.bd/.
275. *Ibid.*

has been working with a vision of developing vibrant software & IT service industry in the country. Currently, there are more than fifteen hundred charter members who account for the lion share of the total software & IT services revenue of the country. Any firm or company registered or incorporated in Bangladesh and running software and ITES businesses commercially can apply for the membership of BASIS can apply for General Membership by paying the membership fee and submitting necessary documents. Every member of BASIS needs to follow the Articles of Association and Code of Conduct and gets various services. The Executive Council of the organization can ask for an explanation and expel a member if that member is found guilty of professional misconduct and/or breach the provisions of the Articles of Association.

§18. Bangladesh Association of Call Center and Outsourcing

294. The BTRC has started providing licenses to the call centres since April 2008. BACCO is the trade association of the business process outsourcing and call centre industry of the country. Any organization involved in providing business process outsourcing and call centre services can be a member of BACCO by following some rules, terms and conditions. The members also receive some services and need to follow the Code of Conduct. Like BASIS, the Executive Council of the organization can ask for an explanation and expel a member if that member is found guilty of professional misconduct and/or breach the provisions of the Articles of Association.

§19. Internet Service Providers Association Bangladesh

295. ISPAB, a non-profit organization, is the association for all the internet service providing organizations in Bangladesh. These ISPs offer access to the internet and related services, i.e., internet access, internet transit, name registration and hosting, dial-up access, leased line access to the customers. The Association, representing over 900 companies, is a strong advocate of industry self-regulation and has been playing important role in developing the sector. An ISP can be a member of the Association by following a process and paying a fee. The members of the Association need to follow the Code of Conduct. Both a consumer and an ISP can lodge a complaint to the ISPAB against an ISP. The Association provides a forum for alternative dispute resolution (ADR) services.

§20. Bangladesh Computer Samity

296. Established in 1987 with eleven founding members, BCS is the ICT Industry Association of Bangladesh with over 2,100 members. This Association represents the ICT business and trade industry, i.e., the distributors, dealers, resellers or computer and allied products, locally assembled computer vendors, software developers and exporters, ISP and ITES providers. The Association is the sole member of the World Information Technology and Services Alliance from Bangladesh and represents in the regional forum of the Asian-Oceanian Industry Organisation. The Association has already adopted two self-regulation policies, i.e., the Warranty Policy, 2018 and the Maximum Retail Policy, 2018. The members of the Association are bound to follow these Policies to ensure the consumers get quality computer products.

§21. OTHER ASSOCIATIONS

297. Bangladesh Domain Hosting Provider's Association was established to facilitate trade and business in web hosting industries in Bangladesh. Even though details could not be found, it seems that there is an association of the IIG organizations known as the IIG Association of Bangladesh. Like other associations of trade bodies, a member of this Association also needs to follow the Code of Conduct containing provisions on relations with clients, other members, employees, public and international community, intellectual property protection, relations with the Association, etc. It is provided that a member will cease to be a member if, *inter alia*, the executive council of the Association finds that the member is involved in anti-state or anti-social activities, and if any member is involved in fraud/scamming activities. Thus, the members need to comply with professional and legal guidelines.

Chapter 2. Regulation of Competition in the Telecommunication Sector

§1. Introduction

298. The regulation of effective and fair competition in any relevant market has huge positive impacts on its overall development. This is because one of the main purposes of competition regulation is, *inter alia*, to prevent business practices which are anti-competitive in nature where the market players enter into agreements among themselves, e.g., to create barriers for the new players to enter the relevant market. Besides, the competition regulations also regulate the abuse of the dominant position of the market players which have adverse effects on the efficient functioning of the market. Moreover, competition regulations also govern the merger and acquisition of market players which may have a detrimental impact on competition or result in anti-competitive effects.

299. Effective and fair competition also benefits the consumers by regulating the conduct of businesses as healthy competition among the market players promises the consumers get better and quality services and products at a lower price from wider choices. Thus, competition helps to break the monopoly, fosters innovation through increased investment by the market players and provides alternatives for the consumers.

300. Effective and fair competition in the telecommunication and ICT sectors are also crucial as this sector is evolving very quickly and is immensely benefitted from the innovative products and services of the market players. It has already been shared in Part I, Chapter 1 on Telecommunication and ICT Regulatory Framework that globally the telecommunication sector has been experiencing the fourth generation of regulation. Historically, like other countries in the world, in the first generation of regulation, the government of Bangladesh had a monopoly in the telecommunication sector initially till the 1990s. During that time, the phone was a luxury and only a selected group of fortunate people could afford or get the connection of a telephone. However, the position started changing when in the 1990s, in the second generation of regulation, this sector was opened for private service providers to provide telecommunication services to the consumers, though the mobile phone tariff was very high initially during this period.

301. Few factors such as an effective regulatory regime and lack of competition policy, etc. were responsible for uncompetitive markets and high tariffs during this time.[276] During this time, the government formulated the National Telecommunication Policy, 1998 which was framed to keep pace with the technological developments in the world, though 'one of the main objectives is for creation of an environment of competition in the field of telecommunication system and services

276. Mohammad Abu Yusuf, Quamrul Alam, & Ken Coghill, *The Mobile Phone Market in Bangladesh: Competition Matters*, 45 J. Asian Afr. Stud., 610–627 (2010).

enhancing rapid development in volume, efficiency and accessibility, shall be ensured to make telecommunication services available within the competitive affordable limit of the general users'.[277] Since the first decade of this century, in the third generation of regulation, the private service providers started to compete against the state-run services in voice telephony, television systems and internet access.

302. Being a member of the WTO, Bangladesh made a commitment to adhere to the Basic Telecommunications Agreement which has established the basis for structural reform of the telecommunication sector aiming at the removal of market entry barriers and encouraging competition.[278] However, Bangladesh has not made any commitment to follow the 'Reference Paper on Regulatory Principles' containing a set of definitions and principles on telecommunication regulations since the Reference Paper is a binding document.

303. Chapter 2 of this monograph has already discussed the history of liberalization of Bangladesh's telecommunication sector while discussing the emergence of this sector and the contribution of this sector to the socio-economic development of the country. Yet, in order to ensure competition in this sector in May 2009, BTRC requested ITU to provide advice on single market power issues. Specifically, Bangladesh sought the assistance of ITU to (i) review the competition provisions in the Bangladesh Telecommunication Act 2001; (ii) define relevant markets and determine whether a licensed operator or operators hold Significant Market Power (SMP); (iii) assess the state of competition in the relevant markets and potential of discrimination and/or anti-competitive behaviour in the market; (iv) examine the concept of SMP and define and identify SMP in each relevant markets; (v) recommend suitable tests to determine abuse of market power and possible remedies; and (vi) draft guidelines and/or determinations in relation to SMP. After the study, the ITU proposed three Drafts on (a) Telecommunications Competition Regulations, (b) Telecommunications SMP Licensed Operator Instruction, and (c) Telecommunications SMP Commission Instruction to consider.[279]

304. Bangladesh has not adopted any separate law to regulate competitions in the telecommunication sector so far; rather this sector is regulated through the general law on competition, i.e., the Competition Act, 2012 (Act No. XXIII of 2012) and the sectorial telecommunication law, i.e., the Bangladesh Telecommunication Regulation Act, 2001, empowers the telecommunication sector regulator, BTRC to take various initiative aiming at an effectively competitive market.[280] This chapter

277. *World Tel Bangladesh Ltd. v. Bangladesh represented by the Secretary Ministry of Post and Telecommunications and others*, 2006, 35 CLC (AD) [284] = 11 MLR (2006) (AD) 65.

278. World Trade Organization, Bangladesh, Schedule of Specific Commitments, Supplement 1, GATS/SC/8/Suppl.1, 11 Apr. 1997.

279. ITU, Report to the BTRC on SMP, ITU Asia-Pacific Ad-hoc Assistance: Action No. 10768, July 2009.

280. For an evaluation of the Competition Act, 2012 (Act No. XXIII of 2012), *see*, Sharmin Tania & Afroza Bilkis, *Competition Law in Bangladesh: Towards Achieving Inclusive Sustainable Development*, 21(2) Australian J. Asian L., Article 10: 159–179 (2021).

will first discuss the regulation of competition in general, followed by the regulation in the telecommunication sector. To this end, the following sections will first provide an overview of 'market' and after that, focus on the three pillars of competition law, i.e., anti-competitive agreement, abuse of dominant position, and merger and acquisition.

§2. Definition of Market

305. An understanding of the concept 'market' or 'relevant market', in the context of competition matters, is fundamental and crucial though critical and complex as well. Market definition, one of the most important analytical tools available in the hands of the competition authorities, is the starting point in the assessment and evaluation of competition problems. The definition of 'market' was implicitly included in the Sherman Act, 1890 which laid down the foundations of modern competition law and was formally introduced in the US in 1982 through the merger guidelines and has evolved since then.[281]

306. The definition of relevant market, a tool to specify the boundaries of competition between the players, plays a decisive role during the assessment of competition cases. According to OECD, '[b]y defining a relevant market, then calculating and assigning market shares, competition authorities seek to assess the market power of firms, which is of central importance to understand competition effects. In addition, the definition of the relevant market helps to identify the market participants, to delineate the boundaries of the market and to determine the area of effective competition'.[282]

307. The UNCTAD Model Law on Competition, 1993 provides that the definition of market 'requires the delineation of the product and geographical lines within which specific groups of goods, buyers and sellers interact to establish price and output' and 'should include all reasonably substitutable products or services, and all nearby competitors, to which consumers could turn in the short term if the restraint or abuse increased prices by a not insignificant amount'.[283]

308. The Competition Act, 2012 (Act No. XXIII of 2012), as in force in Bangladesh, has included a statutory definition of 'relevant market' in section 2(s) of the law and has included both the two fundamental dimensions of market definition, i.e., the product market and the geographic market in the definition. According to section 2(s), 'relevant market' means: '(i) a market of goods or services which are exchangeable or changeable by the consumer on the basis of characteristics, price and intended use of the goods or services; (ii) a market comprising the area in which

281. OECD, Market Definition, Background Note, 12 Oct. 2012, DAF/COMP(2012)19, at p. 22.
282. *Ibid.*, at p. 21.
283. UNCTAD is the United Nations focal point on all work related to consumer policy and consumer welfare. This UNCTAD Model Law on Competition contains substantive possible elements for a competition law. Part 2 is regularly updated with commentaries and cases reported by the Member States.

the conditions of competition for the supply of goods or provision of services or demand of goods or services are homogenous and are distinguished from the conditions prevailing in the neighbouring areas'. A close look at this definition of market will reveal that it has included the main issues to justify the influence of a similar definition proposed by the European Commission, which is believed to have the influence of the US's Hypothetical Monopolistic Test.[284]

309. Chapter 2 of this monograph while discussing the telecommunication infrastructure and emergence of a telecommunication system in Bangladesh has highlighted the market players of the country in the field of telecommunication, mobile network providers, satellite, submarine cable, television, radio, and mobile telecommunication infrastructure, etc. Chapter 3 of this monograph has also provided a glimpse of the ICT and telecommunication market players of Bangladesh.

§3. Competition and National Legal Framework

310. Keeping in mind the purpose and importance of competition law, it can be revealed that a few domestic laws of Bangladesh have already contained some isolated provisions on different aspects of competition.[285] Besides, the Apex court of the country also time to time ruled in favour of a competitive market.[286] However, there was no single piece of legislation containing the most relevant issues covered in modern competition law in one place. To fill in the gap, in 2012, the Competition Act, 2012 (Act No. XXIII of 2012) was enacted by repealing the Monopolies and Restrictive Trade Practices (Control and Prevention) Ordinance, 1970 (Order V of 1970), which prohibited undue concentration of economic power, unreasonable monopoly power or unreasonably restrictive trade practices. The government had to take this initiative, i.e., amend and update the relevant provisions in this regard since the provisions of this Ordinance of 1970 were not effectively implemented.

---

284. European Commission Notice on the definition of relevant market for the purposes of Community competition law (97/C 372 /03).

285. The list of such laws containing provisions on some aspects of competition to protect the consumers includes: the Penal Code, 1860 (XLV of 1860), the Essential Commodities Act, 1957 (Act No. III of 1957), the Control of Essential Commodities (Extension to the Chittagong Hill-Tracts) Ordinance, 1970 (East Pakistan Ordinance No. I of 1970), the Special Power Act, 1974 (Act No. XIV of 1974), the Procurement Regulation, 2003 formulated under the Public Procurement Act, 2006 (Act No. 24 of 2006), the Trademark Act, 2009 (Act No. 19 of 2009), the Consumers' Right Protection Act, 2009 (Act No. 26 of 2009), the Pure Food Act, 2013 (Act No. 43 of 2013), the Breast-Milk Substitutes, Baby Foods, Commercially Manufactured Supplementary Baby Foods and Its Equipment (Regulation of Marketing) Act, 2013 (Act No. 35 of 2013), the Standards of Weights and Measures Act, 2018 (Act No. 56 of 2018), etc.

286. In *World Tel Bangladesh Ltd. v. Bangladesh*, 2006, 35 CLC (AD) [284], the AD confirmed that '… allowing monopoly … is also void as opposed to public policy under the provision of section 23 of the Contract Act, for monopolies being prejudicial to the public welfare' and '… the maintenance of exclusivity or monopoly rights reduces efficiency of competitive markets'. It was also held in the same case that the BTRC, the telecommunication regulator of the country, can also 'amend any condition or content in the licence agreement is inconsistent with any provisions of the Act in order to ensure healthy competitive environment, prohibition of anti-competitive and discriminatory practices in the telecom sector … '

311. It will be relevant to share here that different jurisdictions enact competition law to attain different objectives, e.g., to ensure effective competition or workable competition, economic efficiency, consumer welfare, etc.[287] The general law applicable in relation to competition in Bangladesh is the Competition Act, 2012 (Act No. XXIII of 2012) which was enacted to make provisions to promote, ensure and sustain a congenial atmosphere for the competition in trade, and prevent, control and eradicate collusion, monopoly and oligopoly, combination or abuse of dominant position or activities adverse to the competition in the context of gradual economic development of the country.[288] It is believed that the lawmakers got their inspiration to enact this law from various provisions of the Constitution of Bangladesh, 1972, which are dealing with certain fundamental principles of state policies and fundamental rights.[289] The provisions of the Competition Act, 2012 (Act No. XXIII of 2012) are in addition to, and not in derogation of, the provisions of these laws in force for the time being.[290] It is pertinent to mention here that while the Competition Act, 2012 (Act No. XXIII of 2012) deals with competition matters in the private sector, competition in public procurement is regulated by the provisions of the Public Procurement Act, 2006.[291]

312. Except for the goods or services which are controlled by the Government for the interest of the national security and not open for the private sector, such as arms and ammunition, defence equipment, forest plantation, nuclear energy, security printing, etc., the provisions of this Competition Act, 2012 (Act No. XXIII of 2012) apply to all enterprises involved in purchase, sale, production, supply, distribution or storage of goods or services for commercial purposes.[292] As such, the provisions of this law shall generally be applicable to regulate competition in the telecommunication and ICT sector also, even though these sectors need to abide by the sectoral laws that govern competition.

313. The Competition Act, 2012 (Act No. XXIII of 2012) is silent about the definition of 'effective competition' and how the regulators should and will assess or measure the adverse effects of anti-competition activities. It can be anticipated that the Bangladesh Competition Commission (BCoC), the regulator and a quasi-judicial body having the power to play the role of a civil court established under the law, will consider these issues when they will come up with the subsidiary legislation or policy guidelines. Before doing so, they also need to consider the potential competitive effect of the proposed policy. To evaluate the effects of the proposed

287. To know the practices of different jurisdictions as to why they enacted their domestic competition laws, *see*, UNCTAD's Handbook on Competition Legislation (Volume II), Consolidated Report 2013–2014, https://unctad.org/webflyer/handbook-competition-legislation-volume-ii-consolidated-report-2013-2014.
288. Preamble, the Competition Act, 2012 (Act No. XXIII of 2012).
289. These provisions are Art. 10 dealing with socialism and freedom from exploitation, Art. 19(2) equality of opportunity and equal distribution of wealth to attain a uniform level of economic development throughout the Republic, and Art. 42(1) dealing with the rights to property. *See* Annual Report, Competition Commission of Bangladesh, 2019–2020, at p. 14.
290. Section 42, the Competition Act, 2012 (Act No. XXIII of 2012).
291. Section 13, the Public Procurement Act, 2006 (Act No. 24 of 2006).
292. Sections 3 & 4, the Competition Act, 2012 (Act No. XXIII of 2012).

policy, the can consider the best practices in this field such as the OECD Competition Assessment Toolkit, 2009 and International Competition Network's Recommended Practices for Competition Assessment, 2014 and Framework of Competition Assessment Regimes, 2015.

314. From the provisions of the Competition Act, 2012 (Act No. XXIII of 2012), it is evident that it has incorporated provisions about all the three pillars of competition law, i.e., anti-competitive agreement, abuse of dominant position, and merger and acquisition. Under the provisions of the Competition Act, 2012 (Act No. XXIII of 2012), other than IPRs and export of goods from Bangladesh, it is prohibited to enter into any direct or indirect agreement or collusion, in respect of production, supply, distribution, storage or acquisition of any goods or services which causes or may cause an adverse effect on competition or creates monopoly or oligopoly in the market.[293] 'Collusion', under this law, means the written or unwritten agreement or understanding with mala fide intention to control the market by destroying the environment of congenial and usual competition.[294]

315. Chapter III of the Competition Act, 2012 (Act No. XXIII of 2012) deals with the anti-competition agreement (section 15) and abuse of dominant position (section 16). It is prohibited to enter into a direct or indirect agreement or collusion between persons in respect of production, supply, distribution, storage or acquisition of any goods or services which causes or is likely to cause an adverse effect on competition or creates monopoly or oligopoly in the market. The Law indicates that some practice or decision of anyone or association through agreement regarding the trade of identical or similar goods or provision of services can have an adverse effect on competition if such agreement: (a) directly or indirectly (i) determines abnormal purchase or sale prices; or (ii) determines the deceptive price in all process including bid-rigging; or (b) limits or controls production, supply, markets, technical development, investment or provision of services; (c) divides the market on the basis of types of goods or services, source of production or provision of services, geographical area of market, or number of customers in the market or any other similar basis.[295] The Law has further identified some agreements and arrangements such as 'tie-in arrangement', 'exclusive supply agreement', 'exclusive distribution agreement', 'refusal to deal', 'resale price maintenance' as an anti-competitive agreement if they have an adverse effect on competition.[296]

316. 'Cartel', i.e., the explicit or implicit agreement between any person or association of persons to limit or control or attempt to limit or control over the production, distribution, sale, price or transaction of goods or services in order to establish a monopoly in trade is a punishable offence under the law.[297]

---

293. Section 15(1) & 15(4), the Competition Act, 2012 (Act No. XXIII of 2012).
294. Section 2(q), the Competition Act, 2012 (Act No. XXIII of 2012).
295. Section 15(2), the Competition Act, 2012 (Act No. XXIII of 2012).
296. Section 15(3), the Competition Act, 2012 (Act No. XXIII of 2012).
297. Sections 2(e) and 20, the Competition Act, 2012 (Act No. XXIII of 2012).

317. Under the Law, any enterprise cannot use its dominant position, i.e., a position of strength enjoyed by the enterprise in the relevant market which enables it to: (1) operate independently of competitive forces prevailing in the relevant market; or (2) affect its competitors or consumers or the relevant market in its favour.[298] The Law provides that in the following circumstances, it shall be deemed to be an abuse of dominant position if an enterprise:

(a) imposes directly or indirectly unfair or discriminatory condition in the purchase or sale of goods or services or discriminatory price or predatory price in the purchase or sale of goods or services;
(b) limits or restricts the production of goods or provision of services or market thereof or technical or scientific development relating to goods or services to the prejudice of consumers;
(c) indulges in practice or continue to do practices which prevent others from accessing the market;
(d) makes the conclusion of contracts subject to acceptance by other parties of supplementary obligations which, by their nature or according to commercial usage, have no connection with the subject of such contracts; or
(e) uses its dominant position in one relevant market to enter into or protect other relevant markets.[299]

318. Two relevant cases are pending before the BCoC. In the first case, *Bangladesh Competition Commission v. E-Valey.com Limited* (Suo Motu Case No. 03/2020), the Commission, while dealing with a cashback offer advertised by E-Valey.com, an e-commerce site issued an interim order. The Commission found that '[a]s per the provisions of clause (ko) of sub-section (1) of section 15 of the Competition Act, 2012, 60% and 40% of cash back offer adjustable to next sales mentioned in the Eid Dhamaka advertisement is violation of the Competition Act'. Accordingly, the BCoC instructed the e-commerce site to make necessary changes in the software within a week and to suspend all sales arrangements related to such conditional cashback offers. Recently, a good number of e-commerce platforms such as E-Valey, E-orange, Dhamaka, etc., have been accused of embezzling millions from customers. Similar to E-Valey, these platforms also collected a huge amount of money in the name of promotional and lucrative offers leaving thousands of consumers ruined and shattered. In this context, though various legal issues, of both civil and criminal nature, are involved and a number of criminal cases are also pending, the decision of this case by the BCoC will be significant as this has the prospect to pave the way in the development of a conducive e-commerce legal regime in the densely populated and developing Bangladesh.

319. In *DNS Software v. Robi Axiata Ltd. and others* (Case No. 06/2020), DNS Software was procuring application-to-person messaging (A2P) SMS services from international outlets (e.g., Facebook, Google, etc.) and was routing those SMS to

298. Section 16(1), the Competition Act, 2012 (Act No. XXIII of 2012).
299. Section 16(2), the Competition Act, 2012 (Act No. XXIII of 2012).

customers through local Mobile Station Integrated Services Digital Network (MSISDNs). As a result, when anyone tried to reset Facebook or Gmail password, he used to receive a one-time password on his mobile phone from Facebook or Google and if this SMS comes through DNS, that SMS originator would show a local MSISDN instead of international numbers. Detecting this practice, GP & Robi stopped DNS's A2P SMS services where SMS is originated outside of Bangladesh as this is similar to VoIP services which are unauthorized, illegal and not mandated by BTRC. By being aggrieved with this decision, DNS brought an allegation against Robi, Grameen Phone and Value First Limited to the BCoC claiming that these companies have formed a cartel to do A2P business themselves limiting the scope of competition and thus, have violated the provisions of the Competition Act, 2012. While this case is also pending before the BCoC, this will also be interesting to see the decision of the BCoC as a better forum for DNS to settle this would be BTRC.

§4. Mergers and Acquisitions

320. Mergers and acquisitions are not unique in the context of the telecommunication sector in Bangladesh as this sector has already witnessed several instances of merger and acquisition. The following Tables project the merger and acquisition by the industry of the target firms and ten largest mergers and acquisitions in Bangladesh completed between 2000–2009. It is also evident that in 99% of cases, foreign companies acquired Bangladeshi companies (*see* Tables 8 and 9).

Table 8 Mergers and Acquisitions by the Industry of the Target Firms, 2000–2009 (Values in Millions of USD)

Country	*Services (%)*	*Manufacturing (%)*	*Financial (%)*	*Natural resources (%)*	*Wholesale Trade and Retail (%)*	*Other (%)*	*Total (%)*
Bangladesh	1,432 (68.6)	73 (3.5)	434 (20.8)	145 (6.9)	5 (0.2)	0 (0.0)	2,089 (100.0)

Source: Thomson Financial Service.[300]

Table 9 Ten Largest Mergers & Acquisitions in Bangladesh, 2000–2009

Rank	*Date Announced*	*Date Effective*	*Target and Nationality*	*Acquirer and Nationality*	*Amount (USD Million)*
1	24 March 2003	11 December 2003	AES Hariput, AES Meghnaghat (Bangladesh)	CDC Globeleq Holdings Ltd. (UK)	437

300. Roger Y.W. Tang & Ali M. Metwalli, *Mergers and Acquisitions in India, Pakistan and Bangladesh*, 23 Inter'l J. Com. Mgmt., 327–338 (2013).

Rank	*Date Announced*	*Date Effective*	*Target and Nationality*	*Acquirer and Nationality*	*Amount (USD Million)*
2	16 June 2008	19 September 2008	TM Intl (Bangladesh) Ltd (Bangladesh)	NTT DoCoMo (Japan)	350
3	29 November 2005	6 September 2006	Rupali Bank Ltd (Bangladesh)	Bandar Bin Mohammad Bin Abdul (Saudi Arabia)	330
4	18 May 2005	2 June 2005	Pacific-Bangladesh Telecom Ltd (Bangladesh)	SingTel (Singapore)	118
5	4 August 2003	30 June 2004	Royal Dutch/Shell-Upstream (Bangladesh)	Cairn Energy PLC (UK)	75
6	5 March 2009	5 March 2009	Beximco Pharmaceuticals Ltd (Bangladesh)	GEM Global Yield Fund Ltd (US)	73
7	26 October 2007	26 October 2007	Cairn Energy Bangladesh Ltd (Bangladesh)	Santos Intl Hldg Pty Ltd (Australia)	70
8	2 June 2005	2 June 2005	Pacific-Bangladesh Telecom Ltd (Bangladesh)	SingTel (Singapore)	65
9	2 September 2004	2 September 2004	Sheba Telecom (Pvt) Ltd (Bangladesh)	Orascom Telecom Holding SAE (Egypt)	60
10	29 February 2008	29 February 2008	Oriental Bank Ltd (Bangladesh)	ICB Financial Group Holding SAE (Switzerland)	51

Source: Thomson Financial Service.[301]

In Bangladesh, non-Bangladeshi firms acquiring Bangladeshi companies accounted for 99% of all M&A transaction value (*see* Table 10).

Table 10 Mergers and Acquisitions Completed in Bangladesh (M&A Value in Millions of USD)

Bangladesh	*M&A Value*	*%*
Bangladeshi firms acquiring other Bangladeshi firms	31	1
Bangladeshi firms acquiring non-Bangladeshi companies	0	0

301. *Ibid.*

Bangladesh	*M&A Value*	*%*
Non-Bangladeshi firms acquiring Bangladeshi companies	2,057	99

Source: Thomson Financial Service.[302]

321. The concept of 'merger' is used in different types of laws in different senses, and also by different jurisdictions in different ways. The word 'merger' is generally used to mean the joining of two things into one, e.g., joining of two or more companies, departments, properties, etc. into one. In the relevant discussion in competition matters in the market economy or antitrust law, the concepts 'merger' and 'acquisition' are often used together, i.e., 'merger and acquisition'. In the Bangladeshi statutes, the word 'merger' is not popularly used; instead, the presence of the words such as 'amalgamation' and 'combination' can be traced in different laws.

322. In the sense of joining two agricultural holdings into one often for the purpose of enlarging it for economic viability, the concept 'merger' has been in use in this part of the world for centuries in the context of land matters. The Transfer of Property Act, 1882 (IV of 1882) contains provisions on mergers of mortgage and charges over an estate under section 111. Such a merger is known as a merger by operation of law. However, a merger can also be completed by the intention of the parties.[303] The Bengal Tenancy Act, 1885, which was repealed by the State Acquisition and Tenancy Act, 1950 (Act No. XXVIII of 1951), included provisions on 'doctrine of merger' under section 22(1) of that law of 1885. The State Acquisition and Tenancy Act, 1950 (Act No. XXVIII of 1951) has included a chapter in Part V, i.e., Chapter XV (sections 116–134A) on, *inter alia*, amalgamation. Besides, a merger is a very common incident in the regular operation of the government when two or more departments join together to meet the need of the time or to serve a better purpose.

323. The Competition Act, 2012 (Act No. XXIII of 2012) prohibits activities having an effect on effective competition in goods and services in the market, anti-competition agreements, abuse of dominant position and combinations, i.e., amalgamations or acquisitions. The law has not defined 'merger' and 'acquisition'. But while defining 'combination' in section 2 of the Act, it provides that 'combination' means the acquisition or taking control or amalgamation or merger in trade. Any combination which causes or may cause an adverse effect on competition in the market of goods and services is statutorily prohibited in the country,[304] though the reality seems to be different.

302. *Ibid.*
303. *Tajim Ali v. Saijuddin Khan* (1954) 6 DLR 25.
304. Section 21, the Competition Act, 2012 (Act No. XXIII of 2012).

324. Even though in various jurisdictions there are separate legal instruments usually in the form of subsidiary legislation on mergers, there is no such instrument yet in the context of Bangladesh though some provisions on mergers can be found in the Companies Act, 1994 (Act No. 18 of 1994). Therefore, a discussion on the relevant provisions of the Companies Act, 1994 (Act No. 18 of 1994) may be considered here to understand the merger process. However, it will be pertinent to mention here that the merger of companies under the Companies Act, 1994 (Act No. 18 of 1994) and the merger of companies under the competition law regime is quite different in essence as both these legal regimes serve different purposes, i.e., while the merger procedure as included in the company law should be followed in general circumstances when two or more companies decide to merge for various reasons, e.g., achieve better and faster growth; merger under the competition law is concerned and comes into the scene so that two or more companies cannot merge together to gain excessive power to control the market to enjoy the monopoly.

325. Sections 228 and 229 of the Companies Act, 1994 (Act No. 18 of 1994) deal with the process of compromise or arrangement which may take the form of either merger or amalgamation, i.e., 'arrangement of amalgamation/merger'.[305] To do so, both the parties need to draft a scheme of amalgamation containing various provisions such as salary and benefits of the employees, the denomination of shares and transfer of assets and liabilities, etc. This draft is to be approved by the Board, and with such approval, the same can be presented before the company bench of the HCD of the Supreme Court. If the HCD allows this, then the Court will instruct the parties to advertise it in the newspapers to bring the matter of the proposed merger to the attention of the general mass. After that, the companies that are parties to this process need to get the approval of the scheme in the General Meeting and move to the HCD for approval. After the HCD is convinced and approves the scheme, it will declare that the transferor company is dissolved and direct the relevant authorities to update the record of a licence, share ownership, etc.

326. Muhammad Khurshid Alam Sarkar, J. in the case of *Kay and Que (BD) Ltd. v. Registrar, Joint Stock Co.* 2019, 2019(2) LNJ, highlighted the most important words in section 228 of the Companies Act, 1994 for the purpose of their application in a legal dispute in the following manner:

> Power to compromise with creditors and members:
>
> 228.(1) Where a compromise or arrangement is proposed between a company and its creditors or any class of them, or between the company and its members or any class of them, the Court may, on the application in summary way of the company or of any creditor or member of the company or, in the case of a company being wound up, of the liquidator, order a meeting of the creditors or class of creditors, or the members of the company or class of members, as the case may be, to be called, held and conducted in such manner as the Court directs.

305. *Kay and Que (BD) Ltd. v. Registrar, Joint Stock Co.* 2019, 2019(2) LNJ.

> 228.(2) If a majority in number representing three-fourths in value of creditors, or of members as the case may be, present either in person or by proxy at the meeting, agree to any compromise or arrangement, the compromise or arrangement shall if sanctioned by the Court be binding on all the creditors or the class of creditors, on or all the members or class of members, as the case may be, and also on the company, in the case of a company in the course of being wound up, on the liquidator and contributories of the company. (underlined by me)

327. In *Chittagong Cement Clinker Grinding Co. Ltd. v. Joint Stock companies and Firms*, 11 BLT (HCD) 81, it was held that in relation to amalgamation and merger of the companies, the following principles emerge:

(i) The scheme satisfies the requirements of law.
(ii) The Court should see that the shareholders, who may be affected by the scheme, have been fairly represented.
(iii) The scheme is passed by the majority of the shareholders in value.
(iv) The scheme should be in the interest of the shareholders of the transferor and the transferee company.
(v) The sanction should be given to such a workable scheme which a man of business would reasonably approve.
(vi) The Court may impose conditions and modify the scheme if so required.
(vii) The sanction should be given to a bona fide scheme which is fair as a whole, to all concerned.
(viii) The scheme should not only be in the interest of the shareholders of the companies but also in public interest.[306]

328. In the case of *Kay and Que (BD) Ltd. v. Registrar, Joint Stock Co.* 2019, 2019(2) LNJ, the HCD attempted to dissect and provide a detailed anatomy of amalgamation under sections 228 and 229 of the Companies Act, 1994 when two companies Kay and Que (Bangladesh) Ltd. and MultiSourcing Ltd. applied the approval of their 'Scheme of Amalgamation' into one, i.e., Kay and Que (Bangladesh) Ltd. and it was objected by Bangladesh Securities Exchange Commission in the general interest of the investors on the grounds that the shareholder directors of these two companies might plan to grab 1.7 million additional shares of BDT 10 each and/or, the shareholder directors had the ill motive of financial gain by winding up of the company. Muhammad Khurshid Alam Sarkar, J. evaluated four issues, i.e., (i) whether a company is competent to undertake a Scheme of Amalgamation/Merger if its Memorandum of Association (MoA) does not contain any provision for amalgamation/merger and whether the MoA of these petitioner-companies authorizes for amalgamation, (ii) whether these petitioners have complied with the requirements of section 228 of the Companies Act, (iii) whether this Court is obligated to take into consideration the public interest at the time of sanctioning any

306. *Chittagong Cement Clinker Grinding Co. Ltd. v. Joint Stock companies and Firms*, 11BLT (HCD) 81.

'Scheme of Amalgamation' taken by the companies and, for that purpose, whether this Court is required to investigate into the bona fides of this Scheme and (iv) whether the Court can modify the Scheme and/or pass any other Order/s or Direction/s.

329. In relation to issue no. (i), i.e., the court revealed that 'any company incorporated under the Companies Act may embody in its object clause the provisions for amalgamation with any other company or body of persons and, in the event that the draftsman of the MoA omits to inscribe the provision, it can be inserted therein with the approval of the Court. If the provision for amalgamation is not contained in the MoA of the company, it cannot take a decision for amalgamation in that, MoA of any incorporated company having the status of law, any act not authorised by the MoA is ultra vires the law ... MoA is the charter of any company and, therefore, a company's activities are circumscribed by its object clause and it has no power to act or contract beyond the objects incorporated therein'.

330. In relation to the issues no. (ii) and (iii), on the process of amalgamation, the court had the following observations '... when two or more companies become desirous to enter into any arrangement of merger with each other towards converting themselves into one single entity, they all, ... would make an application to the Court under sub-Section (1) of Section 228 of the Companies Act for directions for convening of the meetings of the members and creditors, if any, for considering the proposed Scheme of Amalgamation, at first. On such an application, the Court would issue directions for convening of separate meetings of the members and/or creditors or different classes of members and/or creditors, as the case may be. In the said meetings of the members and/or creditors, the Scheme of Amalgamation is required to be approved by majority in number representing three-fourths in value of the creditors or class of creditors or members or class of members, as the case may be. After the Scheme is approved by all concerned in their respective meetings, a separate petition then would be presented to the Court for sanctioning of the Scheme of Amalgamation. However, if the prayer for sanctioning of the Scheme of Amalgamation has already been made in the original application, there is no need to file a separate application, but in that event, the fact as to the approval by the three-fourths in value of the members/creditors should be brought to the notice of this Court by way of filing a supplementary affidavit'.

331. The Court also observed that:

> Sub-Section (2) of the Section 228 of the Companies Act is about making the decision of amalgamation binding upon the all concerned. The Section warrants that the decision approving the Scheme of Amalgamation should be passed by majority in number representing three-fourths in value of the members or class of members and/or creditors or class of creditors, as the case may be, in order to make the said decision binding upon all the shareholders, creditors and the company. The aforesaid provision, however, does not specifically state that if the Scheme of Amalgamation is approved by the shareholders/creditors less than 'majority in number representing three-fourths in value of

members/creditors', it would be invalid; it simply says that it shall not be binding upon the members, creditors and the company. Here, the Legislature has put two concurrent conditions; one is majority in number and the second condition is that the value of shares/credits of the said majority in number should be three-fourths. The Legislature's intention for, and the purpose behind, imposing the condition of majority in number representing three-fourths in value is to ensure the fairness and transparency in dealing with the merger of companies by the directors. Because, it is the Board of Directors which initiates the process of merger and it is not unlikely that they may design it for their ulterior purpose.

42. The plain meaning and scheme of Section 228(2) of the Companies Act, as can be gathered from the Bengali text of this piece of legislation, which is written in a clearer version without keeping any ambiguity in understanding the same, is that three-fourths of the shareholders/creditors means three-fourths of the entire shareholders/creditors; there is no scope for any company to interpret the law that three-fourths of the shareholders/creditors means three-fourths of the presentees in the AGM/EGM. It follows that until and unless the three-fourths of the entire shareholders remains present in the AGM/EGM and approves the Scheme of Amalgamation, the requirements envisaged in Section 228(2) of the Companies Act are not fulfilled. An argument is advanced before this Court that since the shareholders of the listed-company are trading their shares every day in the stock market, it is an impossible task for the listed-company to ensure the presence of the three-fourths shareholders in number in the AGM/EGM to be held for approval of the Scheme of Amalgamation. Since the stock market is now digitized and the CDBL [Central Depository Bangladesh Limited] keeps the record of the latest transferees of the shares of the listed- companies, it is not a difficult task for the listed-companies to notify their general shareholders by sending notice through e-Mails, message or registered post. In any event, no provision of law can be interpreted taking into consideration the convenience or inconvenience of the stakeholders of the said law. In other words, any arrangement (be it merger or something else) must be approved by the three-fourths number of the shareholders/creditors and, at the same time, it should also be at least three-fourths from the perspective of value of the company's shares/credits. Therefore, any Scheme would not be approved by the Court, if the resolution granting approval to the Scheme of arrangement is passed by more than three-fourths in value of the shareholders/creditors but, is not carried by the majority in number of the creditors and/or members. Similarly, no Scheme would be approved by this Court when a resolution is passed by the majority in number of shareholders and/or creditors, for example, more than 75% of the entire shareholders/creditors in number favoured the Scheme, but the value of the 75% shares/credits is less than three-fourths of the entire shares/credits. While the purpose of providing majority in number of the creditors and members in the Section is to safeguard the interests of the large number of small creditors and/or shareholders whose voice is often lost amongst small number of big shareholders/ creditors, the reason behind putting the condition of three-fourths in value is that a company should not bow down to any unlawful, unethical and unfair demand by the majority in number at the cost of

jeopardizing the interest of the shareholders/creditors who possess three-fourths in value of the shares/ credits in the company. Thus, the conditions of approval by the majority in number and three-fourths in value of share/credit are cumulative.

43. However, this Court by exercising its discretionary power may pass a direction that the Scheme shall be binding upon all concerned in spite of the poor turn-over of the shareholders in the AGM/EGM held for approval of the Scheme, if the Court finds that it is not contrary to any provisions of law and it does not violate any public policy and is satisfied that the Scheme is reasonable, just, fair and not prejudicial to the interests of the members or class of members or creditors or a class of creditors, as the case may be. By virtue of the inherent power a Court of law possesses, it is competent to examine the 'just and fair' aspect of a remedy sought for by the petitioner in course of dealing with any type of case. This Court, therefore, is required to consider the pros and cons of the Scheme to see whether the Scheme is in favour of public interest. When the listed-company would show the Court that despite taking all the steps to ensure sending of notices to all the shareholders through e-Mail, mobile message, registered post in addition to publishing the notice of the AGM/EGM in two widely circulated national newspapers, the turn-up of the general shareholders in the AGM/EGM for approval of the Scheme of Amalgamation was less than three-fourths, in that scenario, the petitioner-companies may legitimately make a prayer before this Court to pass an Order to the effect that the Scheme shall be binding upon all the shareholders and other stakeholders. And if this Court finds the contentions of the petitioner-companies to be reasonable, fair, just and overall in favour of public interest, it may sanction the Scheme. Therefore, it is my considered view that at the time of sanctioning a Scheme of Amalgamation, while this Court is competent to sanction a Scheme despite the same being not approved by 'the majority in number representing three-fourths in value of the shareholders and/creditors', this Court is also empowered to decline sanctioning of a Scheme despite being approved by the three-fourths shareholders and/creditors if it is found to be against public interest. In other words, while this Court should not act merely as a rubber stamp to simply endorse the *ipse dixit* of the majority of the shareholders or creditors inasmuch it is the solemn duty of this Court to find out whether the big shareholders/creditors have voted for the Scheme for the benefit of the company or only for their personal gain by depriving the 1/4th shareholders/creditors and, at the same time, this Court also should not mechanically refuse the sanctioning of a Scheme merely on the ground of non-approval of the same by the 3/4th of the shareholders and/creditors without delving deep into the matter by carrying out an investigation as to whether the petitioner-companies have put their best effort to ensure the presence of 3/4th shareholders. In both the situations, this Court is under an obligation to take into consideration the public interest upon embarking on the issues as to (i) whether the Scheme of Amalgamation is undertaken by the companies violating any law or public policy, (ii) whether the interest of all types of shareholders, creditors, employees and public at large are well protected, (iii) whether it is designed to benefit only the directors of the companies and (iv) whether the

> Scheme has been prepared for the purpose of dodging the Government revenue or with an ill-motive of evading any Government or non Government dues or depriving any individual/group of individuals.

332. On the issue of (iv), the court held that:

> 53. … anyone with ordinary prudence can understand that when an application for any type of arrangement or compromise, be it for amalgamation or for other purpose, is presented before this Court, the Court, before or after sanctioning the Scheme, may pass any type of incidental, consequential order/s whatever would appear to it to be necessary in order to give full effect to the Scheme; meaning that for the purpose of protecting the interest of all concerned, the Court may pass necessary order/s. Since all the provisions of Section 229(1) are permissive empowering this Court to pass any order for the purpose of protecting the interests of all concerned and, more importantly, there is no prohibitive provision limiting this Court's power, I am of the view that either in course of hearing the application for sanctioning the Scheme, or at the time of passing the Order of sanctioning the Scheme or after sanctioning the Scheme, this Court is competent to pass necessary order and/or direction upon any person, Government authority and non-Government entity towards ensuring the interest of all concerned.
> 54. It follows that although there is no separate provision in the Companies Act for dealing with the amalgamation-application of the public limited companies, however, for the purpose of protecting the public interest by determining the fair valuation of the assets of the petitioners-companies, this Court is armed with sufficient power to pass orders whatever it may deem fit and proper, which may include (i) directing the companies to submit their previous 5-10 years' Financial Reports before the Court and, at the same time, directing the directors of the companies to produce their personal income tax returns so that the data and information contained in the Financial Reports can be checked up by the Court, (ii) directing the C/A Firms, who have prepared the Financial Reports, to explain before the Court their basis for valuation of the assets which are alleged to have been overvalued, (iii) directing the relevant Government and non-Government functionaries, namely, Sub-Registrar of the concerned area, Deputy Commissioner of Tax of the concerned zone assigned by the National Board of Revenue (NBR), the FRC, BSEC, RJSC, DSE and CSE to provide necessary information, and (iv) directing the petitioner-companies to do and/or to refrain from doing certain work/s.

333. It may be relevant to share here that BB, the Central Bank of the country, has issued Guidelines for Merger/Amalgamation of Banks/Financial Institutions. This is because of section 76 of the Bank Companies Act, 1991 (Act No. 14 of 1991) which prohibits the compromise or arrangement between a bank company and its members without the certification of the BB. Similar kinds of provisions on mergers and acquisitions can also be found in section 28 of the Financial Institutions Act, 1993 (Act No. 27 of 1993) regarding the financial institutions. The Bangladesh Securities and Exchange Commission (BSEC) has also formed a Committee on Merger and Acquisition in 2016. The Committee has recently decided to come up with the Acquisition Rules as the Merger culture is not yet popular in the country. On 22 July 2019, the BCoC, through an office order formed a six-member Merger and Acquisition Committee to deal with the merger and acquisition application, its consequence on the market and relevant matters.

§5. Competition Authority in Bangladesh

334. Various sectoral regulators such as BTRC, BB, Bangladesh Energy Regulatory Commission and BSEC have been enjoying the statutory authority and responsibility to ensure competition in their respective markets. Yet, the Competition Act, 2012 (Act No. XXIII of 2012) provides for the establishment of a general competition authority for Bangladesh, i.e., BCoC in Chapter II of the Law. Accordingly, the BCoC, the regulator and a quasi-judicial body having the power to play the role of a civil court, was established. The BCoC has started to function formally in 2016 and properly from March 2020. It has been reported that the BCoC has been working to finalize the subsidiary legislation relating to their working procedure, inspection, appeal, review, and combination (merger and acquisition), etc.

335. Under the Competition Act, 2012 (Act No. XXIII of 2012), the BCoC is responsible and empowered to:

(a) eliminate practices having an adverse effect on competition in the market, to promote and to sustain competition and to ensure freedom of trade;
(b) inquire into, either on receipt of any complaint or on its own initiative, all anti-competition agreements, dominant position and practice of the enterprises;
(c) inquire, without prejudice to section 18, into other offences specified under this Act and to sue and conduct them accordingly;
(d) determine the combination and matters relating to combination, to inquire into for combination and conditions of combination and approval or disapproval of combination;
(e) make rules, policy, instructions of notifications or administrative directions relating to competition, and to give advice and to assist the Government for implementation thereof;
(f) set up appropriate standards for the promotion of competitive activities and to provide training for the matters relating to competition;
(g) take the necessary plan of actions for developing awareness among the people about the matters relating to competition by way of dissemination, publication and any other means;
(h) develop mass awareness by way of conducting research, seminar, symposium, workshops and other similar means about the anti-competition agreement and activities and for publishing and disseminating the result of such research and giving recommendations to the Government for their effective implementation;
(i) implement, follow or consider any matter relating to competition sent by the Government;

(j) review the actions taken under any other law for consumer rights protection and implementation;
(k) sign and execute any agreement or MoU with any foreign organization, with prior approval of the Government order to discharge the duties under this section or for the efficient performance of its functions;
(l) fix fees, charges or any other expenses for carrying out the purposes of this Act; and
(m) do any other act prescribed by rules for carrying out the purposes of this Act.[307]

336. The law provides that the Commission shall act as a Civil Court and follow the provisions of the Code of Civil Procedure, 1908 (Act No. V of 1908) regarding (a) summoning and ensuring the attendance of any person before the Commission; (b) discovery and production of any document; (c) examining and inspection of any information; (d) requisitioning any necessary document or its copy from any office; and (e) issuing notice for examination of witness and document, etc.[308]

337. It may be relevant to share here that to enforce the law, it is necessary to formulate subsidiary legislation such as Rules or Regulations under section 18(2) of the Competition Act, 2012 (Act No. XXIII of 2012). But, the Ministry or the Commission has not yet framed such subsidiary legislation. Nevertheless, the Competition Commission has issued an Office Order on 30 October 2017 containing the procedure to be followed if any complaint is lodged with the Commission.

338. With the continuous economic progress of the country, this is high time that the BCoC becomes more active to exercise some of the powers given by the law and take some strict actions in anti-competitive business practices as there are so many cases available in the country where the practice of 'syndicate' (statutorily 'collusion' and 'cartel') of businessmen is quite normal and kind of open-secret. The consumers, as a result, have been suffering badly due to such anti-competitive business practices. Almost a decade ago, in 2012, Professor William E. Kovacic of George Washington Law School and former Chairman of the Federal Trade Commission, US, highlighted the common initial challenges all emerging economies face, e.g., resource limitations, fragile administrative process, excessive state involvement, etc.; shared some guidelines for the competition authority of Bangladesh to consider.[309] Professor William, with all his experiences for years, emphatically assured that strong systems will build gradually and therefore, the habit of improvement is common. Therefore, the competition authority should follow the cycle- experiment, assess and improve. It is very unfortunate and from the activities of the BCoC, it can be said that the suggestions and guidelines provided by Professor William are largely ignored. Considering the suggestions of after Professor William, the researchers can consider exploring if the two Parliaments formed as a

307. Section 8(1), the Competition Act, 2012 (Act No. XXIII of 2012).
308. Section 8(3), the Competition Act, 2012 (Act No. XXIII of 2012).
309. Kovacic, W.E., *Effective Implementation of Competition Law in Other Developing Countries: Lessons for Bangladesh*, Moving the Competition Law Agenda Forward in Bangladesh – Possible Implementation Concerns, Launch Seminar, Monday, 2 Jul. 2012.

consequence of seriously questionable and controversial national elections held in 2014 & 2018, has any role to play as this has been reported that the nominations were sold and the majority of the Members of the Parliaments elected were businessmen.

§6. Competition Regulation in Telecommunication Sector

339. Most countries regulate competition in the telecommunication sector to prohibit the operators from engaging in anti-competitive conduct, enter into collusive arrangements with the target to control market share, fixation of rate, a boycott of another competitor or supplier of telecommunication system or equipment, etc. In Bangladesh, the National Telecommunication Policy and Bangladesh Telecommunication Regulation Act, 2001 (Act No. 18 of 2001) collectively lay down the foundation of competition regulation in this sector. Based on the above Policy and legislative provisions, the BTRC has a key role in establishing effective competition in the telecommunication sector of Bangladesh under the Act.[310]

340. The national telecommunication regulator, BTRC, has been playing a pivotal role in promoting competition in the sector. The BTRC has established the System and Service division which is responsible for ensuring competition in the area. All the Telecommunication Policies formulated so far have encouraged competition in this sector. The adoption of the ILDTS Policy, 2007 introduces competition in the telecommunication sector in Bangladesh.[311] BTRC has also introduced licensing obligations, QoS standards, and fines for selling SIM cards without proper registration, etc. On 11 September 2011, BTRC has included the Market Competition Factor as an additional charge applicable to all MNOs depending on the quantum of their market share. However, such a charge cannot be imposed retrospectively.[312] Besides, BTRC has also issued the Guidelines on Infrastructure sharing in 2008 and amended them in 2011 to promote competition.

341. The NTTN Licensing Guidelines as framed under the Licensing (Procedure) Regulations, 2004 has considered the principles of transparency, fairness, and non-discrimination, etc. Article 25 of the Regulatory and Licensing Guidelines for NTTN, 2008 deals with 'Anti-Competitive Conduct, Unfair Competition and Discrimination'. It provides that the Licensee(s) shall not engage in anti-competitive conduct which inhibits or impedes fair competition including exploiting a position of dominance such as to unreasonably restricting competition. The Regulatory and Licensing Guidelines for NTTN, 2008, has listed some acts of anti-competitive conduct.

---

310. Relevant provisions can be found in ss 29(c) and (d), 30(1)(e), 30(2)(l), 30(2)(m).
311. ITU, Report to the BTRC on SMP, ITU Asia-Pacific Ad-hoc Assistance: Action No. 10768, July 2009, at p. 1.
312. *Grameen Phone Ltd v. Bangladesh Telecommunication Regulatory Commission* (BTRC) and others, 2012, 41 CLC (HCD) [8826] = 18 BLC (HCD) (2013) 401.

342. According to the Regulatory and Licensing Guidelines for NTTN, 2008, engaging in predatory price cutting may be implied where: (i) a service is priced at less than marginal costs for two consecutive months; and (ii) such costs are likely to price competitor out of the market or deter competitors from entering the market. Besides, the Licensee(s) can (a) recoup the full amount of the loss incurred during the period of price cutting; (b) engage in cross-subsidizing where the revenues for service is used to unfairly cross-subsidize the price of other services or equipment; (c) engage in unfair pricing such as to reduce or eliminate competition including fixing prices for services or equipment at a level which cannot be re-sold with a margin of profit to subscribers; and (d) enter into exclusive arrangements which deny competitors access to services or equipment.[313]

343. In the Guidelines, it is further provided that the Licensee(s), on his own or through a third party, shall not engage in any practice which unfairly restricts or is likely to restrict existing competition in the national telecommunication industry or which deters or restricts or may deter or restrict new Licensee(s) into the national telecommunication industry including, but not limited to, engaging in the following practices:

(a) asserting false or misleading claims on the availability, price or quality of its services or systems or the services or systems of any other Licensee(s) or competitor(s);
(b) degrading the availability or quality of a Licensee(s) or competitor's services or systems or unfairly raising their business, operational or technical costs;
(c) unlawfully interfering with the suppliers or subscribers of the Licensee(s) or its competitor(s); or
(d) providing false or misleading information to other Licensee(s) or competitor(s) or to any third party.

§7. Numbering

344. BTRC, as the principal regulator of the telecommunication sector, has adopted the Bangladesh Numbering Plan 2005 and has recently updated this in 2017 with provisions on the control, planning, administration, management and assignment of numbers and electronic addresses of network and application services. It was formulated to ensure that the number allocation process is fair and transparent to provide a level playing field for competition.

345. BTRC has decided to introduce the inter-operator number exchange, i.e., Mobile Number Portability (MNP) system in October 2018. BTRC has framed the Regulatory and Licensing Guidelines for MNP Services in Bangladesh, 2017 in this regard and this was amended in September 2018. Now, mobile subscribers are free to change their phone operators keeping the existing numbers. It has been reported

313. Article 25.01, the Regulatory and Licensing Guidelines for NTTN, 2008.

that in 2018, in the month of October, November and December 44,312, 32,773 and 29,258, respectively and in January 2019, a total of 27,448 users used the MNP service. Even though this initiative was applauded by the users, it seems that this has created some problems regarding banks and mobile financial services as they stopped getting various notifications attached to the previous numbers.

§8. Single Market Power

346. In order to create a level playing field for the players of the telecommunication sector in the country, to regulate and break monopoly or oligopoly if the activities of an operator are found to have wage anti-market activities and to encourage competition among them, the BTRC started initiative formulating the SMP Guidelines in 2009 by seeking assistance from the ITU.[314] At the beginning of this century, in 2002, the European Commission released the guidelines on market analysis and the assessment of SMP under the Community regulatory framework for electronic communications networks and services to assist the national regulatory authorities to carry out their duties to ensure effective competition and control the abuse of dominance position by the market players.[315] The said Guidelines were recently revised in 2018.[316]

347. Though the market share can give a preliminary indication of a dominant position, this should not be the sole basis to consider. In this recently revised SMP Guidelines of 2018 of the European Commission, it is provided that very large market shares, i.e., in excess of 50% held by an undertaking for some time generally presents evidence of the existence of a dominant position.[317] Whereas, generally, 'dominance is not likely if the undertaking's market share is below 40 % in the relevant market' though there may have exceptional cases.[318] The European Commission suggests that when the market share is high but below the 50% threshold, the regulators should consider other key structural market features, e.g., the overall size of the undertaking, control of infrastructure not easily duplicated, technological advantages or superiority, absence of or low countervailing buying power, easy or privileged access to capital markets/financial resources, product/services diversification (e.g., bundled products or services), economies of scale, economies of scope,

314. ITU, Report to the BTRC on SMP, ITU Asia-Pacific Ad-hoc Assistance: Action No. 10768, July 2009, at p. 2.
315. OJ C 165, 7.11.2002, pp. 6–31. The Guidelines were released in accordance with Article 15(2) of the Directive 2002/21/EC of the European Parliament and of the Council of 7 March 2002 on a common regulatory framework for electronic communications networks and services OJ L 108, 24.4.2002, p. 33.
316. Communication from the Commission – Guidelines on market analysis and the assessment of significant market power under the EU regulatory framework for electronic communications networks and services, C/2018/2374, OJ C 159, 7.5.2018, pp. 1–15.
317. *Ibid.*, para. 55.
318. *Ibid.*, para. 57, footnote No. 55.

vertical integration, a highly developed distribution and sales network, absence of potential competition, and barriers to expansion.[319]

348. In the Bangladesh context, in 2011, the Draft of the SMP Guidelines was developed and shared with the relevant stakeholders such as the MoPT and Board of Investment for review and feedback. Finally, the BTRC finalized the SMP Guidelines in the form of Regulations, i.e., the Bangladesh Telecommunication Regulatory Commission (Significant Market Power) Regulations, 2018 through gazette notification of 14 November 2018. The Regulations defines 'Significant Market Power' as 'the individual capacity of the telecommunication system or service operator or the joint capacity with another operator by the capability of which it can conduct at its own convenience in such a manner, without taking into account of the conduct of other competitors or customers' that can have a negative impact on other competitors or customers'.[320] As per the provisions of the Regulations, if any service provider of retail mobile service-related market controls at least 40% of the total market of any of the criteria, namely: (a) number of subscribers; (b) earned annual revenue; (c) Spectrum allocated by the Commission and other resources, the BTRC shall define this as the SMP for that market.[321]

349. The BTRC declared GrameenPhone as the operator with the SMP on 10 February 2019, issued two directives and proposed to impose a total of twenty conditions.[322] With this decision of BTRC, which is the first of its kind in Bangladesh, the business growth of GrameenPhone may be restricted as the regulators may impose an additional charge for customer acquisition besides the normal charge. BTRC proposed to impose a few conditions on the operation of GrameenPhone and of these conditions, conditions such as a bar on market communication and signing of an exclusive agreement with any goods and service providers, permit the customers to change operator within thirty days instead of ninety days under mobile portability service and bring the mandatory set call drop below 2% were subsequently withdrawn after one month. BTRC asked GrameenPhone to submit its comments on these conditions within fifteen days. GrameenPhone challenged the legality of the decision of BTRC in the HCD. BTRC withdrew and cancelled the two directives and asked for GrameenPhone's response which was submitted on 31 March 2019. On 18 February 2019 and 12 May 2019, BTRC attempted to impose restrictions on GrameenPhone as an SMP operator, but could not do so as the HCD

319. *Ibid.*, para. 58.
320. Regulation 2(7), the Bangladesh Telecommunication Regulatory Commission (Significant Market Power) Regulations, 2018.
321. Regulation 7(11), the Bangladesh Telecommunication Regulatory Commission (Significant Market Power) Regulations, 2018.
322. The list of these conditions include: asymmetric mobile termination rate, cross subsidy, MNP lock-in period, spectrum pricing, infrastructure sharing, exclusivity, loyalty campaign, product and service approval process/automatic approval of retail tariffs of non-SMP operators, social obligation fund, voice tariff, data floor price, parallel pricing or ante approval of retail tariffs, green technology or renewable energy, merger and acquisition threshold, corporate social responsibility, number of product, QoS, revenue sharing and market communication. *See,* 'BTRC withdraws 4 SMP conditions on GP after 1 month', The New Age, 20 Mar. 2019, http://www.newagebd.net/article/67858/btrc-withdraws-4-smp-conditions-on-gp-after-1-month.

imposed injunctions of BTRC's directives as BTRC did not take the response of GrameenPhone into account. The HCD instructed the BTRC to re-issue the conditions. BTRC issued directives with lighter restrictions to GrameenPhone imposing conditions regarding the MNP lock-in period, approval of service/package and Mobile Termination Rate. The BTRC has also communicated the said directives to other MNOs.

§9. Recent Developments

350. Recently, two mobile operators, i.e., Robi-Airtel were merged, and this is the largest merger in the history of Bangladesh. Robi Axiata Ltd. and Airtel Bangladesh Ltd. both applied to the Commission for company merger on 17 September 2015. In response, the Commission decided to conduct a survey regarding the technical and financial effect of the merger, to take public opinion through hearing and to discuss this with the other four operators.

351. Thereafter, the Commission sent recommendations to the Posts and Telecommunications Division. After that, the Government approved the merger of Robi Axiata Ltd. and Airtel Bangladesh Ltd. subject to compliance of fifteen terms and conditions through a letter submitted by the Posts and Telecommunications Division to the Commission on 1 August 2016. Finally, the merger scheme of these two companies was permitted through the judgment of the HCD on 31 August 2016. Finally, the Commission approved the merger of these two companies subject to compliance with twenty-one terms and conditions.[323] Though the value of the merger was undisclosed, it is believed that high tax rates, mandatory government fees and increased competition from other market players contributed to this sensational telecom merger in the history of Bangladesh.[324]

323. BTRC, Annual Report 2016–2017, p. 126.
324. Zaman, M. & Rahman, M., *Surviving a Corporate Telecom Merger: Case Study on Robi Axiata and Airtel Bangladesh* (2018).

Chapter 3. Regulation of Cryptography and Other Dual-Use Goods

§1. INTRODUCTION

352. Cryptology, derived from the Greek words *'Kryptos'* and *'logos'*, is the art and science of code-making and code-breaking.[325] Cryptography is a technique to protect data in storage and message in communication by way of coding or encryption and by using this technique, any message or data can be transferred 'into a form that can't be understood (decrypted) without knowledge of some secret information'.[326] As a discipline, cryptography 'embodies principles, means, and methods for the transformation of data in order to hide its information content, establish its authenticity, prevent its undetected modification, prevent its repudiation, and/or prevent its unauthorised use'.[327] Encryption is generally regulated for its 'dual-use' nature, i.e., this technique can be used for both commercial and military purposes.

353. The art or technique of encryption or cryptography is not an innovation of recent times; rather, people have been using this for centuries. The Roman emperor Julius Caesar used this technique, known as Caesar cipher or Caesar's cipher, to communicate with his army. Due to its 'dual-use' nature, cryptography is being regulated around the world, though there is no binding international instrument on this. The area of law that regulates cryptography is also known as the 'key disclosure law' or 'mandatory key disclosure', and by using the provisions of such laws, the members of the law enforcement agencies can require the owner of encrypted data to share the decrypted data.

354. Even though there is no specific international instrument on the governance and regulation of cryptography, the OECD Council has adopted the Recommendation regarding the Guidelines for Cryptography Policy on 27 March 1997. Different countries that have adopted domestic law on this have considered the OECD Guidelines. These Guidelines contain the following principles:

(a) Cryptographic methods should be trustworthy to generate confidence in the use of information and communications systems.
(b) Users should have a right to choose any cryptographic method, subject to applicable law.
(c) Cryptographic methods should be developed in response to the needs, demands and responsibilities of individuals, businesses and governments.
(d) Technical standards, criteria and protocols for cryptographic methods should be developed and promulgated at the national and international levels.

---

325. Simon A. Price, *Understanding Contemporary Cryptography and Its Wider Impact upon the General Law*, 13 Inter'l Rev. L. Computers & Tech., 95–126 (1999).
326. Stewart A. Baker, *Decoding OECD Guidelines for Cryptography Policy*, 31 Inter'l L., 729–756 (1997).
327. OECD, Recommendation of the Council concerning Guidelines for Cryptography Policy, OECD/LEGAL/0289.

(e) The fundamental rights of individuals to privacy, including secrecy of communications and protection of personal data, should be respected in national cryptography policies and in the implementation and use of cryptographic methods.
(f) National cryptography policies may allow lawful access to plaintext, or cryptographic keys, of encrypted data. These policies must respect the other principles contained in the guidelines to the greatest extent possible.
(g) Whether established by contract or legislation, the liability of individuals and entities that offer cryptographic services or hold or access cryptographic keys should be clearly stated.
(h) Governments should cooperate to coordinate cryptography policies. As part of this effort, governments should remove, or avoid creating in the name of cryptography policy, unjustified obstacles to trade.

§2. Cryptography Regulation in Bangladesh

355. There is no specific law on the regulation of cryptography in Bangladesh though there are various general provisions available in the domestic law using which the law enforcement agencies may compel anyone to disclose the decrypted data of encrypted data.[328] For example, section 46 of the Digital Security Act, 2018 (Act No. 46 of 2018) provides that 'While conducting an investigation under this Act, an Investigating Officer may request any person or entity or service provider to provide information or assist in the investigation, and if any such request is made, the concerned person, entity or service provider shall be obliged to provide the necessary information and assistance.' Similarly, in the case of money laundering related offences, it is provided that it is an offence to decline to supply the information without any reasonable ground.[329] Thus, these provisions are so wide and general that these can be interpreted to also compel anyone to disclose the decrypted data.

356. In Bangladesh, the issue of adoption of encryption standard was included in the first National ICT Policy, 2002, where it is provided that 'Data security ... should be ensured through actions such as setting of encryption standards ... ' Unfortunately, a similar provision is not included in the latest ICT Policy of 2018. However, while dealing with the 'Strategic Priorities of Digital Bangladesh', in January 2011, the issue of Public Key Infrastructure (PKI), cryptography and encryption were discussed.

328. It may be relevant to share here that the Code of Criminal Procedure, 1898 (Act No. V of 1898) is the principle criminal procedural law of the country s. 161 of the Code, 1898 (Act No. V of 1898) provides that an investigating police officer may examine anyone orally if he has the reason to believe that the persona so examined may be acquainted with the facts and circumstances of the case. It is further provided that 'Such person shall be bound to answer all questions relating to such case put to him by such officer, other than questions the answers to which would have a tendency to expose him to a criminal charge or to a penalty or forfeiture.'
329. Section 7(1)(b), the Money Laundering Prevention Act, 2012 (Act No. 5 of 2012).

357. In the Sixth Five Year Plan (2011–2015), the Planning Commission of Bangladesh while setting the Sectorial Strategies, Programmes and Policies authorized the Ministry of Science and ICT, and BTRC, being the responsible agency and the public key custodian for ensuring network security, to develop encryption standard and security-related laws in the country. The Secretariat Instructions, 2014, while containing important provisions on the introduction of information and communication technologies in the government offices, includes a provision on cypher messages. Besides, the government has recently formulated the Government Email Rules, 2018 to properly perform the government activities by ensuring confidentiality, efficiency and transparency in electronic communications. The Rules provide that the BCC, as the implementing authority of the Rules, will publish a manual containing information regarding the use of digital signature and encryption features in the email account of the government officials.

358. In May 2015, the Central Bank of the country, BB issued the Guideline on ICT Security for Banks and Non-Bank Financial Institutions (NBFIs) (version 3.0) as the minimum control requirements that must be adhered to by every Bank and NBFIs. The provisions of the Guideline cover all electronically generated, received, stored, replicated, printed, scanned and manually prepared information. Chapter 5 of the Guidelines, while dealing with Infrastructure Security Management provides, *inter alia*, that 'Confidential or sensitive information that stored in laptops must be encrypted', 'Email shall not be used to communicate confidential information to external parties unless encrypted using approved encryption facilities' and 'the Bank or Non-Bank Financial Institutions (NBFI) shall encrypt backup data in tapes or disks, containing sensitive or confidential information, before transported offsite for storage'.

359. In 1991, the former Telegraph & Telephone Board drafted the 'Amateur Radio Service related Guideline of Bangladesh', which was approved by the MoPT in 1992. Recently, on 30 July 2019, the BTRC has issued the amended 'Instructions for Amateur Radio Usages and Procedures in Bangladesh'. These Instructions were issued as the amateur radios, which are known as voluntary non-commercial communication services, are used for various purposes such as non-commercial exchange of messages, wireless experimentation, self-training, private recreation, and emergency communication. Under these amended instructions, any resident and non-resident Bangladeshi with more than 18 years of age and Bangladeshi entities such as government organizations, schools colleges, universities and Amateur Radio Society/clubs in Bangladesh can apply for a maximum of one Amateur Radio Licence. It is expressly included as a condition of the licence that a Licensee 'will not use/buy/import any amateur Radio with encryption Mode'.[330]

330. Instruction No. 6.13, 'Amended Instructions for Amateur Radio Usages and Procedures in Bangladesh', BTRC, 30 Jul. 2019.

360. Part 20 of the Government of Bangladesh Information Security Manual (GoBISM) contains provisions on cryptography.[331] It is provided that the government agencies should use secure encryption products when they communicate over insecure or unprotected networks such as the internet. Moreover, these agencies should not use any version of Secure Sockets Layer (SSL) and should use the current versions of Transport Layer Security (TLS) as different problems were found in SSL. In line with the GoBISM, in July 2019, the Planning Commission of Bangladesh has adopted the Information Security Policy for Electronic Government Procurement (e-GP) System containing various provisions on encryption to ensure the security of data. Therefore, it is evident that even though the government and various agencies are encouraged to use encryption techniques to protect sensitive data and messages, no prohibition could be identified which expressly prohibits the private use of encryption. Nevertheless, the BTRC in its instructions issued on 18 September 2013 regarding the issuance of registration certificate for the operation of Call Centre provides that the international call centre operators may be permitted to create VPN or apply encryption, but appropriate monitoring facilities are to be made available to BTRC.

361. Finally, it is apparent that the issues on encryption and cryptography in Bangladeshi laws are generally covered, to a limited scale, to ensure data security by way of a digital signature or digital certificate. Cryptography used to develop virtual or cryptocurrency, is not permitted in Bangladesh as per the warning notice issued on 24 December 2017 by BB regarding the legality of the transaction using virtual currencies. Thus, all these initiatives are isolated, and there is so far, no comprehensive legal framework on encryption regulation. The government has not taken any initiative like her neighbour India who took the initiative to formulate a National Policy on Encryption under section 84A of the Information Technology Act, 2000. A draft was released in September 2015 in this regard, though it has not been finalized yet.

362. Regarding the dual-use goods, Bangladesh, though a member of most of the arms-related international instruments, is not a party to the Wassenaar Arrangement on Export Controls for Conventional Arms and Dual-Use Goods and Technologies, 1996.[332] The Import Policy Order (2015–2018) prohibits the import of all goods, including military weapons by anyone other than the Ministry of Defence.

331. The provisions of the GoBISM is discussed in an elaborated fashion under the discussion on cyber security in the later part of this monograph.

332. The Wassenaar Arrangement is a voluntary export control arrangement where forty-two Member States to this Arrangement exchange information on transfers of conventional weapons and dual-use goods and technologies.

Chapter 4. Legal Status of Standardization

§1. Introduction

363. Standards are important in the telecommunication and ICT sectors as they facilitate the interoperability of the internet, telecommunication and computer network technologies, and assist both the regulators and market players in implementing and following the market regulation properly. As a result, consumers can get the products developed following approved standards at a better and competitive rate. Internationally, ITU, founded in 1865, the oldest intergovernmental agency which subsequently became the specialized agency of the UN is primarily responsible for developing telecommunication standards, though there are other recognized standard-setting bodies, such as ISO too. Without standards, the market players and consumers would have to develop and use different devices for different networks. Realizing the importance of the standards, this matter has been included in all the national policies on telecommunication and ICT formulated so far.

§2. Standard-Setting Organizations

364. The Bangladesh Standards and Testing Institution (BSTI), the only National Standards body of the country under the MoI, was established by the Government through the Bangladesh Standards and Testing Institution Ordinance, 1985 (Ordinance No. XXXVII of 1985) for standardization, testing, metrology, quality control, grading and marking of goods. With the establishment of this body, the previous two institutions, i.e., Bangladesh Standards Institution and the Central Testing Laboratories, were abolished. For the purpose of this monograph, it may also be relevant to share here that the telecommunication regulator of the country, BRTC play an important role in relation to the development and introduction of telecommunication-related technical standards in the country following the guidelines and standards of ITU and other international and regional organizations.

365. Being a member of ISO since 1974, Bangladesh is a Technical Committee member in the guidelines on consumer warranties and guarantees (ISO/PC 303), community-scale resource-oriented sanitation treatment systems (ISO/PC 318), leather products (ISO/TC 120/SC 3) and food products (ISO/TC 34) Committees. BSTI is a participating member of the Technical Committee on consumer policy and developing country matters. Moreover, BSTI is an Observing Member in at least twenty-two Technical Committees of ISO, including in Committees on, *inter alia*, leather tanned leather, footwear, ceramic tile, environmental management, floor coverings, foundry machinery, cereals and pulses, tea, textiles, devices for administration of medicinal products and catheters, fibres and yarns, and spices, culinary herbs and condiments.

366. At present, BSTI is the Member/Affiliate Member/Contact Point/ Nodal Point of the following International/Regional Organizations:

(a) International Organization for Legal Metrology.
(b) Codex Alimentarius Commission.
(c) International Electrotechnical Commission (IEC).
(d) Asia Pacific Metrology Programme.
(e) Asian Forum for Information Technology.
(f) ISO Information Network (ISO NET).
(g) Standing Group for Standardization, Metrology, Testing and Quality.[333]

367. BSTI performs its activities through a few wings such as Administrative Wing, Standard Wing, Certification Marks Wing, Chemical Wing, Physical Wing and Metrology Wing. While performing its activities, the Institute was guided by the BSTI Ordinance of 1985 and the Standards of Weights and Measures Ordinance, 1982 (Ordinance No. XII of 1982). However, these Ordinances were recently repealed and replaced by new laws. Therefore, BSTI is now governed by the provisions of the following laws:

(a) The Bangladesh Standards and Testing Institution Act, 2018 (Act No. 67 of 2018).
(b) The Standards of Weights and Measures Act, 2018 (Act No. 58 of 2018).
(c) The BSTI Employee Service Rules, 1989.
(d) The Standards of Weights and Measures Rules, 1982 (as amended in 2006).
(e) The Bangladesh Standards of Weights and Measures (Packaged Commodities) Rules, 2007.

368. Moreover, two subsidiary legislations were formulated under the previous Ordinance, 1985, i.e., the Bangladesh Standards and Testing Institution Rules, 1989, and the Standards of Weights and Measures Rules, 1982. As the primary laws were recently replaced, it can be anticipated that these subsidiary legislations will also be updated soon.

369. As the country is moving from an agro-centric economy to a manufacturing one, the importance of a national standard body such as BSTI is felt increasingly. Along with some regulatory measures, BSTI is primarily responsible for making standardization of services and products (S); introducing the international unit system of weights and measures and promotion of metrology services (M); promoting quality assurance activities; rendering testing facilities for services and products; and preparing, promoting and adopting national standards. Besides, BSTI plays an important role in making different bodies and entrepreneurs aware and adopting key international standards. This Organization has also signed the IEC's affiliate country programme pledge in 2001. The Institution has been functioning as a self-financing organization as its budget is fully supported by its own income.

370. Besides preparing Standards for all articles, products, methods and services, BSTI can bring any product under BSTI's Compulsory Certification Marking

333. Bangladesh Standards and Testing Institution, Vision and Mission, http://bstibds.com/dynaic_pages/2.

system. BSTI marks received through this system cannot be used by anyone other than the original recipient without the prior approval of BSTI. Standards approved by BSTI, known as Bangladesh Standards, are generally voluntary though there are some compulsory standards in place which are published in the Official Gazette. On the other hand, every manufacturer and dealer of commercial weights and measures have to obtain a licence from BSTI, and these are to be verified and stamped by BSTI every year. Moreover, the exporter and importer of weights and measures are to be registered with BSTI, and the use of non-metric weights and measures is strictly prohibited.

371. BSTI is empowered to ban the sale, distribution and commercial advertisement of goods if they do not comply with the relevant Bangladesh standards. For example, on 27 February 2019, the MoI through S.R.O. No. 50-Law/2019 published the list of 101 types of goods with corresponding standards. These categories of goods need to follow these standards. Otherwise, BSTI can ban the sale, distribution and commercial advertisement of these goods.

372. With the general functions to regulate the establishment, operation and maintenance of telecommunication services in Bangladesh, the BTRC is specifically responsible to:

(a) assist the concerned Ministries in matters of the ITU and other international and regional organizations relating to the standards and procedure to be followed in telecommunication;
(b) set the technical standards and standards of telecommunication services, to monitor the standards of telecommunication services provided by operators and to ensure that such services are conformed to the standards set by the Commission; and
(c) set up standards for monitoring arrangements by the Commission and their compliance.[334]

373. The BTRC is also empowered to make and publish, from time to time, a directory containing the names and specifications, technical standards and related matters of the terminal apparatus and everyone has to follow the directory in manufacturing, importing and marketing terminal apparatus and installing them in a telecommunication system.[335]

§3. Standard Making Process

374. At the BSTI, the standard making process follows six different stages. These are (1) *proposal stage* (proposal for new standard is received from the public and private sector and is approved by the Divisional Committee), (2) *preparatory*

---

334. Section 30, the Bangladesh Telecommunication Regulation Act, 2001 (Act No. 18 of 2001).
335. Section 52, the Bangladesh Telecommunication Regulation Act, 2001 (Act No. 18 of 2001).

stage (technical or select Committee prepares the draft), (3) *committee stage* (technical or select Committee reviews the draft), (4) *enquiry stage* (draft is circulated among the stakeholders for feedback), (5) *approval stage* (the final draft, after inclusion of feedbacks, is placed before the Divisional Committee), and (6) *publication stage* (approved standard is published as Bangladesh Standard). All such standards are reviewed every five years to meet the demand of the time and either confirmed, revised or withdrawn after such review. In the case of revision, the standard must follow all the six stages shared above.

375. With regard to the telecommunication standards, the BTRC is empowered to determine the telecommunication standards, by making regulations or by publishing a notice at least in two widely circulated national dailies.[336]

§4. Standards on ICT

376. In relation to e-governance standards, the Office Information and Service Framework (OISF) was established under the A2I Programme of the Prime Minister's Office to function as a mediator of different systems that follow various norms or requirements, i.e., standards. This OISF has either developed or has been working to develop various standards on, e.g., Data Standards, Integration Standards, Security Standards, Deployment Standards, Technology Standards, Application Standards, Payment Standards, CCDS, and Biometric Standards, etc. The Bangladesh National Digital Architecture has adopted several standards on (a) application, (b) architecture, (c) mobile service delivery platform, (d) security, (e) business architecture, (f) data architecture, (g) e-GIF, and (h) technology architecture.

377. The BSTI has already adopted the Bangladesh Standard Specification for Mobile Phone Bangla Keypad on 15 February 2011 after the recommendation by the Committee on standardization of Bangla for use in ICT and approval of the Electrical and Electronics Divisional Committee. The Committee on standardization of Bangla for use in ICT under the Ministry of Science and ICT formulated the standard for Mobile Phone Bangla Keypad with the technical assistance of the A2I program of the Prime Minister's Office.

378. The BCC has taken the initiative to determine the standard of the Bangla alphabet and sign to expand the Bangla language on the computer. Already, the existing code set for the Bangla alphabet (BDS 1520: 2000) has been updated, and a new standard BDS 1520:2011 was announced.

379. The standard of mobile Bangla keypad BDS 1834:2011 has been upgraded to use Bangla in mobile phones. The standard will help to expand the use of the Bangla language in IT, including Bangla language-based software development, mobile application development, SMS in Bangla. A fresh initiative has been taken to expand Bangla Language in the computer world. This includes fixation of sorting

336. Section 54, the Bangladesh Telecommunication Regulation Act, 2001 (Act No. 18 of 2001).

order, improvement of Bangla font converter, Text to Speech and Speech to Text Conversion tools, Bangla Corpus, Bangla spell check and other tools like this.

380. This standard was adopted as the government has been providing several mobile-based services, such as admission procedures for educational institutions of various levels, results, railway ticker reservation, etc. This standard incorporates Bangla alphabets, numbers, signs and symbols in a mobile phone in a scientific manner to facilitate the use of Bangla in all ICT applications in mobile phones.

381. Bijoy Keyboard Layout (BDS 1738:2018) and Bijoy Coding System (BDS 1935:2018) were declared as the national standard Bangla Script Writing in Bangladesh. It is the only standard for Bangla scriptwriting in the world.[337]

382. So far, BSTI has adopted twenty-three ICT-related standards developed by ISO/IEC as Bangladesh Standards and developed four Standards. While from the text of these Standards, this is uncertain about their legal status, BCC encourages all public Institutions and private organizations, especially IT & ITES provider companies to follow these Standards while taking up IT-related projects for developing IT Products or services.[338] The list of these twenty-seven ICT-related standards are shared below:

(1) Information technology – Identification cards – On-card biometric comparison [BDS ISO/IEC 24787:2013].[339]
(2) Information technology – Vocabulary – Part 1: Fundamental terms [BDS ISO/IEC 2382-1: 2011].[340]
(3) Information technology – Vocabulary – Part 25: Local area networks [BDS ISO/IEC 2382-25: 2011].[341]
(4) Information technology – Vocabulary – Part 27: Office Automation [BDS ISO/IEC 2382-27:2011].[342]
(5) Information technology – Program constructs and conventions for their representation [BDS ISO/IEC 8631: 2005].[343]

---

337. Localizing Technology: The Story of Bijoy, https://www.wipo.int/ipadvantage/en/details.jsp?id=2624.
338. The descriptions about these Standards are collected from BSTI Standards Catalogue, 2018, which contains the descriptions about more than 4,000 national standards of Bangladesh.
339. This Standard contains requirements for performing comparisons of biometric samples and returning decisions on an integrated circuit card, and security policies for on-card biometric comparison. It also establishes commands and rules to permit pre-comparison computations to be done off-card.
340. This Standard intends to facilitate international communication in information technology. It presents, terms and definitions of selected concepts relevant to the field of information technology and identifies relationships among the entries.
341. This Standard intends to facilitate international communication in information processing. It presents terms and definitions of selected concepts relevant to the field of information processing and identifies relationships between the entries.
342. This Standard intends to facilitate international communication in office automation. It presents, terms and definitions of selected concepts relevant to the field of office automation and identifies relationships between the entries.
343. This Standard is concerned with the expression of procedure-oriented algorithms.

(6) Information technology – Security techniques – Entity authentication – Part 1: General [BDS ISO/IEC 9798-1:2011].[344]
(7) Information technology – Security techniques – Entity authentication – Part 2: Mechanisms using symmetric encipherment algorithms [BDS ISO/IEC 9798-2:2009].[345]
(8) Information technology – Security techniques – Entity authentication – Part 3: Mechanisms using digital signature techniques [BDS ISO/IEC 9798-3:2009].[346]
(9) Information technology – Representation for human communication of state transition of Software [BDS ISO/IEC 11411: 2007].[347]
(10) Information technology – Software packages – Quality requirements and testing [BDS ISO/IEC 12119:2006].[348]
(11) Information technology – Procedure for the registration of identifiers and attributes for volume and file structure [BDS ISO/IEC13800:2006].[349]
(12) Information technology – Software product Evaluation Part 1: General Overview [BDS ISO/IEC 14598-1:2008].[350]
(13) Software engineering – Product evaluation – Part 2: Planning and Management [BDS ISO/IEC 14598-2:2008].[351]
(14) Software engineering – Product evaluation – Part 3: Process for developers [BDS ISO/IEC 14598-3:2008].[352]

---

344. This Standard specifies an authentication model and general requirements and constraints for entity authentication mechanisms which use security techniques. Used to corroborate that an entity is the one that is claimed. An entity to be authenticated proves its identity by showing its knowledge of a secret. The mechanisms are defined as exchanges of information between entities and, where required, exchanges with a trusted third party.
345. This Standard specifies entity authentication mechanisms using symmetric encipherment algorithms. Four of the mechanisms provide entity authentication between two entities where no trusted third party is involved; two of these are mechanisms to unilaterally authenticate one entity to another, while the other two are mechanisms for mutual authentication of two entities. The remaining mechanisms require a trusted third party for the establishment of a common secret key and realize mutual or unilateral entity authentication.
346. This Standard specifies entity authentication mechanisms using digital signatures based on asymmetric techniques. Two mechanisms are concerned with the authentication of a single entity, while the remaining are mechanisms for mutual authentication of two entities. A digital signature is used to verify the identity of an entity. A trusted third party may be involved.
347. The underlying concept is that diagrams and symbols defined herein be helpful in representing software functions and transitions and in improving human communication. The areas covered are development, communication and review of software requirement analysis and design.
348. This Standard is applicable to software packages.
349. This Standard specifies the procedure to be followed by a Registration Authority in preparing, maintaining and publishing an International Register of attributes and one or more International Registers of identifiers for volume and file structure.
350. This Standard Introduces the other parts and explains the relationship between ISO/IEC 14598 and the quality model in ISO/IEC 9126.
351. This Standard provides requirements, recommendations and guidelines for a supporting function which is responsible for the management of software product evaluation.
352. This Standard provides requirements and recommendations for the practical implementation of software product evaluation when the evaluation is conducted in parallel with the development and carried out by the developer.

(15) Software engineering – Product evaluation – Part 4: Process for acquirers [BDS ISO/IEC 14598-4:2008] [353]
(16) Information technology – Software product evaluation – Part 5: Process for evaluators [BDS ISO/IEC 14598-5:2008].[354]
(17) Software engineering – Product evaluation – Part 6: Documentation of evaluation modules [BDS ISO/IEC 14598-6:2008].[355]
(18) Information technology – Software Maintenance [BDS ISO/IEC 14764:2007].[356]
(19) Information technology – Security techniques – Information security management systems – Requirements [BDS ISO/IEC 27001:2015].[357]
(20) Information technology – Security techniques – Code of practice for information security management [BDS ISO/IEC 17799:2011].[358]
(21) Information technology – Guidelines for the management of software documentation [BDS ISO/IEC TR 9294:2006].[359]
(22) Information technology – Categorization of Software [BDS ISO/IEC TR 12182:2006].[360]
(23) Information technology – Software engineering – Guidelines for the adoption of Computer-Aided Software Engineering (CASE) tools [BDS ISO/IEC TR 14471:2007].[361]
(24) Specification for Computer Bangla Keyboard [BDS 1738:2018].[362]

---

353. This Standard contains requirements, recommendations and guidelines for the systematic measurement, assessment and evaluation of software product quality during acquisition of 'off-the-shelf' software products, custom software products, or modifications to existing software products.
354. This Standard provides requirements and recommendations for the practical implementation of software product evaluation when several parties need to understand and trust evaluation results.
355. This Standard defines the structure and content of the documentation to be used to describe an Evaluation Module.
356. This Standard describes in greater detail management of the Maintenance process. It also establishes definitions for the various types of maintenance. This provides guidance that applies to planning, execution and control, review and evaluation, and closure of the maintenance process. The scope includes maintenance for multiple software products with the same maintenance resources.
357. This Standard specifies the requirements for establishing, implementing, maintaining and continually improving an information security management system within the context of the organization. It also includes requirements for the assessment and treatment of information security risks tailored to the needs of the organization.
358. This Standard establishes guidelines and general principles for initiating, implementing, maintaining, and improving information security management in an organization. The objectives provide general guidance on the commonly accepted goals of information security management.
359. This Standard offers guidance on the management of software documentation to those managers responsible to produce software or software-based products.
360. This Standard categorizes software that are produced by software engineering processes. It describes a categorization scheme for software that encompasses different points of view and significant characteristics and attributes that describe and define software and software categories.
361. Since CASE adoption is a subject of the broader technology transition problem, this Technical Report addresses the adoption practices appropriate for a wide range of computing organizations.
362. This Standard defines layouts for input of Bengali characters, signs, symbols and currency marks using industry standard keyboard hardware and be useable in all known Unicode compliant operating system.

(25) Bangla Coded Character Set for Information Interchange [BDS 1520:2018].[363]
(26) Bangla Keypad for Mobile Phone [BDS 1834:2011].[364]
(27) Bangladesh Standard Code for Information Interchange [BDS 1935:2018].

383. The Digital Security Agency recently established under section 5 of the Digital Security Act, 2018 (Act No. 46 of 2018) is responsible to set the standards of goods and services used in computer hardware, software and human resources involved in ensuring digital security in the critical information structure.[365] Besides, it is also stipulated that the digital forensic lab established under the provisions of the Act of 2018 will follow some standards such as ISO/IEC/BDS 17025, ISO/IEC/BDS 15489, ISO/IEC/BDS 27037, ISO/IEC/BDS 27041, ISO/IEC/BDS 27042, ISO/IEC/BDS 27043 and ISO/IEC/BDS 27050.

384. In July 2018, the government established the Software Quality Testing and Certification Centre at BCC, Agargaon, Dhaka with the aims to verify and validate the software system in government offices, to create awareness and elevate the software testing industry in the country, to build the capacity of resources to support desired growth in the software testing arena. Initially, the Centre will test software, mobile phone apps and computer hardware made or bought by the government and later on, these services will be made available for the private sectors.

§5. Standards on Telecommunication

385. BTRC is responsible to specify the national standards and technical aspects of telecommunication apparatus used in telecommunication systems to provide telecommunication services. Chapter VII of the Bangladesh Telecommunication Regulation Act, 2001 (Act No. 18 of 2001) contains detailed provisions in this regard. The Law provides that BTRC, with the aim to ensure a safe, modern and efficient telecommunication service and interconnection, may determine different standards for different classes of apparatus and criteria and methods for verifying their compliance.[366] These standards of telecommunication are binding on the service operators and providers.[367] However, before doing so, BTRC shall publish a notice in the Official Gazette and two national dailies mentioning its intention in this regard specifying such standard, criteria and method and, invite comment or suggestion and the intended date of effectiveness of these. Once finalized, upon consideration of the comment or suggestion, if any, shall finalize these and publish them in the

363. This Standard specifies Bangla version of character code which are included in the Unicode version 6.0.0 and specification of the codes and with their coded representations.
364. This Standard defines layouts for input of Bangla characters, signs, symbols and currency marks using industry standard 3 X 4 Mobile Keypad. This standard specifies Bangla Characters intended for the definition and implementation of standards for localization of ICT.
365. Rule 3(c), the Digital Security Rules, 2020.
366. Section 51(1) & 51(3), the Bangladesh Telecommunication Regulation Act, 2001 (Act No. 18 of 2001).
367. Section 54, the Bangladesh Telecommunication Regulation Act, 2001 (Act No. 18 of 2001).

same manner. BTRC may also determine the standards of radio method and interference causing apparatus and technical conditions applicable thereto.[368] Besides, BTRC shall from time to time publish a directory containing the details and specifications of such technical standards which the manufacturers, importers and marketing agents of telecommunication apparatus need to follow.[369] However, these standards shall not have any retrospective effect.[370]

§6. Standards on e-Government Activities

386. It has been discussed earlier that the government has already established NEA, the coordinated framework of national e-services, to assist interoperability and operation of e-government activities. As all the agencies of the government will be following the same standards, the government has also released some standards relating to application architecture, business architecture, data architecture, e-GIF, mobile service delivery platform, security, technology architecture and hardware specification, etc.[371]

368. Section 51(2), the Bangladesh Telecommunication Regulation Act, 2001 (Act No. 18 of 2001).
369. Section 52, the Bangladesh Telecommunication Regulation Act, 2001 (Act No. 18 of 2001).
370. Section 51(4), the Bangladesh Telecommunication Regulation Act, 2001 (Act No. 18 of 2001).
371. *See*, for details, Standards, Bangladesh National Digital Architecture, https://bnda.gov.bd/Standards.

Chapter 5. Legal Status of Out-of-Court Dispute Settlement in the ICT Sector

§1. Introduction

387. Disputes in the ICT and telecommunication sector may arise between different parties, i.e., disputes between ICT and telecommunication players, between ICT and telecommunication players with the consumers, and between the ICT and telecommunication players with the regulators or government bodies. For these various types of disputes, the parties involved need to follow different legal procedures, usually stipulated in the relevant statutes, before the matters reach the court of law. However, this is not very common so far that these players or parties involved in these sectors bring their disputes in the court of law. As a result, one may find only a very few case(s) reported in the popular law reports on these matters.

388. Usually, disputes of civil nature in the ICT sector will have to follow the same route as other suits of civil nature where the civil courts will have the jurisdiction to try these suits unless their cognizance is either expressly or impliedly barred.[372] Thus, unless the dispute is settled outside the court, the parties involved in the dispute will have to follow the lengthy procedure of civil courts. The courts of laws in Bangladesh are overburdened with a huge amount of pending cases[373] and settlement of the cases the courts take a huge amount of time.[374] Besides, the World Bank's recent 'Doing Business Report, 2019' revealed that contract enforcement takes 1,442 days, i.e., almost four years and costs 66.8% of the value of the claim. As a result, the government has been encouraging the parties to settle their disputes outside the court by way of conciliation or negotiation, mediation and arbitration, which are otherwise collectively known as ADR methods. This Chapter will first share the general legal provisions on ADR methods under the domestic laws and then shall discuss the important provisions of the Arbitration Act, 2001 (Act No. 1 of 2001), which deals with various aspects of commercial arbitrations.

---

372. Civil Courts, as established under s. 3 of Civil Courts Act, 1887 (Act No. XII of 1887), would not have jurisdiction to entertain suits under special law. Where a right is created by a special law and a method of enforcing the right is pointed out by the law creating such right, the general remedy by way of suit under the Code of Civil Procedure, 1908 will be impliedly barred. In such a case the method provided by the special law must be followed. *See Jalaluddin Ahmed v. Matiur Rahinan and others*, 9 BLD (HCD) 446.

373. The Law Minister informed in the Parliament that as of 29 Oct. 2018, a total of 3,453,353 cases were pending in the higher and lower courts of the country. Of these pending cases, 495,415 cases (civil-88,718, criminal-312,205 and other-88,718) were pending in the HCD and 19,493 cases were pending in the AD. This number is ever increasing.

374. According to Bangladesh International Arbitration Centre (BIAC), a case may be solved in 388 days by using ADR, whereas it takes 15.3 years to resolve the case in civil courts. *See* BIAC Quarterly Bulletin, October–December 2018.

§2. Alternative Dispute Settlement under Domestic Law

389. People of this part of the world has been settling disputes outside the court in civil and in ordinary criminal matters for time immemorial. Settlement of disputes by the family or local elders in the name of *Salish* (arbitration) through the Panchayat system has been in practice for years.[375] Arbitration in its institutional form started only in 1772 during the time of the East India Company when the West Bengal Regulation was enacted. Subsequently, the dispute settlement by way of arbitration was also included in the Bengal Regulation of 1780, 1781 and Cornwallis Regulation, 1787. The Legislative Council for India, which was established in 1834 included the provision of arbitration in the Civil Procedure Code, 1859 and Civil Procedure Code, 1882. Following the English Arbitration Act, 1889, the Indian Arbitration Act was also enacted in 1899. Subsequently, the Arbitration (Protocol and Convention) Act, 1937 and the Indian Arbitration Act, 1940 were enacted.[376] Both these laws were in force in Bangladesh until they were repealed by the Arbitration Act, 2001 (Act No. 1 of 2001). This Act of 2001 deals with the provisions relating to international commercial arbitration, recognition and enforcement of the foreign arbitral award and other arbitrations.

390. Apart from the Act of 2001, various domestic laws contain provisions on the settlement of disputes outside the court in the form of ADR as there are several benefits of ADR methods. These methods are faster, informal, relatively cheaper, and parties to the dispute can enjoy a win-win situation, which is somehow impossible if the same dispute is settled in the formal courts of law. As a result, ADR methods are encouraged through the provisions of various statutes in Bangladesh.

391. The Code of Civil Procedure, 1908 (Act No. V of 1908), the main law relating to the procedure of civil suits, was amended and new provisions were included in section 89A, 89B, 89C, 89D, and 89E to introduce provisions of mandatory mediation or arbitration. ADR or more precisely arbitration-related provisions can be found in Chapter 10 (section 40) of the Bangladesh Energy Regulatory Commission Act, 2003 (Act No. 13 of 2003), section 36 of the Real Estate Development and Management Act, 2010 (Act No. 48 of 2010), Chapter four (sections 29–38) of the Acquisition and Requisition of Immovable Property Act, 2017 (Act No. 21 of 2017). The Companies Act, 1994 (Act No. 18 of 1994) has, in several places, included provisions on arbitration in different stages of the company affairs.[377] Moreover, the government has also framed the *Aingoto Sohayata Prodan (Aini Poramorsho o Bikalpo Birodh Nishpotti) Bidhimala*, 2015 (the Legal Aid (Legal Advice and ADR) Rules) under section 22A of the Legal Aid Act, 2000 (Act No. 6

375. A brief history of arbitration in this part of the world is briefly shared by Mr. Justice Muhammad Khurshid Alam Sarkar in the case of *Corona Fashion Ltd. v. Milestone Clothing Resources*, 2019(1) LNJ [Arbitration Application No. 05 of 2018]; *Southern Solar Power Ltd and another v. Bangladesh Power Development Board and others and ors.*, 2019(2) LNJ [Arbitration Application No. 13 of 2018].

376. Bansal, A.K., *Arbitration & ADR*, Second Edition 11 (2009).

377. *See* s. 227 (Power of companies to refer matters to arbitration), s. 294 (Power of liquidator to accept shares, etc. as consideration for sale of property of company).

of 2000) containing detail provisions on dispute settlement outside the court by the legal aid officer appointed under section 21A of the Legal Aid Act, 2000 (Act No. 6 of 2000).

392. Besides, it may be relevant to share here that in family matters, especially in relation to the dissolution of marriage, the parties must try to reconcile the matter under the Family Courts Ordinance, 1985 (Ordinance No. XVIII of 1985) before the dissolution is declared final.[378] Furthermore, ADR related provisions can be found in the Village Court Act, 2006 (Act No. 19 of 2006), the Contract Act, 1872 (Act No. IX of 1872), and the Survey Act, 1875 (Act No. V of 1875).

393. Section 210 of the Bangladesh Labour Act, 2006 (Act No. 42 of 2006) contains detailed provisions regarding the use of ADR techniques to settle industrial disputes between workers, employers and between workers and employers. Sections 124–130 of the Export Processing Zone *Sramik Shongha abong Shilpa Shamparka Ain*, 2019 (Act No. 2 of 2019) (the Export Processing Zone Trade Welfare Society and Labour Industrial Relation Act) also contains provisions on the application of ADR regarding industrial disputes.

394. ADR related provisions are also included in various fiscal laws such as the Customs Act, 1969 (Act No. IV of 1969),[379] the Income Tax Ordinance, 1984 (Ordinance No. XXXVI of 1984),[380] the VAT Act, 1991 (Act No. XXII of 1991),[381] Value Added Tax and Supplementary Duty Act, 2012 (Act No. 47 of 2012)[382] and the Artha Rin Adalat Ain, 2003 (Act No. 8 of 2003).[383] Under section 125 of the VAT Act, 1991 (Act No. XXII of 1991), even during the pendency of any suit, any party can apply for ADR with the permission of the AD or HCD of Bangladesh Supreme Court. Regarding income tax, the government has also formulated the Income Tax ADR (Procedure) Rules, 2012. ICT entrepreneurs can consider these provisions in relation to their fiscal matters.

395. From the discussion above it is apparent that the disputes are encouraged to be settled outside the court of law in various matters such as fiscal, family, labour, and civil, etc. through the provisions of these sectorial laws. However, the provisions of the Arbitration Act, 2001 (Act No. 1 of 2001) which was enacted to assist the parties to a commercial agreement to settle their disputes amicably without the intervention of the court will be relevant for the discussions in this monograph. The salient features of this Act, 2011, are discussed below.

---

378. Sections 10(3), 10(4) and 13, the Family Courts Ordinance, 1985 (Ordinance No. XVIII of 1985).
379. Section 192A–192K, the Customs Act, 1969 (Act No. IV of 1969).
380. Section 152F, the Income Tax Ordinance, 1984 (Ordinance No. XXXVI of 1984).
381. Section 41A, the VAT Act, 1991 (Act No. XXII of 1991).
382. Section 125, the Value Added Tax and Supplementary Duty Act, 2012 (Act No. 47 of 2012).
383. Chapter V (ss 22–25), the Artha Rin Adalat Ain, 2003 (Act No. 8 of 2003).

§3. The Arbitration Act, 2001 (Act No. 1 of 2001)

396. The Arbitration Act, 2001 (Act No. 1 of 2001) was enacted by repealing the previous laws in this field, i.e., the Arbitration (Protocol and Convention) Act, 1937 and the Arbitration Act, 1940 to make provisions relating to international commercial arbitration, recognition and enforcement of the foreign arbitral award and other arbitrations.[384] There were some obvious shortcomings of the Arbitration Act, 1940 as the latest developments and complexities of the present time could not be anticipated. One of the main limitations of that law was the extensive supervisory role of the national courts which used to frustrate the real purpose of out of the court settlements. Before the drafting and enactment of the law, the opinion of the Law Commission of Bangladesh was taken.[385] With the opinion of the Law Commission, the Law was drafted following the provisions of the United Nations Commission on International Trade Law (UNCITRAL) Model Law on International Commercial Arbitration (1985), with some improvements. The law of 2001, along with including the main provisions of the New York Convention on the Recognition and Enforcement of Foreign Arbitral Awards, 1958, has included the fundamental tenets of modern international arbitration regime such as '(i) party autonomy; (ii) minimal judicial intervention in arbitration; (iii) independence of the arbitral tribunal; (iv) fair, expeditious and economical resolution of disputes, and (v) effective enforcement of arbitral awards'.[386] It is believed that the drafters of the law were also influenced by the English Arbitration Act, 1996 and the Indian Arbitration and Conciliation Act, 1996.[387] It is a special law, and it has been enacted for the sole purpose of resolving commercial international disputes between the parties through arbitration.[388]

397. The law defines 'International Commercial Arbitration' as an Arbitration relating to disputes arising out of legal relationships, whether contractual or not, considered as commercial under the law in force in Bangladesh and where at least one of the parties is:

---

384. In the Indo-Pak subcontinent, the first specific law on arbitration was enacted in 1899. The drafting history of the enactment of the Arbitration (Protocol and Convention) Act, 1937 and international commercial arbitration in the Bangladesh context has eloquently been depicted by Justice Mustafa Kamal in the judgment of *Bangladesh Air Service (Pvt.) Ltd. v. British Airways Plc* (1997) 49 DLR (AD) 187.
385. The Law Commission, Government of the People's Republic of Bangladesh, Report on Proposal for enacting a Comprehensive Arbitration Act by repealing the Arbitration (Protocol and Convention) Act, 1937, the Arbitration Act, 1940, Report No. 19, date of submission 13 Apr. 1999. Unfortunately, on the website of the Law Commission, the Report is not available rather the Draft Bill of the Law can be found.
386. For a comprehensive analysis of the Arbitration Act, 2001 (Act No. 1 of 2001), *See*, A.F.M. Maniruzzaman, *The New Law of International Commercial Arbitration in Bangladesh: A Comparative Perspective*, 14 Am. Rev. Int'l Arb., 139–174 (2003).
387. Khaled Hamid Chowdhury, *Introduction to International Commercial Arbitration and Investment-Treaty Arbitration in Bangladesh*, in Encyclopedia of Public International Law in Asia, vol. 3 (Central and South Asia), 81–83 (2021).
388. *Md. Nurul Abser v. Alhaj Golam Rabbani & ors.*, 6 SCOB [2016] AD 54, at p. 60.

(i) an individual who is a national of or habitually resident in, any country other than Bangladesh; or
(ii) a body corporate which is incorporated in any country other than Bangladesh; or
(iii) a company or an association or a body of individuals whose central management and control is exercised in any country other than Bangladesh, or
(iv) the Government of a foreign country.[389]

398. An arbitration agreement is an agreement between the parties to submit all or certain disputes which have arisen, or which may arise between them in respect of a defined legal relationship, whether contractual or not.[390] Thus, such an agreement does not need to be executed before the dispute arises; it can be executed even after the dispute arises. Such an agreement may be in the form of an arbitration clause in an existing contract or in the form of a separate written agreement.

399. Section 89B of the Code of Civil Procedure, 1908 (Act No. V of 1898) provides that the parties to a civil suit with the aim to refer any dispute or disputes in the suit to arbitration for settlement, can at any stage of the proceeding, apply to the Court for withdrawal of the suit. The Court shall allow such application and permit the suit to be withdrawn and such a dispute shall be settled in accordance with the provisions of the Arbitration Act, 2001 (Act No. 1 of 2001). Such an application of the parties shall be deemed to be an arbitration agreement under section 9 of the Arbitration Act, 2001 (Act No. 1 of 2001).

400. An arbitration agreement shall be deemed to be in writing if it is contained in a document signed by the parties. It will also be so deemed if a record of the agreement can be found in the exchange of letters, telex, telegrams, fax, email or other means of telecommunication; or in an exchange of statement where one party claims the existence of such agreement the other party does not deny.[391] Therefore, it is evident that even though an agreement relating to any other lawful issues can be reached orally by the parties, an agreement on commercial arbitration cannot be made orally rather it must be written irrespective of the form.[392]

401. It may be relevant to share here that whether an arbitration clause/ agreement is incorporated into another underlying contract is a contentious issue in many jurisdictions. For example, A (an Employer) enters into Contract 'X' with B (Main Contractor). B then enters into another Contract 'Y' with C (Sub-Contractor). Contract Y does not have an arbitration clause but has a clause which provides that 'the terms of the Contract X applies' and Contract X has an arbitration clause. In such instances, the dispute may arise as to the validity of the previous

389. Section 2(c), the Arbitration Act, 2001 (Act No. 1 of 2001).
390. Section 2(n), the Arbitration Act, 2001 (Act No. 1 of 2001). It may be relevant to share that even though under s. 28 of the Contract Act, 1872 (Act No. IX of 1872), an agreement in restraint of legal proceedings is void, such an agreement in relation to arbitration is not.
391. Section 9, the Arbitration Act, 2001 (Act No. 1 of 2001).
392. *Globo Piu, Import and Export ltd v. Bangladesh Chemical Industries Corporation (Civil)*, 71 DLR 513.

contract in the context of the subsequent contract; for example, in this example, this may be an issue whether C is bound to follow the contractual provisions of the Contract X entered into between A and B. Generally speaking, incorporation by reference is accepted and parties do not need to sign such arbitration clause/agreement.

402. Chapter 4 of the Law (sections 11–16) deals with the establishment of the arbitration tribunal, while Chapter 5 (sections 17–22) deals with the jurisdictions of arbitration tribunal and Chapter 6 (sections 23–35) contains provisions on the arbitration procedure. The parties, under section 11 of the Act, have the liberty to select the number of arbitrators. If such a number is not selected, then three arbitrators will form the tribunal and if the parties agree to select two arbitrators, then they will collectively appoint another arbitrator who will be the Chairman of the tribunal. An arbitral tribunal may rule on its own jurisdiction on any questions regarding the existence of a valid arbitration agreement, the proper constitution of the tribunal, the severity of the arbitration agreement, whether the arbitration agreement is against the public policy, and if proper procedure is followed in accordance with the arbitration agreement.[393] The parties are free to select the place of arbitration. If they fail to select such a place, the arbitration tribunal shall determine the place after considering the circumstances of the case and the convenience of the parties.[394]

403. Jurisprudentially, there is a legal distinction between the 'place' of arbitration and the 'seat' or 'forum' of arbitration. While 'place' would refer to the geographical location (e.g., the hearing to be held at Meeting Room 1 at Sonargaon Hotel, Dhaka, Bangladesh), the concept 'seat' or 'forum' is used to mean the place where the procedural laws/rules would take place, i.e., if the arbitration is 'seated' in Bangladesh, then the 'seat' would be the law of Bangladesh in respect of the procedures of the arbitration. Similarly, the parties are free to decide the seat of arbitration in another country, e.g., in Kuala Lumpur, Malaysia. Nevertheless, the parties can still agree to have the terms of the contract to be determined according to Bangladeshi law. So, if any terms of contract are breached by a party, although the whole arbitration can physically take place in Kuala Lumpur, the Bangladeshi court can determine the legality of the terms of contract according to the provisions of Bangladeshi law.

404. During the existence of an arbitration agreement, no judicial authority shall hear any legal proceedings even though such proceedings are filed except in some instances permitted by the law.[395] However, the HCD, even in such cases, can make interim orders regarding some matters.[396] It was held that the purpose of any section 7Ka application is for the protection and preservation of the subject matter of arbitral proceedings with a view to ensuring that any future award may remain effectively executable.[397]

393. Section 17, the Arbitration Act, 2001 (Act No. 1 of 2001).
394. Section 26, the Arbitration Act, 2001 (Act No. 1 of 2001).
395. Section 7, the Arbitration Act, 2001 (Act No. 1 of 2001).
396. Section 7A, the Arbitration Act, 2001 (Act No. 1 of 2001).
397. *KA Latif v. Olam International Ltd (Statutory)* 13 BLC 457.

405. When there exists an arbitration agreement between the parties and one party initiates a legal proceeding before the court of law, then the other party before submission of written statement[398] can inform the court regarding the existence of such agreement. In such a case, if the court is satisfied in this regard, it will refer the parties to the arbitration and stay the proceedings unless the Court finds that the arbitration agreement is void, inoperative or is incapable of determination by arbitration.[399] Besides, arbitral proceedings can be commenced by the actions of the parties, i.e., one party may send a notice to the other party to refer the dispute to the other party.[400] In such instances, the Court would, in principle, play a supervisory role over the arbitration. Once the arbitration proceeding is initiated between the parties before the initiation of a suit, the dispute in the arbitration proceeding should be settled first.[401] This provision shall equally apply to international commercial arbitration, whether held in Bangladesh or in any other country.[402]

406. The arbitral award is generally not open to review by the Courts for any error in finding facts and applying the law for the simple reason that it would defeat the very purpose of the arbitration proceedings.[403] Once an award is given by the Arbitrator(s), it is not allowed to challenge the award in a civil suit, as, if it is allowed then the arbitration proceeding shall become a mockery and the whole purpose of the arbitration scheme as envisaged in the Act, 2001 shall fail.[404]

407. A combined reading of the provisions of sections 42, 43 and 39 of the Act, 2001 will reveal that the only remedy open to a person who wants to set aside an arbitral award is to file an application under section 42 of the Act, 2001 within sixty days from the date of receipt of the award. After the expiry of the period of sixty days as envisaged in the section, the award becomes enforceable within the meaning of section 44 of the Act, 2001 and thus, the jurisdiction of the civil Court has impliedly been barred.[405]

408. The Supreme Court of Bangladesh has considered various aspects of commercial arbitration and interpreted different provisions of the Arbitration Act, 2001

398. A written statement can be treated as the reply of the defendant against the claims made by the plaintiff through plaint in a civil suit. A written statement is the averments of the defendant in answer to the plaint either in denial of the plaint case or admitting the plaint in part or whole and constitutes his defence in the suit. what should be the contents of a written statement, and how, where and when it should be filed, etc., have been in detail provided in Order 8 of the Code. *See Narayan Chandra Saha and another v. Jatindra Chandra Saha and others*, 52 DLR (HCD) (2000) 5.

The statement in the plaint or in the written statement is not evidence in the eye of law unless it is proved by a witness. *See Sreejukta Haladhar Karmakar and ors v. Bangladesh and ors.*, 16 BLD (HCD) 519.

399. Section 10, the Arbitration Act, 2001 (Act No. 1 of 2001).
400. Section 27, the Arbitration Act, 2001 (Act No. 1 of 2001).
401. *Mosharaf Composite Textile Mills Ltd & ors v. ECOM Agro. Corp. Ltd & ors.*, 4 SCOB [2015] AD 28.
402. *HRC Shipping Ltd. v. MV X-Press Manaslu and others,* 12 MLR (2007) (HC) 265.
403. *TATA Power Company Ltd v. M/S Dynamic Construction*, 2 SCOB [2015] AD 15.
404. *Md. Nurul Abser v. Alhaj Golam Rabbani & ors.*, 6 SCOB [2016] AD 54, at p. 60.
405. *Ibid.*

(Act No. 1 of 2001). It was held that a party cannot rely on a term of the contract to repudiate it and still say that the arbitration clause should not apply. Where the plaintiff sues to recover the price under the contract, as a valid and binding contract, he cannot repudiate the terms of the contract relating to arbitration, while seeking to rely on the contract in support of his claim.[406]

409. It is pertinent to share here that if the parties to a contract include an arbitration clause stating that the arbitration shall be conducted in accordance with the Arbitration Act, 2001 (Act No. 1 of 2001) of Bangladesh, as, at present in force and the place of arbitration shall be in Dhaka, Bangladesh, then section 7 of the Arbitration Act, 2001 restricts judicial intervention in matters covered by the arbitration agreement and no petition will be entertained to interpret the contract in the writ petitions since the petitioner has a remedy to go for arbitration under the contract signed by the petitioner. This is because the petitioner would have signed a contract with open eyes after reading the terms and conditions, and therefore, it is unconscionable to raise these kinds of contention in the writ petitions.[407] The writ petition is not maintainable on two counts: first, due to the reason that the dispute arose out of simple commercial contract and not out of statutory contract, and second, there is no scope to avail writ jurisdiction as there is an equally efficacious alternative forum to settle the dispute through amicable settlement.[408]

410. It may be relevant to share here that in 2018, the government took initiatives to amend the Arbitration Act, 2001 and the Law Commission of Bangladesh proposed at least fifty-three new amendments in the law aiming to ensure transparency and neutrality in the disposal of cases. The draft contains provisions on: the fee of the arbitrator and time limit to dispose of the matters, explicit and precise jurisdictions of arbitrators and court, and the clear definition of arbitrator and court.[409] Moreover, one of the clearer advantages of arbitration is that the selected arbitrators believe to have better knowledge or technical know-how than the general courts. Thus, for example, if the disputes involve ICT or telecommunication issues, then it can be anticipated that if the lawyer/academic/specialist of these areas is selected as arbitrators, then the parties will have further confidence about better qualitative hearing.

§4. Disputes Between the ICT and Telecommunication Players

411. In case of any dispute between the industry players, one may consider any of the two avenues available to settle the dispute without bringing the matter to the court of law. The players can seek remedy from the regulator, most importantly BTRC, and the regulator can settle the disputes between the industry players on

---

406. *ECOM Agroindustrial Corporation Ltd. & another v. Mosharaf Composite Textile Mills Ltd*, 2014, 43 CLC (HCD) [9656] = 67 DLR (HCD) (2010) 330.
407. *Energy Prima Ltd. v. Bangladesh & ors.*, 8 SCOB [2016] HCD 84.
408. *Mark Construction Ltd v. Chief Engineer, REB & ors.*, 3 SCOB [2015] HCD 37.
409. Muhammad Yeasin, Plan to amend arbitration act, the Independent, 17 Jul. 2018, http://www.theindependentbd.com/post/158199.

various issues, e.g., infrastructure sharing,[410] within the scope of their authority as derived from the existing law. BTRC is also empowered to issue guidelines on matters of interconnection among the operators and to determine, in appropriate cases, the conditions applicable thereto, and to resolve disputes among them.[411] The BTRC can also settle disputes regarding the right to way.[412] The Legal and Licensing Division of the BTRC performs the responsibility to resolve disputes between the parties.

412. If an operator, licensee or a subscriber lodges a well-founded complaint to BTRC about another operator, the Commission may, within seven days of receipt of such complaints, direct the concerned party to redress/resolve the grievance/matter and ask the concerned operators to resolve the dispute amicably.[413] An operator or licensee must abide by the decision of the Commission regarding any dispute.

413. The Interconnection Regulations, 2004 contains provisions on Interconnection disputes between two operators or between an operator and an access provider. Disputes can be related to terms and conditions of the interconnection agreement, especially to the capacity of circuits, provision of services/facilities, QoSs, standards, traffic recording/monitoring, hindrance to traffic flow, anti-competitive & discriminatory practices, charging and pricing of interconnection services/facilities, non-compliance of the terms & conditions of agreement, commercial & legal issues and provisions contrary to the Act, Regulations, Guidelines, orders & directives, issued from time to time by the Commission.[414]

414. Apart from seeking assistance from the regulators to settle the disputes, an industry player can also consider bringing the disputed matter in the forums or association of the industry players such as BASIS, AMTOB, ISPAB, and Federation of Bangladesh Chambers of Commerce and Industries (FBCCI), etc. These bodies have dedicated wings to deal with the disputes between the members.

§5. Disputes Between the Market Players with Consumers

415. The national telecommunication regulator has been playing an important role in relation to disputes settlement between the telecommunication players and consumers, i.e., anyone who takes telecommunication services from an operator.[415] BTRC, by virtue of different provisions of the Bangladesh Telecommunication

410. Guideline No. 4 of General Terms and Conditions for Infrastructure Sharing and Guideline No. 5.8, the Guidelines for Infrastructure Sharing, 2008, Bangladesh Telecommunication Regulatory Authority.
411. Section 31(2)(h), the Bangladesh Telecommunication Regulation Act, 2001 (Act No. 18 of 2001).
412. Sections 42, 44(2) and 44(3), the Bangladesh Telecommunication Regulation Act, 2001 (Act No. 18 of 2001).
413. Section 31(2)(f) and 31(2)(r), the Bangladesh Telecommunication Regulation Act, 2001 (Act No. 18 of 2001).
414. Regulation No. 10, the Interconnection Regulations, 2004.
415. Section 2, the Bangladesh Telecommunication Regulation Act, 2001 (Act No. 18 of 2001).

Regulation Act, 2001, has the statutory authority to consider the issue of consumer protection very seriously. In May 2016, the BTRC established a call centre for the telecom subscribers to register any complaint relating to telecom services. Now, using the short code '100', any person aggrieved can contact the Commission for that purpose. Between 1 July 2019 to 30 June 2020, BTRC received 555,653 complaints made through the short code '100' and resolved 545,454, i.e., 98.16% of these complaints.[416]

416. The Consumers' Right Protection Act, 2009 (Act No. 26 of 2009) provides for an alternative avenue to settle disputes regarding goods, such as ICT goods and services, such as telecommunication services. Under the provisions of this law, any person aggrieved can make a complaint to the National Consumers' Right Protection Directorate regarding any anti-consumer right practice under the Act. If such complaint is proved to be true after investigation or inquiry, the Director-General or any officer empowered by him may, in his administrative action, impose a fine upon the convicted person and 25% of such realized fine shall immediately be paid to the complainant.[417] However, though the Consumers' Right Protection Directorate is relatively active in market monitoring, it is not very common that they inspect services provided by telecommunication service providers.

417. Moreover, it has been reported that BTRC has been working to develop Guidelines on 'Do Not Disturb' and 'National Telecommunication Consumer Protection Guidelines',[418] and it can be anticipated that such guidelines, if finalized, will pave the way to settle disputes outside the courts as there are reasons to believe that these Guidelines will create an alternative forum to dispute settlement.

§6. Disputes Between the ICT and Telecommunication Players with the Regulators

418. It is not uncommon that the market players sometimes find the decision of the regulators unacceptable. In such instances, they can consider settling the issue outside the court and the government has introduced a forum, i.e., Grievance Redress System, in this regard. Using the System, any aggrieved person or organization, including ICT and telecommunication player, can submit a complaint against any government office, including the regulators and seek remedies. Though it is not possible to draw a clear picture of how the whole system works in this regard, the government has already formulated the Grievance Redress System Guidelines, 2015 and introduced an online platform in this regard,[419] using which one can report a complaint or opinion regarding services of various government agencies.

416. BTRC, Annual Report, 2019–2020 [Bangla], p. 39.

417. Section 76, the Consumers' Right Protection Act, 2009 (Act No. 26 of 2009).

418. WSIS+10: Overall Review of the Implementation of the WSIS Outcomes, WSIS 10 Year Country Report by the People's Republic of Bangladesh, May 2014, https://www.itu.int/net/wsis/review/inc/docs/rcreports/WSIS10_Country_Reporting-BGD.pdf.

419. Grievance Redress System, http://grs.gov.bd/.

419. Finally, there can be disputes between the telegraph authority and local authority in consequence of the local authority refusing permission regarding maintenance of telegraph lines and posts, *inter alia*, in any property under the control and management of local authorities. In such cases, the disputes shall be determined by the government-appointed officer.[420]

§7. Recent Developments

420. Usually, when the commercial disputes in Bangladesh are determined in the court of law, it is a time-consuming process and demands a huge amount of money. Therefore, the policymakers have been working to provide for an effective alternative forum so that the parties to a dispute can settle the dispute amicably within a short period of time. Already a few laws have been enacted or adapted to this end, yet, it seems that the existing laws are not sufficient, and therefore, Bangladesh Law Commission has recently drafted the Bill of a law titled 'the Commercial Dispute Resolution Act'.

421. In the Bill, 'commercial dispute' is defined as all disputes arising out of business, financial, banking and commercial transactions, import and export trade and service, matters arising out of the Admiralty Act and maritime law, purchase of aeroplane and parts, lease financing, transportation, building construction agreement and tender, contract relating to immovable property exclusively used for trade and business, distribution and licensing, management and consultation related agreement, joint-stock agreement, share ownership agreement, investment treaty on outsourcing industry and financial services, commercial agency and commercial custom, partnership agreement, technology improvement agreement, IPRs, trademark, copyright, patent, design, domain name, geographical indications and semiconductor integrated circuits, agreement relating to sale of goods and services, exploration of oil and gas and other natural resources, insurance and re-insurance, agreement relating to agency, disputes decided by the government, dumping and anti-dumping. It is evident that this definition has not specifically mentioned about the disputes of ICT and telecommunication sectors even though it has widely included various general activities that may arise in these sectors too, and therefore, the stakeholders will have another alternative forum once the law is passed based on the Bill.

422. This draft Bill proposed for the establishment of a separate tribunal and appellate tribunal to settle the matters airing out of commercial disputes. It is further provided that all disputes must be settled within 120 days. The settlement of such disputes within these proposed 120 days seems to be very optimistic as some commercial disputes are highly technical involving a huge amount of money. The Bill further provides that the party that will get the judgment against them will have

420. Sections 12, 13, 15 and 16, the Telegraph Act, 1885 (Act No. XIII of 1885).

to bear all the expenses. The only issue of concern here is that under the draft, one can move to the proposed court if and when the value of the suit is more than BDT 50 million. Thus, it may only entertain the large companies preventing the ordinary consumers to apply for remedies.

Part II. Protection of Intellectual Property in the ICT Sector

423. Bangladesh, or this part of the world, looking at the list of member countries of OECD which is a forum of industrialized nations, is not historically projected in the literature as a country that promotes the technological innovation culture even though this part of the world has produced some of the finest and world-renowned individual scientists. The country's over-reliance on agriculture due to her geographical location and the availability of cheap labour in one of the most densely populated countries in the world coupled with the socio-economic condition in the war-ravaged time after her Independence have significant contributions in this regard. As a result, the country has been importing mostly technological solutions from outside. Nevertheless, the policymakers have started to realize the importance of innovation and have been taking initiatives to popularize a knowledge-based economy in recent decades thanks to the telecommunication and the ICT sectors. Being a developing country, Bangladesh has been facing similar kinds of problems as other developing countries in terms of protection of IPRs due to the lack of awareness to protect IPRs, inadequate legal frameworks, even the non-implementation or improper implementation of IPRs related laws.

424. Protection of IPRs or the use of genuine products is not widely practised in various sectors, including ICT and telecommunication. In relation to ICT products, existing literature suggests that the use of pirated software is rampant, and users hardly know about licensed software. One research found that only 5% of the study venues used licensed software.[421] Since this has serious diversified consequences, the regulators and responsible government bodies are seen to have taken some sudden drives, the news of which is reported in media.[422] These drives can be considered as a tip of an iceberg and thus, really have any meaningful impacts on the improvement of the situation. As a result, it is not spurring that Bangladesh was

421. The study designed to assess the public's A2I and communication venues, as well as to examine the role of ICTs across the overall economic, political, and regulatory framework of the country. Raihan, A., *Public Access ICT in Bangladesh*, in Gomez, R. (ed.), *Libraries, Telecentres, Cybercafes and Public Access to ICT: International Comparisons: International Comparisons*, 249–266 (2011).

422. From example, the IPR Task Force and Copyright officials initiated a drive and recovered sixty-nine laptops installed with pirated software of Microsoft from a very reputed supplier, Flora Telecom. *See*, Ishtiaq Husain, Bangladesh Launches Drive Against Pirated Software of Microsoft, 12 Sep. 2015, Dhaka Tribune, https://www.dhakatribune.com/uncategorized/2015/09/12/bangladesh-launches-drive-against-pirated-software-of-microsoft.

listed at the bottom of the table and ranked 126 out of 128 countries in the International Property Rights Index, 2016, ranked 122 out of 125 countries in the report of 2018, ranked 125 out of 129 countries in the report of 2019, ranked 126 out of 129 countries in the report of 2020 of the same Index.[423]

425. Intellectual property, according to the WIPO, 'refers to creations of the mind – everything from works of art to inventions, computer programs to trademarks and other commercial signs'.[424] IPRs are classified into two main areas: copyright and related or neighbouring rights, and industrial properties. Copyright law deal with the rights of the authors of literary and artistic works including computer programs. On the other hand, issues such as trademarks, patents, etc. are discussed as industrial properties.

426. IPRs are again classified, based on their protection methods, as formal and informal. In formal IPRs, the rights of the owners are granted and protected by the particular legal system; whereas, in informal IPRs, the rights are protected though not through a legal procedure. Examples of formal IPRs are patents, copyrights, trademarks, industrial designs, sui generis database rights, topography of semiconductors, domain names, etc. On the other hand, examples of informal protection include trade secrets, lead time advantage, complexity of design and digital rights management, etc.[425] This chapter will shed light mainly on patents, trademarks and copyright matters in relation to ICT and telecommunication sectors.

427. It may be relevant to share here that the British rulers introduced the IPR system in this part of the world. The first law on IPR was passed in undivided India in 1856 titled the Protection of Inventions Act (Act No. VI of 1856) which was drafted based on the British Patents Law of 1852 and an innovator used to get the exclusive monopoly over his innovation for fourteen years. The law was amended in 1859 to encourage technology transfer into colonial India. Two more laws on patent & design protection and invention protection were enacted in 1872 and 1883 respectively in British India, and in 1888, these two laws were consolidated into one enactment with the title 'the Inventions & Designs Act, 1888'. Subsequently, based on the British Statute of Monopolies, Patents, Design and Trade Marks Act, 1883 and the Patents and Designs Act, 1907, the British rulers enacted the Patent and Designs Act, 1911.[426] This law of 1911 is sadly still in force in Bangladesh though the government has taken the initiative several times to revise and update the law.

---

423. The International Property Rights Index is published by Property Rights Alliance, an affiliate of American's for Tax Reform, stands as an advocacy organization dedicated to the protection of innovation, IPRs, and physical property around the world. *See*, for more, https://www.propertyrightsalliance.org/.

424. World Intellectual Property Organization, What is Intellectual Property?, https://www.wipo.int/publications/en/details.jsp?id=4528.

425. European Commission, Intellectual Property Rights and Competitiveness: Challenges for ICT-Producing SMEs, Study report No. 08/2008, version 4.0, 2008, p. 21.

426. Mohammad Sayeedur Rahman, *Consistency of Bangladesh Patent Law with TRIPS*, 30 Mgt. Dev., 74–86 (January–June 2016).

428. In 1847, a Literary Copyright Act was enacted in British India modelled on the British Literary Copyright Act of 1842.[427] The discussion to enact a copyright law was started in the mid-1870s and a Bill was drafted in 1885, even before the Berne Convention for the Protection of Literary and Artistic Works, 1886 was signed.[428] The first law on copyright in colonial India was enacted in 1914 based on the English Copyright Act of 1709. This law was subsequently adapted during the Pakistan period in 1962 and the Copyright Rules, 1967 were formulated. The Central Copyright Office during this time was established in Karachi, Pakistan and a regional office was established in Dhaka. This law was subsequently adapted in Bangladesh with some modifications and adjustments after independence. That Dhaka regional copyright office was upgraded to national office and initially placed under the Ministry of Education and subsequently under the Ministry of Cultural Affairs.[429] Finally, the Copyright Act, 2000 (Act No. XXVIII of 2000) was enacted and the law was substantially revised in 2005. Subsidiary legislation under this Act, i.e., the Copyright Rules were formulated in 2006.

429. The legal regime of trademark came much later than patents or copyright. There was no system of registration or statutory title for trademarks in British India until 1940 when these were incorporated into the Trade Marks Act, 1940 even though attempts were made to enact such laws in the 1870s and the Merchandise Marks Act was enacted in 1889.[430] The Trade Marks Act, 1940 was adapted in the then Pakistan and subsequently in Bangladesh. It was only in 2009 that the law of 1940 was revised, updated and replaced through the enactment of the Trade Marks Act, 2009 (Act No. 19 of 2009).

430. The implementation of intellectual property related laws is still a challenge and concern for the members of the law enforcement agencies. Many IP infringed goods and products are introduced through different borders. The Customs Authority could not take adequate actions because of the absence of provisions in the domestic law. Fortunately, very recently in November 2019, the NBR framed the Enforcement of Intellectual Property (Import and Export) Rules, 2019 prohibiting the import and export of any intellectual property protected goods and products without the permission or authorization of the right holder. These Rules empower the Customs authority to take actions regarding the export or import of any IPRs under the existing patents, copyright, trademarks and geographical indications law of Bangladesh.

---

427. Lionel Bently, *The 'Extraordinary Multiplicity' of Intellectual Property Laws in the British Colonies in the Nineteenth Century*, 12(1) Theoretical Inquiries L., 161–200 (2011).
428. Lionel Bently, *Copyright, Translations, and Relations Between Britain and India in the Nineteenth and Early Twentieth Centuries*, 82 Chi.-Kent L. Rev. 1181 (2007).
429. Banglapedia, Copyright, http://bn.banglapedia.org/index.php/%E0%A6%95%E0%A6%AA%E0%A6%BF%E0%A6%B0%E0%A6%BE%E0%A6%87%E0%A6%9F.
430. Lionel Bently, *The 'Extraordinary Multiplicity' of Intellectual Property Laws in the British Colonies in the Nineteenth Century*, 12(1) Theoretical Inquiries L., 161–200 (2011).

Chapter 1. Application of Copyright in the Area of ICT

§1. Introduction

431. The right to acquire, hold, transfer and dispose of property, subject to any restrictions imposed by law, is a constitutionally guaranteed fundamental right in Bangladesh.[431] Copyright is moveable property,[432] and 'moveable property' means property of any description.[433] Copyright in literary and artistic works is different from property in a physical thing. Therefore, someone can buy a book from the market and do whatever she wishes with it as a physical object, but someone else, e.g., the author or publisher or someone having the licence of the author of the book will have the copyright of the content of the book.[434]

432. Copyright protects creative intellectual creations in, e.g., books, songs, movies, software, etc. The main purpose of copyright protection is to protect the 'expression' and not the 'ideas, procedure, methods of operation or mathematical concepts' as ideas can be protected through the provisions of the law of patent.[435] In order to get copyright protection, any work should be fixed in a material form, created by a human author, original and capable of expressing ideas. ICT tools and applications, though facilitate intellectual creativity and are inevitable to some extent in modern times, can negatively be used to make pirated copies of copyrighted creations also. Thus, the regulation of ICT tools, applications, human actors behind the use and application of these, and in many cases, the use of artificial intelligence and the authorship of copyrightable works in the context of copyright protection is one of the hotly debated issues in the study of ICT law and policy.

433. The Berne Convention for the Protection of Literary and Artistic Works, 1886, the oldest and most significant treaty in this area, contains some minimum standards, e.g., types of works protected, copyright duration, scope of exceptions, limitations, principles of 'national treatment' and 'automatic protection', etc. The Convention, along with its several amendments, aims to automatically protect the rights of the copyright holders of 'literary and artistic works', e.g., books and other writings, a musical composition, a film, a software program, a painting and expressions of creative ideas from the date of the first publication of the work.[436]

434. In 1996, the WIPO Copyright Treaty, signed in December 1996 and came into force in March 2002, was introduced as a special agreement under the Berne Convention to protect the works of the authors in the digital environment. This Convention gives some economic rights, apart from the rights recognized by the Berne Convention, to the copyright holders of computer programs and databases. Such

431. Article 42, the Constitution of the People's Republic of Bangladesh, 1972.
432. *S. Sibtain Fazil v. Star Film Distributors* (1962) 14 DLR 307.
433. Section 3(34), the General Clauses Act, 1897 (Act No. X of 1897).
434. Professor Vaver, D., *Principles of Copyright: Cases and Materials*, 11 (2002).
435. Article 9(2), the Agreement on Trade-Related Aspects of Intellectual Property Rights, 1995.
436. Articles 2(1) & 6, the Berne Convention for the Protection of Literary and Artistic Works, 1886.

economic rights are the right of distribution, the right of rental and the broader right of communication to the public. The WIPO Performances and Phonograms Treaty, 1996 deals with the rights of two types of beneficiaries, particularly in the digital environment. These beneficiaries are: performers (e.g., actors, singers, musicians, etc.) and producers of phonograms (i.e., persons or legal entities that are responsible for fixing sounds). This Treaty gives the performers some economic rights, e.g., the right to reproduction, distribution, rental, etc. The WIPO Copyright Treaty and the WIPO Performances and Phonograms Treaty, 1996 are collectively known as 'the Internet Treaties'. The Agreement on Trade-Related Aspects of Intellectual Property Rights (TRIPS Agreement), 1994 (effective in 1996) of the WTO provides guiding principles on effective enforcement of IPRs including copyright for national jurisdictions.

435. Bangladesh has signed, accessed to and ratified relevant important international instruments on copyright protection. With the responsibilities and obligations derived from these international instruments, Article 23 of the Constitution of Bangladesh, 1972 imposes responsibilities on the State to adopt measures to foster literature and arts to enable people of all sections to participate in the enrichment of the national culture. In 2000, the government of Bangladesh enacted, almost immediately after the internet was made available for private and commercial use, the Copyright Act, 2000 (Act No. XXVIII of 2000), replacing the previous law in this field, i.e., the Copyright Ordinance, 1962 (Ordinance No. XXXIV of 1962). It is believed that the newly enacted law has incorporated the relevant provisions of the Berne Convention[437] and TRIPS Agreement, in the domestic context of Bangladesh. However, Bangladesh has not signed the WIPO Copyright Treaty, 1996 and the WIPO Performances and Phonograms Treaty, 1996.

§2. Important Definitions

436. The legal regime of copyright is essentially a domestic matter and therefore, some introductory discussion on some of the important definitions as encapsulated in the Copyright Act, 2000 (Act No. XXVIII of 2000) deserve special attention. The Law of 2001 has defined 'copy' as the reproduction in the form of words, pictures, sounds, letters, written form or in the form of sound recordings, cinematograph films, graphics or in the material or non-material form, digital code (fixed or moving) or whether in two or three or surrealistic dimensions.[438] Whereas 'infringing copy', under the law, means (a) regarding a literary, dramatic, musical or artistic work, a reproduction of the whole work or a part thereof, except in the form of a cinematograph film; (b) regarding a cinematograph film or a photograph embodying the whole or a part thereof, made on any medium by electromagnetic device or any other equipment or process; (c) regarding a sound recording, any other recording embodying the same sound recording made by any means; (d) regarding

437. Bangladesh accessed to the Convention on 4 Feb. 1999 and the provisions of the Convention entered into force for Bangladesh on 4 May 1999.
438. Section 2(1), the Copyright Act, 2000 (Act No. XXVIII of 2000).

a programme or performance in which a broadcast reproduction right or a performer's right subsists under this Act, a cinematograph film or a sound recording of such programme or performance in whole or in part thereof, if such reproduction, copy or sound recording is made or imported in contravention of the provisions of this Act; and (e) regarding a computer programme, reproduction or use of the whole work or a part thereof.[439]

437. The law has defined 'work' as (a) a literary, dramatic musical or artistic work; (b) a cinematograph film; (c) a sound recording; and (d) a broadcast,[440] and the law provides that copyright subsists throughout Bangladesh on (a) original literary, dramatic, musical and artistic works; (b) cinematograph films; and (c) sound recording.[441]

438. Generally speaking, in order to get copyright protection, a work must be created independently with or without having a contractual obligation, minimally creative and fixed in a tangible form. Moreover, the subject of the copyright need not share the expression of any original or novel idea; rather original skills or labour in the expression of an idea is required. According to the Copyright Act, 2000 (Act No. XXVIII of 2000), 'copyright' is the right to do or to authorize the doing of some works in whole or in part listed in section 14 of the Law. A combined reading to section 14(1) and 14(2) of the Law will reveal that the 'copyright' permits the owner the right or authority to (a) reproduce the work in any material form including the storing of it in any medium by electronic means; (b) issue copies of the work to the public except copies already in circulation; (c) perform the work in public, or communicate it to the public; (d) produce, reproduce, perform or publish any translation of the work; (e) make any cinematograph film or sound recording in respect of the work; (f) broadcast the work or the communication of the broadcast of the work to the public by a loudspeaker or any other similar instrument; (g) make the adaptation of the work; and (h) regarding a translation or adaptation of the work, to do any of the acts specified above. Moreover, in relation to 'computer programme', such right includes any of these above works and shall also include any act relating to sell or give on hire, or offer for sale or hire any copy of the computer programme, regardless of whether such copy has been sold or given on hire on earlier occasions. However, in the case of cinematograph film and sound recording, copyright shall not be subsisted if a substantial part of the film or part of the recording is an infringement of other copyrighted work.[442] Usually, copyright subsists for in any literary, dramatic, musical or artistic work (except a photograph) published within the lifetime of the author until sixty years from the beginning of the calendar year following the year in which the author dies.[443]

---

439. Section 2(8), the Copyright Act, 2000 (Act No. XXVIII of 2000).
440. Section 2(11), the Copyright Act, 2000 (Act No. XXVIII of 2000).
441. Section 15(1), the Copyright Act, 2000 (Act No. XXVIII of 2000).
442. Section 15(3), the Copyright Act, 2000 (Act No. XXVIII of 2000).
443. Section 24, the Copyright Act, 2000 (Act No. XXVIII of 2000).

§3. INFRINGEMENT OF COPYRIGHT

439. Any user of a copyrighted work generally needs permission or authorization before its use. The making of any copy of such copyrighted work for the purpose of commercial sale will be treated as infringement.[444] The law provides that the copyright in work shall be deemed to be infringed:

(a) when any person, without a licence granted by the owner of the copyright or the Registrar under this Act or in contravention of the conditions of a licence so granted or of any condition imposed by a competent authority under this Act:
  (i) does anything, the exclusive right to do which is by this Act conferred upon the owner of the copyright; or
  (ii) permits for profit any place to be used for the performance of the work in public where such performance constitutes an infringement of the copyright in work unless he was not aware, and had no reasonable ground for believing, that such performance would be an infringement of copyright; or
(b) when any person:
  (i) makes for sale or hire, or sells or lets for hire, or by way of trade displays or offers for sale or hire; or
  (ii) distributes either for the purpose of trade or to such an extent as to affect prejudicially the owner of the copyright; or
  (iii) by way of trade exhibits in public; or
  (iv) imports into Bangladesh, any infringing copies of the work.[445]

440. Nevertheless, the law, in section 72, provides for many exceptions when the use of the copyrighted work will not be treated as infringement. According to this provision, the fair use of a copyrighted work for the purpose of: (i) private study or private use including research; or (ii) criticism or review, and reporting current events: (i) in a newspaper, magazine, or similar periodical; or (ii) by broadcast or in a cinematograph film or by means of photographs shall not constitute an infringement of copyright. However, the publication of a compilation of addresses or speeches delivered in public is not a fair dealing of such work.[446] Besides, the reproduction of a copyrighted work shall not constitute copyright infringement if this is done for some legal reasons such as, *inter alia*:

- for the purpose of a judicial proceeding or reporting of a judicial proceeding;
- exclusive use of the Members of Parliament when such work is made or supplied by the Secretariat of Parliament;
- in accordance with any law in force;
- reading or recitation in public;
- for the use of educational institutions by a teacher or a pupil in the course and for the sole purpose of instruction and evaluation;

444. Section 39, the Copyright Act, 2000 (Act No. XXVIII of 2000).
445. Section 71, the Copyright Act, 2000 (Act No. XXVIII of 2000).
446. Section 72(1) and 72(2), the Copyright Act, 2000 (Act No. XXVIII of 2000).

- non-commercial use of the work in public by non-profit organizations with or without the intention to benefit a religious, charitable or educational institution;
- reproduction in a newspaper, magazine or other periodical of an article on current economic, political, social or religious topics, unless the owner of copyright of such article has expressly reserved to himself the right of such reproduction;
- the publication in a newspaper, magazine or other periodical of a report a lecture delivered in public;
- reproduction of unpublished work for the purpose of research or private study;
- the making of up to three copies of the copyrighted work by or under the direction of the person in charge of a non-profit library available for use by the public free of charge or a library attached to an educational institution if that copyrighted work is not available for sale in Bangladesh;
- reproduction or publication of any matter published in any Official Gazette except an Act of Parliament; the report of any committee, commission, council, board or such other bodies appointed by the Government unless the reproduction is expressly prohibited; any Act of Parliament with any commentary; any judgment or order of a court, tribunal or other judicial authority unless the reproduction is expressly prohibited;
- the production or publication of a translation with clear notice about its unofficial nature in any language of an Act of Parliament and of any rules or orders made thereunder if no official translation is made by the Government or available for sale to the public;
- the making or publishing of a painting, drawing, engraving or photograph of architecture or the display of a work architecture;
- the making of copies or adaptation of a computer programme by the lawful possessor from such copy: (i) in order to utilize the computer programme for the purpose for which it was supplied; or (ii) to make backup copies purely as temporary protection against loss, destruction or damage in order only to utilize the computer programme for the purpose for which it was supplied; (iii) for further upgrading of a computer programme, etc.

§4. Registration of Copyright

441. The domestic law of Bangladesh does not make it compulsory to register copyrightable creations as this is not also required under the Berne Convention. Nevertheless, in order to get better protection in any future disputes or legal proceedings and considering the practical challenges posed by the ICT tools and applications coupled with the cultures of ineffective implementation of the law and competence of the law enforcement bodies, the copyrightable creation should ideally be registered with the authority, i.e., Bangladesh Copyright Office, a body under the Ministry of Cultural Affairs as such official registration thus form a part of public record. The Law contains provisions on the registration procedure, and the Copyright Office maintains a register containing the details, i.e., the names or titles of works, and the names and addresses of authors, creators, publishers and owners of copyright, etc.[447] Rule 3 of the Copyright Rules, 2006 provides that there shall be seven parts of the register. These are literary, computer, software, dramatic and musical works (Part 1); artistic works (Part 2); cinematograph works (Part 3); records (Part 4); broadcasts (Part 5); telecasts (Part 6); emails, websites and other modes of communications (Part 7). This register is considered as the prima facie evidence and is admissible in evidence in all courts without further proof or production of the original work.[448]

442. The Copyright Rules, 2006, as framed under section 103 of the Copyright Act, 2000 (Act No. XXVIII of 2000), contain provisions on the registration of work for copyright in Rule 4. Nevertheless, since the registration of work for copyright is not mandatory rather voluntary, and the regulators do not take sufficient measures to encourage the stakeholders in this regard, most of the authors or owners of such creations are not aware of this and do not take initiative to register their creations even though the registration fee is very nominal, i.e., only BDT 1600 (approximately USD 18). As a result, the government has been losing revenue, whereas the owner of copyrightable creation becomes prone to infringement and deprived of benefits arising out of his creation.

443. Originally, there was no provision on the computer program in the law. Subsequently, in 2005, the Copyright Act, 2000 was amended to include relevant provisions regarding the protection of the computer program. Software, as a computer program, can be copyright protected as literary work under section 2(46) of the Copyright Act, 2000 (Act No. XXVIII of 2000). Section 2(10) of the Copyright Act, 2000 defines 'computer program' as 'a set of instructions expressed in words, codes, schemes or in any other form, including a machine readable medium, capable of causing a computer to perform a particular task or achieve a particular result'. Software is a computer program as the instructions are expressed in words and codes through a machine-readable medium, capable of causing a computer to perform a particular task or achieve a particular result. The locally developed software is covered under the Copyright Rules as framed under the Copyright Act, 2000 and can get legal protection if duly registered.

444. In case of a computer program, the person or persons or institution appointed for creating the program shall be the first owner of the copyright, if there is no other agreement,[449] and the copyright subsists for sixty years from the beginning of the calendar year following the year in which the program is published.[450] Similar to other copyrightable creations, the registration of copyright of software is not mandatory under domestic law; however, registration of copyright provides

447. For detail information, *see*, Rule 3(2) and First Schedule, Form-1: Register of Copyright, the Copyright Rules, 2006.
448. Sections 55 & 60, the Copyright Act, 2000 (Act No. XXVIII of 2000).
449. Section 17, the Copyright Act, 2000 (Act No. XXVIII of 2000).
450. Section 28A, the Copyright Act, 2000(Act No. XXVIII of 2000).

some benefits to the owner or his heirs in terms of ownership and other benefits airing out of these. It is believed that the Bijoy Bangla Script System is the first software which received copyright protection as literary work in 1989.[451]

445. Even foreign software, if duly registered, can get similar protection like a locally developed software under the IP law of Bangladesh. In order to register software, either locally developed or software developed aboard but introduced in the local market should ideally be registered with the Copyright office following some simple steps.[452] An individual or any organization can apply for registration of software, website or mobile phone application. A prospective applicant needs to apply for registration addressing the Registrar of Copyrights in the Copyright Office, Dhaka under section 56 of the Copyright Act, 2000. A prospective applicant should use Form-2 in this regard. In the Form-2, an applicant should mention the name, address and nationality of both the applicant and author, whether the applicant is an owner or heir or licensee, etc., nature, title, language of the work, information about the status of the publication and first date and place of publication and name, address and nationality of the publisher, etc.

446. The applicant, in the application, must also mention whether the work is original or translated or additional work. Three sets of all the required documents can be submitted either personally or through registered post. In addition to all these, an individual software owner needs to submit two copies of the software in the form of a compact disc and two printed versions. In case an organization is the applicant, it should additionally submit an attested photocopy of its MoA, Trade licence, Tax Identification Number, appointment letter of the employee if an employee has developed the software during the course of his employment and an attested photocopy of his/her NID or Passport and two copies of passport size photos. An applicant should further declare in a non-judicial stamp that there is no legal case or cases pending with regard to the software, website or mobile phone application in any court of law.[453] It may be relevant to share here that an association or body is not required to be incorporated to own the copyright. In the case of an unincorporated association or body, individuals constituting the body will own the copyright as tenants-in-common.[454]

§5. Copyright Ownership

447. ICT and ITES entrepreneurs should consider including the issue of copyright ownership in the employment or service contract of their software developers.

451. World Intellectual Property Organization, Localizing Technology: The Story of Bijoy, https://www.wipo.int/ipadvantage/en/details.jsp?id=2624.
452. http://www.copyrightoffice.gov.bd/site/page/3e7467fa-aabe-4590-8a8e-be38a796e73a/%E0%A6%B8%E0%A6%AB%E0%A6%9F%E0%A6%93%E0%A7%9F%E0%A7%8D%E0%A6%AF%E0%A6%BE%E0%A6%B0.
453. *Ibid.*
454. *Mrs. Suraiya Rahman v. Skill Development for Underprivileged Women, represented by its Project Directors, and others*, 17 BLD (HCD) 284.

If an employed person is an employee of his employer for remuneration, he is under a contract of service. But if such a person is an independent contractor under the employer, he is not under a contract for service.[455] When any work is done or made in the course of the author's employment under a contract of service or apprenticeship, the employer of the employed person, in the absence of any agreement to the contrary, will be the first owner of the copyright therein.[456]

§6. REMEDIES

448. The Law provides for two types of remedies: judicial and administrative. The Copyright Act, 2000 allows the copyright holder or heirs to bring a civil suit for the violation of his copyright and a suit of such nature can be filed in the court of a District Judge.[457] In case of infringement of copyright, the owner of the copyright is entitled to have remedies by way of injunction, damages, accounts, etc., as are or may be conferred by law. Any person aggrieved can apply to the Registrar to prohibit the ban of import of any pirated or infringed copy in Bangladesh.[458] The law provides for punishment of imprisonment for a minimum of six months to a maximum of four years and a fine for a minimum of BDT 50,000 (approximately USD 585)–BDT 200,000 (approximately USD 2334) for the infringement of copyright of any work other than cinematograph. Whereas, for the infringement of cinematograph works, the punishment is imprisonment for a minimum of one year to a maximum of five years and the fine is a minimum of BDT 100,000 (approximately USD 1167)–BDT 500,000 (approximately USD 5,835).[459] The law also provides for enhanced penalty for second and subsequent offences in section 83. However, if the defendant can prove that at the date of the infringement he was not aware or had reasonable ground to believe that copyright subsisted in the work, the plaintiff, at the discretion of the court, will only get remedy by way of an injunction in respect of the infringement and a decree for the whole or part of the profits made by the defendant by the sale of the infringing copies.[460]

449. Anyone who infringes the copyright in a work of computer program, publishes it in any medium, sells or distributes it more than one copy, shall be punished with imprisonment for a term between six months to four years or with a fine which may extend to a minimum of BDT 100,000 (approximately USD 1,167) to a maximum of BDT 400,000 (approximately USD 4,667).[461] Whereas, anyone who uses an infringed copy on a computer shall be punished with imprisonment, which may extend between six months to three years or with a fine which may extend to a minimum of BDT 100,000 (approximately USD 1,167) to a maximum of BDT 300,000

455. *Ibid.*
456. *Ibid.*
457. Section 81, the Copyright Act, 2000 (Act No. XXVIII of 2000).
458. Section 74, the Copyright Act, 2000 (Act No. XXVIII of 2000).
459. Section 82, the Copyright Act, 2000 (Act No. XXVIII of 2000).
460. Section 76(1), the Copyright Act, 2000 (Act No. XXVIII of 2000).
461. Section 84(a), the Copyright Act, 2000 (Act No. XXVIII of 2000).

(approximately USD 3,500).[462] However, if it can be proved to the satisfaction of the court that the infringement has not been made for gain in the course of trade or business, the court may impose any sentence of imprisonment for a term of less than three months and a fine of less than BDT 25,000 (approximately USD 300).[463]

450. The related source code, compilation, data, design documentation and relevant charts, shall be deemed to be the property of the owner of the copyright, who accordingly may take proceedings for the recovery of possession thereof or in respect of the conversion.[464] However, the owner of the copyright shall not be entitled to any remedy in respect of the conversion of any infringing copies, if the opponent can prove (a) that he was not aware and had no reasonable ground to believe that copyright subsisted in the work of which such copies are alleged to be infringing copies; or (b) that he had reasonable grounds for believing that such copies or plates do not involve infringement of the copyright in any work.[465]

§7. Conclusion

451. Easily available and circulated pirated software in the local market seems to create a bar to attract FDI in the country and leave the consumers at risk as this software is believed to contain malware, virus and suspicious programs through which the cybercriminals may obtain sensitive personal information of the consumers and use these to commit various serious cybercrimes. Therefore, like other parts of the world, it is suggested that the users use genuine software collected from authorized dealers or sources.

452. Since the use of genuine software may be found to be expensive to some, in order to solve the issue of the use of pirated software, young entrepreneurs can be encouraged to use open source software developed by reliable bodies, though the issue of security will remain a concern. Bangladesh Open Source Network (BdOSN) is a non-profit, voluntary organization. It was launched on 24 October 2005 in Dhaka to create a broad organization where the Open Source and Open Content volunteers and professionals can exchange their ideas and embark on new initiatives.[466] Besides, BASIS has been using the Linux operating system to discourage people from using pirated software.

462. Section 84(b), the Copyright Act, 2000 (Act No. XXVIII of 2000).
463. Proviso to s. 84, the Copyright Act, 2000 (Act No. XXVIII of 2000).
464. Section 79, the Copyright Act, 2000 (Act No. XXVIII of 2000).
465. *Ibid.*
466. Bangladesh Open Source Network, https://bdosn.org/about-bdosn.

Chapter 2. Legal Protection of Software

§1. Introduction

453. The software industry is a very promising sector in the Bangladesh context and can facilitate the country to earn a huge amount of foreign currency by exporting the same and creating employment opportunities along with assisting the government in fulfilling the national vision to make the country digitalized. Bangladeshi developers and entrepreneurs have been developing software for both foreign and domestic clients. Nevertheless, looking at some of the contracts executed between these parties, i.e., developers and clients, it has been revealed that the issue of the legal protection of the software in a formal manner has not received enough importance in their deals.

§2. Software Protection Law

454. Software, as a computer program, is eligible to be protected under copyright law as literary works under the Berne Convention for the Protection of Literary and Artistic Works. The same is the position under the European Directive 2009/24 on the Legal Protection of Computer Programs. It has already been discussed in the previous Chapter that registration of the copyrightable creation is voluntary in Bangladesh. To protect such creation, one does not need to follow any stringent procedure, and the regulator encourages the registration of such creations to avoid future legal challenges. Nevertheless, it should be remembered that only the source code of the software, and not the algorithm or functionality of a computer program or programming language or format of data files used in a computer program should ideally receive the copyright protection since these are not an expression of the creativity of its author. In Bangladesh, the legal position of this issue is uncertain, and the regulator does not make any distinction between these two things and welcomes the registration of both published and unpublished software.

455. The legal regime of software or computer program or computer-implemented inventions varies from jurisdiction to jurisdiction. The findings of the studies conducted in the context of the European Patent Office, the US Patent and Trademark Office and Japan Patent Office (JPO) have, due to the peculiarities of computer program inventions, made some distinctions between software patent eligibility, software patentability and software patenting.[467] It is found that Japan explicitly recognizes patent protection of software, though every single idea having

467. Dragoni, M., *Software Patent Eligibility and Patentability: An Overview of the Developments in Japan, Europe and the United States and an Analysis of Their Impact on Patenting Trends*, Stanford-Vienna TTLF Working Paper No. 72 (2021), http://ttlf.stanford.edu.

a claim of invention is examined to evaluate if that deals with a 'creation of technical ideas utilizing laws of nature'. Japan has clarified this issue in the JPO Examination Guidelines and Handbook also.[468]

456. In Europe, the purely conceptual aspects in the design and development of software do not fulfil the inventive step to be eligible to get patent protection. However, the case will be different if an invention is a 'computer-implemented invention', i.e., an invention which involves the use of the computer, computer network or other programmable apparatus, where one or more features are realized wholly or partly by means of a computer program.[469] In such cases, software that has a technical character inside along with inventive steps and novelty may be patented. Thus, because of economic and technological factors, patentability will not be denied merely because a computer program is involved. In the case of IBM Corporation [T1173/97], the Board of Appeal of the European Patent Office held that a computer program product is not excluded from patentability if it produces a further technical effect which goes beyond the 'normal' physical interactions between computer software and hardware when it is run on a computer. In the US, based on the 'Mayo-Alice test', it seems that patenting software is significantly harder compared to Japan and Europe.[470] The courts consider such claims following a case-by-case approach and the ultimate outcome is unpredictable.

§3. Patent Law

457. A patent protects inventions, ideas, processes, methods, concepts, machines and devices. Century-old Patents and Designs Act, 1911 (Act No. II of 1911) enacted during the British regime in the then Indian sub-continent is the present law that deals with patent-related issues in Bangladesh. The Patent and Design Rules, 1933, containing detailed provisions as to patent registration, was also formulated under the law of 1911. In accordance with this Law, the Department of Patents Designs and Trademarks under MoI is authorized to manage and administer the patent-related matters in the country. Generally speaking, in order to be patentable, a subject matter has to be an invention, i.e., any manner of new manufacture including improvement and an alleged invention.[471] However, the issue of software patentability is not included in the law for the obvious reason that the law was enacted long ago.

---

468. *Ibid.*, p. 44.
469. Index for Computer-Implemented Inventions, Guidelines for Examination, European Patent Office, https://www.epo.org/law-practice/legal-texts/html/guidelines/e/j.htm.
470. In the *Alice Corp. v. CLS Bank International*, 573 U.S. 208, the US Supreme Court introduced two-part test about software patentability. Using this framework, the Court first determines whether the claims at issue are directed to a patent-ineligible concept. If so, the Court then asks whether the claim's elements, considered both individually and 'as an ordered combination,' 'transform the nature of the claim' into a patent-eligible application.
471. Section 2(8), the Patent and Design Act, 1911 (Act No. II of 1911).

458. Although the Patents and Designs Act, 1911 (Act No. II of 1911) stipulates the procedure to be followed for making the patent application, it does not contain any provision highlighting the subject matters that cannot be patented.[472] Such a stand enables the patent authority to exercise discretion while dealing with any patent application in changing circumstances. A patent is granted, subject to payment of prescribed fees, for sixteen years with the scope of possible extension. The payment of a fee for patent registration is crucial and if an infringement of any patent is committed when the owner failed to pay the fee, the Court may refuse to award any damages for such infringement.[473]

459. Despite the absence of a specific provision on the issue of software patenting under the existing law, there are instances when the patent was granted for the computer program in Bangladesh. Apparently, patents are granted in the case of computer programs as these are capable of producing some technical effects. Locally developed Bijoy Bangla typing software is copyright protected since 1989 as original expression, and it was subsequently granted a patent in 2004 under the existing law as a method that is capable of producing technical effects.[474] Besides, this software has received trademark protection too.

460. The issue of Bijoy Bangla seems to be a unique one and is not generally practised in the country in the case of other software. Thus, it is evident that software as a computer program per se is not eligible to be patented under existing Bangladeshi laws though the same can be patented as an idea or method when it produces technical effects. Nevertheless, there are not many examples of patented local software in Bangladesh.

§4. New Patent Bill, 2018

461. Since the existing patent law was drafted and enacted long ago, the limitations of the law in the present context were revealed on several occasions, and it was suggested to update and revise the Law to meet the needs of the time. The government has also paid attention to the calls, and the Law Commission of Bangladesh reviewed the existing law. The Commission finally, in 2001, proposed to introduce a new law replacing the present one instead of suggesting the incorporation of amendments in the present law.[475] Accordingly, a draft of the law on Patents and Designs was developed to overcome the shortcomings of existing Patent Law as well as to fulfil the TRIPS obligation. That said draft was reviewed by the stakeholders, including WIPO experts but did not get the light of enactment even in almost two decades. Recently, in November 2018, the government released a Bill

472. Azam, M.M., *Intellectual Property WTO and Bangladesh, New Warsi Book Corporation* 175 (2012).
473. Section 14, the Patent and Design Act, 1911 (Act No. II of 1911).
474. World Intellectual Property Organization, Localizing Technology: The Story of Bijoy, https://www.wipo.int/ipadvantage/en/details.jsp?id=2624.
475. Final Report on the Patent and Design Act, by Bangladesh Law Commission, p. 2.

on Patents, repealing the Patents and Designs Act, 1911 (Act No. II of 1911).[476] This is a significant development as the Draft has reached the Bill stage. The Bill will turn to be an Act of Parliament when it will be passed by the Parliament. The Parliament has not considered it yet, though it is expected to be passed soon.

§5. Software Patentability under the Patent Bill, 2018

462. With the recent emphasis of the Bangladesh government on digitalized systems, it may be significant and relevant to examine how far digital technological applications, especially software, are protected by the draft Patent Law.

463. On the issue of patentability, one of the main concerns is to settle whether the alleged subject matter is an invention or not. The patent authority decides about an innovation as per the existing guidelines or rules. It is apparent that the Bill, in section 3, has extended the existing definition of the invention and has defined 'a patentable invention' as the innovation of any product or process of technology having novelty, innovative step and industrial application. Besides, any invention that can be created or used in the industry shall be considered as an innovation.[477]

464. It may be relevant to share here that the draft law, which was proposed by the Law Commission in 2001, also had a concern with the definition of 'a patentable innovation' and so, the definition of the invention was widened. Accordingly, an 'invention' was defined as any new, sufficiently inventive and useful (a) art, process, method or manner of manufacture; (b) machine, apparatus or other article; and (c) substance produced by manufacture and includes any new, sufficiently inventive and useful improvement of any of them and an alleged invention.[478] This wide definition of 'invention' was also applauded by the WIPO experts. In a discussion with the Bangladesh delegation held in 2003, the WIPO experts found the definition acceptable and in line with the TRIPS Agreement.[479] Unfortunately, it is apparent that while developing the Bill in 2018, this wide definition, as suggested by the Law Commission, was excluded from the Bill.

465. The Bill of 2018 has listed a few subject matters as non-patentable in section 4 of the Bill. Like the TRIPS Agreement, the Bill does not contain any specific provision on the patentability of a computer program. However, it explicitly excludes 'business practices, conventions or methods of performing fully mental work and any such computer program' as non-patentable subject matter.[480] Besides,

476. It may be relevant to share here that the Ministry of Industries released a draft titled 'the Bangladesh Industrial Designs Act, 2016' to deal with the design part of the Patents and Designs Act, 1911.
477. Section 3, the Patent Bill, 2018.
478. Section 16, Draft Patent and Design Act, 2001.
479. Report on discussion between Bangladesh delegation and WIPO experts on proposed Patents and Designs Act, Trade Marks and Merchandise Marks Act, Copyright Act, 2000 and other subjects of IPRs within the purview of WTO, p. 5.
480. Section 4(1)(b), the Patent Bill, 2018.

a few things are excluded from patentability on different grounds including a discovery, scientific theory or mathematical method.[481] Hence, the issue of software patents might be opposed on the ground that it is a pure algorithm or mathematical issue and the grant of patents for mathematical algorithms would exclude others from performing the same process.[482]

§6. CONCLUSION

466. The MoI has recently released the Innovation and Intellectual Property Policy, 2018 aiming to, *inter alia*, modernize the domestic intellectual property legal regime. Under this Policy, the decade (2018–2028) is projected as the innovation decade. Bangladesh is known as one of the lucrative destinations for software development and IT process outsourcing. Therefore, the country should consider adopting some specific policy measures regarding software patenting, even though the issue is a subject of debate in the major patent offices in Europe, the US and Japan.[483] After evaluating the possible options as available in these three jurisdictions, the Policymakers can make their stand clear by issuing guidelines that will reflect if they favour the 'flexible' or 'restrictive' approach in relation to software patenting. While this issue in the Bill may not be a concern for the time being as the Bill is not passed yet in Parliament, non-patentability of the software completely will invite new problems in future. Therefore, the European approach, i.e., keeping the scope of patentability of 'computer-implemented inventions' seems to be a better choice that promises to promote innovations.

481. Section 4(1)(a), the Patent Bill, 2018.
482. Talat Kaya, *A Comparative Analysis of the Patentability of Computer Software under the TRIPs Agreement: The U.S., the E.U., and Turkey*, 4 Ankara L. Rev., 22 (Summer 2007).
483. Dragoni, M., *Software Patent Eligibility and Patentability: An Overview of the Developments in Japan, Europe and the United States and an Analysis of Their Impact on Patenting Trends*, Stanford-Vienna TTLF Working Paper No. 72 (2021), http://ttlf.stanford.edu.

Chapter 3. Legal Protection of Databases

§1. Introduction

467. Databases are developed with aims, *inter alia*, to provide faster services in all service sectors like recreation and tourism, legal, healthcare, banking, insurance, education, real estate, etc.[484] Such databases contain data on basic information collected, arranged, classified and stored targeting these service sectors. The references of Yellow pages, different kinds of directories and online databases, etc., can be shared here as examples of such databases.

468. Databases can be both original and non-original, i.e., copied from an original database and used for a similar or different purpose. Databases play an instrumental role in the development of global information infrastructure. The prospect of e-commerce, based on information structure, in Bangladesh, has repeatedly been applauded and reiterated. This has also encouraged entrepreneurs to develop databases of different nature.

§2. Database Protection Law

469. Original databases, if they satisfy the criteria of copyright, can be copyrighted and get similar protection. Several European countries and Mexico have introduced sui generis form of the legal protection of such 'non-original' databases, and therefore, the owner gets legal protection for the sui generis database. In some jurisdictions, these databases can be protected through unfair competition or misappropriation law.[485]

470. The EU Directive 96/9/EC on the legal protection of databases defines 'database' in Article 1(2) as 'a collection of independent works, data or other materials arranged in a systematic or methodical way and individually accessible by electronic or other means'. The exact same definition is incorporated in the WIPO's proposed Convention on Legal Protection of Database, which is in the consultation process for years. The same is the position under the Copyright, Designs and Patents Act, 1988 of the United Kingdom (UK).[486]

471. Under Article 3(1) of this EU Directive, 'databases which, by reason of the selection and arrangement of their contents only, constitute the author's own intellectual creation shall be protected as such by copyright'. Therefore, it is apparent that if any data is systematically or methodically arranged in a way that their contents constitute the author's own intellectual creation that shall be protected by

484. Karim, M.E., *Legal Protection of Databases*, The Daily Star, 7 Jun. 2016, https://www.thedailystar.net/law-our-rights/legal-protection-databases-1235332.
485. *Ibid.*
486. *Ibid.*

copyright. Pertinent to mention here that the very content of the database can be protected under general copyright law, and the same is confirmed by Article 3(2) of the EU Directive.

472. In the US, under the concept of 'compilation copyright', the compilation of works is similarly protected if the work is selected, coordinated, or arranged in such a way that the resulting work as a whole constitutes an original work of authorship. The TRIPS Agreement has considered the word 'compilation' in Article 10(2) and provides that compilation of data, which by reason of the selection and arrangement of their contents constitute intellectual creations shall get copyright protection. The Berne Convention for the Protection of Literary and Artistic Works, 1886 (as amended in 1979) has used the word 'collections' and covers collections of literary or artistic works like encyclopaedia and anthologies under copyright protection as they constitute intellectual creations by reason of the selection and arrangements of contents. Similar language is adopted in Article 5 of the WIPO Copyright Treaty, 1996.[487] However, it has already been shared that though Bangladesh has ratified the Berne Convention and the TRIPS Agreement, but has not signed the WIPO Copyright Treaty, 1996 yet.

§3. Database Protection under National Law

473. In Bangladesh, the government has also been developing various kinds of databases, e.g., databases on voter registration. Non-commercial nature of these government databases keeps them away from the copyright domain. Whereas, other databases mentioned above are easily accessible online and can be copied without the permission of the owner or developer, and can further be modified and re-used by others using sophisticated devices. Even though in some jurisdictions, such databases enjoy copyright protection once they meet some criteria, the status of these databases which are 'non-original' in nature is somehow obscure in the Bangladesh context as they lack the requisite of originality or creativity to qualify for copyright protection, even though they require a substantial amount of investment and intellectual input and effort of the creators.[488]

474. It will be relevant to share here that back in 1890, the Calcutta High Court declared that the compilation of poems is subject to copyright and thus, can be protected. In the case of *Macmillan and another v. Suresh Chunder Deb*, ILR 17 Calcutta 951, Wilson, J, in the absence of any precedent, pointed out that '[i]n the case of works not original in the proper sense of the term, but composed of, or compiled or prepared from materials which are open to all, the fact that one man has produced such a work does not take away from anyone else the right to produce another work of the same kind, and in doing so to use all the materials open to him'. Using the same principle, maps, road books, guide books, street directories, dictionaries,

487. *Ibid.*
488. *Ibid.*

compilations on scientific and other subjects, and a selection of poems are produced. However, it does not mean that someone can easily take away the result of another's labour. In a subsequent case, in *Macmillan and Company Limited v. K and Cooper*, AIR 1924 Privy Council 75, the Privy Council Judge Lord Atkinson, referring to a decision from the US, pronounced that 'any new and original plan, arrangement or combination of material will entail the author to copyright therein, whether the materials themselves is old or new'. Moreover, the judge further mentioned that 'to constitute piracy of a copyright it must be shown that the original has been either substantially copied or to be so imitated as to be a mere evasion of the copyright'.

475. In Bangladesh, within the ambit of the Copyright Act, 2000 (Act No. 28 of 2000), the copyright of literary, dramatic, musical or artistic work, cinematograph film or photograph, sound recording and computer program and broadcast reproduction right or performer's right, etc. can be protected. From the forms available on the website of the Copyright Office of Bangladesh, it is also certain that the copyright applications can be made for software, website, and mobile apps. Albeit, the status of these 'non-original' databases developed by the systematic and methodical arrangement of contents is certainly uncertain. As a result, the status of the US's 'compilation copyright' or internationally recognized 'collection' are not clear in the Bangladesh context also as it is apparent that the word 'compilation' as used twice in the Copyright Act, 2000, i.e., sections 72(1)(2) explanation and 79, and the word 'collection' as used in a number of instances in the Act do not intend to include these non-original databases.[489]

476. Earlier, section 54(2)(b) of the ICT Act, 2006 defined the words 'computer database'. Yet, with this provision, it was uncertain if the same provision could be applied in the case of online databases. This provision was repealed recently through the provision of the Digital Security Act, 2018 (Act No. 46 of 2018) and an attempt was made to remove the uncertainty. As a result, databases are now apparently protected though it is still uncertain if the law intends to protect commercial online databases or not. Instead of 'computer database', the new law has included the definition of 'database' and has defined it as 'information, knowledge, facts, fundamental concepts or instructions by way of texts, image, audio or video prepared in a formalized manner through computer, computer system or computer network' for use in any computer, computer system or computer network. The law provides punishment for downloading, copying or extraction of data from any computer, computer system or computer network without permission.[490] It is also a punishable offence to enter any computer, computer network, internet network, computer database knowingly and with the intention to endanger the integrity, security and sovereignty of the state.[491]

477. It can be anticipated that with this specific legal provision on database protection, computer data will remain protected and secured. This provision can be

489. *Ibid.*
490. Section 19(1)(a), the Digital Security Act, 2018 (Act No. 46 of 2018).
491. Section 27(1)(d), the Digital Security Act, 2018 (Act No. 46 of 2018).

used for cyber security purposes as well. However, it is still uncertain if these databases will receive copyright protection. In the absence of any such provision, the entrepreneurs may face huge financial loss, which may ultimately discourage them from taking similar ventures leading to slow progress towards the government's aspiration of a 'digital Bangladesh'. Even though this issue has not been contested in the domestic courts of law, due to the wide use of computers and the internet and the development of the database industry, it may be anticipated that such things will be an issue of contention in the near future. Besides, due to Article 10(2) of the TRIPS Agreement, with Bangladesh being promoted as a middle-income country very soon, the country will then have to provide protection to databases. Therefore, the copyright authority can take the initiative to clarify its stand regarding the status of copyright protection of the databases.

478. An aggrieved person in Bangladesh may, for the time being, find recourse in different provisions of the Penal Code, 1860. In order to prevent existing employees from copying and using the content of the database in the future, the employment contract should be drafted carefully to prevent data theft. The public, in general, can have access to the database, and they will also be able to copy the content of the database for possible future use. For them, the database entrepreneurs can think to introduce stricter terms and conditions in the database, where a prospective user needs to complete an online agreement containing the rights, obligations, duties, and responsibilities of the parties in a very clear and precise manner even before the use of the content of the database.[492] As click-wrap agreements are declared to be valid in different jurisdictions, such an initiative from the database entrepreneurs may protect them under Bangladesh laws too if they develop the terms and conditions following the basic requirements of a valid agreement.

492. Karim, M.E., *Legal Protection of Databases*, The Daily Star, 7 Jun. 2016, https://www.thedailystar.net/law-our-rights/legal-protection-databases-1235332.

Chapter 4. Legal Protection of Computer Chips

479. Chips are sometimes referred to as the engine in a digital device. Even though the application of computers and other digital devices has increased in many folds in recent years, Bangladesh is not very well-known as a country that produces computer chips. As a result, the legal system has not covered this issue of protection of computer chips, semiconductors or integrated circuits in any law explicitly. From a general online search, it is evident that some local companies have been developing or producing computer chips. But, it is not certain what legal framework that they follow in this regard.

480. Different countries have enacted specific laws in this regard. For example, Malaysia has enacted the Layout-Designs of Integrated Circuits Act, 2006, which defines 'integrated circuit' as a product, whether in its final form or in an intermediate form, in which the elements, at least one of which is an active element, and some or all of the interconnections are integrally formed in and on, or in or on, a piece of material and which is intended to perform an electronic function.

481. The existing patent and design-related law of Bangladesh, i.e., the Patents and Designs Act, 1911 (Act No. II of 1911) is very old, and there was almost no substantive revision in the law even after the independence of the country in 1971. That's why, for obvious reasons, it does not contain any provision on integrated circuits or computer chips or microchips.

482. Section 15 of the Customs Act, 1969 (Act No. IV of 1969) was amended in 2012, and some isolated but relevant provisions were included. Accordingly, it is prohibited to bring into Bangladesh goods or items produced outside Bangladesh involving infringement of layout design of integrated circuits that are intended for sale or use for commercial purposes within the territory of Bangladesh.

483. It may be relevant to share here that the Bangladesh Law Commission prepared the working paper on Patents and Designs Act, 1911 on 14 March 2001 with a view to make the law in line with the TRIPS Agreement which binds Bangladesh as a member of WTO and rightly identified that there is no law on Layout Designs of Integrated Circuits.[493] Nevertheless, when the Final Report on the Patents and Designs Act was submitted in 2003, the provision on 'computer chip' was unfortunately not included. This issue is not even included explicitly in the Draft of the Bangladesh Industrial Design Act, 2016 and in the recently released Patent Bill, 2018. However, in the recently drafted law on 'the Commercial Dispute Resolution Act', the issue of dispute on semiconductor integrated circuits was included within the definition of commercial dispute.

493. Bangladesh Law Commission Report on discussion between Bangladesh delegation and WIPO experts on proposed Patents and Designs Act, Trade Marks and Merchandise Marks Act, Copyright Act, 2000 and other subjects of IPRs within the purview of WTO, Report No. 65, date of submission 11 Dec. 2003.

Chapter 5. Internet Domain Name Registration

§1. Introduction

484. Domain names serve different purposes in the internet ecosystem: they are important in the discussion of internet regulation and governance, they again carry the brand value and function as part of the trademark of the owner. In this modern networked and borderless world, computers and all other digital and IT devices exchange information and respond to each other using IP addresses. An IP address is a series of unique numbers assigned for every single device. Since it is difficult for human beings to remember these unique numbers due to the availability of a burgeoning number of devices, domain name system (DNS) was invented in 1984. The way email address works as an online identity of an individual, domain names and websites serve similar purposes for the organizations.

485. Technically speaking, there are differences between domain names and websites. Moreover, having a domain name is not enough for anyone to make and complete online presence visible. One must need to develop and host a website also to help the netizens to find out the content of a website developed on the domain name. It, again, means that one may own a domain name without having a website. However, a website cannot be hosted without a domain name, free or paid. In the vast ocean of the internet, a Uniform Resource Locator (URL), containing useful information, describes unique addresses about the location on the web. For example, in a URL, i.e., https://www.abc.com/index.html, 'https://' means the language, 'www' indicates server, 'abc.com' is the domain name and 'index.html' indicates the precise location of the page. A URL can be with or without 'www', i.e., in such cases, the 'www' indicates the sub-domain. A URL can even come with or without 'www', and a URL without 'www' indicates the primary server. Moreover, it may be relevant to share here that a URL can contain 'ww2', 'www2', 'www3'.

486. Domain names can be of different types: *generic top-level domains* (gTLDs), e.g., .com (for commercial entities), .org (for organizations), etc., *country-code top-level domains* (ccTLDs), e.g., .bd (for Bangladesh),.my (for Malaysia), etc., and *sponsored top-level domains,* e.g., .gov (for government), .edu (for educational institutes), etc.[494] In any web address or uniform resource locator, e.g., in the web address of Bangladesh National Portal, i.e., https://bangladesh.gov.bd/index.php, 'bangladesh' is the second-level domain within the gTLD and it carries the brand value; '.gov', indicating 'government' is the sponsored top-level domain within the gTLD, and '.bd' is ccTLD.

487. At the international level, a not-for-profit organization of people from all over the world dedicated to keeping the internet secure, stable and interoperable, ICANN was formed in 1998. ICANN, through the Internet Assigned Numbers

---

494. A complete list of domain names is available on the website of Internet Assigned Numbers Authority (IANA). *See*, Root Zone Database, https://www.iana.org/domains/root/db.

Authority (IANA), is responsible for coordinating DNS and thus, play a pivotal role in the expansion and evolution of the internet.[495]

488. ICANN has already assigned more than two thousand registrars who sell domain names to interested persons or organizations.[496] For example, NeuStar, Inc. is the registrar for the.biz domain, VeriSign, Inc. is the registrar for.com domain. The Registrar Accreditation Agreement govern the relationship of ICANN with the registrars.[497] Under the registrars, there are resellers too who, based on their agreements with the registrars, sell domain names and provide web hosting and email mailboxes services. Anyone interested to register a domain name needs to abide by the terms and conditions as mentioned in their agreements with the registrars or resellers. It is important to remember that domain names, by paying the stipulated fees, can be registered for a certain period of time. The registrars allocate a domain name in favour of someone on a 'first come first serve' basis subject to availability of the domain name. For example, one can only register a domain name if none has already registered the same. Again, even if someone has already registered the domain name, it may happen that that domain name is available after the expiry of the registration time if the present owner decides not to continue the domain name. This is how ICANN actually govern billions of websites.

§2. CYBERSQUATTING

489. Since domain names carry the brand value and are seen as a part of the trademark of any company or organization, this has turned to be a matter of serious concern as people have been registering, selling and using domain names based on someone else's trademark in bad faith for making profits later on. Such practice is known as 'cybersquatting' or 'domain squatting' in the legal language. As two identical second-level domain names cannot co-exist under the same gTLD, cybersquatters target the second-level domain name, which carries the brand value and register a confusing second-level domain in bad faith for illegal purposes, such as counterfeit sales, fraud, phishing and online trademark abuses. Cybersquatters sometimes use the 'typosquatting' technique too using which they register a confusingly similar domain of a popular company to cheat netizens. For example, one may register a domain 'SAMSONG' with the aim to cheat general netizens to believe it be the domain of 'SAMSUNG'. Therefore, the issue of 'bad faith' is very important in any dispute of alleged cybersquatting.

490. It has already been shared that the domain name is registered for a certain period of time and a certain amount of fee is to be paid as the registration fee for that purpose. It means that after that certain period, the domain name can be free to

495. ICANN, https://www.icann.org/.
496. ICANN, List of Accredited Registrars, https://www.icann.org/en/accredited-registrars?filter-letter=a&sort-direction=asc&sort-param=name&page=1.
497. The most current Registrar Accreditation Agreement, 2013, https://www.icann.org/resources/pages/approved-with-specs-2013-09-17-en.

register and a cybersquatter may register that domain name if the original owner fails to renew the registration. Moreover, as the law favours the 'prior user' of a trademark in any legal battle,[498] a domain name dispute may arise when two different companies, even without bad faith, want to register the same domain name.

491. In order to resolve the domain name disputes, ICANN has already listed some approved dispute resolution service providers. These are: Arab Center for Domain Name Dispute Resolution, Asian Domain Name Dispute Resolution Centre (ADNDRC), Canadian International Internet Dispute Resolution Centre, the Czech Arbitration Court Arbitration Center for Internet Disputes, and WIPO's Arbitration and Mediation Center. Off these dispute resolution service providers, WIPO the global regulator of trademark revealed that in 2018, with a record 3,447 cases, the cybersquatting cases grew by 12%.[499] In November 2020, WIPO registered 50,000 cybersquatting cases.[500] ADNDRC functions through four operating offices based in Hong Kong (Hong Kong International Arbitration Centre), Seoul (Korea Internet Address Dispute Resolution Committee), Beijing (China International Economic and Trade Arbitration Commission) and Kuala Lumpur (Asian International Arbitration Centre).

492. These dispute resolution service providers follow ICANN's Uniform Domain Name Dispute Resolution Policy (UDRP) to settle domain name disputes between parties and follow the general but very speedy dispute settlement procedure. That is, a complainant will file a complaint in the office of any of the approved dispute resolution service providers, then the provider will review the complaint about formalities, payment, etc., then the respondent will be notified about the complaint and the respondent will get twenty calendar dates to reply, a panel of sole or three members will be appointed, the panel will decide the complaint within fourteen days and notify the decision to parties, ICANN and concerned registrars. The panel may decide to deny the complaint or cancel or transfer the domain name. An appeal can be made within ten days. Finally, ICANN will implement the decision of the panel.

493. It may be relevant to share here that after February 2013, ICANN started a new dispute resolution system known as 'Uniform Rapid Suspension System (URS)', as complements to the UDRP, for the new 'generic' TLD, such as .play,

---

498. In the very recent case of *Md. Anwar Hossain, Proprietor of M/s. Pride Knit Wear Ltd. v. Registrar, Patents, Designs and Trade Mark, Dhaka and another*, 14 SCOB [2019] HCD, the HCD reiterated that '[p]rior use of trade mark and prior application for registration in case of identical marks will go in favour of the prior user'.

499. World Intellectual Property Organization, WIPO Cybersquatting Cases Grow by 12% to Reach New Record in 2018, https://www.wipo.int/pressroom/en/articles/2019/article_0003.html.

500. World Intellectual Property Organization, WIPO's Anti-'Cybersquatting' Service: 50,000 Cases and Growing amid COVID-19 Surge, https://www.wipo.int/pressroom/en/articles/2020/article_0026.html.

.law, .digital, etc. So far, three URS service providers have been selected by ICANN and following the procedure, parties can settle their disputes online.[501]

§3. BANGLADESH AND DOMAIN NAME REGISTRAR

494. Based on the ISO's list, since 2003, ICANN assigned dot bd (.bd) ccTLD name for Bangladesh. Besides, the government started the process to incorporate .বাংলা (dot Bangla) as the International Domain Name (IDN) ccTLD on 21 February 2010.[502] Though the Indian state of West Bengal and Sierra Leone also applied for IDN label – dot bangla (.bangla), ICANN resolved the issue and allocated d .বাংলা (.bangla) as the country's own Unicode domain label in October 2016.

495. The BTCL, formerly known as BTTB and mandated to provide basic telecommunication services throughout the country as it has the largest telecom infrastructure comprising of copper cabling, microwave links, satellite links and optical fibre networks, etc., is an accredited registrar with the IANA,[503] works both as the focal point for ICANN and the registration authority of the ccTLD .bd, .bangla and .বাংলা. BTCL registers domains such as .com.bd (regarding commercial entities and purposes), .org.bd (for not-for-for profit entities), .info.bd (for personal websites of individuals), .net.bd (for ISPs), .edu.bd (for educational institutes, college and universities), .ac.bd (for academic institutes, schools) and .gov.bd (for Bangladesh government entities).

496. Other than BTCL, Bangladeshi firm Innovadeous Pvt. Ltd. (www.rezistro.com) became the first-ever ICANN accredited private domain registrar of the country and anyone interested can register a domain name following certain procedural steps. Purple IT Ltd. (https://www.purpleit.com/) also provides the same service. Bangladesh Domain Hosting Providers Association is an industry association.

497. The domain registration process with BTCL starts with Domain Checker.[504] If the desired domain is available, an individual or an organization needs to sign in to create an account. An individual can start the process by uploading a scanned copy of the National Identification Card or Passport. Additional documents are to be provided for .edu, .gov and .mil domains. For the .edu domain, an approval letter from the Education Board or University Grants Commission is required; for a .gov domain, a forwarding letter from the concerned government office is needed; and for a .mil domain, a forwarding letter from Bangladesh Armed Force is to be submitted.

---

501. Uniform Rapid Suspension System, Internet Corporation for Assigned Names and Numbers, https://newgtlds.icann.org/en/applicants/urs.
502. BTRC Annual Report 2009–2010, p. 24.
503. IANA performs the global coordination of the DNS Root, IP addressing and other IP resources.
504. http://bdia.btcl.com.bd/domain/domainQueryForBuy/searchDomain.jsp.

§4. OFFENCES AND DISPUTE SETTLEMENT

498. No explicit definition of cybersquatting, i.e., the offence of registering the names of a well-known company or brand name with the intention of making a subsequent profit is available in Bangladeshi domestic law. Apparently, the offence is not that rampant in the country too and therefore, even though there are reports of fake or clone websites of popular websites, i.e., spoofing websites published in new media, not a single instance of cybersquatting could be traced.

499. While the issue is not serious for the time being, or the member of Bangladeshi law enforcement agencies have not faced this challenge till now, it may be an issue soon since more and more companies and business entities are taking initiatives to make their online presence visible. Moreover, when the policymakers have been giving emphasis on digital commerce in the country, business entities should be aware of their trademark to maintain the trust and confidence of the consumers. Therefore, it will be relevant to share some relevant issues relating to internet domain name registration here.

500. As the domain name is as good as a trademark, in a country where there is no specific law on deceptive domain name registration or cybersquatting, the law on a trademark can be used in this regard. It can be anticipated that in Bangladesh if such a dispute arises, similar steps will be followed too. If the domain name dispute is the sole matter in the dispute, the parties can decide to follow the UDRP and settle the dispute through the service providers. However, if there are other issues in the trademark dispute and the domain name is one of them, an aggrieved can follow the ordinary court procedure. Trademark related provisions can be found in the Penal Code, 1860 (XLV of 1860) and the Trademark Act, 2009 (Act No. 19 of 2009).

501. The Penal Code, 1860 has contained various provisions prohibiting the use of false trademark and property mark, counterfeiting of a trademark or property mark used by others, making or possession of any instrument for counterfeiting a trademark or property mark, selling of goods marked with a counterfeit trademark or property mark, and making of a false mark upon any receptacle containing goods.[505] Anyone shall be criminally liable for all these activities, and the law provides for punishment by way of imprisonment and fine.

502. In *Nabisco Biscuit and Bread Factory Ltd. v. Baby Food Products Ltd. and another*, 2005, 34 CLC (HCD) [4780] = 58 DLR (2006) 287, Md Imman Ali J pronounced that:

> The purpose of registration of trade marks is to enable a seller's merchandise to be protected from unscrupulous and dishonest copy, which would then be supplied to the market by other traders. The system is geared to protecting the items under registered trade mark and also for protecting the reputation of the

505. Sections 478, 479, 480, 481, 484, 485 and 486, the Penal Code, 1980 (XLV of 1860).

manufacturer of those registered items. The system is also geared to protect the expense and trouble taken by the manufacturer to establish the goodwill of his business and product, so that others will not steal away that goodwill and reputation by producing a commodity and registering a trade mark for it, which is so similar to that of the earlier registered trade mark that the consumer is deceived and/or confused.

503. Since the word 'mark' is defined as device, brand, heading, label, ticket, name, signature, word, letter, symbol, numeral, figurative elements, a combination of colours or any combination under the Trademark Act, 2009 (Act No. 19 of 2009), any domain name registered to offer goods and services to deceive people may be treated as 'false trade description'.[506]

504. Anyone interested may consider registering one or more tradename of her registered trademarks as her domain name and use the same on the website created. However, it seems that BTCL will be careful in registering any domain name which uses or contains a well-known trademark, even if of a different class, and has the scope to confuse others. Yet, if such a domain name is mistakenly registered, it will not be sustained in the court of law if contested. In the case of *Sunil Kumar Das v. Deputy Registrar of Trade Marks and another*, 27 BLD (HCD) (2007) 423=36 CLC (HCD) [8473], a Bangladeshi manufacturer and merchant of Hosiery product wanted to register his trademark 'CANNON' and opposed by the owner of trademark 'CANON', belonging to Canon Kabushiki Kaisha, Japan that has been using the trademark 'CANON' and LOGO since 1954 throughout the world and obtained registration of the said mark in many countries, including Bangladesh. Moreover, they have been using the mark already in different kinds of goods including hosiery goods. Therefore, it was argued that this Japanese company became the absolute owner of the said trademark in Bangladesh for all kinds of hosiery goods and as such nobody else in Bangladesh has any right to adopt or use the word 'CANON' or any other word or words which are likely to cause, confusion and deception in the course of trade for hosiery goods. The Registrar of Trade Marks found grounds in the claim of the Japanese company and denied the application of the petitioner. The Deputy Registrar of Trade Marks and the HCD were convinced that the Japanese owner of CANON trademark is the prior user of the mark and held that the petitioner 'adopted the mark by way of imitation, and between the two marks Canon and Cannon there has been no difference phonetically and in pronunciation', the use of the mark by the petitioner is not 'bona fide', without any 'appreciable reason', such a practice 'will give rise to confusion' and the conduct of the petitioner is not 'proper'. When the petitioner, being aggrieved by the decision of the HCD, made an appeal in the AD, the AD dismissed the appeal and upheld the decision of the HCD as such use of the same name 'Cannon' 'will create confusion in the minds of the consumer who are likely to be misled by such name of a foreign company'.[507]

---

506. Section 2(23), the Trademark Act, 2009 (Act No. 19 of 2009).

507. *Sunil Kumar Das v. Deputy Registrar of Trade Marks and another*, V ADC (2008) 202=37 CLC (AD) [2553]. *See also*, *Md. Nazrul Islam v. National Fans Limited and another*, 2009, 38 CLC

505. As we have been living virtually in a borderless world where due to the presence of giant e-commerce sites, which can be accessed through the internet, it will be interesting to see how the registrar of trademark or the domestic court interprets a situation when a well-known trademark is registered in other parts of the world, but not in Bangladesh and the products are sold online by Bangladeshi consumers from home or by a relative from abroad and bring the product for use in Bangladesh. In the case of *Bally Schutrabriken Ag, Switzerland v. Hosnara Begum*, 1999, 28 CLC (HCD) [4721] = 52 DLR (2000) 546, in a dispute relating to the registration of a trademark of shoes with the name 'BALLY' was challenged by Bally Schutrabriken Ag, Switzerland when the Bangladesh trader, Messrs Hosnara Begum applied for the registration of the trademark with the same name. It was claimed that the trademark 'BALLY' had been in use in products, including shoes, since 1851 first in Switzerland and became their property as it had been registered in more than 100 countries of the world and initiative was taken for its registration, after the respondent, in Bangladesh also. The respondent denied the claim by stating her good faith and adoption of the mark in the same name which means a flower, Jasmine in Bangla. Besides, it was contended that the petitioner had never used the marks in Bangladesh and had never sold their goods with the trademark in dispute in the Bangladesh market. The court revealed that the petitioner could not establish that they had ever exported or marketed their products in Bangladesh, their products were popular in the country because of their high quality, their trademark was never in use in Bangladesh and they failed to produce any sale figure to show that they have any local market of the trademark. Thus, according to Syed Amirul Islam J., mere registration of their trademark in foreign countries will not allow anyone to stop someone registering the same in Bangladesh unless it can be established, along with the above-mentioned grounds, that 'the public or a common man in this country will in any way be deceived or confused while' purchasing such goods.

506. BTCL in .bd & .বাংলা domain name registration agreement makes this clear in the very beginning by specifically mentioning that it is the responsibility of the prospective registrant to check and investigate if his selected domain infringes the legal rights of others. It should be remembered that BTCL's authority lies only with .bd & .বাংলা domain names even though the use of these domain names, unfortunately, are not very popular in the country, and leading local companies of most of the sectors have been using gTLDs.

507. It is to be noted that the registration of a trademark is important as registration of a trademark gives the registrant thc cxclusive right to the use of the trademark, subject to any terms and conditions, in relation to those goods or services, and to obtain relief in respect of infringement of the trademark.[508] Nevertheless, section 30 of the Trade Marks Act, 2009 (Act No. 19 of 2009) provides that priority of use of this mark gets paramount consideration compared to registration.[509] The

---

(AD) [3562] = 16 MLR (AD) (2011) 420; *Baby Food Products Ltd. v. Nabisco Biscuit and Bread Factory and another*, 2008, 37 CLC (AD) [2760] = 28 BLD (AD) (2008) 210.

508. Section 25(1) and 25(3), the Trademark Act, 2009 (Act No. 19 of 2009).

509. *BBC v. Registrar, DPDTM & ors State*, 4 SCOB [2015] HCD 89.

right created in favour of a registered proprietor of a trademark is not an absolute right and is subservient to other provisions of the Act. In other words, registration of a trademark does not provide a defence to the proceedings for passing off as stipulated under section 24 of the Act, 2009. A prior user of a trademark can maintain an action for passing off against any subsequent use of an identical trademark including a registered user thereof.[510]

508. As per the conditions stipulated in the domain name registration agreement, the registrant must agree to use BTCL services only for lawful purposes. BTCL, as the registration authority of .bd and .bangla domain name has the authority to cancel or suspend the licence if BTCL services are used to post, *inter alia*, copyright, trademark, patent, trade secret or other intellectual property infringement, including but not limited to, offering pirated computer programs or links to such programs, serial or registration numbers for software programs, copyrighted music, copyrighted images; copyrighted texts, etc.

509. Recently, the Facebook authority started a legal action against one domain name 'facebook.com.bd', owned by A1 Software Limited, which was registered by BTCL. While investigating, it was revealed that BTRC registered the domain name in 2008 when Facebook was not that popular in the country and BTRC used to manage the register manually and that's how the domain name was registered. However, it can be anticipated that this issue will be taken care of and the domain name of 'facebook.com.bd' will be cancelled.

510. This is apparently a good solution as the domain name was registered with BTCL. However, affected parties have to suffer if such domain names are not registered with BTCL and in such instances, BTCL has nothing to do. Besides, suspension or termination of the domain name may not be an effective solution as these can be re-registered almost immediately using the services of other registrars. In such a situation, the avenues offered by UDRP can be considered. For the Bangladeshi organizations, it may be easy to proceed to ADNDRC, which has been operating its businesses from four different offices located in four Asian cities, i.e., Kuala Lumpur, Beijing, Hong Kong and Seoul.

510. *Ibid.*

Part III. ICT Contracts

§1. Introduction

511. This Part will cover discussion on the general principles of the law of contract, sale of goods and product liability in the Bangladesh context. These issues are primarily covered through the provisions of the Contract Act, 1872 (Act No. IX of 1872), the Specific Relief Act, 1877 (Act No. I of 1877), the Sale of Goods Act, 1930 (Act No. III of 1930), the Partnership Act, 1932 (Act No. IX of 1932) and the Consumers' Rights Protection Act (Act No. 26 of 2009), etc. This part will also shed light on various aspects of an agreement, which are common for all kinds of agreements, including telecommunication and ICT-related agreements covered in this part.

§2. Law of Contract in a Nutshell

512. The Contract Act, 1872 (Act No. IX of 1872), principally based on the common law of England having its roots in the real estate property law,[511] is one of the very old legislation still in force in Bangladesh. It was enacted in 1872 and contains important provisions on various aspects of agreements and contracts. The provisions of this law do not affect the provisions of any Statute, Act or Regulation not expressly repealed, nor any usage or custom of trade, nor any incident of any contract, which are not inconsistent with the provisions of this Act.[512]

513. It can be seen that the parties to general ICT contracts such as software contracts in Bangladesh tend to execute MoU instead of a formal contract which can be seen as usage or custom of trade and thus, can serve the purpose of a contract. Under domestic law, for its enforceability, an agreement does not need to follow any specific format and thus, an agreement can be made orally also.[513] Moreover, even though registration has a positive impact and consequence in protecting the rights

511. Law Commission of India, Contract Act, 1872, Thirteenth Report, p. 1 (1958).
512. Section 1, the Contract Act, 1872 (Act No. IX of 1872).
513. In *Rezanur Rahman and others v. Al-haj Ahmed Hossain Khan*, 6 BLD (HCD) 14, it was held that oral contract is as valid as written contract. But in the matter of oral contract, once it is denied by one of the parties, a very heavy onus of proof lies on the other party in proving the contract.

of the parties to the contract, the Registration law of the country, i.e., the Registration Act, 1908 (Act No. XVI of 1908) does not require the mandatory registration of an agreement unless the subject matter of the agreement is an immovable property.

514. In the available literature, the two terms, i.e., 'agreement' and 'contract' are used as synonyms frequently. Nonetheless, under the Contract Act, 1872 (Act No. IX of 1872), these two terms have different meanings with different legal consequences. The law only considers any 'agreement' as a 'contract' if that is enforceable by law.[514] However, in order to be an agreement which can be legally enforceable; in an agreement, there needs to have a proposal, which is the expression of willingness of one person to do or to abstain from doing anything with a view to obtain the assent of that other to such act or abstinence.[515] Once such a proposal is accepted by the person to whom it was made, it becomes a promise.[516] The basic principle of offer and acceptance is that the offer is binding upon the offeror (proposer) the moment the offeree (acceptor) puts the acceptance into motion.[517] An acceptance, under section 7 of the Contract Act, 1872, must be expressed in some usual and reasonable manner and communicated unless the proposal prescribes a particular manner in which it is to be accepted.[518] Finally, the law says that 'every promise and every set of promises, forming the consideration for each other, is an agreement',[519] and an agreement which can be enforced legally shall be treated as a contract.

515. In simple terms, a contract starts with (a) a proposal, which is the willingness of one party to do or to abstain from doing something, followed by (b) a promise, which is the acceptance of the proposal. The promise turns to (c) an agreement, which, if can be enforced legally, becomes a contract.

516. Under the Contract Act, 1872 (Act No. IX of 1872), along with the valid agreement, which is enforceable by law, an agreement can be either *void*, i.e., not enforceable by law or *voidable*, i.e., enforceable by law at the option of one or more of the parties, but not at the option of the other.[520] For example, it is provided that every agreement in restrain of the marriage of any person, other than a minor, is void.[521]

517. It may be relevant to share here that the Competition Act, 2012 (Act No. XXIII of 2012) has adopted the definition of 'contract' as defined in section 2(h) of

514. Section 2(h), the Contract Act, 1872 (Act No. IX of 1872).
515. Section 2(a), the Contract Act, 1872 (Act No. IX of 1872).
516. Section 2(b), the Contract Act, 1872 (Act No. IX of 1872).
517. *Fatema Enterprise v. Bangladesh & ors.*, 8 SCOB [2016] HCD 59.
518. *Bangladesh Muktijoddah Kalyan Trust, represented by the Managing Director v. Kamal Trading Agency and others*, 18 BLD(AD) 99.
519. Section 2(b), the Contract Act, 1872 (Act No. IX of 1872).
520. Section 2(g) & 2(i), the Contract Act, 1872 (Act No. IX of 1872).
521. Section 26, the Contract Act, 1872 (Act No. IX of 1872).

the Contract Act, 1872 and extended the definition for the purpose of the Competition Act, 2012 to mean the understanding or consensus, formal or informal, written or unwritten, explicit or implicit, whatever it may be, and whether it may be enforceable by law or not, for purchase, sale, production, supply, distribution, control, or storage, as the case may be, of goods or services; and also includes the followings, namely:

(1) tie-in-arrangement;
(2) exclusive supply agreement;
(3) exclusive distribution agreement;
(4) refusal to the transaction;
(5) resale price maintenance.[522]

§3. Elements of a Contract

518. There are some elements of a valid contract. First of all, the parties to a contract must attain the age of majority, have sound mind, i.e., at the time of making the contract he/she should be capable of understanding the contract and form a rational judgment about the contract as to its effect, and should not be disqualified from contracting by any law.[523] Moreover, there must have free consent of the parties competent to contract, lawful consideration[524] and a lawful object. With these elements, it is also required that a contract cannot be declared to be void expressly.[525] With regard to free consent, it is provided that consent will be treated as a free consent if it is not caused by coercion (as defined in section 15), undue influence (as defined in section 16), fraud (as defined in section 17), misrepresentation (as defined in section 18), or mistake (subject to the provisions of sections 20, 21 and 22).[526] With all these, the meaning of the agreements must be or capable of being made certain.[527] Moreover, an agreement is to be made regarding an act which is possible to perform.[528]

519. It must be remembered that a contract or a term thereof may be invalid because its substance or purpose is contrary to public policy or because of its coercive method of procurement, which is contrary to public policy.[529] The word 'public policy' is not easy to define but may include any injustice, oppression, restraint of liberty, commerce and natural or legal right, whatever tends to the obstruction of

522. Section 2(g)(ii), the Competition Act, 2012 (Act No. XXIII of 2012).
523. Sections 11 & 12, the Contract Act, 1872 (Act No. IX of 1872).
524. Section 25, the Contract Act, 1872 (Act No. IX of 1872).
525. Section 10, the Contract Act, 1872 (Act No. IX of 1872).
526. Section 14, the Contract Act, 1872 (Act No. IX of 1872).
527. Section 29, the Contract Act, 1872 (Act No. IX of 1872).
528. Section 56, the Contract Act, 1872 (Act No. IX of 1872).
529. *World Tel Bangladesh Ltd v. Ministry of Post and Telecommunications*, 11 BLC (AD) 37.

justice or to the violation of the statute and whatever against good morals when made the object of a contract and therefore, void and not susceptible of enforcement.[530]

§4. Breach of Contract and Remedies Available

520. The law regulating contractual obligations, i.e., the Contract Act, 1872, plays a crucial role in various stages in the ICT and telecommunication landscape. The breach of contractual terms may have adverse consequences of various nature. When the term of a contract is breached, it gives rise to two reliefs, namely, compensation or specific performance. Where the contract cannot be specifically enforced, the relief available is compensation. Such compensation is not to be given for any remote and indirect loss or damage sustained by reason of the breach.[531]

521. In a case involving the treatment of the patient by a physician and subsequent surgery by another physician by taking a false consent letter and applying forceful anaesthesia, the AD of Bangladesh Supreme Court evaluated the elements of, *inter alia*, breach of contract. According to the AD, in a case of breach of contract, it is to be considered that a mere breach of contract cannot give rise to criminal prosecution. The breach of contract depends upon the intention of the accused at the time of alleged inducement, which must be judged by his subsequent actions. The vital factor to be considered is whether, at the time of the agreement, there was an intention to carry out the terms of the contract or not. If there is nothing to show that there was no intention at the time of agreement which was arrived at, but the failure to fulfil the terms of the agreement was the subsequent event, it would only be a case of breach of contract.[532]

522. If any party to a contract fails to perform his obligations under the contract/agreement, the aggrieved person has a few remedies available under the domestic law of the land. First of all, the aggrieved person may prefer to file a money suit or civil suit for damages as a suit of civil nature under section 9 of the Code of Civil Procedure, 1908. Besides, he can file a suit for specific performance of the contract under section 12 of the Specific Relief Act, 1877 (Act No. I of 1877). Under this section, the specific performance of any contract may, in the discretion of the Court, be enforced when (1) there exists no standard for ascertaining the actual damage caused by non-performance of the act agreed to be done, and (2) the act agreed to be done is such that pecuniary compensation for its non-performance would not afford adequate relief; or (3) it is probable that pecuniary compensation cannot be got for the non-performance of the act agreed to be done.[533] It is to be noted that unless and until the contrary is proved, the Court shall presume that the breach of

530. *World Tel Bangladesh Ltd. v. Bangladesh & Ors*, 20 BLT (AD) 108.
531. Section 73, the Contract Act, 1872 (Act No. IX of 1872).
532. *Prof. Dr. Motior Rahman v. The State & anr.*, 3 SCOB [2015] AD 1, at pp. 3–4.
533. Section 12, the Specific Relief Act, 1877 (Act No. I of 1877).

a contract to transfer immovable property cannot be adequately relieved by compensation in money and that the breach of a contract to transfer moveable property can be thus relieved.[534]

523. Nevertheless, there are some contracts which cannot be enforced specifically. These are the contract (a) for the non-performance of which compensation in money is an adequate relief; (b) which runs into such minute or numerous details, or which is so dependent on the personal qualifications or volition of the parties, or otherwise from its nature is such, that the Court cannot enforce specific performance of its material terms; (c) the terms of which the Court cannot find with reasonable certainty; (d) which is in its nature revocable; (e) made by trustees either in excess of their powers or in breach of their trust; (f) made by or on behalf of a corporation or public company created for special purposes, or by the promoters of such company, which is in excess of its powers; (g) the performance of which involves the performance of a continuous duty extending over a longer period than three years from its date; (h) of which a material is part of the subject matter, supposed by both parties to exist, has, before it has been made, ceased to exist. Moreover, subject to the Arbitration law, no contract to refer present or future differences to arbitration shall be specifically enforced; but if any person who has made such a contract other than an arbitration agreement to which the provisions of the said Act apply and has refused to perform it sues in respect of any subject which he has contracted to refer, the existence of such contract shall bar the suit.[535]

524. In the country, many people have been working to provide outsourced services. The HCD has covered the whole issue in the following manner. Outsourcing services is a new concept in our country. Both labour and professional services may be procured through outsourcing. It is a process by which the recipient of service enters into an agreement with a contractor/service provider who engages persons to render services to the service recipient. In such a situation, there is an employment contract between the service recipient and the service renderer. The contract exists between the service recipient and the contractor and consideration for the services are provided by the service recipient to the contractor. If the service recipient is not satisfied with the service rendered by the persons engaged by the contractor, then his remedy lies for breach of the terms and conditions of the agreement against the contractor. Likewise, if the contractor does not receive adequate consideration for providing his service through his appointed employees, his remedy lies against the service recipient. The service recipient is generally not concerned about who renders the service to him as long as the service sought is rendered adequately. As can be reasonably expected, the service recipient may set certain criteria and conditions to be observed by the service renderer, and he has the discretion to reject any person through whom the service is provided by the contractor, but in all such cases, the matter is governed by the contract between the service recipient and contractor. It is a contract of services as opposed to a contract of employment.[536]

---

534. Explanation to s. 12, the Specific Relief Act, 1877 (Act No. I of 1877).
535. Section 21, the Specific Relief Act, 1877 (Act No. I of 1877).
536. *Grameenphone Ltd. v. Chairman, First Labour Court, Dhaka & ors.*, 10 SCOB [2018] HCD 7.

525. For the remedies of the individuals against any organization, it will be relevant to settle whether that person is a worker or an employee. If someone works or is recognized as a worker, he should avail the remedies available under the labour law of the land, i.e., the Bangladesh Labour Act, 2006, and file a case against the organization in the Labour Court. However, if he is recognized as an employee, he should move to the civil court for his service or employment-related remedies.

526. There are professional bodies for both the organizations such as BASIS, ISPAB, BACCO and e-CAB, and the individuals such as the Institute of Engineers, Bangladesh. All these organizations are at liberty to take disciplinary actions against their registered members, if and when needed, as per the rules and regulations of the professional body. These rules and regulations are self-regulatory in nature, and so, any aggrieved can also consider exploiting these forums to settle their disputes regarding the breach of contract.

527. It is always advised that for professional services, one should follow proper formalities to make the contract. Even though registration of contract for service or moveable property is not required under the Registration Act, 1908 (Act No. 16 of 1908), the terms and conditions of the agreements should ideally be incorporated in the non-judicial stamp valued BDT 300,[537] and the choice of law should be mentioned as Bangladesh explicitly. Most importantly, in the case of the software and ITES development agreement, the issues of intellectual property, e.g., copyright and patent, should be mentioned explicitly.

528. Under the Limitation Act, an aggrieved party must move to the court within one year of the date of the breach of contractual terms.[538] However, in the case of a continuing breach of contract and in the case of a continuing wrong independent of contract, a fresh period of limitation begins to run at every moment of the time during which the breach or the wrong, as the case may be, continues.[539] For specific performance of a contract, for the recession of a contract and for compensation for the breach of any contract, express or implied, not in writing registered and not herein specially provided for, the limitation period is three years. But, the limitation period will be six years for compensation for the breach of a contract in writing and registered.[540]

529. The organization, Business Initiative Leading Development, carried out a problem-tree analysis regarding the enforcement of business contracts in Bangladesh. It was revealed that the main problems are: (1) faulty drafting of a contract can leave the room open for arising of disputes; (2) unscrupulous business entities sometimes make false or vexatious claims to inconvenience their counterparts; (3) case management by the court has certain shortcomings, e.g., lack of distinction

---

537. Section 3 & First Schedule, the Stamp Act, 1899 (Act No. II of 1899). It may be relevant to share here that under s. 35 of the Stamp Act, 1899, an instrument which is not duly stamped is not admissible in evidence.
538. Section 3 & First Schedule, the Limitation Act, 1908 (Act No. IX of 1908).
539. Section 23, the Limitation Act, 1908 (Act No. IX of 1908).
540. Section 3 & First Schedule, the Limitation Act, 1908 (Act No. IX of 1908).

between complex and simple cases; (4) forum shopping and interlocutory matters, i.e., parties can drag a case through several levels of the judiciary; (5) repeated adjournments and low penalty for non-abidance with time limits; (6) lack of use in digital technology; (7) lack of adequate coverage on commercial law in curriculum; and (8) lack of wider usage of ADR, etc.[541]

530. After identifying these problems, the Organization has come up with some short- and long-term recommendations to resolve the problems with contract enforcement. The short-term recommendations included: (1) establishment of a multi-tier system for case management; (2) establishment of specialized Commercial Courts at divisional level; (3) organizing pre-trial case management conference; (4) reducing the number of permissible adjournments and forum shopping as well as appeal; (5) raising of cost orders; (6) clearer understanding about enforcing contracts among key stakeholders; (7) a detailed study on enforcing contracts; and (8) reform of ADR.[542]

531. Looking at the drafting history of the Contract Act, 1872, it may be relevant to share here that Sir James Stephen who moved the Indian Contract Bill, did not intend it to be a complete code and expected that supplementary chapters would be enacted later on.[543] Unfortunately, this did not happen, and therefore, except for repealing the parts on sale of goods and partnership and replacing them with the specific statute, i.e., the Sale of Goods Act, 1930 and the Partnership Act, 1932, one may be shocked to note that Contract Act, 1872 has not been updated at all in the last one hundred and fifty years. It is therefore high time to revisit the law immediately considering the complexities of modern time.

---

541. Ferdaus Ara Begum, Policy change needed for enforcing business contracts, the Financial Express, 3 Mar. 2018, https://www.thefinancialexpress.com.bd/views/policy-change-needed-for-enforcing-business-contracts-1520092759.
542. *Ibid.*
543. Law Commission of India, Contract Act, 1872, Thirteenth Report, p. 3 (1958). To know the historical background of the Indian Contract Act, 1872, please *see*, Atul Chandra Patra, *Historical Background of the Indian Contract Act, 1872,* 4(3) J. Indian L. Inst., 373–400 (1962).

Chapter 1. Hardware and Software Contracts

532. The term 'hardware' is generally used to mean the physical parts of a computer which can be touched. Hardware is the devices that are used to give input and output and to store and process data and information. Examples of such physical parts or hardware include a keyboard, mouse, headset, printer, digital camera, monitor, etc.

533. Regarding any computer hardware-related contracts and their consequences, it can be inferred that the parties need to follow the relevant provisions of the Contract Act, 1872 (Act No. IX of 1872), the Sale of Goods Act, 1930 (Act No. III of 1930) and the Competition Act, 2012 (Act No. XXIII of 2012) discussed in previous Chapters along with other government and industry-specific regulations. For example, BTRC has issued an Instruction regarding the establishment of a factory to produce or assemble mobile phone handsets locally in August 2017. Besides, the BCS, the IT Industry Association of Bangladesh, has introduced the MRP Policy, 2018 and Warranty Policy, 2018 relating to computer hardware.

534. The MRP Policy, 2018, a self-regulation tool, came into force on 22 July 2018, applicable for all members of BCS and all businessmen dealing with ICT products, was adopted to protect the interest of the producers, importers, distributors and retailers dealing with computers, computer hardware and accessories and the interest of the consumers to ensure their satisfaction. Therefore, while developing ICT hardware-related contracts, these documents should be considered.

535. Bangladesh is a lucrative destination for software development projects. It is a popular practice that the companies, before developing software, will usually draft a formal vendor agreement or contract or MoU containing important and relevant provisions. Depending on the nature of the assignment, any software-related contract usually contains provisions relating to the rights and obligations of the parties, dispute settlement, and payment etc. In so doing, like hardware contracts, all the relevant provisions of the Contract Act, 1872 (Act No. IX of 1872), the Sale of Goods Act, 1930 (Act No. III of 1930), the Limitation Act, 1908 (Act No. IX of 1908), and the Competition Act, 2012 (Act No. XXIII of 2012) discussed in previous chapters along with other government and industry-specific regulations should be followed for the execution of software-related agreements.

536. It, however, should be remembered that a software contract has some distinctive features compared to other types of contracts as the purchasers or customers may need to get the services and/or assistance of the developers even after the completion of the work. Also, during the development stage, the developers should perform various tests, e.g., integration tests, system tests and user acceptance tests, etc., to ensure that the software under the development process is capable to serve the intended purposes. Moreover, the uniques issues involved in the online supply of software without any physical hardware and cloud-based software-as-a-service should also be considered.[544] Therefore, both the parties to such a contract need to be careful before setting the terms of the contract to avoid the consequences of breach of contract. Otherwise, it may happen that the customers may include some provisions which will bind the developer to serve even after the termination of the contract without payment or the customer may face problems in running the software properly but needs to enter into another contract.

537. Subject to the provisions relating to void agreements as available in different laws of the land, generally in the Contract Act, 1872, parties to a software contract are free to incorporate any provisions in the agreement to reflect and give effect to their agreed terms and conditions. Nevertheless, it can be seen that, along with the general provisions common to all agreements, a software agreement specifically contains provisions on- (a) commencement date of the agreement, (b) the deliverables or scope of services, (c) specifications on the use of technological architecture e.g., provisions relating to application model, database server, development tool, reporting tools, etc. (d) duration of service including testing, after sales support and maintenance services, (e) cost or charges and modes of payment for the services, support and maintenance, (f) handover of source code and relevant documents, (g) provisions relating to new releases or updates of the software during the period of agreement, (h) requests for changes in the future, (i) termination of the agreement, (j) confidentiality, ownership and protection of personal data/information, (k) governing laws, (l) indemnity and limitation of liability, (m) force majeure, (n) warrenties, and (o) dispute resolution, etc. Moreover, following standard business ethical practices, provisions prohibiting the undertaking of similar software development assignments in the future from the competitors can also be included.

538. The contract law or registration-related law of the country do not require that the contract of service such as a single software development contract should be registered mandatorily since such services are not related to immovable property. However, even though it is not legally required to register any such contract relating to immovable property mandatorily and the parties also do not do so, the parties to the contract should consider following the legal requirements and formalities and carefully stipulate them in the terms and conditions of the agreement to avoid future legal hassles.

539. Any person/ victim in relation to software contract can consider filing a money suit or suit for specific performance of contracts against other parties to the contract if that party fails to perform the terms of the contract. With regard to employees, along with taking care of the requirements of the existing labour laws containing provisions on the rights and responsibilities of an employee, e.g., safe

544. In an interesting recent landmark decision and in the context of software providers and resellers when software are supplied by electronic means and not though any physical hardware, the Court of Justice of the EU, held that the supply, in return for payment of a fee, of computer software to a customer by electronic means where that supply is accompanied by the grant of a perpetual licence to use that software will be considered as 'goods' under Article 1(2) of Council Directive 86/653/EEC of 18 December 1986 relating to self-employed commercial agents. See, *The Software Incubator Ltd. v. Computer Associates (UK) Ltd*, Case C-410/19, ECLI:EU:C:2021:742.

and healthy working environment, salary, benefits, working hours, it will be important to include provisions in the employment contract on breach of trust, breach of confidence, trade secrets, ownership of the copyright of software coding and patent, protection of personal information, etc.

Chapter 2. Turnkey Contracts

540. Theoretically, in a 'turnkey contract' which can be related to any goods or services or the combination of goods and services, the contractor takes the whole responsibility to complete the project and make it operational for the client who can use the service immediately. Turnkey contracts are more popular in the case of energy-related matters where a contractor assumes all responsibilities, designs and constructs any facility relating to drilling and operation of oil or gas reserve and handover the project fully operational to the client for immediate use.

541. In relation to ICT, turnkey contracts can be seen in developing and installing software or computer system at an agreed price, within the duration of a contract period. It has been revealed that some local companies have developed expertise in such agreements. For example, Bangladeshi company 'Dataedge' has completed some major turnkey ICT projects such as Bangladesh Automated Clearing House (BACH), Machine Readable Passport and VISA, Payment Card Solutions and Core Banking Systems for Banks and Call Centre Solutions for Telco's, etc.

542. Turnkey contracts can be seen in the case of large or complex contracts of goods and related services and/or works and physical services. For example, the design, construction, installation of equipment for manufacturing process plants, commissioning of a new refined edible oil bottling factory, industrial plants or the procurement of major computer and communications systems or construction and commissioning of a planetarium.[545] For the private sector ICT turnkey contracts, there is no specific or separate law. Nevertheless, for obvious reasons, the provisions of the contract law, as discussed above, shall be applicable.

543. In Bangladesh, the Public Procurement Rules, 2008 as formulated under section 70 of the Public Procurement Act, 2006 (Act No. 24 of 2006) describes the nature of Turnkey. It is provided that in a turnkey contract, a Contractor is responsible for design, construction, procurement and installation of equipment and commissioning may require additional qualification information. Similarly, a contract for the provision of operational services, such as security or catering services may require additional or different information to be provided.[546]

544. In relation to public procurement, it is provided that the two-stage tendering method can be used by a procurement entity in the case of turnkey contracts or contracts for large complex facilities, such as the supply, installation and commissioning of processing plants, or works of complex nature or communication technology, etc.,[547] and procurement of major computer and communications systems.[548] The two-stage tendering can be considered as it may be impractical to

545. Regulation 19, the Procedures for Implementation of the Public Procurement Regulations 2003.
546. Rules 50, the Public Procurement Rules, 2008.
547. Rules 65, the Public Procurement Rules, 2008.
548. Regulation 19, the Public Procurement Regulations, 2003.

prepare complete technical specifications in advance and where alternative technical approaches may be available to meet a procuring entity's needs.[549]

545. Regulation 39 of the Public Procurement Regulations, 2003 provides for the steps to be followed in the two-stage tendering method. It says:

(1) When a procuring entity engages in two-stage tendering, it shall, in the first stage, invite unpriced technical proposals on the basis of a tender document outlining a conceptual design and/or a stipulated performance specification. In addition to indicating the contractual terms and conditions of supply, the tender document shall establish the criteria for determination of tender responsiveness, which shall include:
   (a) the relative managerial and technical competence of the tenderer;
   (b) the effectiveness and future adaptability of the proposal submitted by the tenderer in meeting the procurement needs of a procuring entity.

(2) In response to the invitation, tenderers shall submit proposals describing the technical performance, quality or other characteristics of the goods, works or services that they consider best suited to meet a procuring entity's procurement needs in addition to commenting on the contractual terms and conditions of supply. A procuring entity shall, at this stage, review all the tenders with the assistance of the Tender Evaluation Committee and retain only the responsive tenders and engage in individual confidential discussions with each of the responsive tenderers concerning any aspect of their proposals excluding price. At the end of these discussions, a procuring entity shall issue a 'Minute of Tender Adjustments' to each individual responsive tenderer that will outline the changes required in its tender's specification and/or design as agreed with a procuring entity for incorporation in the second stage tender. A procuring entity shall treat all first stage tenders, including the discussions with individual tenderers, in such a manner so as to avoid disclosure of their contents to any other competing tenderer.

(3) In the second stage, a procuring entity shall revise the tender document and stipulate the detailed evaluation criteria for the second stage tenders which shall include cost of ownership during the useful lifetime of the object of the procurement, where applicable, and invite all responsive tenderers from the first stage to submit their priced 'best and final' tenders in accordance with the requirements of the second stage tender documents and the individual 'Minutes of Tender Adjustments' issued to each tenderer.

(4) Notwithstanding Regulations 39(1), 39(2) and 39(3) all other steps in processing such competitions including the award of a contract based on tenders submitted in the second stage shall follow the provisions of Chapter V.

---

549. *Ibid.*

Chapter 3. Other Contracts

§1. Distribution Agreements

546. The distributors perform their duties in the same way as an agent of any business entity. In Bangladesh, the law of distribution or agency is covered under Chapter X (sections 182–238) of the Contract Act, 1872 (Act No. IX of 1872). A distributor as an 'agent', is a person employed to do any act for another or to represent another in dealings with third persons.[550] The person or business entity for whom or which an agent works is known as 'principal'. Both the agent and principal must have similar legal qualifications as are required to enter into an agreement except consideration is not necessary.[551]

547. The authority of an agent can be *express*, i.e., established by way of spoken or written words, or *implied*, which is to be inferred from the circumstances of the case.[552] An agent has the authority to do every lawful thing, as stipulated in the terms and conditions of the agreement, necessary for the purpose of carrying on a business.[553] Moreover, in an emergency, an agent as an ordinary person of prudence can do anything to protect the principal from loss.[554] For an act for which the agent undertook the responsibility to act personally, he cannot appoint another as a sub-agent. On several grounds, an agency can be terminated. These are: revocation by the principal or agent, when the assignment is completed, death or unsoundness of the parties, insolvency of the principal, etc.[555]

548. An agent is paid by his principal only, to whom he owes his contractual duty. An agent will be in a situation of conflict of interest and dishonesty, and it will be tantamount to an underhand dealing if he receives any remuneration from a third party unless it is stipulated between the principal and another party that the responsibility of making payment of commission to the agent shall lie on the other party.[556] In the absence of a contract regarding the liability of the agent, the agent cannot personally be liable for the work done by him on behalf of his principal and an agent is not liable to answer the claims arising out of wrong done by their principals.[557]

550. Section 182, the Contract Act, 1872 (Act No. IX of 1872).
551. Sections 183–185, the Contract Act, 1872 (Act No. IX of 1872).
552. Sections 186 and 187, the Contract Act, 1872 (Act No. IX of 1872).
553. Section 188, the Contract Act, 1872 (Act No. IX of 1872).
554. Section 189, the Contract Act, 1872 (Act No. IX of 1872).
555. Section 201, the Contract Act, 1872 (Act No. IX of 1872).
556. *See*, ss 217 and 226, the Contract Act, 1872 (Act No. IX of 1872). *S.M. Faziul Haque v. Salahuddin Ahmed and another*, 22 BLD (HCD) 155.
557. *Bangladesh Chemical Industries Corporation and another v. M. V. Kayo Alkyon and others*, 7 BLD (HCD) 1.

549. Usually, in any distribution agreement, all the general provisions relating to agreement/contract under the law of contract as discussed above should be followed. Apart from these general provisions, such an agreement should contain provisions on the rights and responsibilities of the parties, payments, and commission, commencement and termination of the agreement, consequences of termination, management of IPRs, a specific legal requirement under other laws of the land governing laws and dispute settlement, etc.

§2. Maintenance and Facilities Management Contracts

550. There is no specific law on these contracts, rather issues relating to these are covered by the provisions of the law of contract. Therefore, the parties are free to set their lawful terms and conditions with regard to these services, taking into account the important security concerns.

551. In any maintenance and facilities management agreement/contract, all the general provisions relating to agreement/contract under the law of contract, as discussed above, should be followed. Apart from these general provisions, such an agreement should contain provisions on the rights and responsibilities of the parties, payments and commission, commencement and termination of the agreement, consequences of termination, management of IPRs, a specific legal requirement under other laws of the land governing laws and dispute settlement, etc.

§3. Network Services

552. ICT network services include *network assets*, i.e., both hardware and software, *technologies* such as routers, switches, load balances, firewalls, intrusion prevention, network access control, etc. and *related services* needed to provide local area network (LAN), metropolitan area network (MAN), and wide area network (WAN).

553. Network services in Bangladesh are provided by the MNOs and the ISPs. They provide services to the clients using wire, wireless and satellite and through cutting edge technologies such as WiMAX, Wi-Fi, SDH and GEPON, etc. Since all these service providers need to obtain a licence from the regulatory authorities of the country such as BTRC, their liabilities are determined by the provisions of the licence. Rights and Obligations of the Operators are mentioned in Regulations No. 4 of the BTRC (Interconnection) Regulations, 2004.

554. In government offices, it seems that they are not properly trained to manage network services. The consumers, customers or service receivers do not have much to do against the service providers for obvious reasons that they have very weak bargaining power. As a result, the issue of service interruption is not brought before the court so far. However, the Bangladeshi regulators have taken some actions against some MNOs on ‘call drop’ recently.

Chapter 4. Government Contracts

555. In the area of ICT and telecommunication, the government enters into many contracts with different bodies. The Constitution of Bangladesh, 1972, being the supreme law of the land, contains an important provision on government contracts. It is provided that the executive authority of the Republic shall extend to, *inter alia*, the making of any contract.[558] Moreover, the Constitution of Bangladesh, 1972 provides that all contracts and deeds made in exercise of the executive authority of the Republic shall be expressed to be made by the President, and shall be executed on behalf of the President by such person and in such manner as he may direct or authorize. If a contract or deed is made or executed in the exercise of the executive authority of the Republic, neither the President nor any other person making or executing the contract or deed in the exercise of that authority shall be personally liable though any person can take proceedings against the Government.[559] The Ministry of Law, Justice and Parliamentary Affairs, with the consultation of the Legislative and Parliamentary Affairs Division, shall issue the instructions for the making of contracts on behalf of the President and execution of such contracts.[560]

556. With regard to government contracts in the field of ICT and telecommunication, it is believed to mean the procurement of goods and services of these sectors. However, there is no direct reference to public procurement in the Constitution of Bangladesh, 1972. It will be relevant to share here that after the independence of the country, before 2000, different ministries of the government used to follow their individual procurement system and procedures, and there was no central and harmonized procurement system in Bangladesh. During this time, these departments used to follow some general principles of contracts as contained in Compilation of General Financial Rules framed under British rule.[561] In 2001, the World Bank and Asian Development Bank released the Country Procurement Assessment Report and identified some of the major challenges of public procurement.

557. In 2002, the Central Procurement Technical Unit was established. To harmonize the public procurement system, several initiatives such as framing of Public Procurement Regulations, 2003, Implementation Procedures for Public Procurement Regulations, 2003, Public Procurement Processing and Approval Procedures, Revised Delegation of Financial Powers and several Standard Tender Documents /Standard Request for Proposal Document for the procurement of Goods, Works and Services. and the Public Procurement Rules, 2003 were taken. The Public Procurement Act, 2006 (Act No. 24 of 2006) was enacted to provide for procedures to be followed for ensuring transparency and accountability in the procurement of goods, works or services using public funds and ensuring equitable treatment and free and

558. Article 144, the Constitution of the People's Republic of Bangladesh, 1972.
559. Article 145, the Constitution of the People's Republic of Bangladesh, 1972.
560. Rules 5 & 14A, the Rules of Business, 1996 (as amended up to July 2012).
561. For a historical background of public procurement, *see*, World Bank. 2002. Bangladesh – Country Procurement Assessment Report (English). Washington, DC: World Bank, http://documents.worldbank.org/curated/en/812041468743656486/Bangladesh-Country-procurement-assessment-report.

fair competition among all persons wishing to participate in such procurement. In 2011, Bangladesh formulated the e-Government Procurement Guidelines.

558. The provisions of the Public Procurement Act, 2006 (Act No. 24 of 2006) applies to, *inter alia*, procurement of goods, works or services by any procuring entity or by a registered company using public funds and by any government, semi-government or any statutory body established under any law.[562] Under the law, 'procurement' means the purchasing or hiring of goods, or acquisition of goods through purchasing and hiring, and the execution of works and performance of services by any contractual means.[563] 'Public funds' is defined as any funds allocated to a procuring entity under government budget, grants or loan, placed at the disposal of a procuring entity through the government by the development partners or foreign states or organizations.[564] Therefore, the provisions of this law shall be applicable if the government, semi-government or any statutory body procure any goods, works or services, including ICT and telecommunication services, using public funds.

559. The Government of Bangladesh may sue or be sued by the name of Bangladesh.[565] Part IV of the Code of Civil Procedure, 1908 (Act No. V of 1908) contains the procedure regarding suits by or against the government. Accordingly, 'Bangladesh' shall be used to be named as plaintiff or defendant in suits by or against the Government. A written notice regarding such intended suit is to be served, and such suits can be instituted after two months after serving the notice.[566] The applicant has to mention a competent official to represent Bangladesh. If the Government or the statutory public authority is not made a party or is not properly described in the application, the opposite parties must raise an objection at the earliest stage so that the applicant may get an opportunity to take necessary steps. If the proper party is not before the Tribunal, irrespective of any objection raised or not, his application may be adjudged as incompetent.[567]

560. It is a general principle of law that the writ jurisdiction of the HCD cannot be invoked in case of disputes arising out of the commercial contract.[568] However, this can be invoked in the case of a statutory contract.[569] In *Bangladesh Power Development Board v. Mohammad Asaduzzaman Sikder*, 9 BLC (AD) 1, the AD of Bangladesh Supreme Court laid down the principles upon which writ jurisdiction can be invoked for breach of contract. It was held that the writ jurisdiction could be invoked for breach of contract in the following circumstances:

562. Section 3, the Public Procurement Act, 2006 (Act No. 24 of 2006).
563. Section 2(7), the Public Procurement Act, 2006 (Act No. 24 of 2006).
564. Section 2(33), the Public Procurement Act, 2006 (Act No. 24 of 2006).
565. Article 146, the Constitution of the People's Republic of Bangladesh, 1972.
566. Sections 79 & 80, the Code of Civil Procedure, 1908 (Act No. V of 1908).
567. *Md. Ali Emdad v. Labour Director and others*, 18 BLD (AD) 137.
568. *Mark Construction Ltd v. Chief Engineer, Rural Electrification Board Dhaka and others*, 3 SCOB [2015] HCD 37.
569. *Shahjibazar Power Company Ltd. v. Bangladesh & ors.*, 8 SCOB [2016] HCD 1.

(a) the contract is entered into by the Government in the capacity as sovereign;
(b) where contractual obligation sought to be enforced in writ jurisdiction arises out of statutory duty or sovereign obligation or public function of a public authority;
(c) where the contract is entered into in exercise of an enacting power conferred by a statute that by itself does not render the contract a statutory contract, but 'if entering into a contract containing prescribed terms and conditions is a must under the statute then that contract becomes a statutory contract. If a contract incorporates certain terms and conditions in it which are statutory then the said contract to that extent is statutory';
(d) where a statute may expressly or impliedly confer power on a statutory body to enter into contracts in order to enable it to discharge its functions and the contract so entered by the statutory body is not an exercise of statutory power, then merely because one of the parties to the contract is a statutory or public body, such contract is not a statutory contract;
(e) when a contract is entered into by a public authority invested with the statutory power, in case of breach thereof relief in writ jurisdiction may be sought as against such on the plea that the contract was entered into by the public authority invested with a statutory power;
(f) where the contract has been entered into in exercise of statutory power by statutory authority in terms of the statutory provisions and then breach thereof gives the right to the aggrieved party to invoke writ jurisdiction because the relief sought is against breach of a statutory obligation.[570]

570. *Government of Bangladesh and others v. Excellent Corporation*, 20 BLC (AD) (2015) 355.

Part IV. Electronic Transactions

Chapter 1. Legal Status of Electronic Transaction

561. ICT is a transformative technology, and with the internet, it has been transforming almost every aspect of our daily life. Sale or purchase of goods and services using the ICT and the internet has been increasing exponentially. Electronic transaction is 'the sale or purchase of goods or services, whether between businesses, households, individuals, governments, and other public or private organisations, conducted over computer-mediated networks. The goods and services are ordered over those networks, but the payment and the ultimate delivery of the good or service may be conducted on or off-line'.[571]

562. In 2002, the Law Commission of Bangladesh submitted the study report with the proposal to enact suitable laws to facilitate electronic commerce and to encourage the growth and development of IT in Bangladesh. While conducting the study and developing the report, the Commission considered, *inter alia*, the UNCITRAL Model Law on Electronic Commerce, and the Electronic Transactions Act, 1998 of Singapore. Finally, the Law Commission proposed to enact a law with the title, i.e., 'the Information Technology (Electronic Transaction) Act' and submitted the text of the proposed law.

563. The government subsequently adopted the major part of the text suggested by the Law Commission with some modifications and enacted the Law with the title 'the Information and Communication Technology Act, 2006 (Act No. 39 of 2006)' ('ICT Act, 2006'). Moreover, the Law Commission proposed to amend some provisions of the existing laws such as the Penal Code, 1860, the Evidence Act, 1872, the Bankers Book Evidence Act, 1891 and the Bangladesh Bank Order, 1972 to include the provisions of electronic transaction and listed those amendments in Schedules to the proposed law. Unfortunately, the words 'Electronic Transaction' were dropped from the title of the law and the amendments of these existing laws in the schedule were not adopted as a part of the ICT Act, 2006 when it was enacted subsequently. As a result, one may find it confusing as to the application of the ICT Act, 2006 in the case of electronic transactions. To add to this, it is provided that 'Nothing contained in this Act shall by itself compel any Ministry or Department of

571. OECD Glossary of Statistical Terms, Electronic Transaction, OECD Expert Group on Defining and Measuring E-commerce, April 2000.

the Government or any authority or body established by or under any law or controlled or funded by the Government to accept, issue, create, retain and preserve any document in the form of electronic records or effect any monetary transaction in the electronic form.'[572] Yet, even with the enactment of the Digital Security Act, 2018 (Act No. 46 of 2018), the ICT Act, 2006 is still the principal law in this regard and the provisions of this law legally recognize electronic transactions. It will be relevant to share here that the government has taken the initiative to amend the ICT Act, 2006 significantly and released a Draft Amendment titled the Information and Communication Technology (Amendment) Act, 2019 available on the website of the ICT Division. It can be anticipated that if the amendments come into force, many provisions in the existing law will be updated.

564. The ICT Act of 2006 recognizes electronic documents and records. Generally, 'document' means anything in which information of any description is recorded.[573] Section 29 of the Penal Code, 1860 (Act No. XLV of 1860) defines 'document' as any matter expressed or described upon any substance by means of letters, figures, marks, or by more than one of those means, intended to be used, or which may be used, as evidence of that matter. Some examples of 'document' are included in the law. These are: writing containing the terms of a contract or directions/instructions, cheque, power-of-attorney, map or plan, etc. Almost the same definition of the word has been included in section 3 of the Evidence Act, 1872 (Act No. I of 1872), though no example has been included. Section 87 of the ICT Act, 2006 provides that- for the purpose of this Act:

(a) The definition of 'document' in section 29 of Penal Code, 1860 (Act No. XLV of 1860) also includes the document generated or prepared by electronic machine or technology.
(b) The definition of 'document' in section 3 of Evidence Act, 1872 (Act No. I of 1872) also includes the document generated or prepared by electronic machine or technology.
(c) The definition of 'bankers books' in section 2, Clause (3) of Banker's Books Evidence Act, 1891 (Act No. XVIII of 1891) also includes the books viz. ledgers, day-books, cash-books, account-books and all other books generated or prepared by electronic machine or technology.

565. Whereas, section 6 of the Law, while dealing with the legal recognition of electronic records, provides that- where any law provides that information or any other matter shall be in writing or in the typewritten or printed form, then, notwithstanding anything contained in such law, such information or matter is rendered or made available in an electronic form. However, such information or matter is to be accessible so as to be usable for a subsequent reference.

566. Besides, section 8 of the Law provides that where any law provides for (a) the filing of any form, application or any other document with any office, authority,

572. Section 11, the Information and Communication Technology Act, 2006 (Act No. 39 of 2006).
573. *See*, s. 13, the Civil Evidence Act, 1995 (UK).

body or agency owned or controlled by the appropriate Government in a particular manner; (b) the issue or grant of any licence, permit, sanction, approval or order by whatever name called in a particular manner; (c) the receipt or payment of money in a particular manner; then, notwithstanding anything contained in such law, filing, issue, grant of the document and receipt and payment of money, as the case may be, is effected by means of prescribed electronic form.

567. Moreover, in relation to the retention of electronic records, section 9 of the Law stipulates that where any law provides that any document, record or information shall be retained for any specific period, then such requirement shall be deemed to have been satisfied if such documents, records or information, as the case may be, are retained in the electronic form if the following conditions are satisfied:

(a) the information contained therein remains accessible to be usable for a subsequent reference;
(b) the electronic record is retained in the format in which it was originally generated, sent or received, or in a format which can be demonstrated to represent accurately the information originally generated, sent or received;
(c) such information, if any, as enables the identification of the origin and destination of an electronic record and the date and time when it was sent or received, is retained. But this provision shall not be applicable to any information which is automatically generated solely for enabling an electronic record to be dispatched or received. It is pertinent to mention here that this provision shall not apply to any law that expressly provides for the retention of documents, records or information. Thus, in such instances, the provisions of that law regarding the retention of printed/paper documents, records or information will have to be followed.

568. In addition to these provisions, the law provides that any law, rule, regulation, order, by-law, notification or any other matter that is required to be published in the Official Gazette, can be published electronically.[574] Chapter 3 of the ICT Act, 2006 (sections 13, 14 & 15) deals with the recognition, acknowledgement and despatch of electronic records. Therefore, it is evident that electronic transactions are legally recognized in Bangladesh subject to fulfilment of some conditions.

569. Finally, it can be said that electronic records and transactions are recognized in Bangladesh. There are instances that court orders were sent through Fax.[575] In case of necessity, an electronic affidavit can also be accepted in a court of law.[576] The HCD has taken the email correspondence into consideration in dealing with the dues unpaid.[577] The HCD has also accepted the 'scanned image/photographs (by

---

574. Section 10, the Information and Communication Technology Act, 2006 (Act No. 39 of 2006).
575. *State v. Secretary, Ministry of Law, Justice & Parliamentary Affairs and others*, 2009, 38 CLC (HCD) [5300] = 30 BLD (HCD) (2010) 369; 15 MLR (HCD) (2010) 59.
576. *M. Anwar Hossain and others v. Government of Bangladesh and others*, 2011, 40 CLC (HCD) [8262].
577. *Captain Md. Abdul Hayee Miah and others v. M.V. Ocean Pearl and others* 2016 (2) LNJ 351.

using the electronic Scanner machine and the computer)' of the original deed of *Heba-bil-Ewaz* (a gift for consideration under Muslim law).[578] Email is also accepted as a piece of evidence in a court of law.[579]

570. It may be relevant to share here that Bangladesh has not yet signed the United Nations Convention on the Use of Electronic Communications in International Contracts, 2005, which entered into force on 1 March 2013 ('Electronic Communication Convention'). Sri Lanka, as the only neighbour of Bangladesh from South Asia, signed the Convention on 6 July 2006 and ratified it on 7 July 2007. This Convention is an update to the UNCITRAL Model Law on Electronic Commerce. However, the Government of Bangladesh became the first country to sign the Framework Agreement on Facilitation of Cross-border Paperless Trade in Asia and the Pacific in 2016.

578. *Nurul Islam Shaikha and others v. Shahadat Hossain & others*, 2011, 40 CLC (HCD) [8160] = 64 DLR (HCD) (2012) 222.
579. *State v. Azam Reza*, 2008, 37 CLC (HCD) [7102] = 62 DLR (HCD) (2010) 399.

Chapter 2. Regulation of Electronic Signatures and Certification Services

571. Digital signatures play a crucial role in this hyper-connected and networked world when the various parties involved have to sign and authenticate regularly a huge volume of important documents and records having contractual effects. The definition of the word 'document' in the Bangladesh context is wide enough and includes various things. A combined reading of section 29 of the Penal Code, 1860 (Act No. XLV of 1860), section 3 of the Evidence Act, 1872 (Act No. 1 of 1872) and section 3(16) of the General Clauses Act, 1897 (Act No. X of 1897) will reveal that the word 'document' means any matter expressed or described upon any substance by means of letters, figures, marks, or by more than one of those means, intended to be used, or which may be used, as evidence of that matter. The means, substance upon which the letters, figures or marks are written and purpose of creating such document are immaterial and anything that is expressed by such document shall be deemed to be expressed even though it is not clearly expressed.[580] The examples of documents include any writing, words printed, lithographed or photographed, writing expressing the terms of a contract, a cheque upon a banker, a power-of-attorney, a map or plan, a writing containing directions or instructions, inscription on a metal plate or stone and caricature, etc.[581] Generally, if there arises any question about the admissibility of such documents as evidence by the contesting parties, the adjudicating judge uses his discretion to accept or reject such evidence based on other documentary and circumstantial evidence.

572. An electronic signature is important for various purposes such as paperless Government correspondence, activities relating to electronic government, procurement, commerce, document signing, internet banking, and device and server signing, etc. and also to prevent cybercrimes. Even though in the available literature and legal documents, both the concepts 'digital' and 'electronic' are frequently used interchangeably, e.g., electronic commerce is also described as digital commerce in the National Digital Commerce Policy adopted recently, these are not technically identical in relation to signature matters. There are differences between 'electronic signature' and 'digital signature'.

573. In Bangladesh, the primary law regarding digital signature is the ICT Act, 2006, and instead of using the words 'digital signature', the law contains a definition of the words 'electronic signature' to define it as data in an electronic form, which:

(a) is related to any other electronic data directly or logically; and
(b) is able to satisfy the following conditions for validating the digital signature:
    (i) affixing with the signatory uniquely;

580. Explanations 1 & 2, s. 29, the Penal Code, 1860 (Act No. XLV of 1860).
581. Section 29, the Penal Code, 1860 (Act No. XLV of 1860), s. 3, the Evidence Act, 1872 (Act No. 1 of 1872) and s. 3(16), the General Clauses Act, 1897 (Act No. X of 1897); *Abdus Sattar Bhuiyan v. Deputy Commissioner, Dhaka*, 17 CLC (HCD) [7659] = 42 DLR (HCD) (1990) 151.

(ii) capable of identifying the signatory;
(iii) created in a safe manner or using a means under the sole control of the signatory; and
(iv) related to the attached data in such a manner that is capable of identifying any alteration made in the data thereafter.[582]

574. This law has not defined 'digital signature', but it seems that the concept of 'digital signature' is already included within the definition of 'electronic signature'. Rules 2(d) of the Information Technology (Certifying Authorities) Rules, 2010 as framed under section 88 of the ICT Act, 2006 has included the definition of 'electronic signature' as given under the ICT Act, 2006 and provides that 'electronic signature' also includes 'digital signature'. However, it has already been shared that these two things are not technically identical.

575. An electronic signature can be an electronic sign, symbol or process attached to a contract or other document used with the intention to sign a record. Thus, this is a representation of an individual's handwritten signature in an electronic form. An electronic signature can take various forms, e.g., a person can use his name in any electronic document such as his personal email, or can simply write his name using computer fonts, or can put his signature on a document and then scan it to use in the electronic documents. All these things will be treated as an 'electronic signature'. In case of any disputes in the court of law to use such signature as evidence, one needs to submit a valid declaration attesting and verifying the said signature. The court can ask for expert opinion in the proper adjudication of the dispute between the parties,[583] and can also use discretion to arrive at a conclusion about the signature.[584] Whereas, in a digital signature, which is a technique of encrypting a document with undetectable digital codes, an algorithm encodes the signature to produce a unique signature certificate. A digital signature, generated to serve very specific purposes, is virtually impossible to change or duplicate. Thus, digital signatures are a sub-set of electronic signatures and it can be said that all digital signatures are electronic signatures, but all electronic signatures are not digital signatures. While digital signatures are strictly regulated, electronic signatures are not.

576. It is pertinent to mention here that the wordings of the ICT Act, 2006 used, i.e., 'electronic signature' to mean 'digital signature' create confusion. The confusion is also evident from the definition of 'electronic signature certificate' as included in section 2(2) of the ICT Act, 2006. It provides that 'electronic signature certificate' means a certificate issued under section 36 of the ICT Act, 2006 after fulfilling some conditions mentioned there. However, we know that we have been

582. Section 2(1), the Information and Communication Technology Act, 2006 (Act No. 39 of 2006).
583. *Masud Haider (Md.) v. Md. Golam Ambia (Harun)*, 2015, 44 CLC (HCD) [9749] = 67 DLR (HCD) (2010) 395.
584. Section 73, the Evidence Act, 1872 (Act No. 1 of 1872); *Shawkat Hossain (Md.) and another v. Golam Mohammad and another*, 2014, 43 CLC (HCD) [8980] = 20 BLC (AD) (2015) 27.

using our electronic signatures in electronic documents without taking any certificate from any authority. Interestingly, the e-GP Guidelines, as formulated under section 65(2) of the Public Procurement Act, 2006, with the aims to provide principle guidelines of the e-GP system of Bangladesh, has included the definitions of both these concepts.

577. According to the e-GP Guidelines, 'electronic signature' or 'e-signature' means a signature in electronic form attached to or logically associated with an electronic record, in the form of an electronic symbol or a process attached to or logically associated with documents, and executed, adopted or agreed upon by a person with the intent to sign the documents. Whereas, 'digital signature' means an electronic signature used through asymmetric cryptography that can be used to authenticate the identity of the sender of a message or the signer of a document, and possibly to ensure that the original content of the message or document that has been sent is unchanged. In the case of *Tariqul Islam v. Bangladesh and Others, 2016, 45 CLC (HCD) [9712]* = 68 DLR (HCD) (2016) 150, while explaining the international historical development of 'passport', Quamrul Islam Siddique J mentioned about 'digital signature' to explain the biometric or machine-readable passport.

578. Under the Guidelines, No. 3, the e-GP System keeps all private information of its users in encrypted form in the database so that it shall not be accessible to any user without sufficient authority and access permissions. However, the users are responsible for maintaining the confidentiality of their password and are fully responsible for all activities that occur using their account (email ID and password as their e-signature).

579. It may be relevant to share here that in Europe, in 1999, the regulators adopted the Electronic Signature Directive 1999/93/EC. There were some limitations of the Directive, and the European countries were using a different set of procedural standards for the enforcement of electronic signatures which were preventing real interoperability. As a result, in 2014, the European Parliament repealed the said Directive and adopted the Electronic Identification and Trust Services for Electronic Transactions (eIDAS) Regulation (910/2014) which entered into force in July 2016. This eIDAS Regulation has included a very simple definition of electronic signature. According to this Regulation, 'electronic signature' means data in electronic form which is attached to or logically associated with other data in electronic form and which is used by the signatory to sign. The Regulation has adopted three levels of e-signature, i.e., simple e-signature, advanced e-signature and qualified e-signature. Besides, there are other 'electronic trust services' which include electronic timestamps, electronic documents, electronic seals to be used by the companies, electronic registered delivery service and website authentication.

580. Under Bangladesh law, to authenticate electronic records, a technology-neutral system or standard authentic signature generating machine or strategy should be used. With these, any subscriber may authenticate an electronic record by affixing his digital signature.[585] Section 7 of the ICT Act, 2006, while dealing with the legal recognition of electronic signatures, provides that where any law provides that (a) any information or any other matter shall be authenticated by affixing the signature; or (b) any document shall be authenticated by signature or bear the signature of any person; then, notwithstanding anything contained in such law, such information or matter can be authenticated by means of an electronic signature affixed in a defined manner.

581. To be a valid electronic signature, its security is to be ensured. An electronic signature shall be deemed to be a secured one if, by application of a security procedure agreed to by the parties concerned, it can be verified that the signature, at the time it was affixed, was (a) unique to the person affixing it; (b) capable of identifying the person affixing it; and (c) created in a manner or using a means under the sole control of the person affixing it. The electronic signature would be invalidated if the electronic record was altered.[586]

§1. Certification Services

582. It has already been discussed that there are differences between 'electronic evidence' and 'digital evidence'. Even though in various sections of the ICT Act, 2006, the word 'electronic signature' are used to provide for various relevant matters, while discussing the certification services, it is apparent from the provisions of Chapter V of the ICT Act, 2006 (sections 18–40) dealing with the Controller and Certifying Authorities (CCAs), and Chapter VI (sections 41–44) dealing with the duties of subscribers that the law has included provisions generally practised for 'digital evidence' in other parts of the world. Chapter V of the ICT Act, 2006 provides for the appointment of one Controller and necessary numbers of Deputy Controller and Assistant Controller. Accordingly, the office of the CCA was established in May 2011 under the ICT Division of the Ministry of Posts, Telecommunications and Information Technology as per the provisions of the IT (Certifying Authorities) Rules, 2010. This CCA, which performs the regulatory duties to monitor the activities of the certifying authorities (CAs), has a crucial role to play in making the country's cyberspace secure, leading and maintaining PKI program within the legal framework and in building public awareness in a secured electronic transaction.

583. The CCA follows the Certificate of Practice Statement (CPS) as the guiding document, which was developed based on RFC-3647: Internet X.509 PKI Certificate Policy and Certification Practices Framework. The office of the CCA has also finalized the PKI Auditing Guideline (first published in December 2010 and updated in 2012) to audit the infrastructures and security measures of prospective licensees and to the activities of the licensees every two years to see if they comply with the rules, procedures and the practices as they need to comply with as per the terms and conditions of the licences.

---

585. Section 5, the Information and Communication Technology Act, 2006 (Act No. 39 of 2006).
586. Section 17, the Information and Communication Technology Act, 2006 (Act No. 39 of 2006).

584. In 2011, the CCA granted licences to be CAs to six organizations, and these are Mango Teleservices Ltd., Dohatec New Media, Data Edge Ltd., Banglaphone Ltd., Computer Services Ltd., and BCC. The BCC CA is the only government CA, and this BCC CA has been providing technology-oriented services such as digital certificates and PKI enablement tools in the country since January 2014. BCC CA has also adopted CPS and Object Identifier Management Guidelines.

§2. The Information Technology (Certifying Authorities) Rules, 2010

585. The Information Technology (Certifying Authorities) Rules, 2010 provide for detailed provisions, *inter alia*, on authentication of information through electronic signature, procedure to create electronic signature, verification of electronic signature, proof of public key, standards to follow, standards to be followed during the issuance of electronic signature, electronic signature certificate, generation and use of electronic signature, issue of electronic signature, preservation of electronic signature, process to follow in case of doubt regarding electronic signature, revocation of electronic signature, and confidential information.

586. Under the Rules, an electronic signature shall be created and verified by such cryptography which will transform electronic records into seemingly unintelligible form and back. To create and verify electronic signature, 'Public Key Cryptography', which employs an algorithm using two different but mathematically related 'keys', i.e., one for creating an electronic signature or transforming data into a seemingly unintelligible form, and another key for verifying an electronic signature or returning the electronic record to original form, shall be used. The hash function process shall be used in both creating and verifying an electronic signature.[587]

587. A public key shall be authenticated when (a) the public key was generated by using secret cryptography; and (b) the Controller authenticates the said public key.[588] The usages and transmission of the Electronic Signature Certificate shall involve (a) the receipt of an approved and verified Electronic Signature Certificate request; (b) the creation of a new Electronic Signature Certificate; (c) binding the key pair associated with the Electronic Signature Certificate to the owner of an Electronic Signature (d) a distinguished name associated with the owner of an Electronic Signature Certificate; and (e) a recognized and relevant name as defined in the Certification Practice statement.[589]

588. A CA, as per the provisions of the Rules, 2010, is responsible to archive (a) application of the applicant for the issue of Electronic Signature Certificates; (b) registration and verification documents of Electronic Signature Certificates; (c)

587. Rule 3, the Information Technology (Certifying Authorities) Rules, 2010.
588. Rule 6, the Information Technology (Certifying Authorities) Rules, 2010.
589. Rule 25, the Information Technology (Certifying Authorities) Rules, 2010.

Electronic Signature Certificates; (d) notices of temporary suspension; (e) information relating to temporary suspended Electronic Signature Certificates; (f) information relating to withdrawal of suspension orders; and (g) information relating to the expiration of Electronic Signature Certificates at least for seven years or for such period as may be required by any other legal proceedings.[590]

§3. The Digital Signature Interoperability Guidelines, 2018

589. The PKI framework helps to perform a secure e-business and e-transactions, and early adoption of the PKI framework helps to save a lot of money as it will be costly to adopt the revised standard in the future. The Digital Certificate Interoperability Guideline, 2013, was developed based on RFC-5280: Internet X.509 PKI Certificate and Certificate Revocation List. When the Guidelines was revised in 2018, along with RFC-5280, Asia PKI Forum Interoperability Guidelines was followed to reduce interoperability issue among Bangladesh CAs. Being the latest document in this area, the provisions of this revised Guidelines, 2018, shall prevail and be interpreted as final over the existing laws, rules and guidelines if there arises any inconsistency.

590. There are various types of PKI Models such as hierarchy model, cross-certification model, cross-recognition model, bridge model and certificate trust list model, etc., available in the world. But, the provisions of the ICT Act, 2006 and IT (CA) Rules, 2010 refer to hierarchical PKI model for Bangladesh where a trusted root CA issues certificates only to accredited CAs and these accredited CAs may subsequently issue certificates to subordinate CAs and/or end-users and/or other relying parties.[591]

§4. The Time Stamping Services Guidelines for Certifying Authorities, 2016

591. A trusted timestamp issued by a trusted third party is used to prove the existence of certain data before a certain point (e.g., contracts, research data, medical records, etc.) without the possibility that the owner can backdate the timestamps.[592] The CCA has formulated the Time Stamping Services Guidelines for CAs in August 2016. Licensed CAs have been operating timestamping services and cannot issue such certificates other than for their own timestamping service.

592. The CCA has also issued the Auditing Guidelines for Certifying Authorities for technical, financial, commercial, physical compliance in 2013. The CA and

590. Rule 28, the Information Technology (Certifying Authorities) Rules, 2010.
591. Office of the Controller of Certificate Authorities, Digital Certificate Interoperability Guideline, 2018.
592. Office of the Controller of Certifying Authorities, The Time Stamping Services Guidelines for Certifying Authorities (CA), August 2016.

impanelled auditor needs to comply with the provisions of the ICT Act, 2006 such as secure electronic record and signature (sections 16, 17), operation of CA (section 31), publication of information by CA (section 35), certificate issuance condition (section 36), assurance for certificate (section 37), certificate revocation and suspension procedure (sections 38, 39 & 40), making the subscribers aware of their responsibilities (sections 41, 42, 43 & 44), actions taken to prevent the issue of fake certificates (sections 64 & 65). Moreover, they need to comply with the certificate issuance condition (Rules 24, 25 & 26), procedure to create digital signature and validation (Rules 4 & 5), standard to be followed by a CA (Rules 7 & 8), CA operation termination procedure (Rule 22), Certificate Repository (Rule 28) and Privacy of Information (Rule 34).

§5. Conclusion

593. In this inter network-connected world and the post-COVID-19 new normal reality when almost everything is done electronically, the importance of electronic and digital signatures cannot be overstated. From the discussion above, it is apparent that there are some confusions in the provisions of the ICT Act, 2006 where the word 'electronic signature' is sometimes used to mean 'digital signature'. Yet, this issue appears to be not so serious in the context of the country as not a single decision of the higher judiciary has been reported on this yet. Nevertheless, since the country has been progressing economically and stakeholders are getting connected to their counterparts from other jurisdictions, it is high time to fix this issue immediately in order to avoid future challenges and difficulties. An extensive review of the existing law is the demand of the time through which it should be evaluated if the provisions of the law are sufficient to meet the needs of modern times. A delay in this move may demand a huge amount of financial loss associated with other catastrophes.

594. The new European eIDAS Regulation has clearly included provisions relating to the legal effects of electronic signatures (Article 25), electronic seals (Article 35) and documents (Article 46). One important innovation of eIDAS Regulation is the introduction of the web authentication service, which can be very promising in the Bangladesh context to promote e-commerce as this initiative promises to increase the trust and confidence of the consumers or customers to get products from genuine service providers. Taking into account the developments of the EU and other parts of the world, lawmakers need to consider removing the existing confusion regarding the definition of electronic signature and digital signature and adopt an easy definition in an understandable language, perhaps in the same manner as it was done in the e-GP Guidelines.

Chapter 3. Legal Aspects of Electronic Banking

§1. Introduction

595. With the economic development of the country and the increasing volume of cross-border trade, the number of commercial activities of the scheduled banks has been increasing, and people have been using formal banking services. The introduction and dynamic use of the internet in offering banking services have facilitated the consumers to get various services in different ways. It was shared that among Bangladeshi adults with bank accounts, 34.1% made digital transactions in 2017, compared to an average rate of 27.8% for South Asia.[593]

596. Electronic banking, also known as internet banking, online banking, virtual banking, etc., enables the customers to access and maintain their accounts and get general information on bank products and services using digital technologies through various devices such as a computer, ATM, mobile handphones and mobile applications, etc. Various issues, e.g., the legal issues of electronic funds transfers, evidential issues, legal issues on specific EFT transactions, privacy and confidentiality, personal data protection, frauds, money laundering, financial terrorism, etc. are some of the important issues covered in any discussion on electronic banking and some of these will be discussed in this chapter.

§2. Electronic Banking in Bangladesh: An Overview

597. In Bangladesh, BB, the Central Bank of the country and the regulatory authority regarding banking and financial activities have the mandate and authority to shape the legal framework of banking activities. BB is responsible to formulate and implement the monetary and credit policies, regulate and supervise banks and NBFIs, promoting and developing domestic financial markets, managing the country's international reserves, issuing currency notes, regulating and supervising the payment system, acting as the banker to the government, prevent money laundering, collect and furnish credit information, regulate foreign exchange and manage a Deposit Insurance Scheme.[594] While doing all these activities, BB plays the main role in the electronic banking system in the country.

593. Mr Shyam Sunder Sikder, Secretary of Ministry of Posts, Telecommunications and Information Technology, Speech delivered at the ITU-BTRC Asia-Pacific Regulators' Roundtable 2018, 6–7 Aug. 2018, Dhaka, Bangladesh, https://www.itu.int/en/ITU-D/Regional-Presence/AsiaPacific/Pages/Events/2018/rr2018/home.aspx.

594. After the independence of the country in 1971, BB assumed all the responsibilities of the Dhaka branch of State Bank of Pakistan on the Victory Day on 16 December 1971 through the BB Order, 1972 (P.O No. 127 of 1972). BB performs its activities and responsibilities through its ten offices located at Motijheel and Sadarghat (Dhaka), Chittagong, Khulna, Bogra, Rajshahi, Sylhet, Barisal, Rangpur and Mymensingh. *See*, About BB, BB, https://www.bb.org.bd/aboutus/index.php.

598. The financial market in Bangladesh consists of the money market, stock market and foreign exchange market.[595] Taking into account the degree of regulation, three different sectors, i.e., formal, semi-formal and informal sectors, provide financial services in Bangladesh. The formal sector includes all institutions such as Banks, Non-Bank FIs, Insurance Companies, Capital Market Intermediaries such as Brokerage Houses, Merchant Banks etc. BB mainly regulates fifty-nine scheduled[596] and five non-scheduled banks, and thirty-four non-bank FIs.

§3. Payment Systems

599. The Payment Systems Department of BB is empowered and entrusted to establish the digital payment system in the country. BB operates four major national interbank payment systems. Of them, three are for retail value and one for high value. Three retail national interbank payment systems are: Bangladesh Automated Cheque Processing System (BACPS), BEFTN and NPSB. BB established two interbank payment systems, i.e., BACH in 2010 to operate BACPS and BEFTN, and the central BACH receives 24/7 transactions (through instruments or instructions) from the member banks. Under the provisions of the BACPS Operating Rules and Procedures, 2010, which applies to all paper-based payment instruments, BACH started its operation in October 2010 in the Dhaka Clearing House area. The BACPS Operating Rules and Procedures was revised on 5 December 2019.

600. BB published the BEFTN Operating Rules in August 2010. Through these Rules, 2010, BEFTN started its operation in February 2011 with a view to establishing an efficient alternative paperless electronic payment method for the secured & cost-effective transaction. Various types of credit transfers, e.g., salary payments can be settled through EFT credits while utility bill payments, loan repayments, insurance premiums, etc. can be accommodated through EFT debits. Bangladesh Government is an early adopter of the EFT network as salaries of most government officials are being paid through this system.[597]

601. The NPSB, introduced on 27 December 2010, facilitates interbank electronic payments originating from different payment channels such as ATMs, POS and the internet, etc. The NPSB was established with the objectives to act as a mother switch and to connect all child switches owned or shared (owned and operated either by the bank or non-bank entity) gradually and to create a common electronic platform for the switches in Bangladesh. Of the fifty-two banks operating card business in the country, NPSB routes interbank ATM transactions of fifty-two

595. Overview of Financial system of Bangladesh, BB, https://www.bb.org.bd/fnansys/index.php.
596. There are four types of scheduled banks: (a) state-owned commercial banks, (b) state-owned development financial institutions, (c) private commercial banks, and (d) foreign commercial banks. As of December 2019, 10,578 branches of 59 banks were operating. The number of branches were 10,286 in December 2018. *See*, BB, Annual Report (July 2019–June 2020), at p. 38.
597. BB, Annual Report (July 2017–June 2018), at p. 130.

banks and POS transactions of fifty-one banks. Besides, BB started the Internet Banking Fund Transfer (IBFT) in November 2017, and so far, twenty-four banks have been exploiting the service.[598]

602. Under the provisions of the BPSSR, 2014, BB has permitted five non-bank entities to work as the Payment Systems Operator, who offered merchant aggregation and payment gateway service and granted a licence to one PSP to provide e-wallet service in the market.[599] In 2018, IPay Systems Limited introduced the first digital wallet service in the country having the licence on PSP obtained from BB.

§4. Automated Teller Machine

603. Some issues relating to ATMs have been already covered in the chapter on e-commerce. ATM was introduced in 1992, and the number of installed ATMs started increasing after 2000. Both debit and credit cards are used in Bangladesh, and the use of the debit card was started in 1999. Though the number of card users has been increasing, the number of installed ATMs all over the country is very limited. According to the recent statistics of the World Bank, there are only 8.07 ATM booths for every 100,000 adults in the country.[600] With this, the regular news of ATM thefts, mostly by foreigners, has turned to be a genuine issue of great concern for the customers, regulators and policymakers. Sometimes, these foreigners visit the country with a tourist visa and use such techniques on which the law enforcement agencies do not have expertise. On 4 March 2016, twelve such criminals along with two local individuals were arrested. On 3 June 2019, just before the Eid festival, six Ukrainians were arrested on the charge of ATM booth fraud, and it was revealed that the techniques these criminals were using were totally unknown to the bank and regulators. Some criminal cases are pending in the subordinate courts.

§5. Credit Card Service

604. The credit card has also gained popularity, at a slow pace, in the country since its inception in 1999. At present, companies such as VISA, Master Card and VANIK are dealing with this computer-based Credit Card Service, which is a safe and easy device for monetary transactions. Very recently a number of foreign banks have introduced the EFT service. The microchip installed Smart Cards are also becoming popular in the country gradually. This device has been proved to be very useful, especially in repaying bills of various service-oriented organizations and

598. National Payment Switch Bangladesh (NPSB), Bangladesh Bank, https://www.bb.org.bd/fnansys/paymentsys/natpayswitch.php.
599. The list of Payment Systems Operator includes- IT Consultants Ltd, SSL Commerz Ltd., Shurjo-Mukhi Ltd. and D Money Bangladesh Ltd (PSP). Whereas only iPay Systems Ltd. is permitted to provide e-wallet service in the country.
600. The World Bank, ATMs (per 100,000 adults), https://data.worldbank.org/indicator/FB.ATM.TOTL.P5?locations=BD.

companies.[601] As of January 2020, there are around 1.6 million subscribers of credit cards who can use this card in around 11,000 ATM booths and in 60,500 POS terminals around the country.[602] These subscribers transact BDT 10 billion every month, and 70% of them pay the instalments on time.[603]

605. It has already been highlighted that the Credit Card service, an essential element of an electronic payment mechanism, was first started in 1996 by the Standard Chartered Bank followed by National Bank Limited. In 1998, Vanik Bangladesh Limited, now Lanka Bangla Finance Limited, started the service. The Citi Bank's AmEx card introduced in 2009 deserves the credit to make Credit Card services popular in the country. In December 2018, Mutual Trust Bank, with the help of MasterCard, introduced a contactless Credit Card, using which the subscribers can use the card for up to BDT 3000 by only tapping it in the Card Reader or POS terminal.

606. In 2014, BB issued the draft of Credit Card service Guidelines and finally in 2017, the Guidelines on Credit Card Operations of Banks was formulated to ensure safe, secure and efficient operations of Credit Cards as a payment instrument. According to the Guidelines, 'Credit Card' generally means a plastic card issued by Scheduled Commercial Banks assigned to a Cardholder, with a credit limit, that can be used to purchase goods and services on credit or obtain cash advances.[604] There are two types of credit cards: general purpose cards and private level cards. No prior approval of BB is required, but the Board of Directors of the issuing bank need to approve the issuance of credit cards. The Guidelines on Credit Card Operations of Banks, 2017 contain some important provisions on the stakeholders to a Credit Card, types of Credit Cards, marketing of Credit Cards, eligibility of customers, issuing principal, supplementary and corporate Credit Cards, terms of contract, interest/profit rate and other charges, billing process, collection/recover mechanism, protection of customer rights, dispute resolution, internal control, monitoring and compliance, fraud control, security of Credit Cards. Accordingly, the Card Issuer needs to arrange an appropriate dispute resolution mechanism, cannot reveal any information of the Cardholders obtained without obtaining specific consent, cannot levy any new/additional charges without the prior consent of the Cardholder. The Card Issuer is further responsible, *inter alia*, to (i) ensure that contractual relationships with all relevant parties, domestic and cross-border, are valid and enforceable in the court of law, and (ii) adhere to the instructions/guidelines on Know Your Customer, Anti Money Laundering and Terrorist Financing.

---

601. Computer, Banglapedia, http://en.banglapedia.org/index.php?title=Computer.
602. Bangladesh Bank, National Payment Switch Bangladesh (NPSB), https://www.bb.org.bd/fnansys/paymentsys/natpayswitch.php.
603. Prothom Alo, 8 Apr. 2019.
604. It may be relevant to share here that Lanka Bangla Finance Limited, a non-banking financial institution, which was earlier known as Vanik Bangladesh Limited till 2005, also provides Credit Card service in the country.

607. Though no security is needed for issuing a credit card, an Issuer Bank normally collects cheques covering the credit amount from the Cardholder and can recover the overdue by encashing that cheque. However, if any such cheque is dishonoured then the provisions of the Negotiable Instrument Act, 1881 (Act No. XXVI of 1881) shall be applicable. Accordingly, following some procedural requirements as mentioned in section 138 of the Act of 1881, if any cheque is dishonoured due to insufficient amount available in the account to honour the cheque or it exceeds the amount arranged to be paid from that account by an agreement made with that bank, this will be treated as a criminal offence for which an accused shall be punished with imprisonment for a term which may extend to one year, or with fine which may extend to thrice the amount of the cheque.

§6. Electronic Fund Transfer

608. The Regulations on Electronic Fund Transfer, 2014, the provisions of which apply to a single EFT and framework contracts and transfers covered by them, is the main law containing provisions on EFT. The Regulation was formulated to promote, regulate and ensure a secure and efficient payment system in the country. But, in the case of any transaction through BEFTN, the provisions of the Operating Rules, 2010 shall be applicable.

609. Under the Regulations, 'electronic fund transfer' means any transfer of funds which is initiated by a person by way of instruction, authorization or order to a bank to debit or credit an account maintained with that bank through electronic means and includes POS transfers, ATM transactions, direct deposits or withdrawal of funds, transfer initiated by telephone, internet and card or other devices.[605] It includes those carried out through or by means of, or a combination of the following:

(a) POS terminals.
(b) ATM.
(c) Kiosks or Self-Service Terminals.
(d) TV, internet, and other communication channels.
(e) Telephonic instruments, including mobile devices.
(f) Credit, Charge, Prepaid and Debit cards.
(g) Card-based and network-based stored value products (electronic money).
(h) Electronic entries initiated by banks or PSPs as per any fully electronic, partly electronic or non-electronic payment instructions by the customers of the banks or PSPs.[606]

610. This Regulation contains provisions on execution of EFT, receipt of payment instruction, irrevocability, transmission of payment instruction through an EFT system, authorization of transfers, erroneous payment instruction, notification of

605. Article 2, the Regulations on Electronic Fund Transfer, 2014.
606. Article 1, the Regulations on Electronic Fund Transfer, 2014.

loss, theft or unauthorized use, liability in cases of system or equipment malfunction, security of deposits at electronic terminals, duty of customers to notify errors, other duties of customers, delay in notification, circumstances where the customer is not liable, right to refund, standard terms and conditions for providing EFT service, records and issuance of receipts, evidentiary value of receipts, complaints and investigation, incorrectly credited or debited account, institution to provide information, information and advice on appeal, records of complaint, audit trails and file retention, privacy and waiver of rights and greater protection.

§7. Mobile Financial Services

611. With the number of mobile phone subscribers compared to the availability of formal banking services in very remote areas of the country, the mobile banking business has started becoming popular for a couple of years. Mobile banking services include cash-in, cash-out, merchant payments, utility payments, salary disbursement, foreign remittances, and fund transfers. There are reports that the personal information of the customers are misused, and some forms of financial crimes have been committed. Nevertheless, some of the important factors such as security, easiness, convenience and low transaction costs have encouraged more financial consumers to use Mobile Financial Services (MFS) in Bangladesh.[607]

612. MFS was introduced in Bangladesh in 2011. The Department of Currency Management and Payment Systems of BB issued 'Guidelines on Mobile Financial Services (MFS) for the Banks' on 22 September 2011. After the robust growth in the number of account holders, volume and amount of transactions in MFS, with a view to providing an orderly, enabling and competitive environment for optimal utilization of the new windows of opportunity for extension of the traditional financial services, BB revised the Guidelines of 2011 on 20 December 2011 and replaced it with the recently formulated Guidelines on MFS for the Banks, 2018. In 2018, BB formulated the Bangladesh MFS Regulation, 2018.

613. BB permits only bank-led MFS providers to run operations in the country. MFS is permitted to conduct the following activities:

(a) Cash-in and cash-out from MFS accounts through agent locations, bank branches, ATM, linked bank account and other methods determined by BB.
(b) Disbursement of Inward foreign remittances. It is pertinent to share here that only the domestic part of the transaction is permitted and the cross-border transaction is not permitted.
(c) Person to business payments, e.g., utility bills, merchant payments, etc.
(d) Business-to-person payments, e.g., salary disbursement, dividend/interest and refund payments, etc.

---

607. Yesmin, S., Paul, T.A. & Uddin, M., *bKash: Revolutionizing Mobile Financial Services in Bangladesh?*, in Sikdar, A. & Pereira, V. (eds), *Business and Management Practices in South Asia*, 125–148 (2019).

(e) Government-to-person payments, e.g., elderly allowances, social safety net, etc.
(f) Person-to-Government Payments, e.g., Tax, Levy payments.
(g) Person-to-Person Payments using which one registered mobile account can transfer money to another registered mobile account.
(h) Business-to-business payments, e.g., vendor payments, supply chain management payment, etc.
(i) Online and e-commerce payments.
(j) Other Payments, such as microfinance, overdrawn facility, insurance premium, deposit pension scheme, etc., approved by BB.[608]

614. As of 30 June 2020, fourteen banks and one subsidiary received permission to provide MFS though only seventeen banks and one subsidiary were in operation.[609] Dutch-Bangla Bank, with its service 'Rocket', started the mobile banking service in the country. The total MFS market is BDT 15 billion, where BRAC Bank's bKash has 75%, and Rocket has 18% of the market share.[610] Examples of some other similar services include mCash (Islami Bank Bangladesh Limited), MYCash (Mercantile Bank Limited), UCash (UCBL), IFIC Mobile Banking (IFIC Bank Limited), Trust Bank Mobile Money (Trust Bank Limited), OK Banking (ONE Bank Limited), FSIBL FirstPay Surecash (FSIBL), and Hello (Bank Asia).[611] As of 30 June 2020, a total of one million agents have been serving 88.70 million registered customers.[612] From the latest statistics of BB, the following information can be shared:

General Information	
Particulars	*January 2020*
No. of Debit Card	18,611,681
No. of Credit Card	1,556,448
No. of prepaid Card	428,910
No. of ATM Booths	10,961
No. of POS terminals	60,474
NPSB certified Banks for ATM transactions	52 Banks
NPSB certified Banks for POS transactions	51 Banks
NPSB certified Banks for IBFT transactions	24 Banks

Source: Bangladesh Bank.[613]

608. BB, Annual Report (July 2019–June 2020), at pp. 139–140.
609. *Ibid.*, at p. 139.
610. Yesmin, S., Paul, T.A. & Uddin, M., *bKash: Revolutionizing Mobile Financial Services in Bangladesh?*, in *Business and Management Practices in South Asia*, 125–148 (2019).
611. *Ibid.*
612. BB, Annual Report (July 2019–June 2020), at p. 142.
613. NPSB, BB, https://www.bb.org.bd/fnansys/paymentsys/natpayswitch.php.

§8. ICT SECURITY FOR BANKS

615. The financial services need to follow the Guideline on ICT Security For Banks and NBFIs issued by the BB in May 2015 with the objectives, *inter alia*, to establish a standard ICT Security Policy and ICT Security Management approach, help the Banks and NBFIs for secured setup of its ICT infrastructure, establish a secured environment for the processing of data, establish a holistic approach for ICT Risk management, aware stakeholders' roles and responsibilities for the protection of information, aware and train the users associated with ICT activities for achieving the business objectives, ensure the best practices (industry standard) of the usage of technology that is not limited to this guideline, analyse security risks against faster adoption of Bring-Your-Own-Devices, and minimize security risks for electronic banking infrastructure including ATM and POS devices, payment cards, internet banking, MFS, etc.[614]

616. The provisions of this Guideline are applicable for Banks and NBFIs for all of their Information Systems and for activities and operations required to ensure data security including facility design, physical security, application security, network security, ICT risk management, project management, infrastructure security management, service delivery management, disaster recovery and business continuity management, alternative delivery channels management, acquisition and development of information systems, usage of hardware and software, disposal policy and protection of copyrights and other IPRs.[615]

617. It should be appreciated that while the legal status of this Guideline is not very certain, it is clearly stipulated that 'this Guideline is to be used as a minimum requirement and as appropriate to the level of technology adoption of their operations'. The guideline containing provisions on ICT Security Management, ICT Risk Management, ICT Service Delivery Management, Infrastructure Security Management, Access Control of Information System, Business Continuity and Disaster Recovery Management, Acquisition and Development of Information Systems, Alternative Delivery Channels Security Management, Service Provider Management, Customer Education has made it mandatory to have an 'ICT Security Policy' for each bank or NBFI in line with this ICT Security Guidelines, and this Policy is to be regularly updated to deal with the changing circumstances. Unfortunately, even after this Guideline and ICT Policies of the Banks, the news of financial crimes exploiting thc wcakness of credit and debit cards, ATM Cards, POS and banks, etc., are quite common in the country. As a result, BB issued a directive for the banks to instal anti-skimming devices.

614. Objectives, the Guideline on ICT Security for Banks and Non-Bank Financial Institutions, May 2015.

615. Applicability of the Guideline, the Guideline on ICT Security for Banks and Non-Bank Financial Institutions, May 2015.

618. In 2020, an independent unit named 'Cyber Security Unit' was established to monitor the IT security, information security and cybersecurity issues of BB. Moreover, BB has instructed all banks and NBFIs to get ISO 27001 certifications.

§9. Status of Cryptocurrency or Virtual Currency

619. Like many other parts of the world, some local people wanted to popularize cryptocurrencies or virtual currencies, such as bitcoin, ether, etc., in the country and usually used social media platforms to advertise the trading of these. Since these can be a part of ongoing scams and general consumers could be the target of a scammer, the BB, Central Bank of the country issued a warning notice on 24 December 2017 regarding the legality of the transaction using virtual currencies, such as Bitcoin, Ethereum, Ripple, Litecoin. BB declared that since these virtual currencies are not legal tenders issued by the valid national authority of any country, any financial claim against such currencies cannot be recognized, and as a result, customers can suffer from various legal and financial risks. The banking regulator believed that transactions using such virtual currencies might violate the provisions of the existing money laundering law and terrorist financing law, so such transactions are not supported through the provisions of the Foreign Exchange Regulations Act, 1947, the Anti-Terrorism Act, 2009 and the Money Laundering Prevention Act, 2012. Nevertheless, there are many recent developments on this, and more and more central banks from around the world have expressed their willingness to consider positively cryptocurrencies as a legal tender. Therefore, it can be anticipated that BB will also re-evaluate its position regarding cryptocurrencies soon.

§10. Conclusion

620. Empirical studies revealed that despite huge investment in e-banking technologies, the banks may experience negative profits; nevertheless, e-banking has a positive impact on the performance of the banks in Bangladesh within two years.[616] Bangladesh faced one of the biggest cybercrimes, in the form of online thefts, in history in 2016 when more than USD 80 million were stolen from BB through the Federal Reserve Bank of New York, US and transferred to the casino of the Philippines through Manila-based Rizal Commercial Banking Corporation. It has been reported that organized criminals have used a very simple technique to heist the bank. This demonstrates the weak security system of the bank and the inability of the Central Bank to properly train and monitor the activities of some of the officials holding responsible posts. The government has formed a Committee to investigate the matter, and the Committee has also submitted its Report, which has not been disclosed for public inspection yet.

---

616. Md upti Alam Siddik et al., *Impacts of E-Banking on Performance of Banks in a Developing Economy: Empirical Evidence from Bangladesh*, 17 J. Bus. Eco. Mgmt, 1066–1080 (2016).

621. Financial Technologies (Fintechs) are inevitable in the present world. Fintechs offer both prospects and unique challenges. In October 2019, BB established Regulatory Fintech Facilitation Office (previously Regulatory Innovation Office) for Fintech to enable the easy entry of the Fintechs in the financial sector. BB issues licences to FinTech entities in two broad categories: Payment System Operator (PSO) and PSP. There are four PSOs and three PSPs functioning in the country with the licences of BB.[617]

622. BB finalized the draft of the primary legislation on National Payment and Settlement Systems in 2018, and this is now under review by the concerned ministry. Recently, in April 2019, BB had taken the initiative to review nine banking-related laws. These are (a) the Bangladesh Bank Order, 1972 (President's Order No. 127 of 1972), which was enacted to establish a central bank in Bangladesh to manage the monetary and credit system of Bangladesh with a view to stabilizing domestic monetary value and maintaining a competitive external par value of the Bangladesh Taka towards fostering growth and development of country's productive resources in the best national interest; (b) the Bangladesh Banks (Nationalization) Order, 1972 (President's Order No. 26 of 1972), which was enacted to provide for the taking over of the undertaking of certain banks in Bangladesh; (c) the Bank Company Act, 1991 (Act No. 14 of 1991), which was enacted to provide for the provisions relating to bank companies; (d) the Negotiable Instruments Act, 1881 (Act No. XXVI of 1881), which was enacted to define and amend the law relating to Promissory Notes, Bills of Exchange and Cheques; (e) the Bankers' Book Evidence Act, 1891 (Act No. XVIII of 1891), which was enacted to amend the Law of Evidence regarding Banker's Books; (f) the Financial Institutions Act, 1993 (Act No. 27 of 1993), which was enacted to provide for licensing of financial institutions and their control; (g) the Money Loan Court Act, 2003 (Act No. 8 of 2003), which was enacted to further amend and consolidate existing laws for loan collection by financial institutions; (h) the Co-operative Societies Act, 2001 (Act No. 47 of 2001), which was enacted to update the Co-operative Societies Ordinance, 1984; and (i) the Insolvency Act, 1997 (Act No. 10 of 1997) which was enacted to make provisions relating to bankruptcy. As can be seen, all these laws are quite old and enacted at a time when ICT services or goods were not introduced. It can be anticipated that after the review of these laws, these will be able to meet the needs of the time and some of the real existing challenges that impede the expansion of electronic banking system in the country.

623. The Bankers' Books Evidence Act, 1891 (Act No. XVIII of 1891) has recently been repealed and updated by the Bankers' Books Evidence Act, 2021 (Act No. 27 of 2021). This newly enacted law contains provisions on certified copies of bankers' books (section 3), evidentiary value of certified copies of bankers' books (section 4), cases in which bank officers are not bound to produce books (section 5), inspection of books by Court's order (section 6), grounds and conditions for publication of information of the customers (section 7), punishment (section 8), trial (section 10) act done in good faith (section 11), costs (section 12), etc. This Law

617. BB, Annual Report (July 2019–June 2020), at pp. 144–146.

has encapsulated the definitions of 'data', 'electronic signature' as available in the ICT Act, 2006 and 'computer system', included in the Digital Security Act, 2018 (Act No. 46 of 2018).

Chapter 4. Protection of Users of Electronic Services

624. The issue of protection of the users of electronic services is still a challenge for the stakeholders in the country. As a result, there is frequent news of fraud on online money transfer, MFS or ATM theft as shared in the previous chapter. There are even instances of credit card forgery and payments done abroad without the knowledge of the customer.[618] Even though there are some isolated provisions in different laws on various aspects of privacy protection, there is no personal data protection law in the country. In the absence of a comprehensive personal information protection law, cybercriminals, MFS agents and in many cases, bank officials are found to be involved in facilitating the commission of these incidents though a PSP is liable to secure the information of customers' EFT.[619] A recent study conducted by the Bangladesh Institute of Bank Management, based on fifty hacking incidents in the banking sector, revealed that bankers and engineers employed with the banks perpetrated 67% of the online banking frauds. Both the bankers and engineers were involved in 40% of the incidents and the bankers alone were responsible for 18% of the incidents.[620]

625. Sometimes the law enforcement agencies become successful in arresting some of these offenders, which can be seen as the tip of an iceberg. The ultimate success of these initiatives is to be evaluated in a great context as many of these accused arrested receive bails within a short period of their arrest and later get involved in similar kinds of criminal activities. In a very few instances, it is reported that the Banks agreed to reimburse the loss of the customers. Nevertheless, in most instances, the customers of these services do not get any speedy and effective remedy.

626. The Regulations on Electronic Fund Transfer, 2014, as formulated under the Bangladesh Bank Order 1972, contains provisions on any transfer of funds initiated by a person by way of instruction, authorization or order to a bank to debit or credit an account maintained with that bank through electronic means and includes POS transfers, ATM transactions, direct deposits or withdrawal of funds, transfer initiated by telephone, internet and card or other devices, etc. The Regulations contains various provisions regarding the protection of electronic banking services. Under regulations, a PSP is responsible for providing a platform so that a customer can contact the service provider in case of any loss, misuse, theft or unauthorized use of a card or other electronic device or breach of a security code.[621] Besides, a PSP shall be liable to its customers for a loss caused by the failure of a system or

618. It has already been shared that as of 30 Jun. 2020, a total of one million MFS agents have been serving 88.70 million registered customers. *See* BB, Annual Report (July 2019–June 2020), at p. 142.
619. Article 26, the Regulations on Electronic Fund Transfer, 2014.
620. Daily Sun, Bankers engineer most online banking frauds Reveals BIBM study, 17 Nov. 2017, https://www.daily-sun.com/printversion/details/269151/Bankers-engineer-most-online-banking-frauds.
621. Article 9, the Regulations on Electronic Fund Transfer, 2014.

equipment malfunction.[622] With all these provisions, the implementation of these, and the regulation and monitoring of electronic services is an important concern.

627. It will be relevant to share here that the Regulations has imposed several duties on the customers in Articles 12 and 13. A customer is responsible for informing his PSP within fifteen days regarding any error in his statement of account or possible unauthorized transaction relating to his card or security access code. Moreover, a customer will be responsible for his negligence if he makes a delay in notification.[623]

628. BB established the Customer Interest Protection system in 2011. Subsequently, a Department, i.e., Financial Integrity & Customer Services Department (FICSD) was created in 2012. In June 2014, this FICSD issued the 'Guidelines for Customer Services and Complaint Management'. These Guidelines, issued by BB under section 45(1) of Bank Company Act, 1991 and applicable to all banks and financial institutions regulated by BB, are supplementary to the standards set by the legislative requirements and will not replace or supersede those. Accordingly, most of the Banks have issued their own customized complaint management. It has been reported that in 2016–2017, the FICSD received 3,521 complaints of which 325 were related to cards and 87 were related to mobile banking.[624] In 2018, the Department received 5,731 complaints of which 1,972 were related to general banking, 502 were related to cards, 36 were related to cheque fraud, and 101 were related to mobile banking. It was claimed that 99% of these complaints were resolved.[625] In FY 2020, 3,570 complaints were received and 99.13% of these complaints, i.e., 3,539 complaints were resolved.[626]

629. Besides, BB and other banks have been running customer awareness campaigns through various events and initiatives. Some bank officials are also brought before the law. To ensure a safe, efficient and digital payment system, the Payment Systems Department of BB is also working to formulate and publish national chip specifications, NPSB Operating Manuals, ATM Operating Guidelines and other regulatory frameworks.

630. There is an important recent development in this regard. The Bankers' Books Evidence Act, 2021 (Act No. 27 of 2021) was enacted repealing the Bankers' Books Evidence Act, 1891 (Act No. XVIII of 1891). This recently enacted law has included provisions on the protection of customers' information in section 7. It is provided that notwithstanding anything contained in any other law for the time

622. Article 10, the Regulations on Electronic Fund Transfer, 2014.
623. Article 15, the Regulations on Electronic Fund Transfer, 2014.
624. Financial Integrity and Customer Services Department, Annual Report (2016–2017).
625. Mehedi Hasan, BB Received 5,731 Complaints Against Banks in 2018, 17 Jan. 2019, Dhaka Tribune, https://www.dhakatribune.com/business/banks/2019/01/17/bb-received-5-731-complaints-against-banks-in-2018.
626. BB, Annual Report (July 2019–June 2020), at p. 51.

being in force, no officer or employee of the bank shall disclose any customer information to any other person, though such information may be disclosed to the concerned authorized person or organization, complying the terms of disclosure of customer information in authorized grounds as included in the Schedule to the law. Besides, customer information collected during the bank inspection by Bangladesh Bank under Section 44 of the Banking Companies Act, 1991 (Act No. 14 of 1991) and Section 20 of the Financial Institutions Act, 1993 (Act No. 27 of 1993), even if it is not necessary, for the control or supervision of such bank, will be treated as confidential. Violation of these provisions shall be deemed to be an offence under this Act, and the officer or employee of the bank responsible for such offence shall be punished with imprisonment for a term not exceeding 3 (three) years or with a fine not exceeding BDT 10,00,000 or both (section 8). However, such an offence will be non-cognizable, bailable and compoundable subject to the consent of the court (section 9).

Part V. Non-contractual Liability

Chapter 1. Non-contractual Liability

§1. Negligence

631. Even though Bangladesh is predominantly an English common law country, the law of tort is not developed satisfactorily and has not taken a mature shape in the country yet even after fifty years of independence; albeit, there are some isolated instances where the court of law considered various tort issues.[627] The Penal Code, 1860 (XLV of 1860), the main substantive criminal law of the country, contains provisions on negligence relating to criminal activities.[628] The justice seekers, however, hardly exploit these provisions since one has to follow a troublesome and complex procedure. Besides, there are general beliefs among the people that they do not get enough cooperation from the members of the law enforcement agencies in these matters. Moreover, the punishments stipulated under these provisions are very nominal as the law was enacted long ago, and civil remedies under negligence cases are not very common.

632. For the purpose of the content of this monograph, it is relevant to share here that section 53 of the Consumers' Right Protection Act, 2009 (Act No. 26 of 2009) provides for liability for negligence, irresponsibility or carelessness which causes the consumer to suffer damage to his health or monitory loss or death arising out of goods and services. The law has included a very wide meaning of the words

---

627. For example, in *British American Tobacco Bangladesh Company Ltd. v. Begum Shamsun Nahar*, 2010, 39 CLC (AD) [8698] = 66 DLR (AD) (2014) 80, in a case for damages for sexual harassment of an employee by another employee, the AD of Supreme Court of Bangladesh held that 'A person can be liable for tort as well and damages may be claimed against him for such wrong doing as well as against an organization or establishment if it fails to ensure the prevention of sexual harassment and bullying to a woman, where she can work with honour and dignity and without being harassed or disturbed by her male boss or other male colleagues.'

628. *See*, for example, public servant negligently suffering such prisoner to escape (s. 129), deserter concealed on board merchant vessel through negligence of master (s. 137), escape from confinement or custody negligently suffered by public servant (s. 223), negligent act likely to spread infection of disease dangerous to life (s. 269), rash driving or riding on a public way (s. 279), rash navigation of vessel (280), negligent conduct with respect to poisonous substance (s. 284), negligent conduct with respect to fire or combustible matter (s. 285), negligent conduct with respect to explosive substance (s. 286), negligent conduct with respect to machinery (s. 287), negligent conduct with respect to pulling down or repairing buildings (s. 288), negligent conduct with respect to animal (s. 289), causing death by negligence (s. 304a), causing death by rash driving or riding on a public way (s. 304b), act endangering life or personal safety to others (s. 336), etc.

'goods', 'services' and 'consumers' and accordingly, the consumers can bring suits against the ICT and telecommunication service providers in case they suffer damage to their health or monetary loss or death.

633. Immediately, after the Independence of the country, in *Abdul Awal and ors v. Mofasiluddin Ahmed and others,* 1975, 4 CLC (HCD) [9518] = 27 DLR (HCD) (1975) 628, in a matter involving the issue of damages and compensation due to certain injuries resulting from the falling of materials from a corridor under construction, D.C. Bhattacharya J. held that '[n]egligence as a tort is the breach of a legal duty to take care which results in damage to the plaintiff. So, it involves three elements *viz.* (1) existence of a legal duty on the part of the defendants to the plaintiff (2) breach of that duty and (3) consequential damage to the plaintiff'.

634. The court of laws attempted to deal with the issue of negligence in different circumstances in recent times. In *Children's Charity Bangladesh Foundation (CCB Foundation) v. Bangladesh & ors.* 10 SOCB [2018] HCD 117, the HCD of the Bangladesh Supreme Court while dealing with the death of a 4 years old boy by falling into a 16 inches uncovered abandoned shaft, discussed the various aspects of negligence in the following manner:

> 49. The word 'negligence' is defined as the breach of a duty caused by the omission to do something which a reasonable man would do or doing something which a prudent and reasonable man would not do. In other words, negligence may arise from non-feasance or from misfeasance.
> 50. An action for negligence proceeds upon the idea of an obligation or duty on the part of the person concern to use care, a breach whereof results in the injury of the aggrieved person.
> 51. However, the standard or degree of care which a man is required to use in a particular situation varies with the obviousness of the risk. If the danger of doing injury to the person or property of another in pursuance of a certain line of conduct is great, great care is necessary. If the danger is slight, only a slight amount of care is required. The care that will be required of them will be the care that an ordinary prudent man is bound to exercise. But, persons who profess to have a special skill, or who have voluntarily undertaken a higher degree of duty, are bound to exercise more care than an ordinary prudent man.
> 52. In order to succeed in an action for negligence, the aggrieved person must prove the followings – 1. that the other party was under a legal duty to exercise due care and skill; 2. That the duty was towards aggrieved person; 3. that in the circumstances of the case, the other party failed to perform that duty; 4. that the breach of such duty was the *causa causans* i.e., the direct and proximate cause, of the damage complained of; and 5. that the injury is caused on account of this breach of duty.
> 53. As a general rule, the onus of proving negligence is on the aggrieved person. He must not merely establish the facts of the other parties' negligence and of his own injury but must show that the one was the effect of thc othcr.
> 54. However, in an action of negligence, the affected person must affirmatively prove negligence but may find hardship in cases where the aggrieved person

can prove the accident, but cannot show how it happened, the fact being solely outside his knowledge and within the knowledge of the other party who causes it. In such cases, it is sufficient for the aggrieved person to prove the accident and nothing more, for, there is a presumption of negligence according to the maxim '*res ipsa loquitur*' (the thing speaks for itself). Such presumption arises when the cause of the mischief was apparently under the control of the other person or his servants. The accident itself constitutes reasonable evidence of negligence in the particular circumstances.
55. Thus, the following are the essential requirements for the application of the said maxim:

(i) The thing causing the damage must be under the control of the other party or his servants; (ii) the accident must be such as would not, in the ordinary course of things, have happened without negligence and (iii) there must be no evidence of the actual cause of the accident.

635. It is a general understanding that any act done in good faith by government officials will get an exemption and cannot be sued in a court of law. Relevant laws also provide that the Government shall not be responsible for any loss or damage which may occur in consequence of any telegraph officer failing in his duty with respect to the receipt, transmission or delivery of any message; and no such officer shall be responsible for any such loss or damage unless he causes the same negligently, maliciously or fraudulently.[629] Similarly, the Bangladesh Telecommunication Regulation Act, 2001 has also extended indemnity to the Minister, government employee, Chairman or officer or employee of the BTRC for any act done in good faith.[630]

636. Even though there are such provisions, in some isolated instances, the courts of law awarded compensations in negligence cases. In *Md. Shahanewas v. Government of Bangladesh,* 18 BLD (HCD) 337, the HCD of Bangladesh Supreme Court awarded 'compensatory' costs of Tk. 20,000/=, against a delinquent police officer for negligently arresting a poor fisherman in place of a convicted criminal merely on the basis of their identical names by observing that the poor victim should be 'well compensated' for his 'immense sufferings' and loss of livelihood for six months due to sheer negligence of the public servant in discharging his public duty. Similarly, in recent times, the Supreme Court of Bangladesh has awarded compensation to the victims in negligence cases.

629. Section 9, the Telegraph Act, 1885 (Act No. XIII of 1885).
630. Section 95, the Bangladesh Telecommunication Regulation Act, 2001 (Act No. 18 of 2001).

§2. Liability of Network Operators

637. Subject to any restrictions imposed by law, the freedom of profession, occupation, trade or business, is a constitutionally guaranteed right in Bangladesh.[631] Thus, the telecommunication and ICT service providers are free to run their trade and business, though they are bound to follow the provisions of the general, special and sectoral domestic laws, sectoral policies, rules, regulations, orders, decisions, guidelines, directives and other relevant documents issued by the Government or BTRC. Apart from these, they are further regulated through the provisions of the licence they obtained from the regulators to run their trade or business. Though there are concerns that the licensing regime is highly fragmented and complex, and there are different provisions regarding the QoS from the NTTN and MNOs,[632] the licensees are still bound to follow the licensing conditions. With regard to the licences, the BTRC has been issuing various Guidelines from time to time, and it is explicitly stated that these Guidelines shall form an integral part of the licence.[633]

638. The MNOs cannot make any discrimination in providing services. Section 50(1) of the Bangladesh Telecommunication Regulation Act, 2001 (Act No. 18 of 2001), provides that 'an operator is not, in relation to a service provided by him or the charge for such service, make any discrimination or create any inconvenience to any person or group or class, nor will he give any unfair or unreasonable preference to himself or any other person'. The BTRC, being the regulator of this sector, is empowered 'to protect the social and economic interests of consumers, respond to their needs, and control and abolish existing and probable oppressive or discriminatory conduct or activities of the telecommunication service providers'.[634]

639. The BTRC (Interconnection) Regulations, 2004 were formulated, *inter alia*, to prevent and abolish discrimination in the provision of services, ensure fair competition, and promote and safeguard the interests of consumers by ensuring reliable and fairly priced modern services with reasonable accessibility. Section 4 of the Regulations, 2004 deals with the rights and obligations of the operators. Under the Regulations, it is mandatory for all operators to ensure logical interconnection among their exchanges and/or networks enabling the subscribers or consumers or users of one operator to communicate with the subscribers or consumers or users of other operators as and when required.

640. Since all these service providers need to obtain a licence from the regulatory authorities of the country, their liabilities are determined by the provisions of the licence. Besides, they are bound to ensure the standards of QoS as specified in the BTRC (ANS Operator's QoS) Regulations, 2018.

---

631. Article 40, the Constitution of the People's Republic of Bangladesh, 1972.
632. Global System for Mobile Communications Association (GSMA), Country overview: Bangladesh, 2018, at p. 46.
633. *See*, Introduction, the Cellular Mobile Phone Operator Regulatory and Licensing Guidelines, 2011.
634. Section 30(d), the Bangladesh Telecommunication Regulation Act, 2001 (Act No. 18 of 2001).

641. There is a definition of ANS Operator in the ILDTS Policy, 2007 and 2010. The definition includes ANS as PSTN, Cellular, Cable Service Providers and ISP Operators who have direct connections with the subscribers. With these, the BTRC (ANS Operator's QoS) Regulations, 2018 has also included broadband access services providers in the definition. Four network operators, i.e., Grameenphone Ltd. (GP), Robi Axiata Ltd. (Robi), Banglalink Digital Communications Ltd. and Teletalk Bangladesh Ltd. (Teletalk), are functioning in the country. Under the general provisions of law, it is an offence to provide telecommunication services without obtaining a licence from the regulators, though it is permitted to operate the telecommunication system, to a limited scale, which is not connected to another telecommunication system.[635]

642. Moreover, in determining the liabilities of the network operators, the terms and conditions of these operators with the consumer will also play an important role. Usually, the terms and conditions are available on the website or service-related documents, such as mobile SIM/Account opening form. Nevertheless, the consumers hardly read these. The network operators need to dispose of consumer complaints in a timely manner about various services. Section 59 of the Bangladesh Telecommunication Regulation Act, 2001 (Act No. 18 of 2001) deals with the provisions on the receipt and disposal of consumer complaints.

643. The BTRC formulated the 'Cellular Mobile Phone Operator Regulatory and Licensing Guidelines, 2011' and under these Guidelines, 2011, the operators have a number of obligations regarding the Spectrum Operation, QoSs, interconnection, infrastructure and facility sharing, MNP, IMEI barring system and SMP, etc. Under the Guidelines, 2011, the Cellular Mobile Phone Licensees have to provide commitments to the consumers with respect to the standard and quality of licensed service. Moreover, Licensees have to establish and maintain a substantial number of Customer Care Centres.

644. The BTRC has issued the 'Regulatory and Licensing Guidelines for Mobile Number Portability Services, 2016' and based on the provisions of this Guidelines; the mobile phone subscribers are permitted to migrate to their preferred operators without changing their mobile phone number. It is believed that such an initiative will encourage the service providers to improve their service quality to retain their existing subscribers and attract new subscribers and will ultimately benefit the telecommunication and ICT industry of the country.

645. In some isolated instances, the court of law has interfered. For example, in a case relating to the use of the national anthem as a mobile phone ringtone, the AD noticed that the mobile phone operators such as Grameen Phone, Bangla Link and Robi were charging revenue for playing the national anthem on the mobile phones. The AD, after referring to Article 4 of the Bangladesh Constitution, 1972 and the

---

635. Section 35, the Bangladesh Telecommunication Regulation Act, 2001 (Act No. 18 of 2001).

National Anthem Rules, 1978, held that there is no scope for commercial use of the national anthem and such commercial use of national anthem shows utter disrespect to the national anthem.[636]

§3. LIABILITY OF SERVICE PROVIDERS

646. The recently enacted Digital Security Act, 2018 (Act No. 46 of 2018) has defined the 'service provider' as any person who through a computer or digital process enables any user to communicate; or any such person, entity or institution who or which preserves or processes data in favour of the service user.[637]

647. Like the network service operators, the ISPs also need to obtain licences for providing services. Generally, the terms and conditions of the licence stipulate duties and responsibilities on the licence holder to follow the relevant legal provisions along with additional conditions as stipulated in the licence. The detailed conditions of the licence that the BTRC can include in the licence are included in section 37 of the Bangladesh Telecommunication Regulation Act, 2001 (Act No. 18 of 2001). Thus, the service providers need to follow both the provisions of law, both general and special, and the terms and conditions of the licence.

648. Section 79 of the ICT Act, 2006 deals with the liability of network service providers, i.e., intermediaries to some extent. It is provided that no person providing any service as a network service provider shall be liable under this Act, or rules and regulations made thereunder, for any third party information or data made available by him if he can prove that the offence or contravention was committed without his knowledge or that he had exercised due diligence to prevent the commission of such offence or contravention.

649. The Digital Security Act, 2018 (Act No. 46 of 2018) has included the safe harbour provisions for the service providers. While the law has reproduced the provision similar to the provision of section 79 of the ICT Act, 2006,[638] it is clearly stated that the investigation officer who is investigating an offence under the law may request, *inter alia*, the service provider to provide information or assistance in the investigation, and such service provider so requested will be bound to assist the investigation officer.[639] The Law further provides that the service provider shall

636. *Orascom Telecom & Chief Executive Officer, Grameen Phone Limited v. Kalipada Mridha & ors.*, 2 SCOB [2015] AD 12.
637. Section 2(v), the Digital Security Act, 2018 (Act No. 46 of 2018).
638. Section 38 of the Digital Security Act, 2018 (Act No. 46 of 2018) provides that '[a]ny service provider shall not be responsible under this Act or any rules enacted under this Act for facilitating access to data-information, if he can prove that the offence or breach was committed without his knowledge or that he had exercised due diligence to prevent the commission of such offence or contravention'.
639. Section 46, the Digital Security Act, 2018 (Act No. 46 of 2018).

maintain the secrecy of the information obtained during the investigation and for such act of the service provider, no civil or criminal proceedings can be brought.[640]

650. Thus, even though under the law, the services providers can enjoy immunity for making third party information or data, e.g., copyrighted materials available, they need to establish two things, i.e., absence of knowledge and exercise of due diligence. While the issue of absence of knowledge may be proved through circumstantial evidence;[641] in order to establish the due diligence, the service providers may be compelled to show the initiatives taken in this regard. Since there is no definition of 'due diligence' in the existing law or interpretation given by the court of law, examples of such initiatives may include the use of adequate technical tools such as software and hardware, training of the employees, sharing of immediate information to the law enforcement body when any doubt or irregularity is noticed, etc. In any case, as per the existing criminal procedure law of the country, the burden to prove an accused guilty will lie on the prosecution.[642]

640. Section 47, the Digital Security Act, 2018 (Act No. 46 of 2018).

641. *In Manzu Sweeper v. The State* (2008) 13 MLR (HC) 417, the court, with regards to the possession of counterfeit currency under s. 25A of the Special Powers Act, 1974, held that since counterfeit currency may come into possession of a person in course of daily transaction without the knowledge of the same being counterfeit, mere possession of a counterfeit currency without the knowledge of the nature thereof does not constitute an offence. Based on this proposition, in the absence of any direct and specific case law, the intermediaries may escape liabilities.

642. Part III, Ch. VII, the Evidence Act, 1872 (Act No. I of 1872).

Chapter 2. Product Liability

§1. Introduction

651. The discussion on consumer protection in the context of product liability for the purpose of this monograph is crucial. Being an agricultural country, the culture of consumer protection has not been properly developed in the country yet even after five decades of independence. As a result, the consumers of the country, like many other parts of the world, having limited bargaining power have a very thin voice in the making of the decisions affecting them. Even though one may notice some news of law enforcement actions against the seller or manufacturers of defective products causing serious injuries to human health, consumers have very few ordinary remedies available under the domestic law compared to the injuries they suffer. This chapter will start by shedding light on the definitions of consumer, goods/products and services. After that, a glimpse of global consumer movements will be provided. Next, the issue of product liability and consumer protection within the domestic legal framework of Bangladesh will be discussed, where the important provisions of the Consumers' Right Protection Act, 2009 (Act No. 26 of 2009) highlighting the definitions of important terms, available remedies and defences under the Act will be evaluated. Finally, an overview of product liability in the context of law of contract, sale of goods and tort will be shared.

§2. Consumer, Goods and Services: Definitional Aspects

652. The term 'consumer' generally denotes a natural person who purchases, acquires or uses any goods or services for personal, domestic or household use or for consumption as opposed to business or commercial use. One exception, in the context of Europe, can be shared here where under the Package Travel Directive (90/314/EEC), the companies and business travellers are also considered as consumers. Otherwise, a consumer is usually a natural person who remains outside the scope of economic and commercial activities and does not include a legal person. Nevertheless, the term 'consumer' is very wide and the European Parliament, in a study conducted in 2015, revealed that at least ninety community legislation contain provisions on consumer protection.[643]

653. The words 'goods' and 'products', generally indicate tangible moveable items as used by the consumers, are used interchangeably in the common parlance. Under the European Council Directive 85/374/EEC of 25 July 1985 on the liability for defective products, 'product' means all movables even if incorporated into another movable or into an immovable and includes electricity (Article 2). On the other hand, under the US Federal Law, i.e., the Consumer Product Safety Law of

643. European Parliament, 'Consumer Protection in the EU: Policy Overview', European Parliamentary Research Service, September 2015, p. 5.

2021 [15 U.S.C. § 2052], the word 'consumer products' means 'any article, or component part, produced or distributed for the personal use, consumption or enjoyment of a consumer in or around a permanent or temporary household or residence, a school, in recreation, or otherwise'. Thus, it is apparent that in the context of the US, the definition has mentioned some sectors more specifically where a consumer uses these products personally. The definition has excluded some articles, e.g., non-customary products used by a consumer such as tobacco and tobacco products, motor vehicles or motor vehicle equipment, pesticides, aircraft, aircraft engines, propellers, or appliances, drugs, devices, or cosmetics and food, etc., from the said definition as there are separate laws to regulate different aspects of these articles or products.

654. One may not find any actual difference between these two words, i.e., 'goods' and 'products' except their usage and context in our daily life. While the common people prefer to use these words in a different context, e.g., consumer goods, financial products, petroleum products, etc., these words have different legal implications, at least in the context of free movement of goods in the EU as the word 'goods' entails addressing different tax or fiscal related consequences. In the case of *European Communities v. Italian Republic*, 1968 (Case 7-68), the European Court of Justice (now the Court of Justice [CoJ]) defined goods as products which can be valued in money and which is capable of forming the subjects of commercial transactions. The term 'good' is very broad and depends on the different contexts. Therefore, a razor-sharp line as to what constitutes a good and what is not is neither very clear nor straightforward. Moreover, the CoJ has extended the definition of 'goods' and included some otherwise unconventional things ranging from electricity, gold and silver coins, bees, waste etc. within the definition of 'goods' (*See*, for example, *Commission v. France* [1997] ECR I-5815 [Case C-158/94]; *R v. Thompson* (1978) ECR 2247 [Case 7/78]; *Bluhme* [1998] ECR I-8033 [Case C-67/97]; *Commission v. Belgium* [1993] 1 CMLR 365 [Case C-2/90]). It may be relevant to share here that in the context of Europe, the word 'object' is also used sometimes as a synonym of goods or products. Thus, from the discussion above, it is evident that these two terms, i.e., 'goods' and 'products' are used interchangeably in the legal texts though they may have a different meaning in a different context. Besides, it is apparent that there are laws containing general provisions regulating goods or products; whereas, there are specific laws also provisions of which govern specific types of consumer products or goods, such as foods, drugs, medicines, cosmetics, children toys, etc.

655. In the legal literature, the terms 'goods' and 'services' are used regularly as a pair, and many legal disputes arise about 'services', at least in the context of Europe concerning the free movement of services. The examples of services include various industry-specific services such as legal services, telecommunication services, hotels, tourism services, etc.

656. The definition of the term 'goods' in the context of sale of goods may create some confusion or uncertainty when the software or electronic book is sold on disks, and when these are sold in electronic format, i.e., delivered through downloading. The judiciary of different jurisdictions has approached the issue highlighting different aspects of goods, property or propriety rights. Understandably, any software or electronic book is sold on disks will be regarded as 'goods'. However, software that is delivered through downloading is not 'goods' for the purpose of sale of goods since there is nothing supplied in the tangible form, e.g., compact disk.[644] Nevertheless, this can be treated as 'service'.[645]

§3. Consumer Protection and Global Move

657. The issue of consumer protection, though can be found indirectly in ancient texts such as the Code of Hammurabi, is more like an idea of recent origin after the advent of capitalism. Initially, it was developed in the Western countries from the mid-nineteenth century, and subsequently, it started expanding in other Asian countries.[646] In the context of the legal history of Bangladesh, the word 'consumer' was even included in the Electricity Act, 1910 which was recently repealed and updated by the Electricity Act, 2018 (Act No. 7 of 2018). In the Act of 1910, the term 'consumer', used more than forty times, was defined as 'any person who is supplied with energy by a licensee, or who is the owner or occupier of the premises which are for the time being connected for the purposes of a supply of energy with the works of a licensee'. Nevertheless, when the Act of 2018 was enacted, the word 'customer' was preferred instead of 'consumer', though the word 'consumer' is included in the Bangladesh Energy Regulatory Commission Act, 2003 (Act No. 13 of 2003), through which the Bangladesh Energy Regulatory Commission was established to implement the provisions of the Act of 2018.

658. Consumers have very limited bargaining power compared to manufacturers or suppliers for various reasons. Former American President, John F. Kennedy realized this and pronounced the 'Consumer Bill of Rights', containing four basic rights of a consumer on 15 March 1962. These four rights are: (a) the right to safety, (b) the right to information, (c) the right to choose, and (d) the right to be heard. Leading consumer protection Non-Governmental Organization (NGO), the Consumer International, formerly known as International Organization of Consumers Unions, proposed four more rights with these, i.e., (a) the right to redress or remedy, (b) right to environmental health, (c) right to service, and (d) right to consumer education. While adopting the United Nations Guidelines for Consumer Protection (UNGCP) through resolution 39/248 of 16 April 1985, the UN General Assembly encapsulated all these eight rights. The UNGCP have turned to be a valuable set of

644. *See* the English decision *Computer Associates UK Ltd. v. The Software Incubator Ltd.* [2018] EWCA Civ 518. Similar was the stand of the New South Wales Supreme Court. *See Gammasonics Institute for Medical Research Pty Ltd v. Comrad Medical Systems Pty Ltd* [2010] NSWSC 267.
645. *Commission v. Luxembourg*, Case C-502/13 (ECJ) and *Commission v. France*, Case C-479/13 (ECJ).
646. For an authoritative history on consumer protection related legal developments, *see* https://consumersinternational.blogspot.my/2011/03/vision-for-consumer-empowerment.html.

principles setting out the main characteristics of effective consumer protection legislation, enforcement institutions and redress systems. The Economic and Social Council later revised and expanded these Guidelines through the resolution 1999/7 of 26 July 1999. Finally, the UN General Assembly adopted the resolution 70/186 of 22 December 2015.

659. The UNGCP have identified the legitimate needs of the consumers. These are, *inter alia*, access to essential goods and services, protection of vulnerable and disadvantaged consumers, promotion and protection of the economic interests of consumers, access by consumers to adequate information to enable them to make informed choices according to individual wishes and needs, consumer education on the social and economic consequences of consumer choices, availability of effective consumer dispute resolution and redress, a level of protection for consumers using electronic commerce, protection of consumer privacy, etc.

660. It will be pertinent to share here that the UNGCP are mere guidelines and therefore, are not legally binding. Nevertheless, they are of high persuasive value since they are accepted as the international benchmark for good practice on consumer protection and were adopted by the UN General Assembly. It is believed that most of the countries in the world have considered these principles while drafting their national laws on consumer protection. Realizing the importance of these principles, UNCTAD has subsequently developed the 'Manual on Consumer Protection' to assist countries in implementing the revised UNGCP.

§4. Product Liability and Consumer Protection

661. Constitutionally, in Bangladesh, the taking of initiative to improve public health is among the primary duties of the state.[647] Therefore, the state is responsible for ensuring that the citizens get quality products which may, in turn, ensure improved public health in the long run. Unfortunately, there is no domestic law which directly deals with defective products, and as such, there is no statutory definition available as to defective products due to which one can be held liable. Instead, some isolated provisions can be found in domestic laws having implications on consumer protection. A list of such laws includes, but is not limited to, the Special Powers Act, 1974 (Act No. XIV of 1974),[648] the Penal Code, 1860 (XLV of

647. Articles 16 & 18(1), the Constitution of the People's Republic of Bangladesh, 1972.

648. Section 2(e) of the Act has defined 'hoarding' as stocking or storing anything in excess of the maximum quantity of that things allowed to be held in stock or storage at any one time by any person by or under any law. Hoarding is a punishable offence under s. 25 of the Act.

Section 25C of the Act deals with penalty for adulteration of, or sale of adulterated food, drink, drugs or cosmetics.

Even an attempt or conspiracy or making preparation to commit or abetment of any offence punishable under this Act shall be punishable with the punishment provided for the offence (s. 25D). Moreover, if offences under this Law is committed by any company then partner, director, manager, secretary or other officer or agent shall, if actively concerned in the conduct of the business of such firm, company or body corporate, be deemed to have committed the offence unless he proves that the

1980),[649] the Drugs (Control) Ordinance, 1982 (Ordinance No. VIII of 1982),[650] the Food Safety Act, 2013 (Act No. 43 of 2013), etc., which prohibit marketing or selling adulterated food, drinks, drugs, cosmetics, etc. The government of Bangladesh has established several institutions such as BSTI and other regulators to ensure that the citizens get a quality product. Besides, the telecommunication regulator of the country, BTRC is also empowered to take initiatives under the Bangladesh Telecommunication Regulation Act, 2001 to ensure that the consumers get quality telecommunication services.[651]

662. The issue of product liability can be discussed by referring to the provisions of the domestic contract law, i.e., the Contract Act, 1872 (Act No. IX of 1872) since the terms and conditions of a contract do not need to be written down and oral agreements are enforceable if all the legal requirements are met. But, unlike the system of product liability focused on consumer protection, there is no specific protection regime for the consumers in Bangladesh. The Sale of Goods Act, 1930 (Act No. III of 1930) implies some implied conditions in the contract for the sale of goods as to title, quality, purpose and merchantability.[652] However, such conditions can be avoided and varied by the traders by express provisions in terms of the contract.[653]

663. Along with the above-mentioned isolated provisions on product liability in many other sectorial laws, the Consumers' Right Protection Act, 2009 (Act No. 26 of 2009), the general law on product liability in Bangladesh, which was enacted to make provisions for the protection of the rights of the consumers and to prevent anti-consumer right practices,[654] is additional to the provisions of other laws for the time being in force.[655] Thus, understandably, the provisions of the law shall be implemented along with other domestic legal provisions. Therefore, the law

---

offence was committed without his knowledge or that he exercised all due diligence to prevent the commission of the offence (s. 25E).

649. The Penal Code, 1860 deals with the punishment for making any article of food or drink adulterated with the intention to sell such article of food or drink (s. 272), sale of noxious food or drink (s. 273), adulteration of drugs (s. 274), sale of adulterated drugs (s. 275), sale of drug as a different drug or preparation (s. 276).

650. Section 16(c) prohibits the manufacturing, import, distribution, stock, exhibition or sell of any drug which is adulterated.

651. It may be relevant to share here that in the official Bangla version of the law, i.e., the Bangladesh Telecommunication Regulation Act, 2001 (Act No. 18 of 2001), a Bangla word is used the English translation of which should be 'subscriber' or 'customer'. However, in the apparent official authentic translation of the law publicly available, the word 'consumer', instead of 'subscriber' or 'customer', is used throughout the law. This Law further says that the Government shall publish an authentic English translation of the law and in case of any conflict between the two versions, i.e., original Bangla version and the authentic English translation, the Bangla version shall prevail.

652. Section 16, the Sale of Goods Act, 1930 (Act No. III of 1930).

653. Section 62 of the Sale of Goods Act, 1930 provides that 'Where any right, duty or liability would arise under a contract of sale by implication of law, it may be negatived or varied by express agreement or by the course of dealing between the parties, or by usage, if the usage is such as to bind both parties to the contract.'

654. Long title and Preamble, the Consumers' Right Protection Act 2009 (Act No. 26 of 2009).

655. Section 3, the Consumers' Right Protection Act 2009 (Act No. 26 of 2009).

enforcement bodies can use the provisions of these general laws along with the sectorial law provisions simultaneously. This is apparently a good move from the policymakers since the liability regime under the Act is not clear yet, and no substantial jurisprudence has developed under the Act yet. Thus, the previous general laws can be used as a guideline for the moment. In any event, if the liability under the Act of 2009 is uncertain or obscure, the prosecution can depend on the provisions of other laws.

664. At the national level, a Directorate of National Consumers' Right Protection under the Ministry of Commerce, with its branches in seven Divisions and sixty-four Districts, was established to monitor the market and to implement the provisions of the Consumers' Right Protection Act, 2009. The market monitoring activities started on 6 April 2010, and a consumer complaint centre was started on 3 August 2014. In FY 2017–2018, a total of 4,077 market monitoring drives were taken around the country, and a fine equivalent to BDT 141,478,200 was imposed on 11,718 business entities. During this time, the Directorate received 9,019 complaints and resolved 8,122 of them with a resolution rate of 90.05%.[656] In FY 2019–2020, a total of 12,351 market monitoring drives were taken around the country, and a fine equivalent to BDT 119,147,200 was imposed on 22,244 business entities.[657] Every year, 15 March is observed as the National Consumer Rights Day in the country. Any victim can contact the Directorate using email, social media, such as a Facebook page or directly using the specific official form developed for this purpose.

§5. Important Definitions

665. The Consumers' Right Protection Act, 2009 (Act No. 26 of 2009) has incorporated a very wide definition of the word 'consumer' to mean any person:

(a) who, without resale or commercial purpose, buys any goods for a consideration – (i) which has been paid or promised to be paid; (ii) which has been partly paid and partly promised; or (iii) under any system of deferred payment or instalment basis;
(b) who uses any goods bought under clause (a) with the consent of the buyer;
(c) who buys any goods and uses it commercially for earning his livelihood by means of self-employment;
(d) who hires or in any other means avails of any service for a consideration:
   (i) which has been paid or promised to be paid; or
   (ii) which has been partly paid and partly promised; or
   (iii) under any system of deferred payment or instalment basis; or

656. Directorate of National Consumers' Right Protection, Ministry of Commerce, Government of Bangladesh, Annual Report 2019–2020, p. 13.
657. Directorate of National Consumers' Right Protection, Ministry of Commerce, Government of Bangladesh, Annual Report 2017–2018, pp. 1–2.

(e) who enjoys any service under clause (d), with the consent of the person who hires or avails it.[658] Thus, the definition includes an individual and a self-employed businessman as a consumer who buys goods or hires services for his personal/family use without the intention of resale or commercial purpose, or for commercial purpose of earning a livelihood.

666. It may be pertinent to mention here that instead of 'product', this law has used the word 'goods'. Under the law, 'goods' means any movable commercial commodities which the buyer buys or contracts to buy from any seller in exchange for money or price;[659] and 'service' means transport, telecommunication, water supply, drainage, fuel, gas, electricity, construction, residential hotel and restaurant and health services, which is made available to its users in exchange of price but does not include the services rendered free of cost.[660] Therefore, the users of ICT products and telecommunication/s services will be treated as a consumer under the Consumers' Right Protection Act, 2009 (Act No. 26 of 2009) and they will be entitled to get the rights and remedies available under the law along with such rights and remedies available under other sectorial laws of these fields. Under section 4 of the Act, 2009, the Government is empowered to exempt any goods or services from the application of this Act.

667. It may be relevant to share here that the consumers when they enjoy the goods or services need to pay the price for it along with the service tax known, in the Bangladesh context, as VAT. In the case of *Azharuddin Ahmed v. TNT Board and Others, VI ADC (2009) 236*, a question was raised, i.e., whether BTTB, being registered under section 15 of the Value Added Tax Act, 1991 as VAT payee and the telephone service provider, can collect VAT from its subscriber or not. Moreover, it was also proposed that if VAT is at all payable, the BTTB should pay this as the service provider and not the subscribers who are also consumers. The AD of the Supreme Court of Bangladesh revealed that 'VAT is payable on goods and services and it is payable by the service provider or trader or manufacturer' and even though importer is liable to pay the VAT at the import stage, 'the incident of VAT is ultimately shifted to the consumers'. On the basis of section 73 of the VAT Act, the AD held that 'It is the consumer or purchaser of the commodity or the subscriber of a telephone who is liable to pay VAT because VAT is leviable on goods or service. Therefore, a person, who does not enjoy the benefit of the goods or service, by no stretch of imagination, can be said that he is to bear the incidence of tax. This would destroy the scheme of VAT Act and frustrate the purpose of the enactment. VAT is a tax leviable on goods and service, it must be paid by the person who purchases goods or enjoys the benefit of service provided by a service provider … VAT is

---

658. Section 2(19), the Consumers' Right Protection Act 2009 (Act No. 26 of 2009).
659. Section 2(11), the Consumers' Right Protection Act 2009 (Act No. 26 of 2009).
660. Section 2(22), the Consumers' Right Protection Act 2009 (Act No. 26 of 2009).

collected fractionally along the whole chain of distribution from the point of importation or production to the supply to the consumers. The incidence of VAT ultimately falls on the consumer but a duty is cast upon the trader or service provider to collect it from the consumer or user of the services and then to account for the same to the Government.'[661]

668. Moreover, a consumer needs to come to the court of law in clean hands, i.e., he needs to complete his part or perform his role as per the terms of the goods/service contract before he moves to the court of law to claim any legal remedies. If he fails to do so, the court will not entertain any such claims.[662]

669. The Consumers' Right Protection Act, 2009 (Act No. 26 of 2009) ('Act of 2009') has not stipulated any explicit rights of the consumers instead it has prohibited some practices as 'anti-consumer right practice' and the enforcement bodies created under the law are empowered to prevent these. These 'anti-consumer right practice' mean to:

(a) sell or offer to sell any goods, medicine or service at a higher price than the fixed price under any Act or rules;
(b) sell or offer to sell adulterated goods or medicine knowingly;
(c) sell or offer to sell any goods containing any ingredient which is extremely injurious to human health and the mixing of which with any food item is prohibited under any Act or rules;
(d) deceive consumers by an untrue or false advertisement for the purpose of selling any goods or service;
(e) not to sell or deliver properly any goods or services promised to sell or deliver in consideration of money;
(f) sell or deliver less quantity of goods than the weight offered to the consumers while delivering or selling any goods;
(g) show more than the actual weight by the weight stone or any other weight measuring instrument used for measuring weight in selling or delivering goods in a commercial enterprise;
(h) sell or deliver less quantity of goods than the promised amount while delivering or selling any goods;
(i) show more than the actual length by the length measuring gauge or anything else used for measuring the length in selling or delivering goods in a commercial enterprise;
(j) make or manufacture any fake goods or medicine;
(k) sell or offer to sell goods or medicine the date of which has expired; or

---

661. Similarly, in the case of *Grameen Phone Ltd. v. Bangladesh Telecommunication Regulatory Commission (BTRC) and others*, 2012, 41 CLC (HCD) [8826] = 18 BLC (HCD) (2013) 401, it was held that ' … the value added tax is called "consumer tax", as it is the consumer who ultimately pays the VAT. The people or person in the middle like the whole-seller or retailer, although pay VAT, but get the same credited or adjusted from the final vat paid by the consumer. Thus, the ultimate burden is on the consumer'.
662. *Titas Gas v. Immense Washing Plant and others*, 2001, 30 CLC (HCD) [4623] = 53 DLR (HCD) (2001) 471.

(l) do an act which may endanger the life or security of the consumer and which is prohibited by any Act or rules.[663]

670. A 'manufacturer' is defined as a person who: (a) makes or manufactures any goods or part thereof; (b) does not make or manufacture any goods but lawfully assembles parts of goods made or manufactured by others and claims the goods so assembled as manufactured by him; (c) lawfully puts or causes to be put his own trademark on any goods made or manufactured by any other manufacturer and claims such goods to be made or manufactured by him; or (d) where the goods are manufactured outside Bangladesh, and the manufacturer of the goods does not have any branch office or business office in Bangladesh, imports and distributes such goods. It is important to note that where the local manufacturer assembles any goods or parts thereof in any of its self-controlled or self-conducted branch offices, such branch office shall not be deemed to be the manufacturer even though the parts are assembled at such branch office.[664]

§6. Remedies Available under the Law

671. Though the system of product liability regime under various laws in Bangladesh focuses mainly on criminal liability of the traders for the defective or adulterated product, under the provisions of the Law of 2009, a consumer is entitled to receive any civil remedy for any damage caused by any anti-consumer rights practices.[665] These remedies may extend to the replacement of the defective product, the return of the defective goods and refund of money, and compensation for any damage caused.[666]

672. Section 66(1) though recognizes/saves the rights of the affected consumer to file a civil suit for civil remedies, it is uncertain whether the liability would be strict or fault-based. It is evident that the Law has not included any provision of strict liability as can be found in some other jurisdiction, especially around the European countries. The overall scheme of the Act shows that liability under the Act would be fault-based. Further, the liability of the seller, manufacturer, supplier or wholesaler under the Act to compensate for any damage caused to a consumer due to any defect in the product or goods is relatively limited to the cases of the defect arising from any of the 'anti-consumer rights practices' under the Act.[667] Further, the liability of compensating is limited to the cases where damage or injury suffered by the consumer is measurable in terms of money, and the amount of compensation to be awarded is limited to five times the monetary value of damage suffered. Civil

663. Section 2(20), the Consumers' Right Protection Act 2009 (Act No. 26 of 2009).
664. Section 2(4), the Consumers' Right Protection Act 2009 (Act No. 26 of 2009).
665. Section 66, the Consumers' Right Protection Act 2009 (Act No. 26 of 2009).
666. Section 67, the Consumers' Right Protection Act 2009 (Act No. 26 of 2009).
667. A seller means any manufacturer, maker, supplier and shall also include wholesaler or retailer (s. 2(16)).

suits for compensation can be filed against the seller. However, the Act is silent about who will bear the liability for any harm or injury done to the consumer arising out of defective products.[668]

673. Apparently, the Consumers' Right Protection Act, 2009 concentrates more on the prevention of anti-consumer rights practices and imposes criminal liabilities on the manufacturers for violating provisions of the Act and do not make them liable to the consumers. Though the Act of 2009 stipulates that provision in the Act will not affect the right of the consumers to get civil remedies, it does not provide explicitly about the liabilities of the manufacturers to the consumers for the products and the time when remedies can be claimed against the manufacturers for the violation of such liabilities.

674. The Act prohibits certain business practices as anti-consumers rights and prescribes punishment in case any such prohibited practice is carried out. It has established some regulatory authorities to monitor and prevent anti-consumer rights practices. The Act also empowers the consumers to bring criminal cases against any of the anti-consumer rights practices only through the Directorate. These can be considered as the successes of the Act as it has come out of the reluctance to criminalize unfair and dishonest commercial practices. The Act is further unique in the sense that it makes the complainant consumer entitled to a share of the fine collected from a person accused of being involved in any anti-consumer rights practice.

675. The Act makes any allegation non-cognizable unless such allegation is brought within thirty days of arising of the cause of action.[669] Given the level of consumer awareness in Bangladesh, it is highly probable that the action may not be taken against a vast majority of anti-consumer rights practices. Further, the Court is barred from taking the allegation in cognizance unless the charge sheet is submitted within ninety days.[670] The present state of criminal prosecution system indicates that in many cases, it will not be possible to submit the charge sheet within ninety days. The Act of 2009 also recognizes the right of the consumer to file civil suits for civil remedies for any damage caused by any of the anti-consumer practices and states the remedies a consumer is entitled to get in a civil suit.[671] However, this right will be hard to implement in practice. The fact that remedies should be claimed in ordinary civil courts which are already overloaded with cases may undermine the purpose of the provision.

676. It is worth mentioning that the Act lags far behind the contemporary concept of 'consumer rights' or consumerism. Though the Act criminalizes some business practices as 'anti-consumer rights practices' instead and recognizes the rights of the consumer to bring civil suits for loss suffered from any anti-consumer rights

---

668. Section 66, the Consumers' Right Protection Act, 2009 (Act No. 26 of 2009).
669. Section 60, the Consumers' Right Protection Act, 2009 (Act No. 26 of 2009).
670. Section 61, the Consumers' Right Protection Act, 2009 (Act No. 26 of 2009).
671. Sections 66 and 67, the Consumers' Right Protection Act, 2009 (Act No. 26 of 2009).

practices, it is completely silent about the list of rights of the consumers against the businesses. It is suggested that the Act should explicitly incorporate specific provisions recognizing various rights of the consumers, especially the rights that are recognized by the UN Guidelines on the Protection of the Consumers.[672]

§7. Product Liability under the Act of 2009

677. Any consumer who has suffered any loss that can be measured in terms of money can file a civil suit against such person for civil remedies. The initiation of criminal action or conviction in any criminal trial for any anti-consumer rights practices will not be a legal bar for claiming any civil remedy. Thus, the claim for compensation is not admissible when the loss suffered cannot be measured in terms of money.[673]

678. Since under section 66(1)(3) of the Act of 2009, a civil action can be taken by a consumer who is injured or has suffered any loss, the definition of 'consumer' merits special consideration. This provision is really appreciable for the reason that the user of a defective product often does not have a cause of action in the absence of any direct contractual relation with the manufacturer or seller of the defective product. Now the problem of establishing liability under the law of contract will be solved to the extent that a third party as a consumer is entitled under the act to remedy his suffering from a defective product.

679. It has already been shared that the liability of the seller for a defective product is not strict; rather, it requires some fault or conduct on the part of the producers. Under section 66, an action for civil remedy can be taken by a person if he suffers loss for any anti-consumer rights practices.[674] All anti-consumer rights practices are not relevant for the purpose of product liability and sections 2(20)(b), (c), (d), (e), (i), (k), and (l) shared above are specifically important. Section 66(3) of the Act, 2009 provides that the seller will be liable when damage is done by any of

672. UN Guidelines for Consumer Protection, 1985.

673. Section 66, the Consumers' Right Protection Act, 2009 (Act No. 26 of 2009).

674. 66. Civil Remedies. – (1) For the reason that a criminal proceeding for any anti-consumer rights practices has been initiated against a person or that such person has been convicted of a criminal offence for any such practices, there shall be no legal bar on any consumer, who has suffered any loss, to file a civil suit to civil court against such person, in appropriate cases, for civil remedies.

(2) The competent Civil Court under this Act shall mean the Court of Joint District Judge of relevant local jurisdiction.

(3) If any consumer suffers any loss by any anti-consumer rights practice by any seller and if such damage is measurable in terms of money, a civil suit claiming compensation not exceeding five times of the money determined.

(4) The Court, after considering the plaint, written statement, evidences and other circumstances, may allow compensation not exceeding five times of the actual damage determined as the Court may think fit, proper and just.

(5) Notwithstanding anything in the Code of Civil procedure, 1908, the Contract Act, 1872 and Civil Courts Act, 1887, the provisions of this section shall apply.

these anti-consumer rights practices. Anti-consumers rights practices contain a fault element in each case. To sell a defective product is not an anti-consumer rights practice unless it falls within any of the practices listed as anti-consumer in the Act.

680. Examination of some of the anti-consumer rights practices listed in the Act of 2009 would make it clear how limited the scope of product liability is in relation to these practices. Under section 2(20)(b), it is an anti-consumer rights practice to sell or offer to sell adulterated goods or medicines intentionally. Liabilities for any damage done to the buyer from adulterated goods or medicines can be incurred by the seller only when he sells such adulterated products intentionally. The seller cannot be made liable when he does have no knowledge that the goods are adulterated. However, at least there should be a strict liability on the manufacturer of the defective product since he is supposed to cure any product before it comes to the market for the use of the consumers. Further, this provision is limited to only adulterated goods, adulteration, which has a specific meaning under the Act and certainly does not cover every 'defect' in the goods or medicine.[675]

681. Liability under section 66(3) may arise only if the damage or loss suffered can be measured in money.[676] Thus, any non-material loss such as pain or stress may be out of reach of the Act of 2009, if the courts interpret the provision restrictively. Further, if death is caused by a defective product, compensation cannot be claimed since loss caused by death cannot be assessed in terms of money. Any loss suffered in the form of physical injury or damage to property seems to be covered under the provision.

§8. Defences

682. Since the liability of the seller under the Act is fault-based and the injured consumer must show that the damage was caused by any anti-consumer rights practice of the manufacturer including supplier-retailer and wholesaler, the manufacturer will always have a defence that he did nothing which constitutes an anti-consumer rights practice under the Act. The manufacturer can argue that though his actions would appear to be an anti-consumer rights practice, he lacked the required mental element, e.g., required intention under section 2(20)(b) and that the damage/loss/injury suffered by the plaintiff was not caused by his anti-consumer rights practice rather it was caused by some other reason. Once the aggrieved consumer proves that there have been one or more of the anti-consumer rights practices on the part of the seller, the focus will be a shift on the issue of causation. It appears that as anti-consumer rights practices are clearly defined under the Act, causation will be tracked to establish liability under the Act.

---

675. Under s. 2(18), 'adulteration' means adulteration as defined in s. 3(1) of the Pure Food Ordinance, 1959 (Ordinance No. LXVIII of 1959) and in s. 25C of the Special Powers Act, 1974 (Act No. XIV of 1974), or adulteration as defined in any other Act.
676. Section 66(3), the Consumers' Right Protection Act, 2009.

§9. Product Liability in the Law of Contract

683. Under the law of contract in Bangladesh, the consumers do not have any special status and the consumer contracts so far have not attracted any special treatment, though initially, the issues relating to sale of goods were part of Chapter VII of the Contract Act, 1872 (sections 72–123), which were subsequently repealed by the Sale of Goods Act, 1930 (Act No. III of 1930). Rights of the consumers in relation to the defective product under the law of contract are the same as anybody – whether it is a business or consumer – as a party to the contract or agreement. However, as consumers are buyers in most cases, a discussion on the relevant provisions of the Sale of Goods Act, 1930 (Act No. III of 1930) demands special attention in this regard.

§10. The Sale of Goods Act, 1930

684. Consumer contracts are not dealt with separately in the Sale of Goods Act, 1930 (Act No. III of 1930). Though some conditions as to description, sample, quality, fitness and merchantability are declared by the Act to be implied into the contract for the sale of goods, such conditions implied by law can be varied or avoided by express provision into the contract.[677] There is no provision in the law to the effect that implied condition as to the quality, fitness or merchantability cannot be waived by an expressed provision in the contract when the contract is between a business and a consumer. The Law does not discriminate between the businesses and the consumers and the contract between a business and/or a consumer is treated equally. It is highly probable that in the contract between a business and a consumer, where a contract is made in the standard form of contract developed by the businessmen, the seller would incorporate into a contract express provisions to exclude any potential liability arising by implication of law. It is worth mentioning that while the Law does not specifically permit the wholesale exclusion of the implied conditions implicated by the Act, it permits variation or negating of any rights, duties or liability arising under a contract for the sale of goods by implication of law. Probably the court would not allow the exclusion of every implied condition.

685. Section 16(4) of the Sale of Goods Act, 1930 (Act No. III of 1930) deserves special attention which provides that '[a]n express warranty or condition does not negative a warranty or condition implied by this Act unless inconsistent therewith'. Thus, though the Act permits the exclusion of conditions or warranty to be implied by express provision in the contract, it provides that the courts should interpret express warranty or condition in a contract as not to exclude the condition or warranty to be implied under the Act unless the former is inconsistent with the latter.

677. Section 62, the Sale of Goods Act, 1930 (Act No. III of 1930).

686. The application of the conditions is made limited in their applications. For example, under the Act, there is no implied condition as to the fitness for the purpose or to the quality of goods except certain conditions prescribed by the Act are fulfilled. Additionally, there is implied condition only as to the purpose for which goods are required, not as to the quality of the goods. Condition as to the quality of goods can be allowed only if the parties to the contract (seller and buyer) agree to incorporate express terms into the contract as to any particular quality.

687. In a B2B contract, this provision would not be a problem unless there is a substantial difference in negotiating capacity between the parties, but there will be a huge scope of potential injustice in cases of B2C contracts where contracts are often made in the seller's standard form of contract. It is usual that the buyer would incorporate into the contract no express condition as to quality. The buyer, under the Act, has the right to terminate the contract, recover the damages and get the price already paid returned in appropriate cases.

688. Product liability system based on 'breach of warranty or condition' in the contract cannot be expected to effectively protect the injured consumers against the defective product for at least two reasons. The first barrier is the 'doctrine of privity' which requires a contractual relationship for enforcing duties or liabilities under the contract. In many instances, there is no contractual relationship between the seller and the consumer who suffers loss or injury due to the defect in the product. The gravity of the breach of condition or warranty about the quality or fitness of the product sold does not matter. Second, it is always open for the seller to incorporate express provisions into the contract which excludes any of the liability of the seller relating to a defect in the product. In such cases, the injured consumer, though could rely on the contract otherwise to recover damages, cannot recover anything due to the express exclusionary provision in the contract itself. This second problem can be easily avoided by enacting a special provision to provide that exclusionary provision in the contract should be fair and reasonable.

§11. Tort

689. Tortuous liability for defective products is not usually welcomed by the courts in Bangladesh unless it is incorporated into any statutory instruments (including primary and delegated legislation). If the courts have ever recognized or are expected to recognize the tortuous liability of the producer or manufacturer or seller of the defective product, the liability is supposed to be analogous to the liability recognized by the common law of England and Wales.

§12. Consumers, Telecommunication Services and BTRC

690. It has already been discussed that the provisions of the Consumers' Right Protection Act 2009 are additional to the provisions of other laws for the time being in force,[678] i.e., a consumer can enforce his rights under any other laws and take the benefits of the provisions of this Act of 2009. To get quality telecommunication services and relevant matters, some important provisions are incorporated in the Bangladesh Telecommunication Regulation Act, 2001 (Act No. 18 of 2001). It is apparent that the protection of the consumers' rights and interests in getting quality telecommunication services from various service providers, some of which are already highlighted in the previous chapter, is an important mandate of BTRC. For example, the law provides that the BTRC shall protect the interest of the local consumers in respect of the charges imposed on them, their access to telecommunication services and the quality and variety of such services.[679] Besides, it is also provided that BTRC shall take initiatives to protect the social and economic interest of the consumers, to respond to their needs, and to control and abolish the existing and probable oppressive and discriminatory conduct or activities of the telecommunication service providers.[680] In addition to these, BTRC needs to ensure the compliance of the provisions of the law keeping in view the public interest in general and protecting the interest of the consumers from the unfair practices of the operators and other persons engaged in providing telecommunication services. Moreover, the law further provides that BTRC needs to introduce a mechanism for receiving the complaints and suggestions of the consumers regularly and to ensure that proper action has been taken accordingly. It is perhaps due to these provisions the Bangladesh Telecommunication Regulation Act, 2001 provides that the five commissioners who are appointed to form BTRC should have at least fifteen years' practical experience on, *inter alia*, the protection of consumer interest.[681]

691. The Bangladesh Telecommunication Regulation Act, 2001 has incorporated one single chapter, i.e., Chapter IX containing provisions on the handling of consumer complaints. It is provided that every telecommunication service providing operator shall establish a sufficient number of complaint-centres so that information on the inconvenience or complain of the consumers in respect of that service or related matters can be collected, and shall, from time to time, publish notice about the location of, and communication with, such centres. In these centres, a consumer should be able to present his inconvenience or complain by telephone message or written complaint. The service provider needs to maintain a register recording all information relating to the complaints received from consumers and disposal of such complaints. Once information or complaint about the inconvenience of a consumer is received, the service provider needs to take immediate necessary action and shall follow the code of practice framed in this regard by BTRC. If the service provider fails to take timely action and properly resolve the inconvenience or the complaint of the consumer, that consumer may in writing apply to the Commission for taking necessary action on the matter. The Commission may, after necessary inquiry, give proper directions to the service provider to take necessary steps for

678. Section 3, the Consumers' Right Protection Act 2009 (Act No. 26 of 2009).
679. Section 30(1)(b), the Bangladesh Telecommunication Regulation Act, 2001 (Act No. 18 of 2001).
680. Section 30(1)(d), the Bangladesh Telecommunication Regulation Act, 2001 (Act No. 18 of 2001).
681. Section 10(1)(c), the Bangladesh Telecommunication Regulation Act, 2001 (Act No. 18 of 2001).

resolving the said inconvenience or complaint, within seven days of receipt of such application. If such direction is not complied with, the Commission may issue a compulsory enforcement order.[682]

§13. FINAL WORDS

692. In a developing country such as Bangladesh, it is difficult for regulators to ensure quality products and services due to various reasons. Yet, the government has been trying and has taken few initiatives to this end in different sectors including ICT and telecommunication, e.g., software certification has been introduced as discussed earlier. Regulators such as BSTI, Bangladesh Safe Food Authority, BCoC and Consumer Protection Directorate have been taking some market drives from time to time. Besides, BCS has formulated MRP Policy, and BTRC has been taking various initiatives so that the consumers get improved ICT and telecommunication services and quality products, etc. The police have also been running some programs to confiscate pirated software and copyrighted materials, etc.

693. On 22 August 2017, the BTRC issued Directives on QoS for Cellular Mobile Telecom Operators. QoS is the ability of a network or service to satisfy the end-user. Except in the event of natural disaster, strikes, war, riots, power outages, etc., the MNOs are bound to accommodate the provisions of these Directives. BTRC has also formulated the (ANS Operator's QoS) Regulations, 2018, which are applicable to all ANS operators providing: (i) Broadband Access Services; (ii) Cellular Mobile Phone Services; (iii) Fixed Telephony Services; (iv) Any other service introduced by BTRC through administrative order from time to time.

694. Any person aggrieved, on behalf of the consumers, may consider initiating public interest litigation in the HCD under Article 102 of the Constitution of Bangladesh, 1972, and the HCD can also direct the business community to recall below standard products. The Consumer Association of Bangladesh, given their mandates and financial constraints, has been playing a very limited role to promote the interest of the consumers, and some of their isolated actions are reported in newspapers.

682. Section 59, the Bangladesh Telecommunication Regulation Act, 2001 (Act No. 18 of 2001).

Part VI. Privacy Protection

§1. INTRODUCTION

695. Historically, the people of different religions have been living in harmony for ages in this part of the world. Nevertheless, when Islam was introduced in the thirteenth century in ancient Bengal, the Muslim community started considering the privacy of their homes and female members very seriously. In various ancient and historical publications, thc solitary nature of abode, especially of Muslim abode, and non-accessibility of the outsiders without proper permission and even meeting of male relatives of the family with the girls and women were described.[683]

696. This situation continued even after the independence of the country and till the 1990s. With the economic development of the country, which mainly started from the 1990s, successive governments took initiatives to make education free for all and allocate special incentives for girls' education to ensure gender equality. With these initiatives, and with the economic progress of the country along with the introduction of computers in printing presses, the issue and understanding of privacy have started evolving differently.

697. This issue of privacy protection in the Bangladesh context can be discussed, taking into consideration the domestic law provisions and interpretation of these provisions, though very few, given by the courts of law. Furthermore, the position of the government regarding privacy protection can also be identified and evaluated from Bangladesh's commitments to international human rights instruments which recognize this right, and through the obligations of the government expressed by adhering to the provisions of these international human rights instruments by way of accession, signing, and ratification. This chapter will first highlight the privacy provisions in core international human rights instruments followed by a discussion on the status of the international law in general and of these human rights instruments in the Bangladesh context as these are already signed or accessed and ratified by Bangladesh. After that, a survey of Bangladeshi laws containing provisions on different aspects of privacy will be provided, and how the higher judiciary has interpreted some of these provisions on different occasions will be discussed.

683. *Abdus Sobhan v. Jamiruddin Jaigirder & Ors.*, 1988 BLD 257.

§2. Privacy, International Human Rights Instruments and Bangladesh

698. Scholars from around the world have been facing difficulties for years to come up with a universally accepted definition of privacy.[684] Unfortunately, it is not possible to reach such a definition of privacy as the understanding of privacy varies from culture to culture, country to country, religion to religion, age to age, person to person, gender to gender, and generation to generation, etc.[685] There are various dimensions of privacy, and this can be discussed, taking into account the economic, social, cultural and religious aspects. Generally speaking, looking at the practices of different jurisdictions, the right to privacy can be recognized either or both as a statutory right and a human right.

699. The right to privacy is recognized as a human right in the core international and regional human rights instruments. Article 12 of the Universal Declaration of Human Rights, 1948 (UDHR) provides that '[n]o one shall be subjected to arbitrary interference with his privacy, family, home or correspondence, nor to attacks upon his honour and reputation. Everyone has the right to the protection of the law against such interference or attacks'. Similar provisions can be found in the International Covenant on Civil and Political Rights, 1966 (ICCPR),[686] the Convention on the Rights of the Child, 1989 (CRC),[687] the International Convention on the Protection of the Rights of All Migrant Workers and Members of their Families, 1990[688] and the Convention on the Rights of Persons with Disabilities, 2006 (CRPD).[689]

700. Bangladesh has either signed or accessed and ratified these treaties.[690] It will be pertinent to mention here that though Bangladesh has either accessed, signed or ratified these treaties with some reservations and/or declarations on the different provisions of these instruments, the country, interestingly, has not put any reservation or declaration on the provisions on the right to privacy as encapsulated in these human rights instruments.

701. As a treaty obligation, Bangladesh needs to submit state reports regarding the progress and development of various provisions of these human rights treaties at the national level. Through the General Comment No. 16, the United Nations

684. Solove J. Daniel, *Conceptualizing Privacy*, 90 Cal. L. Rev., 1087 (2002); Solove J. Daniel, *A Taxonomy of Privacy*, 154 U. Pa. L. Rev., 477–564 (2006).
685. *See* generally, Munir, A.B., Mohd, S.H. & Karim, E., *Data Protection Law in Asia* (2018).
686. Article 17, the International Covenant on Civil and Political Rights, 1966.
687. Article 16, the Convention on the Rights of the Child, 1989.
688. Article 14, the International Convention on the Protection of the Rights of All Migrant Workers and Members of their Families, 1990.
689. Article 22, the Convention on the Rights of Persons with Disabilities, 2006.
690. Bangladesh accessed the International Covenant on Civil and Political Rights, 1966 on 6 Sep. 2000, signed the Convention on the Rights of the Child, 1989 on 7 Jan. 1998 and ratified it on 3 Aug. 1990, signed the International Convention on the Protection of the Rights of All Migrant Workers and Members of their Families, 1990 on 7 Oct. 1998 and ratified the Convention on 24 Aug. 2011 and signed the Convention on the Rights of Persons with Disabilities, 2006 on 9 May 2007 and ratified it on 30 Nov. 2007.

Human Rights Committee, formed through the provisions of ICCPR to monitor the implementation of its provisions, has made it clear that 'as all persons live in society, the protection of privacy is necessarily relative' and '[s]urveillance, whether electronic or otherwise, interceptions of telephonic, telegraphic and other forms of communication, wire-tapping, and recording of conversations should be prohibited. Searches of a person's home should be restricted to a search for necessary evidence and should not be allowed to amount to harassment'.[691] Nevertheless, the General Comment has listed down few things to be included in the content of state reports to be submitted by the state parties to ICCPR.

702. A combined reading of paragraphs 7, 8 and 10 of the General Comment 16 will reveal that the state reports should contain information regarding: (a) the laws and regulations that govern authorized interferences with information relating to individual's private life the knowledge of which is essential in the interests of society; (b) reference of legislation on interferences mentioning in detail the precise circumstances in which such interferences may be permitted and authorized; (c) reference of legislations body search of persons by State officials, or medical personnel acting at the request of the State only be examined by persons of the same sex; (d) reference of laws that personal information on computers, databanks and other devices are gathered or hold, whether by public authorities or private individuals or bodies, are regulated by law and reference of measures taken to ensure that information concerning a person's private life does not reach the hands of persons who are not authorized by law to receive, process and use it, and is never used for purposes incompatible with the Covenant.[692] Thus, it can be understood that the state report of Bangladesh under the ICCPR will take these matters into consideration and therefore, one should reveal the position of privacy protection in the Bangladesh context from the submitted state reports.

703. The framers of the Constitution of Bangladesh, 1972, while stipulating various provisions in the Constitution, were greatly influenced, *inter alia*, by the provisions of core international human rights instruments such as UDHR, ICCPR and International Covenant on Economic Social and Cultural Rights, 1966 (ICESCR), etc. As a result, it can be presumed that they have incorporated most of the human rights as encapsulated in these human rights instruments in the Constitution of Bangladesh, 1972.

704. In *Dr Shipra Chaudhury and another v. Government of Bangladesh and others*, 2009, 38 CLC (HCD) [9178] = 29 BLD (HCD) (2009) 183, the HCD found that '[t]he framers of the Constitution were particularly impressed by the formulation of the basic rights in the Universal Declaration of Human Rights. If we make a comparison of Part III of the Constitution with the Universal Declaration of

691. Paragraphs 7 & 8, Human Rights Committee, General Comment 16 (Twenty-third session, 1988), Compilation of General Comments and General Recommendations Adopted by Human Rights Treaty Bodies, U.N. Doc. HRI/GEN/1/Rev.1 at 21 (1994).
692. Paragraphs 7, 8 & 10, Human Rights Committee, General Comment 16 (Twenty-third session, 1988), Compilation of General Comments and General Recommendations Adopted by Human Rights Treaty Bodies, U.N. Doc. HRI/GEN/1/Rev.1 at 21 (1994).

Human Rights (UDHR), we shall find that most of the rights enumerated in the Declaration have found a place in some form or other in Part III and some have been recognised in Part II of the Constitution'.

705. It is evident that the Preamble of the Constitution, being the beacon light, has included it explicitly that– 'it shall be a fundamental aim of the State to realize through the democratic process a socialist society, free from exploitation a society in which the rule of law, fundamental human rights and freedom, equality and justice, political, economic and social, will be secured for all citizens'. Moreover, in Article 43(2) of the Constitution, 1972, the framers have incorporated the fundamental right to be secured in the home against entry, search and seizure and privacy of correspondence and other means of communication, subject to any reasonable restrictions imposed by law in the interests of the security of the State, public order, public morality or public health. Hence, it is reiterated that this right to privacy is not an absolute right and can be curtailed by the state by imposing reasonable restrictions on the grounds of security of the State, public order, public morality or public health.

706. In the initial state report submitted to the Human Rights Committee on ICCPR,[693] the government has claimed that the right to privacy is guaranteed.[694] It is explicitly mentioned that the right to privacy is constitutionally guaranteed under Article 43 subject to any reasonable restrictions imposed by law in the interest of the security of the state, public order, public morality or public health. The state report has shared the decision of the Apex Court delivered in *Government of Bangladesh and Others v. Hussain Mohammad Ershad* [2000] 52 DLR (AD) 162 where the Supreme Court has reaffirmed the right of a person to be secured in his home against entry, search and seizure as per Article 43(a) of the Constitution. However, the state report is silent about the issue of the protection of personal information, etc.

707. Similarly, in the Fifth Periodic State Report under the CRC submitted in 2012, even though it was claimed that the National Children Policy, 2011 had made provisions for the protection of privacy and image of the children who had come into contact with the law and to protect other children,[695] it was very difficult to precisely identify such provision in the National Children Policy, 2011.[696] This uncertainty was cleared in the subsequently enacted Children Act, 2013 (Act No. 24 of 2013), where it is prohibited explicitly to publish or broadcast the image, news, report or any description in print or electronic medium or on the internet relating to

693. United Nations, Human Rights Committee, Initial Report of Bangladesh, CCPR/C/BGD/1, 3 Sep. 2015.

694. *Ibid.*, pp. 10 and 31.

695. United Nations, Committee on the Rights of the Child, Fifth Periodic Report of Bangladesh, CRC/C/BGD/5, 16 Dec. 2014.

696. It seems that the Government in the State Report wanted to mean Policy No. 6.7.2 which provides for making and implementation of specific plan and programs for ensuring and protecting the rights of the children coming in conflict with law or keep in touch with same and rights of the children to participate in the judicial process pertaining to them.

any child involved in any suit pending in the Child Court. Though such activities can be permitted by the responsible court if it is believed that such publication will not be against the interest of the child.[697]

708. According to the same Report, the Children Act, 2013 (Act No. 24 of 2013) clearly spelt out provisions to protect the privacy and image of children that come into contact with the law that includes: (i) formation of a children's desk in each police station; (ii) separate charge sheet for children and adults; (iii) formation of children's courts; (iv) separate trial for children and adults; (v) children's participation in judiciary process; (vi) in camera trials; and (vii) prohibition of dissemination of information regarding ongoing trials in children's courts through print and electronic media.

709. In the Initial Report submitted under the International Convention on the Protection of the Rights of All Migrant Workers and Members of their Families, 1990, the government only referred to Article 43 of the Constitution of Bangladesh, 1972 while sharing the position of the country on Privacy.[698] Bangladesh submitted the initial report under the CRPD in 2017.[699] Along with the reference of Article 43 of the Constitution of Bangladesh, 1972, it is also mentioned that the only law as in force in Bangladesh which contains a specific provision on the protection of personal information, one aspect of personal privacy, is the Rights and Protection of the Persons with Disabilities Act, 2013 (Act No. 39 of 2013).[700]

710. Bangladesh is not a member of the organizations that have developed and adopted instruments on the protection of personal data, one category of personal privacy, such as OECD,[701] EU,[702] Asia-Pacific Economic Cooperation (APEC),[703] or Association of Southeast Asian Nations (ASEAN).[704] Moreover, as there is no data protection authority so far, the country had not joined in the development of the Madrid Resolution when data protection authorities of more than fifty states joined

697. Section 28, the Children Act, 2013 (Act No. 24 of 2013).
698. United Nations, Committee on the Protection of the Rights of All Migrant Workers and Members of Their Families, Initial Report of Bangladesh, CMW/C/BGD/1, 29 Feb. 2016.
699. United Nations, Committee on the Rights of Persons with Disabilities, Initial report submitted by Bangladesh under Art. 35 of the Convention, CRPD/C/BGD/1, 30 Aug. 2018.
700. Section 16(1)(r), the Rights and Protection of the Persons with Disabilities Act, 2013 (Act No. 39 of 2013).
701. OECD Guidelines governing the Protection of Privacy and Transborder Flows of Personal Data, 1980 (revised in 2015).
702. The General Data Protection Regulation (EU) 2016/679, adopted on 27 Apr. 2016 and entered into force on 25 May 2018. With its extraterritorial effect, this Regulation is the most comprehensive data protection law in the world. For its implication on Bangladesh, please *see*, Jewel N. & Karim, M.E., *European General Data Protection Regulation Its Implications for Bangladesh, Law & Our Rights,* The Daily Star, 19 Jun. 2018.
703. APEC Privacy Framework, 2004 (revised in 2015).
704. ASEAN Framework on Personal Data Protection, 2016 (According to Art. 2, this Framework serves only as a record of the Participants' intentions and does not constitute or create, and is not intended to constitute or create, obligations under domestic or international law and will not give rise to any legal process and will not be deemed to constitute or create any legally binding or enforceable obligations, express or implied.).

together in 2009 to develop international standards on the protection of personal data and privacy. Nevertheless, Bangladesh is a very active member of the UN, which has adopted the Guidelines for the Regulation of Computerized Personal Data Files adopted by General Assembly resolution 45/95 on 15 December 1989. Even though the implementation of the Guidelines relating to the Regulation of Computerized Personal Data Files is left to each state, more than a hundred countries in the world have already enacted personal data protection laws. Recently, the UN High-Level Committee on Management has also adopted the Principles on Personal Data Protection and Privacy in October 2018. But, these principles will be applicable for persons working for, associated with or under the care of the UN system.

711. It may be relevant to share here that Bangladesh is a part of the Bali Process on People Smuggling, Trafficking in Persons and Related Transnational Crime, which was a voluntary and non-binding regional consultative process of forty-five member countries and organizations established in 2002. A Report on 'Privacy and data protection laws of Bali Process member States' was published in May 2015. In this Report, while discussing the position of Bangladesh, along with the Constitutional provision on privacy, as mentioned in Article 43, the provisions of the Right to Information Act, 2009 were mentioned. This law is often mistakenly referred to, perhaps due to the title of the law, as one of the personal information protection laws available in Bangladesh by different corners and therefore, deserves an elaborated discussion.

712. The Right to Information Act, 2009 (Act No. 20 of 2009) is not a law that deals with the citizen's privacy protection; rather, this law was enacted to make provisions for ensuring the free flow of information and people's right to information which is manifested both in the long title and preamble to the law. In the preamble, it is stated that- right to information is an inalienable part of freedom of thought, conscience and speech recognized by the Constitution of Bangladesh and it is necessary to ensure the right to information for the empowerment of the people, who own all powers of the Republic. The preamble further stipulates that if people's right to information is ensured, the transparency and accountability of all public, autonomous and statutory organizations and of other private institutions constituted or run by a government or foreign financing shall increase, corruption of the same shall decrease and good governance of the same shall be established.

713. Besides, section 4 of the Act, 2009, which provides that '[s]ubject to the provisions of this Act, every citizen shall have the right to information from the authority, and the authority shall, on demand from a citizen, be bound to provide him with the information'. The sharing and a close look at some definitions as encapsulated in the law is necessary. The Law defines 'information' as 'any memo, book, design, map, contract, data, log book, order, notification, document, sample, letter, report, accounts, project proposal, photograph, audio, video, drawing, painting, film, any instrument done through electronic process, machine readable record, and any other documentary material regardless of its physical form or characteristics, and any copy thereof in relation to the constitution, structure and official activities of any authority'. 'Authority', under the law, means: (i) any organization constituted in accordance with the Constitution of Bangladesh; (ii) Ministry, Division or office established under the Rules of Business; (iii) any statutory body or institution established by or under any Act; (iv) any private organization or institution run by government financing or with aid in grant from the government fund; (v) any private organization or institution run by foreign aid in grant; (vi) any organization or institution that undertakes public functions in accordance with any contract made on behalf of the Government or made with any public organisation or institution; or (vii) any organization or institution as may be notified in the Official Gazette from time to time by the Government. Additionally, the 'right to information', as per the law, means the right to obtain information from any authority. Thus, this is clear that this law was enacted to fulfil a different purpose and not to ensure the protection of citizens' personal information.[705]

§3. Status of International Law in Bangladesh

714. Before we discuss the privacy-related national laws, it may be relevant to share the status of international law in Bangladesh as the country has signed, ratified or accessed many of the international human rights instruments shared above having provisions on privacy. Article 25 of the Bangladesh Constitution, 1972 provides that the 'state shall base its international relations on the principle of, *inter alia*, respect for international law and the principles enunciated in the UN Charter'. Therefore, this is a constitutional obligation upon the state to respect international law.[706]

715. In *Bangladesh National Women Lawyers Association (BNWLA) v. Government of Bangladesh*, 2011, 40 CLC (HCD) [4739] = 1 BLD (HCD) (2011) 324, 18 BLC (HCD) (2013) 290, the HCD while framing directives/guidelines on 'eve-teasing' reiterated that '[w]hen there is a gap in the municipal law in addressing any issue, the courts may take recourse to international conventions and protocols on that issue for the purpose of formulating effective directives and guidelines to be followed by all concerned until the national legislature enacts laws in this regard'. While delivering the judgment, Mr Justice Sheikh Hassan Arif shared the highly regarded observation of Mr Justice Bimalendu Bikash Roy Chowdhury shared in *Hussain Mohammad Ershad v. Bangladesh & others*, 21 BLD (AD) 2001, 69 where Justice Chowdhury stated as below:

> The national courts should not, I feel, straightway ignore the international obligations, which a country undertakes. If the domestic laws are not clear enough or there is nothing therein, the national courts should draw upon the principles

705. Various provisions of the law, in the context of political parties, were evaluated in the case of *Badiul Alam Majumdar and others v. Information Commission and others*, 2017 (1) LNJ 251.
706. *Professor Nurul Islam v. Bangladesh* [2000] 52 DLR (HCD) 413.

incorporated in the international instruments. But in the cases where the domestic laws are clear and inconsistent with the international obligations of the state concerned, the national courts will be obliged to respect the national laws but shall draw the attention of the law makers to such inconsistencies.

716. Moreover, in *Dr Shipra Chaudhury and another v. Government of Bangladesh and others*, 2009, 38 CLC (HCD) [9178] = 29 BLD (HCD) (2009) 183, Justice Syed Mahmud Hossain opined that 'Our courts will not enforce those Covenants [ICCPR and ICESCR] as treaties and conventions, even if ratified by the State, are not part of the corpus juris of the State unless these are incorporated in the municipal legislation. However, the court can look into these Conventions and Covenants as an aid to interpretation of the provisions of Part III, particularly to determine the rights implicit in the rights like the right to life and the right to liberty, but not enumerated in the Constitution.' In addition to this, in *Anika Ali v. Rezwanul Ahsan*, 2011, 40 CLC (AD) [5145] = 17 BLC (AD) (2012) 77, 17 MLR (AD) (2012) 49, Mr Justice Muhammad Imman Ali held that 'unless provisions of international instruments are contrary to our domestic laws, the beneficial provisions may profitably be referred to and implemented in appropriate cases'. Thus, Bangladeshi courts are free to refer to the beneficial provisions of the international instruments in appropriate cases if they are not contrary to the national laws.

§4. Protection of Privacy under Domestic Law

717. As the Privacy Act, 1974 of the US or the Privacy Act, 1988 of Australia, there is no specific and exclusive privacy legislation in Bangladesh. Nonetheless, some domestic laws of Bangladesh contain some isolated provisions having privacy implications.[707] Though the scholars may find it difficult to define privacy, some of them have attempted to classify privacy as: (a) bodily privacy, (b) privacy as to the home or territorial privacy, (c) privacy as to correspondence and communication, and finally, (d) information privacy.

718. The right to bodily privacy, which allows a human being to take and make an exclusive decision about his body and to remain free from any sort of interference is recognized under the provisions of various laws in Bangladesh. The right to privacy as to a home, correspondence and communications subject to some limitations are a constitutionally guaranteed right under Article 43 of the Constitution of Bangladesh, 1972. With the enactment of the Digital Security Act, 2018 (Act No. 46 of 2018), the government has claimed to protect the personal information or information privacy of the citizens. This part will shed light on some of these various aspects of privacy, such as breach of confidence, defamation and harassment, trespass, nuisance, surveillance, etc., as included in several laws of the land.

707. Mohammad Ershadul Karim, *Citizen's Right to Privacy: Reflection in the International Instruments and National Laws*, 9 Bangladesh J. L., 35–65 (2005).

719. Section 4 of the Partition Act, 1893 (Act No. IV of 1893) gives the preference of a member of an undivided family to buy the share of a dwelling house belonging to that undivided family over an outsider who is not a member of such family. It was revealed that to make this provision, the legislator intended to preserve the 'purdah and privacy of the members and inmates of the undivided dwelling-house'[708] so that 'the stranger purchaser who is not acceptable to other members of the family cannot come into the undivided dwelling house and possess it forcibly'.[709] In *Sreemati Sobita Rani Bonik v. Sree Gouranga Prasad Acharjee & Ors*, 17 BLT (HCD) 470, it was held that '[t]he very purpose of Section 4 is to protect and preserve the sentiment of the co-sharers and attachment to their ancestral property and also preserve the privacy of the members of the undivided family'.

720. Passing off dishonestly the trade secrets of business or information is a criminal offence under the Penal Code, 1860 (XLV of 1860). The Penal Code, 1860 contains various provisions (sections 441–462) on criminal trespass. Section 509 of the Penal Code, 1860 provides that whoever, intending to insult the modesty of any woman, utters any word, makes any sound or gesture, or exhibits any object, intending that such word or sound shall be heard, or that such gesture or object shall be seen, by such woman, or intrudes upon the privacy of such woman, shall be punished with simple imprisonment for a term which may extend to one year, or with fine, or with both.

721. The Code of Criminal Procedure, 1898 (Act No. V of 1898), in Chapter V, contains detailed provisions as to search of place and arrested person, breaking open zanana and mode of searching women. It is provided that if a police officer needs to enter a place to arrest anyone and if such place is an apartment in the actual occupancy of a woman (not being the person to be arrested) who, according to custom, does not appear in public then the police officer shall, before entering such apartment, give notice to such woman that she is at liberty to withdraw and shall afford her every reasonable facility for withdrawing, and may then break open the apartment and enter it.[710] Section 52 explicitly provides that whenever it is necessary to cause a woman to be searched, the search shall be made by another woman, with strict regard to decency. In civil matters also, the Code of Civil Procedure, 1908 (Act No. V of 1908) contains various provisions respecting the privacy of a woman.[711] Similar kinds of provisions on pardanashin lady can be found in section 17(2) of the Birodh Mimangsha (Pouro Alaka) Board Ain, 2004 (Act No. 12 of 2004). Besides, if the town planning authorities require to enter any place to discharge their responsibilities, they need to give sufficient notice in every instance even when any premises may otherwise be entered without notice, to enable the

708. *Sayesta Bibi and others v. Juma Sha and others*, 1989, 18 CLC (AD) [1973] = 42 DLR (AD) (1990) 53; *Noorjahan Akhter v. A Motaleb & ors.*, 2000, 29 CLC (HCD) [3757] = 53 DLR (2001) 256; *Hazi Shamul Alam v. Dr. Ashim Sarkar and others*, 2006, 35 CLC (HCD) [8027] = 13 MLR (HCD) (2008) 199.

709. *Amena Khatun and others v. Md. Afsaruddin being dead his heirs 1(ka) Maleka Khatun and others*, 1997, 26 CLC (HCD) [6339] = 50 DLR (HCD) (1998) 156.

710. Section 48, the Code of Criminal Procedure, 1898 (Act No. V of 1898).

711. Sections 55(1), 62(3), the Code of Civil Procedure, 1908 (Act No. V of 1908).

inmates of any apartment appropriated to females to remove to some part of the premises where their privacy need not be disturbed.[712]

722. The Evidence Act, 1872 (Act No. 1 of 1872) contains several provisions on the protection of confidential information having privacy implications. It is prohibited to compel to the disclosure of or permitted to disclose any communication made by anyone during the existence of marriage without consent.[713] It is also prohibited for anyone, including a public officer, to share or disclose any evidence derived from unpublished official records of any affairs of the state or disclose any communication made to him in the official confidence.[714] Similarly, any magistrate, police office or revenue officer is not bound to disclose the source of any information regarding the commission of an offence.[715]

723. Sections 126–129 of the Evidence Act, 1872 (Act No. 1 of 1872) deal with the protection of professional communication subject to certain conditions. Generally, no lawyer (including the interpreters, clerks or servants of the lawyer) shall at any time be permitted unless with his client's express consent, to disclose any communication made to him in the course and for the purpose of his employment, as such Advocate by or on behalf of his client, or to state the contents or condition of any document with which he has become acquainted in the course and for the purpose of his professional employment, or to disclose any advice given by him to his client in the course and for the purpose of such employment.

724. Under the Bangladesh Labour Act, 2006 (XLII of 2006), wrongful disclosure of any information relating to any manufacturing or commercial secret coming to his knowledge in the course of his official duties or any result of an analysis made under any provision of this Act is a punishable offence.[716] Anyone empowered to exercise any power or discharge any duty under the Bangladesh Labour Act or under any rules, regulation or scheme cannot, while in service or after leaving the service, disclose other than in connection with the administration of this Act any information relating to any manufacturing or commercial secret which may come to his knowledge in the course of his official duties. Such activities are permitted with the prior written consent of the employer.[717] The law also provides for keeping certain matters confidential.[718]

---

712. Section 181, the Town Improvement Act, 1953 (East Bengal Act No. XIII of 1953).
713. Section 122, the Evidence Act, 1872 (Act No. 1 of 1872).
714. Sections 123 & 124, the Evidence Act, 1872 (Act No. 1 of 1872). Regarding the application of s. 123 of the Evidence Act, 1872 (Act No. 1 of 1872), the AD of Bangladesh Supreme Court has set the guidelines and directions in the case of Government of Bangladesh represented by the Secretary, *Ministry of Law, Justice and Parliamentary Affairs v. Md. Shamsul Huda and others*, 60 DLR (AD) (2008) 108.
715. Section 125, the Evidence Act, 1872 (Act No. 1 of 1872).
716. Section 304, the Bangladesh Labour Act, 2006 (XLII of 2006).
717. Section 341, the Bangladesh Labour Act, 2006 (XLII of 2006).
718. *Ibid.*

725. Besides, the Right to Information Act, 2009 (Act No. of 2009) which was enacted to ensure the free flow of information and people's right to information also prohibits the publication of any such information that may if disclosed, offend the privacy of the personal life of an individual.[719]

726. In the recently enacted the Investment Corporation of Bangladesh Act, 2014 (Act No. 12 of 2014), the managing director, director, members of the executive committee, members of the committee, adviser, auditor, consultant, agent, deputy managing director and Chairman of the Investment Corporation of Bangladesh have to take an oath regarding the trustworthiness and confidentiality of information regarding the activities of the corporation. With this oath, is prohibited to transfer, inspect or see such information, file or documents to someone who is not legally entitled to know such information.[720]

727. There is no explicit provision on the regulation and governance of Closed-circuit Television (CCTV) in Bangladesh, though the Dhaka Metropolitan Police has encouraged residents to instal CCTV in premises to assist the police in crime detection and prevention. After the commission of some serious criminal offences in recent times, it is a practice to instal CCTV everywhere in urban areas through individual initiatives. Some of the sensation criminal cases were decided based on the footage captured through CCTV. However, in the absence of any law, privacy and personal data such as images, etc. collected through CCTV are at stake and can be misused.

728. The HCD held that the identity of the victim of sexual harassment offences should be kept confidential.[721] Even in the case of a child offender since the matter involves a child, the HCD, based on section 17 of the Children Act, 1974,[722] provides that the picture, name and identity of a child offender shall not be published in the media and any such publication would be an offence under the said Act. Hence, the publication of any photograph or the real name, address and identity of the detenu is strictly prohibited in any form or manner whatsoever in any electronic, print or other media.[723] There are provisions of camera trials in domestic laws, and it can be presumed that these provisions were included in the legal system to protect the privacy of the litigating parties.[724]

---

719. Section 7(h), the Right to Information Act, 2009 (Act No. XX of 2009).
720. Declaration of Trustworthiness and Secrecy, Schedule and s. 16, the Investment Corporation of Bangladesh Act, 2014 (Act No. 12 of 2014).
721. *Naripokkho & ors. v. Bangladesh & ors.*, 10 SCOB [2018] HCD 140.
722. The Children Act, 1974 was repealed through the provisions of the Children Act, 2013 (Act No. 24 of 2013) and the said provision was incorporated in s. 28 of the new law.
723. *Fahima Nasrin v. Government of Bangladesh and others*, 2009, 38 CLC (HCD) [5284] = 61 DLR (HCD) (2009) 232.
724. Section 11, the Family Courts Ordinance, 1985 (Ordinance No. XVIII of 1985), s. 10, the International Crimes (Tribunals) Act, 1973 (Act No. XIX of 1973), s. 25, the Prevention and Suppression of Human Trafficking Act, 2012 (Act No. 3 of 2012), s. 54, the Children Act, 2013 (Act No. 24 of 2013).

729. It may be relevant to share here that some laws of the country contain provisions on the retention of business data such as tax records, payment details and records, balance sheets, vouchers, all books, transaction details, all sorts of licences which may contain some personal information. These documents need to be preserved for three to twelve years.[725]

§5. PROTECTION OF PRIVACY AND DOMESTIC COURTS

730. The Supreme Court of Bangladesh has from time to time mentioned the issue and importance of privacy in different judgments. As early as at least in 1986, Mr Justice Abdul Bari Sarker considered the issue of customary easement right of privacy filed under section 18 of the Easement Act, 1882 (Act No. V of 1882)[726] in *Abdus Sobhan v. Jamiruddin Jaigirder & Ors.*, 1988 BLD 257. In this case, the plaintiff filed a suit for permanent injunction restraining the defendant from setting up, fixing and opening out any doors or windows on one side of the wall of a new hotel building which was under construction in the land adjacent to the plaintiff's homestead. The plaintiff submitted that they have been observing and maintaining purdah, especially for the female folks to protect their privacy. It was further claimed that 95% of the local people were Muslims and they observed purdah and the observance of privacy of neighbouring houses had been practised since ancient times and thus, had acquired a right of easement by immemorial and local customs prevalent since ancient times. The plaintiff also submitted that the neighbours among themselves scrupulously avoided the invasion of each other's privacy. The trial court, which was a Munsif court, shared an interesting observation on the protection of privacy and Mr Justice Abdul Bari Sarker reproduced that part in this judgment.

731. The trial court observed that '[t]here is ample evidence to show that plaintiff [plffs.] as a custom, observe parda and maintain privacy. It's true that one has the duty to protect one's own privacy. It's equally true that there is a mutual customary obligation not to invade each other's privacy … the plaintiff [plffs.] … have a customary right to protect and preserve the privacy of their house and to maintain the same un-invaded'. The appellate court, i.e., the court of Subordinate Judge thought that the ingredients of customary right to maintaining privacy had not been proved legally. Unfortunately, Mr Justice Abdul Bari Sarker did not directly comment on the issue of the right to privacy or invasion rather set aside the judgment and decrees of the courts below and ordered to send the case for remand, i.e., ordered the subordinate court for re-trial by stating, '[w]hether the plaintiffs have failed or succeeded in establishing their claim of customary right of easement of privacy needs to be decided afresh'.

---

725. *See*, for example, s. 33 of the VAT Act, 1991; s. 107, the VAT and Supplementary Duty Act, 2012; s. 181, the Companies Act, 1994; s. 25(b), the Money Laundering Prevention Act, 2012; s. 211, the Customs Act, 1969.

726. Illustration (b) of s. 18 provides that 'By the custom of a certain town no owner or occupier of a house can open a new window therein so as substantially to invade his neighbour's privacy … .'

732. In *Imtiazur Rahman Farooqui (Md.) (MI Farooqui) v. Bureau of Anti-Corruption and Others*, 1998, 27 CLC (HCD) [7457] = 51 DLR (HCD) (1999) 421, the petitioner, a senior lawyer of Bangladesh Supreme Court was asked to submit, *inter alia*, information containing the names and addresses of all clients and case numbers of all cases which had been dealt with by the petitioner during the period from 1 March 1993 to 20 March 1994. The respondent believed that they had the authority to ask for that information under section 94 of the Criminal Procedure Code and Articles 31/50 of the Anti-Corruption Manual. Mr Justice Mainur Reza Chowdhury found that these legal provisions spoke of production of documents and '[s]uch information as asked for does not … constitute a document'. Therefore, the respondent's act was unauthorized and illegal since these two legal provisions 'do not confer any power to direct a person to give information' and 'the information asked for the purpose of the inquiry was of a roving nature and was merely fishing for information … only to harass the petitioner'.

733. In *State v. Mostafizur Rahman and another*, 2013, 42 CLC (AD) [9154] = 67 DLR (AD) (2015) 218, a case involving the rape of victim Shefali, a domestic worker, Mr Justice Imman Ali, while giving dissenting judgment shared the findings of a judgment pronounced by the Indian Supreme Court, i.e., *Md. Iqbal v. State of Jharkhand* reported in AIR 2013 SC 3077 where it was held that an act of rape was a violation of the right to privacy of the victim.

734. In *Chairman, RAJUK and other v. Parvin Akter*, 7 BLC (AD) 167, in relation to a dispute involving the construction of … the petitioner claimed, *inter alia*, that if such construction is allowed, her privacy rights would be violated. Though the AD had commented on other grounds to reach its decisions, did not comment on the privacy right of the petitioner as it was claimed. In similar incidents involving construction works, the issue of privacy was raised but was not treated as the main issue of contention.[727] Similarly, in *Dr Ismat Mirza and other v. Md Mosaddek Hossain and ors,* (2002) 7 BLC 90, in a dispute relating to the partition of inherited property, the plaintiff claimed that if the partition was allowed and the sale of the defendant's portion to a stranger was allowed to be sold, it would infringe the right to privacy of the plaintiff. The Court found from the circumstantial evidence that there was no allegation of inconvenience to the enjoyment and possession of the plaintiff's property and held that 'the claim of the plaintiff as regards infringement of privacy does not stand to reason'.

735. In *State v. Secretary, Ministry of Law, Justice & Parliamentary Affairs and others*, 2009, 38 CLC (HCD) [5300] = 30 BLD (HCD) (2010) 369; 15 MLR (HCD) (2010) 59, involving the rape of a minor, Mr Justice Imman Ali, while commenting on the needs of a child rape victim held that '[l]aws are required to be formulated for victim and witness protection in order to avoid harassment of the victim children and to ensure effective prosecution of offenders, keeping in mind the need to maintain confidentiality, privacy and dignity'.

---

727. *See*, for example, *Anowar Hossain (Md.) and another v. Bangladesh and others*, 2005, 34 CLC (HCD) [8918] = 57 DLR (2005) 512.

736. In *Safazuddin and another v. State*, 2007, 36 CLC (HCD) [8407] = 27 BLD (HCD) (2007) 321, 13 BLC (HCD) (2008) 271, Justice AK Badrul Huq held that '[r]ape apart from being a dehumanizing act is an unlawful intrusion on the right of privacy and sanctity of a women/girl'.

737. In *Bangladesh Society for the Enforcement of Human Rights (BSEHR) and Others v. Government of Bangladesh and others*, 2000, 29 CLC (HCD) [3662] = 53 DLR (2001) 1, the sex workers were lifted and dislodged from their residence at Tanbazar and Nimtali, Narayanganj, by the District Administration with the help of the Police in the early hours of 23 July 1999. In the name of rehabilitation, some of them were taken to the Kashimpur Vagrant Home, where they were physically abused in the private parts of their bodies. Justice Md Fazlul Karim of the HCD found that the police at least had failed to resist the owners of the houses at Tanbazar and Nimtali and their hoodlums in preventing the eviction of the sex workers from their dwelling house and the action of house owners did not have any sanction of law, not being the due process of law. In this regard, the Honourable Court found that 'It should be remembered that nobody could violate the privacy of the inmates of any house or trespass into it except in accordance with the law.'[728]

738. In relation to a case on the forceful imposition of dress codes both by private persons and extremist political organizations, claiming to act on the basis of religion, and by persons in authority, including those in public office, the HCD found that:

> Arbitrary and intrusive gender-based codes for acceptable demeanour and dress also violate the rights to privacy and to free expression protected under international law, as well as the right of women to protection from violence. These obligations of the state have been set out in reports of the United Nations Special Rapporteur on Violence against Women, which are summarized below: As a party to the International Covenant on Civil and Political Rights (ICCPR), Bangladesh has agreed to bar interference with the right to privacy (Article 17) and protects freedom of expression (Article 19). Bangladesh has an obligation to respect and ensure these rights, and to do so in a non-discriminatory manner as set forth in Article 2 of the treaty.[729]

739. Very recently, in relation to a death reference, criminal and jail appeal arising out of sections 7 and 8 of the *Nari-o-Shishu Nirjatan Daman Ain* (Act VIII of 2000) [Prevention of Violence Against Women and Children Act, 2000 (Act VIII of 2000)] and sections 302 and 34 of the Penal Code, 1860, Mr Justice Md Ruhul Quddus of the HCD has laid down some observations having implications on the protection of citizens' telecommunication privacy under Article 43 of the

---

728. *Bangladesh Society for the Enforcement of Human Rights (BSEHR) and Others v. Government of Bangladesh and others*, 2000, 29 CLC (HCD) [3662] = 53 DLR (2001) 1.
729. *Advocate Md. Salahuddin Dolon v. Government of Bangladesh and Others*, 2010, 39 CLC (HCD) [3765] = 63 DLR (HD) (2011) 80.

Constitution.[730] This is the first time a Bangladeshi court has come up with some specific observations and provided some directions in this regard and this case will be discussed in detail at the end of Chapter 2 of this Part on the protection of telecommunication privacy.

730. *The State v. Oli*, 2019 [Death Reference No. 61 of 2011].

Chapter 1. Regulation of Personal Data Processing

§1. Introduction

740. The notion of privacy is apparently the most desired by almost everyone. The issue of privacy, more specifically, information privacy, which is also known as 'personal data' or 'personal information' protection, is invaluable in this present interconnected and networked world. It is the oil of the internet, and in this age of the fourth industrial revolution and IoT, the collection, use, processing and importance of personal information is only growing.

741. It has already been shared that there is no specific law that can protect an individual's right to privacy in Bangladesh. Nevertheless, several domestic laws contain some isolated and inadequate provisions dealing with different aspects of privacy. Article 43 of the Constitution of Bangladesh, 1972 only explicitly provides for the protection of correspondence and other means of communication, and a citizen's right to be left alone in his house against entry, search and seizure. However, these rights can be curtailed on the grounds of security of the State, public order, public morality or public health, etc. Thus, this is not an absolute right and being a part of the fundamental rights under the Constitution, 1972; this cannot be enforced against private individuals.

742. In *Tarique Rahman v. Director-General, Bureau of Anti-Corruption*, 1999, 28 CLC (HCD) = 52 DLR (2000) 518, it was held that:

> There is no fundamental right to privacy or secrecy in respect of property and wealth of a person and therefore, calling upon the petitioners to submit a statement of their properties do not violate any fundamental right guaranteed by the Constitution. The petitioners by the impugned notices have not been accused of possessing properties disproportionate to their known sources of income. Therefore, they cannot be said to interfere with the fundamental right guaranteed by Article 35(4) of the Constitution.

743. The United Nations General Assembly Resolution A/HRC/38/L.10 of 2 July 2018, affirms that the same rights that people have offline must also be protected online, in particular, freedom of expression, which is applicable regardless of frontiers and through any media of one's choice, in accordance with Article 19 of the UDHR and of the International Covenant on Civil and Political Rights. Therefore, in Bangladesh, the online privacy rights under Article 43 of the Constitution will be protected in the same way it is protected offline.

§2. Domestic Law on Personal Data

744. Before the enactment of the Digital Security Act, 2018 (Act No. 46 of 2018), only one law, i.e., the Rights and Protection of the Persons with Disabilities Act, 2013 (Act No. 39 of 2013) contained a specific provision where the protection of personal information of a disabled person is identified as his right.[731] Besides, there are provisions which have indirect relations on the protection of personal data in the name of confidentiality and privileged communication.

745. Though one may find the definition 'data' and 'information' in a few Bangladeshi laws, there is no definition of personal data or information available in the Bangladesh context. The passport of Bangladesh has included some information as personal information. Besides, the newly enacted Digital Security Act, 2018 has included a definition of 'personally identifiable information'.

746. The Passport of Bangladesh, on page No. 3, contains some information under the heading of 'personal data' and these are: name, parents' name, spouse's name and permanent address. On page No. 2, some other information, i.e., date of birth, gender, place of birth, national identification number, etc., are also included. This is obviously personal information and is usually included in the personal data protection law as in force in other countries. There is a scope of interpretation as to whether this information on page 2 will be included within the definition of 'personal data' when page 3 has explicitly included a few things as 'personal data'.

747. Section 26 of the Digital Security Act, 2018 (Act No. 46 of 2018) has attempted to define 'personal information', under the heading 'identification information'. This section has included a long list of information as information. Explanation to the section provides that 'identification information' means any external, biological, physical information or any other information which alone or jointly can detect an individual or system, whose name, photograph, address, date of birth, parent's name, signature, NID, birth and death registration number, fingerprint, passport number, bank account number, driving licence, e-Tax Identification Number, electronic or digital signature, user name, debit or credit card number, voice print, retina image, Iris image, DNA profile, security questions or any other identity which are easily available for the advancement of technology.

748. One may identify some limitations in this definition of 'identification information'. A standard definition of 'personal data' will provide a clear outline as to which information would be considered as 'personal data'. Usually, this is information using which an individual can be *identified* (i.e., name, ID number, Passport etc.) and/or *identifiable* (IP address, website browsing history, etc.) electronically and manually. Personal data are also categorized into sensitive and non-sensitive data to ensure appropriate protection mechanisms. Thus, though the explanation to section 26 has included some examples of personal data, it cannot be considered as a proper definition.

749. Since March 2016, the Dhaka Metropolitan Police has started collecting seventeen types of personal information to develop a 'central database' to curb

731. Section 16(1)(r), the Rights and Protection of the Persons with Disabilities Act, 2013 (Act No. 39 of 2013).

crimes; information like individual's name, father's name, date of birth, marital status, the type of the house, present and permanent addresses, religion, occupation, work address, educational qualification, mobile phone number, email ID, national ID number, passport number, contact person, and names and details of the house helps, drivers, and security guards with their photos are considered as 'personal information'. Of these seventeen types, while some of the information is personal information, from the legal and regulatory point of view, some others are obviously not personal information.

750. The word 'processing' has a special and distinctive meaning under the existing personal data protection laws. According to the EU General Data Protection Regulation (GDPR), 'processing' means any operation or set of operations which are performed on personal data or on sets of personal data, whether or not by automated means, such as collection, recording, organization, structuring, storage, adaptation or alteration, retrieval, consultation, use, disclosure by transmission, dissemination or otherwise making available, alignment or combination, restriction, erasure or destruction.[732] Some examples of 'processing' include staff management and payroll administration, access to/consultation of a contacts database containing personal data, sending promotional emails, shredding documents containing personal data, posting/putting a photo of a person on a website, storing IP addresses or MAC addresses, video recording (CCTV).[733]

751. Since there is no law to use, collection and processing of personal data, service providers have been collecting an excessive amount of personal data of Bangladeshi individuals. Moreover, though they are obliged to protect and ensure the safety of this personal data, there is regular news of illegal use or criminal use of personal data.

752. Before the general election in 2007, there was a huge controversy that the then government led by BNP included a huge number of fake voters in the electoral roll. As a result, the National Identity Registration Act, 2010 (Act No. III of 2010) was enacted for the registration of the national identity. Under this law, initiatives were taken to introduce an electronic database of voters with photographs and other relevant personal information or data. Under this law, 'information or data' means, for the purposes of the registration of national identity, any information or data collected from or given by any citizen at the time of preparing, amending or updating the electoral rolls in accordance with the Electoral Enrolment Act, 2009 (Act No. VI of 2009), and shall also include biometrics features of such citizens.

753. Subsequently, the government has made it mandatory to use the NID for verification purposes in getting and providing at least twenty-two types of various services. The Election Commission has entered into an agreement with eighty-two

732. European Regulation on the protection of natural persons with regard to the processing of personal data and on the free movement of such data, Regulation (EU) 2016/679.

733. European Commission, What constitutes data processing?, https://ec.europa.eu/info/law/law-topic/data-protection/reform/what-constitutes-data-processing_en.

institutions including the passport office and banks, and through this agreement, these institutes can access the NID Databases to check services, such as e-TIN, Pay-Fixation, banking activities, withdrawal of foreign remittance, registration of mobile SIM cards, vehicle registration, driving licences, identification of bodies, terrorist and criminals.

754. When it was found that the criminals have been making fake voter lists since the NID was merely laminated, then in 2011, the government initiated the project, Identification System for Enhancing Access to Services with the financial support of the World Bank to introduce Smart NID containing several pieces of biometric data, including an impression of all ten fingers and iris scans. In developing the Smart NID, twenty-five international certifications and standards were ensured, and three levels of security features were added to prevent forgery.

§3. Recent Developments

755. In the ITU's recently published Global Cyber Security Index, 2018, it was suggested that Bangladesh should enact a comprehensive national personal data protection law, which will bestow the data subjects some rights and the control and sovereignty over the collection, use and processing of their personal data. Even before this suggestion, enough has already been written and discussed in various forums highlighting the importance to enact such a law in the Bangladesh context though there is apparently no genuine endeavour from the policymakers in this regard.[734]

756. The Digital Security Act, 2018 (Act No. 46 of 2018) was enacted to ensure digital security and to identify, block, prevent, trial digital crimes, etc. The high-profile government spokesmen claimed that the drafting of this law was necessary to, *inter alia*, protect the citizens' data and privacy. It is apparent from the review of relevant provisions of the law that even though one may identify some scattered provisions in the Digital Security Act, 2018 which may be used to protect some aspects of information privacy, an intentionally designed personal data protection law is something very different.

757. Section 26 has made it an offence to collect and use, etc. of 'identification information' and it is provided that if anyone, without having the legal authority, collects, sells, possesses, supplies or uses such information, he will commit an offence for which he will be responsible for imprisonment up to five years or fine up to BDT 500,000 (approximately USD 5834) or both for the first time offence; and for the subsequent similar offence, he will be responsible for imprisonment up to seven years or a fine of up to BDT 10,00,000 (approximately USD 11667) or both.

---

734. Karim, M.E. & Jewel, N., *The Digital Security Act, 2018: How Far Does It Protect Our Privacy?*, The Daily Star, 8 Jan. 2019, https://www.thedailystar.net/law-our-rights/law-analysis/news/how-far-does-it-protect-our-privacy-1684342.

758. Unfortunately, this section has not defined 'persons with or having legal authority' or 'process or instances to get legal authority', 'use' and 'collection', etc. for the purpose of this section. No distinction is made between 'identification information' collected and used for social, family or recreational purposes, and such information collected or used for commercial purposes. Moreover, there is no distinction made between general and sensitive information. There is no scope for future Rulemaking under section 60 of the Digital Security Act, 2018 (Act No. 46 of 2018) in this regard. Without this, such acts of collection and use of 'identification information' is made cognizable, i.e., anyone can be arrested even without a warrant and a non-bailable offence under section 53. Thus, it can be anticipated that, given the technological knowledge of the members of the law enforcement agencies of the country, there are enough scopes of misuse and abuse of this section.[735]

759. The reality is that under the existing personal data protection laws, the data subject enjoys sovereignty before and during the collection, use and processing of his personal information. Simultaneously, even with legal authority, anyone cannot simply collect and use such data unless he obtains the consent of the data subject, who can at any time withdraw his consent and the data processor is bound to cease further activities with such data of the data subject. Moreover, even with such consent, data collected for one purpose cannot be used for another purpose.

760. Moreover, the provisions of data protection law generally encapsulate guidelines on the *legal basis* of the data processing under which conditions/circumstances anyone can collect, use and process personal data of an individual. Additionally, '*data controller*' and '*data processor*' have to comply with some duties, responsibilities and obligations to protect the personal information collected. However, the Digital Security Act, 2018 (Act No. 46 of 2018) has no provision on the *legal basis* of data processing, obligations of '*data controller*' and '*data processor*' and compliance issues.

761. In 2019, a draft titled the Information Privacy and Protection Rules, 2019, as per the power under section 60(2) Jha and containing forty provisions and two schedules, was released and available on the website of the ICT Division. This Draft Rules, 2019 has defined personal data as any information relating to a person using which that person can be identified directly or indirectly and included sensitive personal information within the definition. Besides, this Rules has also included definitions of other terms, such as communication, data, information controller, data processing, processing, anonymization, portability, profiling, surveillance, biometric, cyber incident, etc. The purpose of releasing this Draft is not very clear and it seems that the draft was prepared in a hurry for some unknown reason, and that is why some serious mistakes in terms of legal drafting can be noticed. However, this Rules is still in the draft form, has not been finalized yet and given the force of law.

735. *Ibid.*

§4. CONCLUSION

762. It is believed that while enacting the ICT Act 2006, the drafters of this law followed the similar law of India, i.e., the Information Technology Act, 2000. The right to privacy was not recognized in India and is not included as a fundamental right in the Indian Constitution, 1949. Nevertheless, the Indian Supreme Court has recently declared that the 'right to privacy' is a fundamental right and ordered the government to enact a personal data protection law.[736] Accordingly, the government of India has taken the initiative, and Bill was presented in the Parliament in this regard.

763. The EU has adopted the GDPR, the most comprehensive data protection legal framework in the world. The provisions of GDPR are applicable to all data processing activities related to personal data of EU individuals, including offering goods and services to the EU and monitoring their behaviour. The location of the data controller, data processor and processing activities is immaterial if the data processing is related to an EU individual. As a result, any Bangladeshi person or company that offers goods or services to the EU or monitors the behaviour of the EU individuals will be obliged to follow GDPR provisions.

764. With around 25% of total trade, the EU is Bangladesh's main trading partner, and Bangladesh is the EU's 35th largest trading partner in goods. Bangladesh is on the way to attaining the status of a developing country soon, and the country will have to face stiffer challenges in terms of business and trade as it will not get duty-free access to the EU as it used to get as an LDC. Bangladesh's competitors in the IT outsourcing business have already taken initiatives in this regard; the Philippines enacted personal information protection law in 2011, Indonesia and Thailand have joined the data protection law club.[737] In such a situation, Bangladesh cannot sit idle anymore and observe the loss of markets only because of the absence of a personal data protection law. The government of Bangladeshi has established the data centre and included some provisions in the recently formulated Digital Commerce Policy and ICT Policy.[738] But these are meant for government use and do not guarantee the processing of personal data by private individuals or organizations for commercial purposes. Therefore, the enactment of a personal data protection law should be considered seriously. Fortunately, it is evident that the government has recognized the importance of this issue and released the Draft of Personal Data Protection Rules in the second half of 2019. As the Rules is still in the Draft stage, it will be better to wait for a while to comment on the Draft. Nevertheless, this is a significant move from the government end and, therefore, should be appreciated with the hope that the process of enacting a national law aiming at the protection of personal data has started to roll.

---

736. *Justice K S Puttaswamy (Retd.), and another v. Union of India and Ors.*, (Writ Petition (Civil) No. 494 of 2012).
737. Karim, M.E. & Jewel, N., *The Digital Security Act, 2018: How Far Does It Protect Our Privacy?*, The Daily Star, 8 Jan. 2019, https://www.thedailystar.net/law-our-rights/law-analysis/news/how-far-does-it-protect-our-privacy-1684342.
738. *Ibid.*

Chapter 2. Protection of Telecommunication Privacy

765. Constitutionally, every Bangladeshi citizen has the fundamental right to privacy as to communication and other correspondence though reasonable restrictions can be imposed by law in the interests of the security of the State, public order, public morality or public health.[739] Hence, the privacy of communication and other correspondence using telecommunication facilities between individuals are protected, the government, however, can intercept and infringe the telecommunication privacy of the citizens on the grounds of security of the State, public order, public morality or public health, etc.

766. Even after having such provisions in the Constitution, the issue of telephone interception or leaked telephone conversation clips has turned to be a normal phenomenon nowadays and, in some cases, these become viral and broadcasted on private television channels. In most cases, one may see a specific trend, i.e., the parties involved in these leaked telephone conversations are people who are critics of government activities. The general people do not have any clue about how and which government agency leaks these, and the victims or parties involved do not have an effective remedy, though there are instances that on the basis of these leaked conversations, people are arrested and convicted on the grounds of public safety and security of the state.

767. Of all these telephone conversation leak instances, at least two deserve special attention. These are often cited as 'cassette scandal' and 'skype scandal' where on two different occasions, the conversation involving two different Judges of the Supreme Court were intercepted and publicized. In the first instance, on 16 September 2000, Bangladeshi tabloid *Dainik Manabzamin* published a secret conversation recorded in an audio cassette between former President of Bangladesh, Mr Hussain Muhammad Ershad and one HCD Justice, Mohammad Latifur Rahman under the news title- '*Ekti Rajokiyo Kelenkkarir Khoshra*' [A Draft of a Royal Scandal].[740] In this conversation, it could be revealed that the former President tried to get a favourable verdict in a famous pending case popularly known as the 'Janata Tower Case' involving him regarding his abuse of power and corruption in allocating a government land in favour of his wife. An allegation was brought against the tabloid and the court 'criticized the sensational media coverage of a scandal involving senior judge … '.[741] In the second instance, London-based 'Economist' obtained 17 hours of recorded telephone conversation and 230 emails where it was found that they were discussing various issues relating to the tribunal.[742] Subsequently, a Bangla

---

739. Article 43, the Constitution of Bangladesh, 1972.
740. *State v. Chief Editor, Manabjamin and others*, 2002, 57 DLR (2005) 359. It may be relevant to share here that this Justice Latifur Rahman is a different than former Chief Justice Latifur Rahman who was the Chief Justice of Bangladesh between 1 Jan. 2000 to 28 Feb. 2001 and led the Caretaker government of Bangladesh before the national election in 2001.
741. United Nations Economic and Social Council, Commission on Human Rights, 'Civil and Political Rights, including Questions of Freedom of Expression', E/CN.4/2003/67/Add.1, 20 Feb. 2003.
742. Anbarasan, E., *Bangladesh War Crimes Judge Nizamul Huq Resigns*, BBC News, Dhaka, 11 Dec. 2012, https://www.bbc.com/news/world-asia-20677752.

daily Amar Desh published the conversation of Justice Nizamul Huq, Chairman of the International Crimes Tribunal-1, a tribunal established to try the war crime offences of Bangladesh Liberation War in 1971, with an expatriate Bangladeshi legal expert on International crimes. In both instances, the judges in question resigned from their role, but the person responsible for these scandals, recording or interception of telephone calls could not be identified.

768. Apart from the constitutional provision recognizing citizens' conditional or qualified right to privacy, section 71 of the Bangladesh Telecommunication Regulation Act, 2001 (Act No. 18 of 2001) has made the intentional listening of a telephone conversation between two other persons as a punishable offence. The 2006 amendment to the law has added an extra clause to this provision which reads: 'Provided that nothing in this section shall apply to any officers of intelligence agencies, national security agencies, investigating agencies and law-enforcing agencies who are authorized by the government under section 97A.'

769. Under section 84 of the Bangladesh Telecommunication Regulation Act, 2001, the BTRC, for the purpose of implementation of the Act, can ask for and collect any information from an operator or other licensees, or the permit or certificate holder or any other person. Such persons are bound to furnish such requested information. Such person shall not be compelled to deliver a document or contents thereof which the person is not bound to deliver to a court in connection with a civil suit, and the burden of proof that he is not so bound shall lie on him.[743] An interpretation of this provision will reveal that the government can collect all information about the subscribers of various telecommunication services. Besides, under section 97 of the said Act, in times of emergency, the government can collect information. In fact, very recently, the BTRC had collected personal data of seventy million mobile number subscribers in the name of biometric SIM registration. Even though there was no emergency in the country and the government initiated the program to reduce the threat of, *inter alia*, Islamic extremists and terrorists, critics believe that the move of the Regulators was political in nature.

770. Section 97A, as has been inserted in the Bangladesh Telecommunication Regulation Act, 2001 through the Bangladesh Telecommunication (Amendment) Act, 2006, provides that for the security of the state and public tranquillity, the Government can authorize any of its agencies to record, prevent and collect information regarding communications made by any person through the telephone. This section further provides that the Government can order any service provider for assistance in this regard, and in that case, the service provider shall be bound to assist the Government. Section 97B of the Act states that any information collected under section 97A shall be admissible under the Evidence Act, 1872, and section 97C deals with punishment to anybody who fails to comply with the order under section 97A. Thus, the government can tap any telephone conversation without the prior order of the government or warrant of the court.

---

743. Section 84(2), the Bangladesh Telecommunication Regulation Act, 2001 (Act No. 18 of 2001).

771. The National Telecommunication Monitoring Center (NTMC), an intelligence agency established as per the provisions of section 97A of the Bangladesh Telecommunication Regulation Act, 2001 as amended in 2006 under the Ministry of Home Affairs, has started functioning since 2013 to tighten the state security and to protect the country from prospective security threats. It provides, through the National Monitoring Center (NMC) established in 2008, for all kinds of monitoring facilities to government authorized law enforcement and intelligence agencies. NTMC assists them in intercepting the telecommunication service providers lawfully, tracking mobile and fixed-line phone calls for identifying and locating suspected criminals, including members of militant outfits in Bangladesh. For example, NTMC has been assisting the Anti-Corruption Commission of Bangladesh in receiving corruption-related information from the phone calls of the suspects. Besides, the Criminal Investigation Department (CID) of Bangladesh Police has also established a Lawful Interception Cell under the organized crime division in this regard, and this Cell performs its duty 24/7 throughout the year.[744] These initiatives are praiseworthy, lawful and constitutionally permitted and also, in line with the activities of the best practices practised around the world as the protection of the security of the state and citizens is one of the prime responsibilities of a modern-day government. Nevertheless, there are some real concerns in these initiatives, e.g., with regard to citizens' privacy rights as bestowed through Article 43 of the Constitution in general and also that, the advantages of initiatives can be used by the government to undermine the political opposition.

772. The Act, unfortunately, is silent about the instances of privileged communication, such as communication between a lawyer and a client or a doctor and a patient. Such communication as a privileged communication, cannot be used as evidence in any court of law. But the Act has given the Government an explicit authority to record, prevent and collect information on personal communication made through telephone under section 97A and such recorded communication shall be admissible under the Evidence Act, 1872 as per section 97B of the Act, 2001. Besides, the Act is also silent about voice identification.[745]

773. A writ petition was moved in the HCD seeking invalidation of the amendment on 18 May 2006. The HCD issued a rule on the government to explain within three weeks the legality of the provisions that entitled the law enforcers and intelligence agencies to tap the telephone conversations of any individual. An HCD Bench which consisted of Justice M Awlad Ali and Justice Zinat Ara also directed the Government to explain why the Bangladesh Telecommunication (Amendment) Act, 2006 should not be declared unconstitutional and void. The hearing on the petition is pending, and the government has not replied to the rules.[746]

---

744. Lawful Interception Cell, Criminal Investigation Department, Bangladesh Police, http://cid.gov.bd/site/content_view/lic.

745. Arafat A., *Bangladesh Telecommunication (Amendment) Ordinance, 2005: National Security or Infringement on Civil Rights?*, The Daily Star, 6 May 2006, https://www.thedailystar.net/law/2006/05/01/index.htm.

746. How Safe Are Your Telephone Conversations?, 20 Nov. 2013, Dhaka Tribune, https://www.dhakatribune.com/uncategorized/2013/11/20/how-safe-are-your-telephone-conversations.

Under section 85 of this Act, 2001, the people can utilize the opportunity to inspect and collect copies of all information that the Commission receives during the performance of its functions under the Act unless the information is confidential in nature.

774. Section 5 of the Telegraph Act, 1885 (Act No. XIII of 1885) provides that on the occurrence of any public emergency, or in the interest of the public safety, the Government or any officer specially authorized in this behalf by the Government, may, *inter alia*, order that any message or class of messages to or from any person or class of persons or relating to any particular subject brought for transmission by, or transmitted or received by, any telegraph, shall not be transmitted, or shall be intercepted or detained, or shall be disclosed to the Government making the order or an officer thereof mentioned in the order. It is further provided that if any doubt arises as to the existence of a public emergency, or whether any act is done under sub-section (1) was in the interest of the public safety, a certificate of the Government shall be conclusive proof on the point.

775. Entry into the signal room of a telegraph office, either government or licensed, or unauthorized access to the boundary of the office, refusal to quit or wilful obstruction or impediment with the intention of unlawfully learning the contents of any message, or of committing any offence punishable under this Act is also punishable. However, the law provides for very nominal punishment, i.e., for unauthorized access BDT 500 and for unlawful learning of the content of any message imprisonment up to one year.[747] Similarly, damaging, removing, tampering with or touching any battery, machinery, telegraph line, post or other thing whatever, being part of or used in or about any telegraph or in the working thereof with the intention to, *inter alia*, intercept or to acquaint himself with the contents of any message is a punishable offence.[748] Moreover, intercepting, detaining or disclosing message by any telegraph officer without the authority of the government or direction of a competent court is an offence.[749] Even mistakenly received messages cannot be retained fraudulently or kept a secret willingly.[750]

776. Finally, the government established BTRC, as the national regulator, on 31 January 2002 under section 6 of the Bangladesh Telecommunication Regulation Act, 2001 (Act No. 18 of 2001), empowered BTRC and made this regulator responsible for ensuring the protection of the privacy of telecommunication.[751] Nevertheless, to what extent this regulator is successful in protecting telecommunication privacy is a matter of contention due to the frequent release of the leaked conversation between political leaders and celebrities in social and mass media. In most cases, the mass media channels that telecast these leaked conversations or videos do not even share the source of these and thus, violate journalistic ethics. With this,

747. Sections 22 and 23, the Telegraph Act, 1885 (Act No. XIII of 1885).
748. Section 25, the Telegraph Act, 1885 (Act No. XIII of 1885).
749. Section 26, the Telegraph Act, 1885 (Act No. XIII of 1885).
750. Section 30, the Telegraph Act, 1885 (Act No. XIII of 1885).
751. Section 30(1)(f), the Bangladesh Telecommunication Regulation Act, 2001 (Act No. 18 of 2001).

there are threats and concerns of artificial intelligence-driven services such as deep fake, using which anyone can be trapped and fake videos can be made to, *inter alia*, undermine the image of the victim and for illegal economic gains. Therefore, it is high time that the government or relevant regulators come forward with relevant rules or guidelines.

777. The basis in this journey of framing relevant rules and regulations can be the judgment of the HCD delivered in the recent case mentioned in the last chapter. In the judgment delivered in the case of the *State v. Oli*, 2019 [Death Reference No. 61 of 2011] Mr Justice Md Ruhul Quddus shared some observations and provided some directions regarding the practice of collection of call lists or audio discussions from public or private phone companies without any formal requisition and formal seizure and also without the knowledge of the phone subscribed while deciding a murder case under the *Druto Bichar Tribunal Ain*, 2002 [The Speedy Trial Tribunal Act, 2002].

778. It can be seen from the fact of the case and complaint of the informant that he made an allegation against the accused, with whom he had enmity and claimed that the accused used an unregistered mobile SIM to make him eleven phone calls. Through the phone calls, the accused informed the informant about the kidnapping of his seven years old son and demanded ransom to release the minor, who was subsequently found murdered even though the demanded ransom amount was paid. A criminal case was started.

779. During the examination process, in cross-examination in the trial court, the first investigating police officer claimed to seize these phone calls list though subsequently denied. Moreover, he also stated that he could not recover the SIM but recovered a mobile set used for making those calls. Again, he did not seize any ownership document of the phone used in this incident too. The second investigating police officer even submitted the photocopy of an unsigned calls list and stated that the SIM of the accused was not registered and so, there was no ownership document.

780. In support to establish the case, the lawyer of one of the accused raised this issue that the informant prosecution did neither submit the original calls list nor mentioned the reasons why the original calls list could not be presented. Also, neither there was any signature or seal of the supplying authority nor anyone from the phone operating company was examined. Therefore, such call lists do not have evidentiary value in the eye of law. While discussing the evidentiary value of such documents produced in these ways, the Judge pointed out that:

> the practice of collection of call list/audio discussion from public/private phone companies without any formal requisition and formal seizure, and also behind the knowledge of the subscriber must be stopped. It is our common experience that nowadays private communications between the citizens including their audios/videos are often leaked and published in social media for different purposes. We must not forget that the citizens' right to privacy in correspondence

and other means of communication is guaranteed under article 43 of the Constitution which cannot be easily violated at the instance of any interested quarter. Bangladesh Telecommunication Regulatory Commission and the phone companies operating in Bangladesh have a great responsibility towards proper compliance of the Constitutional mandate of maintaining privacy in communication. They cannot provide any information relating to communication of their subscribers and the citizens of the Country, unless it is permissible in law matched with the Constitution. So, when the Investigating Officers in relation to particular investigation/inquiry require any call lists or information relating the one's communication, they must make a formal request to the concerned authority of the respective company/office stating the reason why it is necessary for that investigation/inquiry, not in a roving and fishing manner. Only in that case the phone companies have obligation to supply the call list or information within the knowledge of the subscriber. Otherwise the supplied documents would lose its evidentiary value and the supplying person/authority would also be liable for aiding violation of one's fundamental right guaranteed under the Constitution.

Part VII. Computer-Related Crime

§1. Cybercrime: An Introduction

781. The functions of modern computers were, in some form, known to human beings since the time of the abacus, which was in existence in 3500 B.C. in Japan, China and India. Since the 1960s, the power and applications of computers have been expanded exponentially impacting almost every single affair and need of our daily lives, directly or indirectly. While the use of computers and their applications are treated as enabling and transformative, these have also increased the chances and number of criminal activities. ICT products and applications are considered as dual-use products, i.e., products that can be weaponized and be used for both good and evil purposes. One of the serious concerns is that these ICT products and applications are very easily available and accessible, and are not expensive like other dual-use products/items such as nuclear technology, arms, and chemicals, etc. As a result, some forms of computer crimes, e.g., physical damage to computer systems and stored data, unauthorized use and access to computer systems and the manipulation of electronic data, computer-related fraud and software piracy, etc., have been recognized as criminal offences since the 1960s.

782. It is claimed that the first computer crime was committed in 1801 AD when a French textile manufacturer designed a technology that could repeat a series of steps in the weaving of special fabrics.[752] Whereas, it is believed that the word 'cyber' is derived from the word 'cybernetics', which was first used by the American mathematician, Nobert Wiener in 1948. The word 'cybernetics' has a Greek origin and it means the theory of control and communication in living beings and machines.[753] In the existing literature, several terms such as 'computer crime', 'computer abuse', 'computer-related crime', 'high technology crime', 'electronic crime', 'digital crime', and 'virtual crime', etc.; and when the internet is used, terms such as 'online crime', 'network crime', 'cybercrime', 'crime in the cyberspace', 'internet crime', etc. are used interchangeably to denote computer-related crime or cybercrime. The terms 'computer crimes', 'computer-related crimes' and 'cybercrime' will be used for the discussion in this chapter.,

752. United Nations Manual on the prevention and control of computer-related crime, International review of criminal policy – Nos 43 and 44 (1994), at p. 5.
753. For a historical background on the origin on how Wirner used the word 'cybernetics' in the context of World War II, *see* Terrell Ward Bynum, *Computer Ethics: Its Birth and Its Future*, 3 Ethics Info. Tech., 109–112 (2001).

§2. Cybercrime: Types and Forms

783. Cybercrimes can generally be of two types, i.e., (a) crimes committed by misuse or abuse of computer, i.e., use of the computer as a target of criminal activity, and (b) commission of traditional crimes, such as theft, fraud, forgery and mischief by use of the computer as a tool or instrument. In the first category, sometimes dubbed as *cyber-dependent crimes*, a computer and the related system can itself be used as a tool and target of the attack, and in the second category, sometimes dubbed as *cyber-enabled crimes*, the computers can be used or abused as incidental to commit traditional crimes. Thus, software or data theft, e.g., copyright infringements, trade secrets, etc., and hardware theft can be committed in the first category, while in the second category, telecommunication crimes such as phone hacking, eavesdropping, etc., can also be committed.

784. The concept 'cybercrimes' are discussed in both a narrow and broader sense.[754] Accordingly, the concept 'cybercrime' is narrower than 'computer-related crimes' as when 'cybercrime' has to involve a computer network with or without the use of the internet, 'computer-related crimes' even cover those offences that bear no relation to a network, but only affect stand-alone computer systems.[755] Thus, the word 'cybercrime' will be used in this monograph to mean crimes committed involving a computer network with the use of the internet. Cybercrimes can take various common forms: fraud by computer manipulation, computer forgery, damage to or modification of computer data or programs, unauthorized access to computer systems and services, and unauthorized reproduction of legally protected computer programs, etc.[756] According to the Council of Europe's Convention on Cybercrime, 2001 (CETS No. 185) (popularly known as 'Budapest Convention'), substantive cybercrimes can be in the form of *Offences against the confidentiality, integrity and availability* (illegal access, illegal interception, data interference, system interference, misuse of devices), *Computer-related offences* (computer-related forgery, computer-related fraud), *content-related offences* (offences related to child pornography), *Offences related to infringements of copyright and related rights.*

785. From the existing domestic, regional and international legal instruments, it can be revealed that these laws generally encapsulate provisions regarding a few substantive offences within the ambit of cybercrime. These are: illegal access to a computer system; illegal access, interception or acquisition of computer data; illegal interference of data or system; production, distribution or possession of malware; breach of privacy or data protection measures; computer-related offences, e.g., fraud or forgery, identity theft, infringement of copyright and trademark offences, defamation, racism or xenophobia, production, distribution or possession of child pornography, child grooming, terrorism offences, etc.

---

754. United Nations Manual on the prevention and control of computer-related crime, International review of criminal policy – Nos 43 and 44 (1994), at p. 5.

755. Gercke, M., *Understanding Cybercrime: Phenomena, Challenges and Legal Response,* 11 (September 2012).

756. United Nations Manual on the prevention and control of computer-related crime, International review of criminal policy – Nos 43 and 44 (1999).

786. In the recently released Bangladesh Cyber Threat Landscape, 2020 by the Bangladesh e-Government Computer Incident Response Team (BGD e-GOV CIRT), a few otherwise known substantive cybercrimes were listed as top cyber threats for Bangladesh. These are spam, ransomware, phishing, malware, information leakage, insider threat, identity theft, web-based attack, data breach, denial of service, web application attacks, botnets, cryptojacking, physical manipulation/damage/theft/loss and cyber espionage.[757] Thus, it is evident that using the computer, various criminal activities such as hacking, malware, gambling, stalking, phishing, harassment, internet extortion, the spread of hate speech, fake news, pornography, cyber terrorism, identity theft, etc., can be committed.

§3. Cybercrimes and International Instruments

787. Generally speaking, there is no exclusive binding international instrument dealing with cybercrime, its substantive, procedural and preventive aspects. Some recent regional initiatives from which some instruments are proposed can be identified and shared. Some of these are in the form of Model Law and some are still in the draft form. The list of such instruments includes- African Union Convention on Cyber Security and Personal Data Protection Convention on Combating, League of Arab States Convention on Combating Information Technology Offences, Caribbean Community Model Legislative Texts of Cybercrime/e-Crimes and Electronic Evidence, Common Market for Eastern and Southern Africa Cybersecurity Draft Model Bill, Commonwealth of Independent States Agreement on Cooperation in Combating Offences related to Computer Information, East African Community Draft Legal Framework for Cyber laws, Economic Community of Central African States Declaration of Brazzaville (adoption of Model Laws in ICT and Cybersecurity), Economic Community of West African States Directive C/DIR. 1/08/11 on Fighting Cyber Crime, EU Directive on Security of Network and Information Systems, Shanghai Cooperation Organisation Agreement on Cooperation in the Field of International Information Security, and Southern African Development Community Model Laws on Cyber Security; Cybercrime, Data Protection and Electronic Transactions.[758]

788. The Budapest Convention, though is a European Convention, is open for all countries in the world to be part of it (Article 36). The Convention was entered into force in 2004 and is the first international treaty to address some of the cybercrimes such as infringements of copyright, computer-related fraud, child pornography and violations of network security, etc.[759] The Convention was introduced as it was found 'necessary to deter action directed against the confidentiality, integrity, and availability of computer systems, networks and computer data as well as the

---

757. BGD e-GOV CIRT, Bangladesh Cyberthreat Landscape, January–December 2020, Risk Assessment Unit, p. 5.

758. For an authoritative reference, *see* United Nations Institute for Disarmament Research, Multilateral Frameworks, https://unidir.org/cpp/en/multilateral-frameworks.

759. The example of another regional instrument is African Union Convention on Cyber Security & Personal Data Protection, which was adopted on 27 Jun. 2014.

misuse of such systems, networks and data by providing for the criminalisation of such conduct, as described in this Convention, and the adoption of powers sufficient for effectively combating such criminal offences, by facilitating their detection, investigation and prosecution at both the domestic and international levels and by providing arrangements for fast and reliable international co-operation'.[760]

789. Though the Budapest Convention is made open for signature/accession and ratification for any sovereign state, it is more like a European regional law on cybercrime, and some non-European countries have already become a member of this Convention by way of signature or accession and ratification. Non-European countries such as Canada, Japan, South Africa and the US signed the Convention when this was open for signature in 2001 and except for South Africa, other these countries have already ratified this Convention. On the other hand, countries such as Argentina, Australia, Chile, Morocco, Paraguay, Senegal and Sri Lanka have accessed and ratified this Convention.[761] Bangladesh has neither signed nor accessed this Convention also. Other than the Budapest Convention, the Commonwealth also drafted the first Model Law on Cybercrime in 2001. This Model Law and Harare Scheme for Mutual Assistance can be considered as international best practice in this field and a practical alternative to the Budapest Convention. In this Part, some of the substantive cybercrimes and their procedural aspects in the context of Bangladesh will be discussed.

760. Preamble, Convention on Cybercrime, Budapest, Council of Europe, 2001.

761. Chart of signatures and ratifications of Treaty 185 Convention on Cybercrime Status as of 23 Apr. 2021, https://www.coe.int/en/web/conventions/full-list/-/conventions/treaty/185/signatures?p_auth=sWlwHNtP.

Chapter 1. General Legal Development

§1. Introduction

790. The word 'crime' denotes an act or omission which is prohibited and recognized by the state as crimes are injurious to the public at large and punished by law. Crime is a wrong of a public character, and it possesses elements of evil which affect the public as a whole and not merely an individual. To put it differently, crime is an act deemed by law to be harmful to society in general, even though its immediate victim is an individual.[762] Crime is the commission of an act specifically forbidden by law, and it may be an offence against morality and social order. Crime subjects the doer to legal punishment.[763]

791. Cybercrimes are frequent, rampant, organized and often multi-jurisdictional and have some substantive and procedural aspects. Substantive aspects of any law deal with the rights and obligations of the individual(s) as a member of society.[764] Substantive law is not retrospective in operation by implications. There are some substantive cybercrimes, i.e., crimes committed involving a computer network with or without the use of the internet. On the other hand, some procedural formalities need to be observed in different stages of investigation and trial of these cybercrimes as procedural laws assist the proper exercise and implementation of the substantive laws.

792. More than 154 countries in the world have already enacted national legislation on cybercrime and the number is growing as more countries are joining the list.[765] From the experience of various countries having cybercrime legislation, it can be revealed that some countries, depending on their socio-legal and cultural background, have enacted specific laws to tackle various cybercrimes, while some countries have amended their penal laws to include cybercrimes. These laws contain provisions on substantive cybercrimes and their procedural and punitive aspects.

793. There is no specific law on cybercrime in Bangladesh similar to the Computer Misuse Act, 1990 of the UK, the Computer Crimes Act, 1997 of Malaysia, or the Computer Crime Act, 2007 of Thailand. Instead, there are general substantive laws on crime such as the Penal Code, 1860 (XLV of 1860) and general law on criminal procedure, i.e., the Criminal Procedural Code, 1898 (Act V of 1898). Both these colonial laws are still in force to deal with modern crimes, including computer crimes or cybercrimes. Besides, there are sector-specific general laws such as the ICT Act, 2006, and the Digital Security Act, 2018 (Act No. 46 of 2018), and

762. *Shamim Hossain v. The State*, 7 BLT (HCD) 89.
763. *Md. Alfu Miah & Anr. v. The State*, 10 BLT (HCD) 331.
764. For example, the Constitution of Bangladesh, 1972 has bestowed a number of rights to the citizens and imposes some general duties on them to observe the Constitution and the laws, to maintain discipline, to perform public duties and to protect public property under Art. 21.
765. UNCTAD, Cybercrime Legislation Worldwide, https://unctad.org/page/cybercrime-legislation-worldwide.

sector-specific special laws, such as the Pornography Control Act, 2012 (Act No. 9 of 2012), etc. These sectorial laws contain some substantive and procedural provisions, and thus, can be used to investigate and try various statutory computer-related crimes and cybercrimes. Moreover, one may also find some important and general provisions on different crimes committed within the metropolitan areas in the metropolitan police laws and if a computer is used to commit any of these crimes the provisions of such laws can be considered in relation to computer-related crimes as well.[766]

794. This Chapter begins by sharing some facts and figures in relation to various cybercrimes in the context of Bangladesh. After that, a brief analysis of the existing Bangladeshi laws on cybercrimes, their strengths and limitations, etc. will be examined. Next, the legal definition of 'computer', which is extremely important in the legal discussion of cybercrime will be considered. Finally, this chapter wraps up by shedding light on the legal framework of some important issues relevant in the discussion of cybercrimes, e.g., cybersecurity and CII.

§2. Facts and Figures

795. With the popularity of computers and availability of the internet even at the grassroots level, with so many success stories, incidents of cybercrimes are almost regularly reported in national dailies. Though there are differences in figures in the available statistics, it is apparent that the incidents of cybercrimes are increasing at an alarming rate. In 2017, the Police received at least 40,000 complaints about cybercrimes, and using the police mobile app, 'Hello City', a total of 5,842 complaints were received.[767] In the last four years, they received around 17,000 complaints through different channels including Facebook messenger, email and this mobile app.[768] The helpdesk of the Ministry of Telecommunications and ICT and BTRC has also been receiving a huge amount of complaints every day where almost 70% of complaints are received from women, and there are incidents of suicides also as a consequence of such incidents. In most cases, the images of the victims are cut out or edited to make them pornographic. The Dhaka Metropolitan Police arrested seventy-two persons in 2017.[769]

796. Another report shows that during 2012–June 2017, a total of 1,417 instances involving cybercrimes were filed (19 in 2012, 48 in 2013, 149 in 2014, 303 in 2015, 546 in 2016 and 352 in 2017) where police submitted charge sheets in

766. For example, s. 92 of the Dhaka Metropolitan Police Ordinance, 1976 (Ordinance No. III of 1976) provides that it is an offence to assemble with others in a street or public place for the purpose of gambling or wagering or joining in any such assembly. Thus, using this provision, the offence of online gambling can be tried as well though the fine is very nominal, i.e., BDT 100 only.

767. https://www.jugantor.com/todays-paper/it-world/41217.

768. Khan, S., *Strengthening Cyber Security Management* (21 Feb. 2021), https://thefinancialexpress.com.bd/views/columns/strengthening-cyber-security-management-1614442872.

769. https://www.jugantor.com/todays-paper/it-world/41217.

748 cases and final report in 179 instances.[770] The Cyber Crime Investigation Center established with a computer forensic lab at the CID received 25 complaints in 2013, 70 in 2014, 217 in 2015, 575 in 2016 and more than 600 till July 2017.[771]

797. In the Cyber Security and Crime Division of the Dhaka Metropolitan Police, on the other hand, a total of 666 cases were filed with the different police stations in Dhaka between 2016 and March 2019. The accused in these cases used to spread defamatory news and disinformation on online platforms and blogs using fake IDs and photos of the victims and blackmail women after hacking or compromising their social media profile. 70% of cybercrime victims were women, where 57% of them were between the age limit of 18–25, and in the case of the remaining 13%, the age of the victims was below 18. The Police revealed that these cases were related to terrorism (1%), blackmailing or extortion (7%), pornography and financial fraud (14% each), hacking (20%), defamation (18%), fraudulent impersonation (20%) and miscellaneous (6%).[772]

798. It was reported that around 73% of women internet users in Bangladesh were subject to cyber-bullying or another form of cyber-crime and 70% of the complainants were women.[773] The latest report suggests that the number has increased and 80% of the victims of cyber-bullying are women aged between 14–22.[774] According to AMTOB, 21% of Bangladeshi internet users use Facebook and 36% use YouTube. Some 84% of the net users are aged between 18–34. Some 41% of school students also suffer from cyber-bullying.

799. The findings of research conducted on 133 victims of cybercrimes revealed that in social media, young people of age between 18–30 are the main victims of cybercrime (73.71%), whereas 10.52% were aged below 18 years, 12.77% were aged between 30–45 years and 3% were above the age of 45 years. Of them, 51.13% were female, and 48.87% were male. It was further revealed that the types of cybercrimes include: (a) identity or data theft, email fraud, mobile banking account hacking, fraud in an online transaction, online threat, dissemination of fake profile/ photograph after editing, harassment in social media creating a fake ID, hacking of online account, pornography, uploading and distribution of personal photographs

770. Under the criminal law system in Bangladesh, a police officer after completion of investigation submits the 'charge sheets' when there are reasons to believe that the accused has committed the crime and 'final report' when during the investigation, the police officer has not received any such grounds that the accused has committed the crime.
771. Rabbi, A.R., *Women Biggest Victims of Rising Cybercrimes* (21 Sep. 2017), https://www.dhakatribune.com/bangladesh/crime/2017/09/21/women-biggest-victims-rising-cybercrimes.
772. Bangladesh Sangbad Sangstha, 'Cybercrimes escalate worries to women internet users', 30 Mar. 2019, https://www.bssnews.net/?p=188875.
773. Legal Action on Cyber Violence against Women, 2017, Bangladesh Legal Aid and Services Trust (BLAST) and BRAC James P Grant School of Public Health, at p. 2.
774. UNB News, *80% of cyberbullying victims are women* (10 Dec. 2020), https://unb.com.bd/category/Bangladesh/80-of-cyberbullying-victims-are-women/61781.

without permission and love scams, etc.[775] It was also revealed that these victims do not take the legal actions due to their ignorance about the process of taking legal actions; they felt that they would not get any remedy even after lodging cases; there are possibilities of further harassment after taking the legal actions to avoid social harassment, and the accused is socially powerful. It was found that 39% of the victims did not make any complaint, 54% were not satisfied with the remedies they received after the complaint was made, and 7% were satisfied with remedies they received.[776]

800. The government has established the BGD e-GOV CIRT, which has been listed as Trusted Introducer of European Computer Incident Response Teams (CIRTs) in September 2018. This BGD e-GOV CIRT is a full member of the Organisation of Islamic Cooperation- Computer Emergency Response Team (OIC-CERT). Instead of cybercrime, the BGD e-GOV CIRT preferred to use the phrase 'security incident' which can be a single or series of security events reported by the computer system or human beings related to the violation of cyber-related law or incident having the significant probability of adverse consequences to an information system or the information that the system processes, stores, or transmits and that may require a response action to mitigate the consequences.[777] Therefore, security-related incidents can be reported to BGD e-GOV CIRT. It can be seen that in 2016, it registered 377 incidents; in 2017, there were 683 incidents, and in 2018, 870 incidents were listed. The number reached 910 and 1,154 in 2019 and 2020 respectively. These incidents are relating to fraud, information gathering, intrusions, information security, availability, intrusion attempts, abusive content, malicious code, vulnerability and service request, virus, Bot, Spam, Trojan, phishing, Distributed Denial of Service (DDoS), worm, security assessment, application compromise, login attempt, loss of confidentiality, and privileged account compromise, etc.[778]

801. Since 2013, a total of 2,669 cases, involving around 3500 accused, were filed in the Cyber Tribunal established in Dhaka under the ICT Act, 2006. Till September 2020, a total of 768 cases were disposed of, and in only 22 cases, i.e., 2.86% cases, sentences were passed and in 97.14% cases, the accused were acquitted of charges or the charges have been dismissed. Of these settled cases, 20, 2 and 1 cases were filed under sections 57, 54 and 66 of the ICT Act, 2006 respectively and the remaining cases are filed under sections 23, 29, and 31 of the Digital Security Act, 2018. Of the 768 cases, final reports were given in 529 cases and out of these cases, in 68.88% of cases, the court dismissed charges against the accused. Of the 2261 cases pending for trial, 94% are under the controversial section 57 of the ICT Act, 2006, and 408 cases are under the Digital Security Act, where almost half of these

775. The Cyber Crime Awareness Foundation, Tendency of Cyber Crime in Bangladesh, Research Report, 20 May 2018.
776. *Ibid.*
777. BGD e-GOV CIRT, https://www.cirt.gov.bd/.
778. BGD e-GOV CIRT, Incident Statistics, https://www.cirt.gov.bd/incident-reporting/statistics/.

cases were filed under sections 25, 28, 29 and 31 of this Law.[779] These have also been reported that after the cyber tribunals are established in the divisional district headquarters, 176, 135, 120, 161, 22 and 58 cases are pending in the tribunals in Rajshahi, Rangpur, Mymensing, Khulna, Sylhet and Chattogram respectively. These cases are filed mostly for defamation, fraud, Facebook posting, spread of political and religious hatred, disinformation, uploading false content on social media, sexual harassment, etc. The reasons for very poor rate disposal include lack of evidence, lack of digital forensic laboratory and compromise between parties, etc.

§3. Cybercrime Legal Regime: Emergence and an Overview

802. Even though the Customs Act, 1969 contains provisions on 'computer system', the BCC Act, 1990 contains a definition of 'information technology' and the Copyright Act, 2000 includes a definition of 'computer', the ICT Act, 2006 is the first special law enacted in Bangladesh containing elaborated provisions regarding the regulation of information and communication technologies. Nevertheless, the ICT Act, 2006, as it was originally enacted, did not contain enough provisions on specific computer crimes or cybercrimes, though some wide and general provisions were included.[780] It may be due to the reason that the law was originally enacted based on a study report conducted by the Law Commission of Bangladesh to give effect to electronic transactions and the use of a computer to commit various crimes could not be anticipated. This law was subsequently amended twice in 2009[781] and 2013[782] to include provisions with increased punishment of cybercrimes. Recently, in 2018, this law was again amended substantially to repeal, *inter alia*, computer crimes related provisions through the provisions of the Digital Security Act, 2018 (Act No. 46 of 2018) (hereinafter 'the DSA, 2018') and the computer crimes or cybercrime-related existing provisions under the ICT Act, 2006 are thus encapsulated in the DSA, 2018. After this amendment in 2018, the ICT Act, 2006 has turned to be more like a law on digital signature or electronic transaction as available in the context of many other countries.

803. The ICT Act, 2006, one of the most important cyber laws of the country, contains provisions on electronic signature (sections 5–12), electronic record (sections 13–15), safe and secured electronic record and signature (sections 16–17), Controller and Certificate Issuing Authority (sections 18–40), responsibilities of the certificate holder (sections 41–44), etc. Chapter VII of the Law (sections 45–53) provides for the punishment and penalty for the certificate holders for the violation

---

779. Asaduzzaman, *Cybercrime: 97 per cent Cases Dismissed* (21 Sept. 2021), https://en.prothomalo.com/bangladesh/crime-and-law/cyber-crime-97-per-cent-cases-dismissed.
780. Part VIII, ss 54–66. The offences included: damage to computer and computer system, etc. (s. 54), tampering with computer source code (s. 55), hacking with computer system (s. 56), publication of fake, obscene or defamatory information in electronic form (s. 57), unauthorized access to protected system (s. 61), disclosure of confidentiality and privacy (s. 63), use of computer for committing an offence (s. 66).
781. The Information and Communication Technology (Amendment) Act, 2009 (Act No. 41 of 2009).
782. The Information and Communication Technology (Amendment) Act, 2013 (Act No. 42 of 2013).

of law and rules. Chapter 8 (sections 54–84) is divided into three parts, where Part One (sections 54–67) deals with offences and penalty, Part Two (sections 68–81) deals with the establishment of Cyber Tribunal, investigation of offences, trial and appeal procedure, and Part Three (sections 82–84) deals with Appellate Tribunal. Though the Law was amended in 2009 to amend section 18, major revisions of the law were made in 2013 when the punishments of various offences under the law were increased, and many of the offences which were originally non-cognizable and bailable were made cognizable and non-bailable and these will be discussed in the next Chapter. Recently, the government has taken another initiative to amend the ICT Act, 2006 and released the Draft Amendment titled the Information and Communication Technology (Amendment) Act, 2019 available on the website of the ICT Division.

804. The wide misuse of the provisions of the ICT Act, 2006, especially section 57 dealing with fake, obscene or defamatory publication in the electronic form, for political and personal reasons became a normal event and had been criticized seriously by all corners, except the government and the law enforcement agencies. After the amendment with the provision of increased punishment, section 57 of the ICT Act, 2006, became more controversial due to its frequent rampant misuse and abuse. It was reported and claimed by various concerns that the members of the law enforcement agencies and some enthusiastic supporters of the government parties were using this section 57 to oppress the opposition voice and take personal revenge. People of various professions were arrested under this section. As a result, the Police Head Quarter even took the initiative and issued instructions to consult the Police Head Quarter before arresting anyone under this section.

805. Recently, the DSA, 2018 was enacted with the aim to ensure National Digital Security and to enact laws regarding Digital Crime Identification, Prevention, Suppression, Trial, etc. The Law defines 'Digital Security' very widely to mean the security of any digital device or digital system. Moreover, 'Digital', according to the Law, means the working procedure based on a binary system (0 or 1) or digit based system, and to fulfil the objective of this Act, electrical, digital, magnetic, optical, biometric, electrochemical, electromechanical, wireless or electromagnetic technology are made part of it. Whereas, 'Digital Device' means any electronic, digital, magnetic, optical or information processing device or system which by using electronic, digital, magnetic, optical or information processing device or system, will perform logical, mathematical and memory programming, and any digital or computer device system or computer network connected with it or all kinds of input, output, processing, accumulating digital software device or communication facilities will be included.[783]

806. Under section 5 of the Law, it is provided to establish a Digital Security Agency to implement the provisions of this law. This is obviously a positive effort

783. Section 2, the Digital Security Act, 2018 (Act No. 46 of 2018).

on the part of the government as this issue is technical and requires technical expertise. Many countries in the world have a separate body like this one to deal with cyber security issues.

807. Moreover, the law provides for the establishment of a thirteen-member National Digital Security Council chaired by the Prime Minister of Bangladesh.[784] Members of the Council include only the member or representatives of the relevant government bodies such as Minister of – Ministry of Posts, Telecommunication and Information Technology; Ministry of Law, Justice and Parliamentary Affairs, Principal Secretary of the Prime Minister's Office; governor of BB, Secretaries of – Posts and Telecommunications Division, ICT Division, Public Security Division, Ministry of Foreign Affairs, Inspector General of Bangladesh Police, Director Generals – Directorate General of Forces Intelligence and National Digital Security Council.

808. The DSA, 2018 is a special law, and it is provided that, except the issue of the right to information under the Right to Information Act, 2009 (Act No. 20 of 2009), in case there is any provision which is in conflict with the provision of this Act with any provision of any other Act, then the provisions of this Act will apply to the extent it is inconsistent with any other Act.[785] For example, the Customs Act, 1969 (Act No. IV of 1969) has also incorporated provisions on the damage and destruction of the 'Customs computer system' through an amendment of the law in 2001. Thus, in case of any conflict on computer systems between the DSA, 2018 and the Customs Act, 1969, the provisions of the DSA, 2018 shall, understandably, prevail.

809. The DSA, 2018 has adopted a similar language like the ICT Act, 2006 regarding the extraterritorial application of the law. It provides that:

(1) If anyone commits an offence within this Act outside Bangladesh which would be a punishable offence if committed inside Bangladesh, then the provisions of this Act would be applicable in such a manner as if those Acts were committed in Bangladesh.
(2) If anyone commits any offence in Bangladesh within this Act from outside Bangladesh using any computer, computer system, or computer, then the provision of this Act will be applicable in such a manner as if the whole process of the offence was committed inside Bangladesh.
(3) If anyone commits any offence outside Bangladesh within this Act from inside Bangladesh, then the provisions of this Act will be applicable in such a manner that the whole process of committing the offence occurred inside Bangladesh.[786]

784. Section 12, the Digital Security Act, 2018 (Act No. 46 of 2018).
785. Section 3, the Digital Security Act, 2018 (Act No. 46 of 2018).
786. Section 4, the Digital Security Act, 2018 (Act No. 46 of 2018).

810. Under the law, the Director-General is empowered to request the BTRC to remove or block any content published or propagated in digital media if such information contains anything that creates threats for Digital Security, i.e., the security of any digital device or digital system.[787] Simultaneously, the law enforcement agencies can also request the BTRC, through the Director-General, to block or remove any data information if it is evident to them that such data information published or propagated in digital media hampers the solidarity, financial activities, security, defence, religious values, public discipline of the nation or any part of it or incites racism and hatred.[788] Once the BTRC receives such information, it takes initiative to block or remove such information by informing the government.

811. It may be relevant to share here that the Systems & Services division of BTRC may block any offensive content simply based on the objection from general public.[789] Sometimes, the HCD can also direct BTRC to block or take down any content. For example, based on the HCD ruling, BTRC has been blocking pornographic and gambling websites.[790] Very recently, the HCD ordered BTRC to take down a sensational investigative report on high-level corruption by Al Jazeera Media Network from online platforms.[791]

812. This provision on removing or blocking content is very wide, and in the absence of further supporting subsidiary legislative documents or guidelines, this part may be misused and abused. Moreover, such blocking or removal may not be a solution technically since such information, if these really contain information targeting national security, can be uploaded to other platforms or websites almost immediately. Moreover, there are concerns too as this law of 2018 was enacted at a very fast speed just before the national election in 2018. Concerned citizens and members of the civil societies apprehended that the government and the supporters of the ruling parties would be using this provision to limit the criticisms of the opposition in a democratic country like Bangladesh. This is because, in many cases, an ordinary statement may be interpreted and treated as news targeting to hamper any of things, i.e., 'solidarity, financial activities, security, defence, religious values, the public discipline of the nation or any of part it'. Some of these concerns are already reflected in the Freedom House's annual flagship report 'Freedom on the Net'.[792]

787. Section 8(1), the Digital Security Act, 2018 (Act No. 46 of 2018).
788. Section 8(2), the Digital Security Act, 2018 (Act No. 46 of 2018).
789. Systems & Services, Bangladesh Telecommunication Regulatory Commission, http://www.btrc.gov.bd/systems-and-services.
790. For more, *see*, Freedom House, *Freedom on the Net, 2020, Bangladesh,* https://freedomhouse.org/country/bangladesh/freedom-net/2020.
791. The Daily Star, Al Jazeera Documentary – Make sure it's taken down: HC to BTRC, https://www.thedailystar.net/frontpage/news/make-sure-its-taken-down-hc-btrc-2046685.
792. Freedom House, *Freedom on the Net, 2020, Bangladesh,* https://freedomhouse.org/country/bangladesh/freedom-net/2020.

813. Critics of this provision often intend to share that the freedom of speech and expression is constitutionally guaranteed under Article 39(2) of the Constitution of Bangladesh, 1972. However, it is pertinent to share here that this constitutional provision does not provide for the absolute right, rather it is clearly mentioned that the right of every citizen to freedom of speech and expression is guaranteed subject to any reasonable restrictions imposed by law in the interests of the security of the State, friendly relations with foreign states, public order, decency or morality, or in relation to contempt of court, defamation or incitement to an offence.

814. Many, from home and abroad, have already termed this DSA, 2018 as a draconian law as the law contains many provisions giving the law enforcement agency apparently unfettered powers in the name of protection of the security of the state. While none will dispute the importance of state security, instances of use and abuse of the provisions of this law have already been reported in media widely, many people had to suffer and have been suffering in prison and police custody, and died also as a consequence of such arrest. Therefore, there are increased demands from the stakeholder, especially the human rights activists to repeal the law.

815. The decision of repealing the DSA, 2018 should not be taken based on popular reactions as one should not doubt the importance of having such a national law aiming at protecting digital security and it is inevitable in this digitally ever increased networked and digitally connected world, instead avenues and options should be explored to amend the law based on international best practices. It will be pertinent to mention here that many countries have been struggling to design a statute that will be able to meet the demand of the time in an area which is ever-changing with so many actors involved and burgeoning devices and systems are introduced every second. There is a high-profile case currently pending before the US Supreme Court involving an accused who exceeded his authorized access to enter the law enforcement database to find information about a dancer for personal use; during the oral hearing, Justice Sonia Sotomayor found the Computer Fraud and Abuse Act, 1986, the oldest law in the world in this field that guided and influenced many similar statutes in different jurisdictions, as a 'very broad' and 'dangerously vague' statute.[793]

816. The DSA, 2018 provides to include necessary issues through the provisions of the rules to be framed under section 60 of this law. The option of removal of the apparent limitations in the primary legislation and their interpretations through the provisions of the subsidiary legislation such as rules to be framed under section 60(1) of the DSA, 2018 can be exploited to remove many of the limitations and concerns as available in the law.

817. It will be relevant to share here that the Digital Security Rules, 2020 that were framed in February 2020 do not contain any provision regarding the interpretation of substantive criminal activities under the DSA, 2018. Instead, the Rules of

793. *Nathan Van Buren v. United States*, United States Court of Appeals for the Eleventh Circuit, case numbers (18-12024).

2020 contain provisions, *inter alia*, on the Digital Security Agency's power (rule 3) and, functions and responsibilities (rule 4); power and responsibilities of the director-general (rule 5) and the national computer emergency response team (rule 6); evaluation (rule 12), audit (rule 18), and identification (rule 19) of CII, establishment of digital forensic lab (rule 13), forensic analysis of digital evidence (rule 15), etc. Nevertheless, there are still scopes under section 60(1) of the DSA, 2018 to frame more rules and using this scope, the policymakers can take initiatives to remove some of the existing challenges and concerns as available in the law. Simultaneously, judicial activism may be an alternative through which the Supreme Court of the country may take the initiative to interpret some of the provisions of the DSA, 2018.

§4. Legal Definition of Computer

818. In the legal discussion of 'cybercrime', the definition of 'computer' is crucial and fundamental. The term 'computer' seems to be statutorily defined first by section 2(9) of the Copyright Act, 2000 which provides that 'computer' means any mechanical, electro-mechanical, electronic, magnetic, electromagnetic, digital or optical or any other impulse or data processing devices or systems which perform logical and arithmetical, any or all functions, by using those devices or systems. The Customs Act, 1969 (Act No. IV of 1969) was amended in 2001 to include provisions on 'Customs computer system', though this law has not defined 'computer' or 'computer system'. It is provided that such computer system means the customs computerized entry processing system established by the NBR for the purpose of the Customs Act, 1969.

819. The ICT Act, 2006 has extended the definition of 'computer' as encapsulated in the Copyright Act, 2000, though the recently enacted Digital Security Act, 2018 has not included any such definition; instead the DSA, 2018 has included the definition of 'computer system', i.e., a process interconnected with one or more computers or digital devices capable of collecting, sending and storing information singly or being connected with each other. Nevertheless, it is provided in section 2(2) of the DSA, 2018 that '[t]he words and expressions used in this Act but not defined shall have the same meaning as are used in the Information and Communication Technology Act, 2006'. Thus, the DSA, 2018 will recognize the definition of 'computer' as included in the ICT Act, 2006, which has broadly defined the term 'computer'.

820. According to the ICT Act, 2006, 'computer' means any electronic, magnetic, optical or other high-speed data processing device or system which performs logical, arithmetical and memory functions by manipulations of electronic, magnetic or optical impulses, and includes all input, output, processing, storage, computer software or communication facilities which are connected or related to the computer in a computer system or computer network.[794] Exactly the same definition of 'computer' was included in section 2 of the Indian Information Technology Act, 2000, which seems to include the definition from the US's Computer Fraud and Abuse Act, 1986. Apparently, ICT, 2006 incorporated this definition from the Indian law. The word 'processing' is crucial in this definition making it technologically neutral to include all types of new devices such as computer servers, desktop computers, laptops, smartphones, tablets, cameras, etc. within the definition.

821. In different jurisdictions, an interesting question was raised, i.e., whether smart mobile phones or tablets should be included within the definition of 'computer' as modern-day smartphones are sophisticated enough to perform almost all the activities that a computer does. A clear stand from the regulators on this matter is also important to settle the debate whether a member of the law enforcement agency can search the mobile phone of anyone and ask to unlock it without a warrant.

822. Even though technologically a mobile phone or tablet can perform the same functions as a computer, two conflicting trends can be observed. For example, the Council of Europe's Cybercrime Convention Committee, having mandate under Article 46 of the Budapest Convention, agreed that new devices, e.g., smartphones, tablets, etc. that procedure, process and transmit data are included within the definition of 'computer system'.[795] Similarly, the courts in the US also have an identical stand that any internet-enabled device, e.g., coffeemakers, microwave ovens, watches, telephones, children's toys, MP3 players, refrigerators, heating and air-conditioning units, radios, alarm clocks, televisions, and DVD players, etc. will come within the statutory definition of a 'computer'.[796] In a case where an issue was raised whether basic 2G phones, used to call and text without having the internet-enabled features, should be treated as a 'computer' or not. Sharing the features of the phone set in dispute, i.e., Motorola JA 1-120 that and considering the terms included in the statutory definition, i.e., 'data processing device' capable to perform 'logical, arithmetic, or storage functions' the US Court of Appeal held affirmatively that such 2G mobile phone also fall within the definition of a 'computer'.[797] However, interestingly, the Federal Court of Australia recently took a different approach and held that mobile phones should not be considered as a 'computer' or a 'data storage device'.[798]

823. In this Australian case, the plaintiff, under the law, was required to provide police with any information or reasonable assistance to help the police access, copy or convert data on a computer or data storage device. The law, though contained the definition of 'data storage devices', did not define 'computer' or things that will be

794. Section 2(13), the Information and Communication Technology Act, 2006 (Act No. 39 of 2009).
795. Cybercrime Convention Committee, Guidance Note # 1 on the notion of 'computer system', T-CY Guidance Notes, Strasbourg, France, 15 Nov. 2016.
796. *US v. Kramer,* United States Court of Appeals, Eighth Circuit. 8 Feb. 2011. 631 F.3d 900 (8th Cir. 2011).
797. *Ibid.*
798. *Luppino v. Fisher* (No. 2) [2019] FCA 1100 (15 Jul. 2019).

included within the definition. One police stopped the plaintiff and found three devices – a laptop, two mobile phones – one with password and another without password. The plaintiff assisted the police and gave the password of the laptop, but refused to provide the password of the mobile phone. In the judgment, the learned Judge, highlighting the legislative history of the law and citing the use of computers in different devices, e.g., motor vehicles, television sets, refrigerators, etc., and sharing the primary purpose of the mobile phone as a communication device held that 'data storage device' may include DVDs, CDs, USB drives and computer servers, but not a mobile phone. In the Bangladesh context, no such case has been reported so far though it can be anticipated that a similar situation is very likely to occur in the near future and therefore, the policymakers can consider clarifying the position to avoid possible future disputes. The example of the US and Singapore can be considered here where the Computer Fraud and Abuse Act, 1986 and the Computer Misuse Act, 1993 respectively clearly mention the things, e.g., automated typewriter or typesetter, portable hand-held calculator, etc., that will not be treated as a computer.

§5. Cyber Security

824. Secured cyberspace is a challenge for every country in the world and a concern for everyone in this networked world. ITU introduced the Global Cybersecurity Index to measure the commitment of countries to cybersecurity at a global level. In the first Global Cybersecurity Index, launched by the ITU in 2014, Bangladesh positioned 53, which should be applauded considering the socio-economic foundation of the nation. Bangladesh ranked 78 in the latest version of this Index. However, the country ranked 74 in the ITU's National Cyber Security Index, 147 in the ICT Development Index and 112 in the WEF's Network Readiness Index.[799] The rankings in these indexes indicate that there are some gaps, limitations, and challenges in Bangladesh's existing cybersecurity legal regime which demand an intensive study.

825. The concept of 'cybersecurity' includes the protection of digital information and also digital assets which are considered non-information, but vulnerable through ICTs, e.g., computer systems and networks, etc. An exact definition of 'cybersecurity' is difficult to craft and even international organizations are unable to succinctly define it, though some features or characteristics can be shared. The ITU's recommended definition considers 'cybersecurity' as the 'collection of tools, policies, security concepts, security safeguards, guidelines, risk management approaches, actions, training, best practices, assurance and technologies that can be used to protect the cyber environment and organization and user's assets' such as 'connected computing devices, personnel, infrastructure, applications, services, telecommunications systems, and the totality of transmitted and/or stored information in the cyber environment'. With the objectives to make assets and properties

799. National Cyber Security Index, https://ncsi.ega.ee/country/bd/.

available while maintaining their integrity and confidentiality, the purpose of cybersecurity is to ensure the 'attainment and maintenance of the security properties … against relevant security risks in the cyber environment'.[800] Thus, the concept of 'cybersecurity' covers all aspects of information, data, technology, server, device, software, hardware, hard disc, cloud, network, the internet, etc., which are digitally connected and can be exploited to ensure data integrity and authenticity. In most of the information landscape, initiatives are taken to ensure the CIA Triangle and these three, along with two additional elements, i.e., authentication with uniquely identified personal information, and the inclusion of logbook through which the presence of anyone in the cyberspace can be identified are the main elements of cybersecurity.

826. An ideal Cybersecurity Framework, promoted by the ITU Global Cybersecurity Agenda (GCA), should have five interrelated and coordinated arms.[801] These are: (a) *legal*, where a country should enact a legislation on cybercrime and cybersecurity containing provisions on spam regulation; (b) *technical and procedural measures*, where a country should establish CERT/CIRT/CSIRT, develop standards implementation framework, appoint a standardized body, adopt technical mechanisms and capabilities to address spam, use cloud for cybersecurity purposes, and employ child online protection mechanisms; (c) *organizational measures/structures* where a country should have a national cybersecurity strategy, along with an established responsible agency, and cybersecurity metrics; (d) *capacity-building measures*, where a country needs to take public awareness campaign, framework for the certification and accreditation of cybersecurity professionals, professional training course, educational program or academic curricular, R&D programs and incentive mechanisms in cybersecurity; and (e) *cooperation measures* where the country should enter into bilateral and multilateral agreements, participate in international fora or associations, foster public-private partnerships, Interagency or intra-agency partnership, and adopt best practices.

827. A cybersecurity framework, therefore, must have clear objectives, action plans, reference of measures (legal, procedural, technological, and institutional), and responsibilities of the institutions designed to safeguard systems, networks, services, and data, etc. While cybercrime legislation deals with rule of law, human rights, crime prevention, and criminal justice, etc., the purpose of cybersecurity legislation is more about national interest and security, trust, resilience, and reliability of ICT. The way different forces have been working in promoting security within the national territory of a state, cybersecurity mechanisms need to be employed similarly to make different stages of cyberspace, such as network, server, application, database, etc., secured.

---

800. International Telecommunication Union, 'X.1205: Overview of cybersecurity' (2008), https://www.itu.int/rec/T-REC-X.1205-200804-I.

801. International Telecommunication Union, Global Cybersecurity Agenda, https://www.itu.int/en/action/cybersecurity/Pages/gca.aspx.

828. One may reveal two aspects of cybersecurity incidents- internal/national and external/international, i.e., some such incidents may arise within the national jurisdiction of a country or an organization and thus, these are relatively easy to detect and investigate by countries or organizations with technical expertise. On the other hand, similar activities may occur from beyond the national border of a country or by an outsider. In such cases, this is extremely difficult to detect and investigate these incidents due to the public international law principles of sovereignty of the state and state jurisdiction, etc.

829. Rooted on the definitions of the terms- 'crime' and 'security-related incidents', there are apparent differences between cybercrimes and cybersecurity incidents. While some crimes, in cyberspace, may be committed by individuals targeting other individuals and may not have direct security threats always, e.g., spam emails; cybersecurity-related incidents are committed in an organized manner and examples of cybersecurity incidents include DDoS attacks, advanced persistent threats, phishing or spear-phishing attack, etc. Thus, it can be said that all cybersecurity-related incidents are cybercrime, but not all cybercrimes have security aspects.

830. Though some initiatives were taken by the government earlier; after the BB cyberheist committed in February 2016, it seems that the government started taking some stern actions to make the national cyberspace more secure. It may be relevant to share here that earlier, the government adopted 'the National Cyber Security Strategy of Bangladesh' on 3 March 2014, containing provisions on the long-term measures for protecting the cyber world against security threats, risks and challenges to the national security of Bangladesh. This Strategy was adopted to create a coherent vision for 2021, keeping Bangladesh secure and prosperous by coordinating government, private sector, citizens and international cyberspace defence efforts. Yet, the country had to face the BB cyberheist.

831. In the context of Bangladesh, it seems that as the government has been using 'digital Bangladesh' as the political slogan and has taken various initiatives to promote the 'digital Bangladesh' brand, the government prefers to use the word 'digital' instead of 'cyber' in all the recently adopted legal and policy documents bypassing the global trend. As a result, a number of initiatives in the name of 'digital security' have already been taken through the effectiveness of these initiatives is seriously doubtful.

832. The government has already assessed the Cybersecurity Maturity capacity of the country based on the Cybersecurity Capacity Maturity Model for Nations developed by the Global Cyber Security Capacity Centre of the University of Oxford (GCSCC) with the help of Norway Registers Development Cyber Security and the GCSCC with the aim to develop the cybersecurity strategy, assess critical infrastructure, provide self-assessment toolkit, and basic cybersecurity package for agencies, etc., to strategically prioritize investment in this area.[802] In the Cybersecurity Capacity Maturity Model for Nations of GCSCC, five dimensions of cybersecurity capacity, i.e., (a) Cybersecurity Policy and Strategy; (b) Cyber Culture and Society; (c) Cybersecurity Education, Training and Skills; (d) Legal and Regulatory Frameworks; and (e) Standards, Organisations, and Technologies are considered and these were also evaluated in the context of Bangladesh. The findings of the study revealed very shocking and unexpected results in all five dimensions and indicated that there needs to introduce significant improvements in all these five sectors. Nevertheless, considering the fact that even the most advanced countries in the world have been suffering in making their cyberspace secured, the government should take initiatives to cybersecurity framework. In this regard, the government may consider the very influential reference guide to developing a national cybersecurity strategy produced through a multi-stakeholder approach facilitated by the ITU in 2018.[803]

833. An important initiative in this regard is the enactment of the Digital Security Act, 2018 which was enacted to make provisions for ensuring digital security and identification, prevention, suppression and trial of offences committed through digital devices, etc. It has already been discussed that in this ever dynamic and internetwork connected internet ecosystem when none will argue about the importance of such a law, the application and abuse of the law has already raised a lot of concerns.

834. The Digital Security Rules, 2020 framed under section 60 of the DSA, 2018 has included a very broad definition of 'digital security-related incidents' to mean the adverse situation involving actual or potential digital security-related incident through which the unauthorized access to any computer, computer system, computer resources, networks or any other device is occurred violating the digital security systems and the provision of the related policies, or as a result of such unauthorized access, the service to be provided is to close or disrupted, or due to such unauthorized access data in any computer, computer system, computer resources, networks or other any device is changed or processed. Thus, broadly speaking, cyber security incidents, within the ambit of this Rules, 2020, generally occur in any of the three ways, i.e., (i) unauthorized access to, (ii) closure or interruption of service of, and (iii) changing or processing of data in any computer, computer system, computer resources, networks or other any device. This broad definition of 'digital security-related incidents' will require further interpretation as the inclusion of such a broad and general definition may frustrate the whole purpose of enacting a special law on cyber or digital security.

835. The DSA, 2018 provides for the establishment of an Emergency Response Team, i.e., National Computer Emergency Response Team (CERT). This law also

802. Cybersecurity Capacity Review Bangladesh, August 2018, https://dsa.gov.bd/documents/magazine-document_69236_2021-02-28.pdf.

803. International Telecommunication Union, National Strategies, Guide To Developing A National Cybersecurity Strategy, https://www.itu.int/en/ITU-D/Cybersecurity/Pages/cybersecurity-national-strategies.aspx.

provides that the CIIs can also form individual CERT with the prior approval of the Digital Security Agency. The detailed responsibilities of the Emergency Response Team are already included in the Digital Security Rules, 2020 framed under this Law. As a result, the CERT will be responsible for performing, *inter alia*, the following duties:

(a) ensure the security of CII;
(b) take immediate required remedial measures in case of any cyber or digital attack or if the cyber or digital security is hampered;
(c) take necessary initiatives to prevent possible and prospective cyber or digital attacks;
(d) take overall cooperation initiatives including the exchange of information with any similar type of international team or organization, in order to fulfil the objectives of this Act, with the prior permission of the government; and
(e) any other activities determined by the rules.[804]

836. Even though the law provides that the government may declare any computer system, network or information infrastructure as CII,[805] the government of Bangladesh, as discussed in the next segment of this chapter, has not yet declared any infrastructure as CII. The Digital Security Rules, 2020 as framed under section 60 of the DSA, 2018, also do not contain provisions on any specific CII; instead, the Digital Security Rules, 2020 contain provisions on evaluation (rule 12), audit (rule 18), and identification (rule 19) of CII.

837. Earlier, the ICT Division of the Bangladesh government established the BGD e-GOV CIRT under BCC in 2016 to support the government efforts to develop and amplify ICT programs by establishing and maintaining cybersecurity incident management capabilities within the environment of the government of Bangladesh.

838. The BGD e-GOV CIRT, which is now serving as the National CERT or N-CERT as per rule 5 of the Digital Security Rules, 2020, was established to: (a) manage cybersecurity incidents in Bangladesh government network and related infrastructure; (b) serve as a catalyst in organizing national cybersecurity resilience initiatives (education, workforce competence, regulation, cyber exercises) among various stakeholders; and (c) make efforts to establish national cybersecurity incident management capabilities in Bangladesh. As such this body will (a) monitor the network for the events that affect the security of the government network; (b) carry out investigations and containment measures for cybersecurity events in order to minimize data loss or service disruption in the government network and e-services; (c) help to solve security-related issues in NDC including provisions of obligatory instructions for BCC personnel to secure NDC information resources; (d) carry out preventive measures in order to minimize disruptions of secure operations of the government network and e-services; (e) participate in international and national cybersecurity initiatives; (f) promote and strengthen cybersecurity environment by

804. Section 9(5), the Digital Security Act, 2018 (Act No. 46 of 2018).
805. Section 15, the Digital Security Act, 2018 (Act No. 46 of 2018).

developing, collaborating and maintaining relationships with other CIRTs and organizations in the country and abroad; and (g) support capacity building of the existing manpower of BCC to establish national CIRT.[806]

839. The BGD e-GOV CIRT, with the aim to secure and protect Bangladesh government unclassified information and systems, has developed an Information Security Manual entitled GoBISM, based on International Standards ISO/IEC 27001:2013, ISO/IEC 27002:2013, and New Zealand Information Security Manual. The GoBISM will allow the BCC to assist the Bangladesh government in providing with, *inter alia*, the needs with a solid, flexible and implementable information security manual covering every important aspect of information security to be implemented by government agencies to protect their systems and information. Moreover, it is intended that some of these information security principles and measures could be translated into government legal acts, policies and Bangladeshi standards on information security. For the time being, compliance with the GoBISM is not a legal requirement for the government departments to follow. Nevertheless, this can be made binding subsequently.

840. The GoBISM contains provisions on: information security governance, system certification and accreditation, information security documentation, information security monitoring, information security incidents, physical security, personnel security, infrastructure (cable management), communication systems and devices (fax machines, multifunction devices and network printers), product security, decommissioning and disposal (media usage, media sanitization, media destruction), software security, email security, access control, cryptography, network security (Network Management, Wireless LANs, Video and Telephony Conferencing and IP Telephony, Intrusion Detection and Prevention, Gateways, Firewalls, etc.), working off-site and enterprise system security.

841. The GoBISM suggests two sets of controls: mandatory and recommended. Mandatory controls are essential to managing identified risks effectively and recommended controls may not be used if agreed and acknowledged by the Accreditation authority with formal auditable record and decision. Various government bodies such as Bangladesh Police, Comptroller and Auditor General, BCC, Ministry of Home Affairs, Ministry of Commerce, National Archives and Ministry of Law are entrusted to provide various services.

§6. Critical Information Structure

842. The protection of CIIs is vital to ensure public safety, financial security, public health, national security, national integrity and sovereignty of any country

806. Office Order, ICT Division, Ministry of Posts, Telecommunication and Information Technology, Government of Bangladesh, Date: 28 Jun. 2016.

and this has been recognized for long.[807] The DSA, 2018, has also rightly recognized this and has included provisions on the protection of CIIs in section 15 of the DSA, 2018. It may be relevant to share here that the protection of important communication structures and essential public service providers from outside physical attacks has been recognized for long, and there is a considerable number of provisions even in the Bangladeshi domestic laws also.[808] Nevertheless, after the expansion of the digitalization process in all sectors, external cyberattacks on CIIs has emerged as a real issue of concern for policymakers.

843. The developed countries have already established very sophisticated CIIs ensuring their protection from cyberattacks. In 1996, the President's Commission on Critical Infrastructure Protection was formed in the US to evaluate the physical and cyber threats to CIIs and to formulate strategies for their protection. Similar initiatives are also taken by different other developed countries, whereas a developing country like Bangladesh has just started the process.

844. Experiences of other countries show that the examples of critical infrastructures include transport/traffic (aviation, navy, railway, road traffic), government (administration, parliament, judiciary), IT & T (telecommunication and IT), media and culture (electronic and print media and national monuments), utilities such as water (water supply and sewerage), energy (electricity, gas, oil), health (medical care, drugs, laboratories), finance and insurance (banks, stock exchange, insurance and other financial services), etc. These are treated as critical as the control, process, circulation or preservation of any information after damaging or compromising may adversely affect: (i) public safety or financial security or public health, and (ii) national security or national integrity or sovereignty. The example of BB cyberheist can be shared here when in February 2016, by exploiting a SWIFT global payment network, the hackers stole USD 81 million of the national reserve. An attack on the national central bank is undoubtedly an attack on the sovereignty of the country.

845. In the effective and efficient management of CII, an operation set up involving a team comprising of government agencies, intelligence service and CERT team that promises to ensure strategic leadership and supervision, with analytical capacity and technical competencies is desirable. The main responsibilities of this team are of four-folds: (a) prevention and early warning, (b) detection, (c) reaction and (d) crisis management. Even though one of the purposes of the protection of CIIs is

807. *See*, in general, National Research Council. 'Critical Information Infrastructure Protection and the Law: An Overview of Key Issues'. (2003).

808. For example, the Telegraph Act, 1885 contains important provisions prohibiting the intrusion into signal room, trespass in telegraph office or obstruction (s. 23), intentionally damaging or tampering with telegraphs (s. 25), injury to or interference with a telegraph line or post (s. 25A). Similarly, the Bangladesh Telecommunication Regulation Act, 2001 also contains provisions prohibiting the cause of interference in radio communication and telecommunication (s. 67), trespass, unlawful stay, causing damage to apparatus, obstruction to operation activity, (s. 72), etc.

to ensure public essential services, it is important to attempt public-private partnerships.[809] In 2008, OECD released a set of Recommendations on the Protection of CII and replaced this with the new one released in 2019 titled 'Recommendation on Digital Security of Critical Activities'.

846. The definition of critical infrastructure is crucial before making any logical plan for its protection. First defined in the US Presidential Decision Directive, 1998, the researchers identified more than twenty versions of definitions of CIIs as available in the national policy documents. These definitions are 'restrictive, static, and local, as they are mainly dictated by the vision of the defender', and therefore, considering the greatest number of possible elements, they proposed a very broad definition from the attacker's point of view. According to them, 'Critical infrastructure can be a company, an institution, an organisation, facilities …, services, and equipment …, whether regional, national, or international, which, if disrupted, damaged, or destroyed, would have a serious impact on the health, safety, security, or economic well-being of citizens or the effective functioning of governments and others infrastructures depending on it. It includes humans, which, if co-opted, diverted, or eliminated, could lead to the disruption, damage or destruction of the critical infrastructure … . In fact, it includes any element which could lead to the disruption, damage, or destruction of the critical infrastructure. These elements can also be found in the political and cultural environment of the infrastructure.'[810]

847. The DSA, 2018 has defined CII as any physical or virtual information infrastructure declared by the government which is capable of controlling, processing, circulating or preserving any information, data or electronic information and which if it is damaged or compromised may adversely affect: (i) public safety or financial security or public health, and (ii) national security or national integrity or sovereignty.[811] The Law empowers the government to declare any computer system, network or information structure as 'Critical Information Infrastructure'.[812]

848. Though the recently formulated Digital Security Rules, 2020 contain important provisions on the identification (rule 19), evaluation (rule 12), and audit (rule 18) of CII, the government has not declared any such CII yet. Nevertheless, it may be pertinent to mention here that in the National Cybersecurity Strategy, 2014, which was adopted following the Pillars of the ITU's GCA, some sectors such as communications, emergency services, energy, finance, food, government, health, transport and water were indicated as critical.

---

809. For more, *see* Suter, M., *A Generic National Framework for Critical Information Infrastructure Protection*, Center for Security Studies, ETH Zurich (2007): 1 [ITU Commissioned Research Paper].

810. C. Gallais & E. Filiol, *Critical Infrastructure: Where Do We Stand Today? A Comprehensive and Comparative Study of the Definitions of a Critical Infrastructure*, 16(1) J. Info. Warfare, 64–87 (2017).

811. Sections 2, 15 & 16, the Digital Security Act, 2018 (Act No. 46 of 2018).

812. Section 15, the Digital Security Act, 2018 (Act No. 46 of 2018).

Chapter 2. Application of Substantive Criminal Law in the Area of ICT

§1. INTRODUCTION

849. Cybercrime legislations generally include provisions on substantive cybercrimes addressing various aspects such as acts against the confidentiality, integrity and availability of computer data and systems (e.g., illegal access or interference to computer system and/or data; DDoS, interception, modification or acquisition of computer data; production, distribution or possession of computer misuse tools, breach of privacy and personal data), computer-related activities for personal or financial gain (fraud, forgery, identity theft, infringements of IPRs, provisions on SPAM emails or texts), and computer-related specific acts (act causing personal harm, e.g., defamation, spread of racism, hate speech, communal violence, discrimination, hostility, etc.; distribution of illicit content, e.g., child pornography; child grooming, terrorism, etc.).[813]

850. In Bangladesh, there is no specific law with the title, e.g., the Computer Crimes Act, 1997 (Malaysia). Instead, the policymakers of Bangladesh decided to enact a law on overall ICT matters where the provisions on substantive and procedural aspects of cybercrimes are included. In the absence of any specific law on cybercrime or computer crime at the domestic level, this chapter will share various substantive cybercrimes in the Bangladesh context as incorporated in various laws. It will be pertinent to share here that earlier Chapter 8, sections 54–67 of the ICT Act, 2006 contained a provision on some substantive cybercrimes.[814] However, these sections 54–57 were subsequently repealed through section 61 of the DSA, 2018, and while doing so, the contents of these sections were extended, updated and incorporated in various provisions of the DSA, 2018. Besides, some sectorial laws were also enacted to deal with specific issues like pornography. It may be relevant to share here that the Customs Act, 1969 (Act No. IV of 1969) was amended in 2001 to include provisions on 'Customs computer system'. With the amendment, the law has incorporated some provisions on substantive computer crimes targeted at the Customs computer system such as unlawful access to Customs computer system, unlawful collection of information from such computer system and disclosure, collection of information with lawful authority but disclosure of information in an unauthorized manner, falsifying any record or information in such computer system, and damaging or impairing the computer system, etc.

---

813. United Nations Office on Drugs and Crime, Approaches in national cybercrime legislation and the UNODC Cybercrime Repository, https://unctad.org/meetings/en/SessionalDocuments/Cybercrime%20Nayelly%20Loya%20(UNODC).pdf.

814. These sections were dealing with penalty for damage to computer, computer system, etc. (s. 54), punishment for tampering with computer source code (s. 55), punishment for hacking computer system (s. 56), and punishment for publishing fake, obscene or defaming information in electronic form (s. 57).

851. It is pertinent to mention here that cybercrimes are a sub-set of law of crimes and therefore, the relevant general principles of criminal law, e.g., legality, *actus rea* and *mens reas*, causation, harm, defences, rules against retroactivity, i.e., the prohibition of imposition of *ex post facto* laws, right of the accused to fair and impartial trial etc. need to be considered automatically and then all these principles need to be established in the context of substantive cybercrimes as encapsulated in the general law of crime, i.e., the Penal Code, 1860 (XLV of 1860) and special law, i.e., the Digital Security Act, 2018 (Act No. 46 of 2018), the Pornography Control Act, 2012 (Act No. 9 of 2012), etc.

852. The defence of rule against retroactivity, i.e., the prohibition of imposition of *ex post facto* laws should not be misunderstood in case of cybercrimes. Due to the nature of some cybercrimes, where sophisticated technologies and innovative techniques are used, some forms of cybercrimes may not be able to be included in the statute explicitly. Nevertheless, from the experience and practices of most countries around the world, it can be revealed that some broad and general provisions are already included there and these can be applied in case of such crimes as well. Moreover, the provisions of the general law of crime of the country, i.e., the Penal Code, 1860 (XLV of 1860) can always be applied by the criminal justice administration. This is because the way the Human Rights Council of the UN in 2012 unanimously resolved that '… the same rights that people have offline must also be protected online …',[815] it can validly be argued that anything that is regarded as a crime offline shall also be regarded as a crime online.

853. The principles of natural justices, i.e., rules against bias, rules relating to, e.g., investigation, arrest, evidence, trial, judgments and punishment shall simultaneously come into the scene automatically as well and will be applied even if these are not mentioned in the cybercrime-related special statute since these are all well recognized in the legal system of Bangladesh. Moreover, these principles demand that an accused shall enjoy some general rights, e.g., right to know the allegation brought against, right to know adverse evidence, right to remain silent, right to examine witnesses, right to have reasoned decisions always, etc.

854. It may also be relevant to share here that in most cases, cybercrimes are organized crimes and some people may simply abet the commission of such crime. In such cases, the abettor will also be charged as abetment is an offence under Chapter V (sections 107–120B) of the Penal Code. Someone may even be 'charged for abetting an offence punishable under a special law even though the word "abetment" may not be mentioned as an offence under the Special Act'.[816]

855. It is, however, a matter of great concern that so far not a single case involving important aspects of interpretation of the provisions of these general or special cybercrime laws has been reported in law reports. In the absence of the availability of such statutory interpretation and supporting subsidiary legislation enacted under

---

815. https://ap.ohchr.org/documents/E/HRC/d_res_dec/A_HRC_20_L13.doc.

816. *Hussain Mohammad Ershad v. The State*, 14 BLD (AD) 178.

the DSA, 2018, the following segment attempts to evaluate some substantive cybercrimes doctrinally in light of the practices of some other countries.

§2. SUBSTANTIVE CYBERCRIMES

I. Illegal or Unauthorized Access and Hacking

856. Illegal or unauthorized access and hacking are the most common forms of cybercrimes recognized in this world and were familiar even before the introduction of the internet for private use in the mid-1990s. For example, the Computer Fraud and Abuse Act, 1986 and the Electronic Communication Privacy Act, 1986 of the US, the Computer Misuse Act, 1990 of the UK and the Computer Misuse Act, 1993 of Singapore contained provisions prohibiting the unauthorized use and access to computers. The US even enacted a law titled the Comprehensive Crime Control Act in 1984 containing three computer-related crimes.

857. Though the words 'illegal' and 'unauthorized' seem synonymous,[817] in the statutes of many countries, such as the UK, Singapore, Malaysia, etc., the word 'unauthorized' is preferred and used. However, Bangladeshi lawmakers included the 'illegal' instead of 'unauthorized' use of computers in the statute, i.e., the DSA, 2018. While the 'illegal' use of the computer may be understandable to some extent and the word 'illegal' is included in the statutes of different countries and regional instruments also, in the absence of a comprehensive list of instances derived from the law to treat any act as 'legal' or 'illegal', how the prosecution and courts deal with this issue and set the boundary of such use will be interesting if this becomes an issue of dispute ever.

858. Instances which make anything 'illegal' is shared in the principal substantive criminal law of the country, i.e., the Penal Code, 1860 where in section 43 it is provided that '[t]he word "illegal" is applicable to everything which is an offence or which is prohibited by law, or which furnishes ground for a civil action … '. Thus, considering the unlimited use of computers and the definition of computer which apparently includes almost all internet-enabled devices, the policymakers need to come up with a catalogue of acts which are offences and prohibited by law. Since this is virtually impossible in this age of ubiquitous computing, looking at the practices of some countries dealing with such offences regularly in a better manner, e.g., the UK, US, Singapore and Malaysia, it seems that the word 'unauthorized' would be a better choice. It will be pertinent to share here that the Digital Security Rules, 2020 formulated under the DSA, 2018 has rightly used the word 'unauthorized' while defining 'digital security-related incidents' in rule 2(1)(b).

859. The Digital Security Act, 2018 (Act No. 46 of 2018) has included the definition of both these terms, i.e., 'Illegal access' and 'hacking' and recognized these

817. In the case of *MA Samad v. Sub-Divisional Officer*, 1977, 29 DLR 198, it was held that anything which is done without any lawful authority is wholly illegal.

as criminal offences. The Law has defined 'Illegal access' as the access into any computer or digital device or digital network system without the permission of any person or authority or entrance in violation of the conditions of permission of entrance by the said person or authority, or by the above-mentioned entrance create hindrance in the exchange of any data information suspend or prevent or stop the process of exchange of data information, or change the data information or add or deduct the data information or collect the data information with the use of a digital device.[818] The understanding of this definition is important as the DSA, 2018 has contained provisions on punishment for the illegal entrance to CII (section 17), computer, digital device, computer system, etc. (section 18) and computer, computer or internet network to commit cyber terrorism (section 27). The law has not included any definition, elements and nature, i.e., oral or written, etc. of such permission in the DSA, 2018 or the Digital Security Rules, 2020. This definition of 'permission' and 'conditions of permission' will be challenging to establish in a country like Bangladesh where the use of written letters containing permission or conditions is not a general practice in computer hardware or software troubleshooting.

860. It has already been discussed that the number of cybercrime cases decided by Bangladeshi courts is very low and apparently not a single case has been decided by either division of the Supreme Court. Nevertheless, an analysis of decisions on unauthorized access to computers by the courts of different common law countries will reveal that some actions such as copying computer files and folders without permission, transfer of computer data through emails, use of the position and privileges of a civil servant to hack women's social media accounts to blackmail for personal gain, researching on and use of secured computer system by an employee for personal interest and purpose, revenge cyberattack by a former employer or business associate, spying on women's webcams to film them secretly, use of colleague's login ID to the damage computer system of a former employer, and access to office pay-role data to find out colleagues' salaries, etc. have already been recognized as 'unauthorised'. In these cases, different forms of punishments ranging from fines, imprisonment, suspension, unpaid community works, etc., were imposed on the accused. Though the DSA, 2018 has not included punishments specifying some of these instances of unauthorized or illegal access, the Customs Act, 1969 (Act No. IV of 1969), which was amended in 2001 to include provisions on 'Customs computer system', has interestingly specifically included some of these.

861. Hacking, on the other hand, is also an offence under the Digital Security Act, 2018.[819] 'Hacking', under the DSA, 2018, is an act: (a) to destroy, change, format, delete any information of the computer data storage or to reduce the value or suitability of it or to damage it in any other way; or (b) to damage any computer, server, computer network, or any other electric system after illegal entrance without ownership or possession.[820] It may be relevant to share that in the US, the author of

818. Section 2(q), the Digital Security Act, 2018 (Act No. 46 of 2018).
819. Section 34, the Digital Security Act, 2018 (Act No. 46 of 2018).
820. Explanation to s. 34(2), the Digital Security Act, 2018 (Act No. 46 of 2018).

the first computer virus Robert T Morris, a graduate student at Cornell University and son of the then chief of National Computer Security Center of National Security Agency, Morris, Jr, was successful, though unintentionally, to distribute worms now often dubbed as 'Morris worm' through the internet and was sentenced for three years' probation and four hundred hours of community services under the Computer Fraud and Abuse Act, 1986.

862. From the statutory definitions of 'illegal access to a computer' and 'hacking' as included in the DSA, 2018, it can be seen that some features, e.g., damage, destruction, changing of data etc. are common in both offences. However, the offence of 'hacking' will occur after illegal access to a computer. Therefore, it can be said that hacking is a kind of illegal access, but all illegal access to a computer may not end in hacking. In other words, illegal access to computers can be committed independently, though hacking cannot be committed without illegal access to a computer.

863. In order to access illegally or hack the computer system, various techniques and programs such as viruses, worms, trojan horses, malware, phishing emails, etc. are used. Technically, all these terms have different meanings, but these are broadly and collectively known as 'malicious software' or 'malware'. These techniques and programs are targeted to a computer to make the host computer to be used as a 'botnet', instal 'spyware' to collect various information in the computer, computer network and system to get illegal advances, e.g., financial, technical (DDoS) and for collecting 'ransomware'. Though Robert Morris received the first statutory punishment for spreading the worms, the theoretical idea of a computer virus was shared in 1949 when John von Neumann in the seminal paper titled 'Theory and Organisation of Complicated Automata' presented the idea that a computer program can be reproduced. Bell Laboratory was successful to introduce a game called 'Core Wars' using Neumann's idea immediately.[821] The history that started with the fatal mistake of Robert Morris has emerged as a constant unbearable headache for most computer users and blessings for the cybercriminals who exploit these for gains of different nature in an organized manner.

864. Instead of defining all these terms individually, the Digital Security Act, 2018 has rightly included a broad definition of the term 'Malware', though both 'virus' and 'malware' are mentioned in section 19(b) of the law. According to the DSA, 2018, 'Malware' is such kind of computer or digital instruction, data information, Program or application which is used to: (i) change, distort, damage any work done by a digital device or computer or to create an adverse effect on the work done; (ii) connect oneself to any computer or digital device and any program of that mentioned computer or digital device, to operate data information or during any

821. For an authoritative history of 'computer virus', *see*, Scientific American, *When did the term 'computer virus' arise?*, https://www.scientificamerican.com/article/when-did-the-term-compute/.

other operation, it becomes autonomously active and by means of which the mentioned computer or digital device causes harmful incidents or changes; or (iii) create the opportunity of automatic entrance to a digital device or to steal information of the said device.[822]

865. The government, under section 15 of the DSA, 2018 can declare any computer, computer system or computer network as a CII, though this has not been declared yet. The DSA, 2018 has made a distinction between illegal access to an ordinary or secured computer, digital device, a computer system with illegal access to any CII. Illegal or unauthorized access to any CII, intentionally or knowingly, is an offence under the law. For the commission of such offence, any person, including an organization, shall be liable for imprisonment up to seven years and/or a fine up to BDT 25,00,000. However, the law provides for a higher amount of punishment if, by means of illegal entrance, any harm or destruction is caused or attempts to cause harm and destruction is made, or the infrastructure is made inactive. In such instances, the law provides for punishment of imprisonment up to fourteen years and/or a fine up to BDT 10 million. Besides, for the commission of a second-time offence or repeated offence, the person shall be responsible for the punishment of life imprisonment and/or fine up to BDT 5,00,000.[823]

866. Under section 18 of the Law, intentional illegal access to a computer, digital device, the computer system is a punishable offence for the commission of which any person can be liable for punishment of imprisonment up to six months and/or a fine of up to BDT 2,00,000.[824] However, access or assistance to access the computer, digital device, a computer system with the intention to commit a crime may make someone liable for punishment of imprisonment up to three years and/or a fine up to BDT 10,00,000.[825] Moreover, under section 18(3) of the Law, if such activities are done in relation to a secured computer, digital device, computer system, then the person shall be liable for a similar amount of punishment, i.e., imprisonment up to three years and/or a fine up to BDT 10,00,000. The law also provides that for a second-time offence or repeated offence, a person shall be liable for double the amount of punishment as mentioned for the original offence.

867. It may be relevant to share here that the word 'hacking' has a positive aspect and should not be treated negatively always. The 'intention' in committing 'illegal access' or 'hacking' is crucial and will be decisive in declaring anyone convicted. For example, the idea of 'ethical hacking' is a very general practice in the tech world and the tech geek ethical hackers, also known as white hat hackers, help people and organizations identify security flaws in a computer, computer system or computer network.[826] It is the 'intention' that primarily differentiates between 'black

---

822. Section 2(1)(t), the Digital Security Act, 2018 (Act No. 46 of 2018).
823. Section 17, the Digital Security Act, 2018 (Act No. 46 of 2018).
824. Section 18(1)(a) and 18(2)(a), the Digital Security Act, 2018 (Act No. 46 of 2018).
825. Section 18(1)(b) and 18(2)(b), the Digital Security Act, 2018 (Act No. 46 of 2018).
826. Based on the consequences of hacking activities, 'hackers' are classified as: (a) black hat hackers, who commits or attempts to commit hacking activities with *mala fide* intention for gains, (b) white hat hackers, (c) grey hat hackers, who are in between the black and white hat hackers.

hat' and 'white hat' hacking. Besides, since the burden of proving hacking offences will rest on the prosecution, this is not yet clear how, in a country where pirated software is freely available and widely used, which may contain a built-in virus that can be executed even without the knowledge of the user, the police or courts will establish the responsibilities of the coder, i.e., virus writer and programmer. If the users practice using genuine software, then the virus writer and programmer, etc., or the local supplier of the software could be identified and arrested for providing defective products. While this is understandable that intention is a question of fact, in the context of technological capabilities of the security professionals and the organized, and multi-jurisdictional coordinated activities of the cybercriminals, these will be clearly challenging.

868. Section 53 of the Law which deals with the scope of cognizance and bail of offences under the law, though has included provisions regarding section 18(1)(a) and 18(1)(b), it has not included what will happen if any offence is committed under section 18(3), i.e., intentional illegal access to a secured computer, digital device, computer system, which is apparently an offence of a more serious nature.

869. Thus, it is evident that the government considers the incident or attempt to harm, destruction or make the computer system ineffective or inactive very seriously and provides for the highest amount of fines. While this is very welcoming and appreciable, the implementation of this provision in instances such as BB cyberheist will be difficult, if not impossible, when the offence will be committed from outside the country.

§3. Damage to Computer and Computer System

870. Under section 19 of the DSA, 2018 apparently deals with punishment for hacking offences. It is provided that it is an offence to:

(a) collect any data or data storage, information or part of it from any computer, computer system, or computer network or collection of transferable information or part of it or copy of it stored in the said computer, computer system or computer network, or
(b) intentional insertion or attempt to insert any virus or malware or any harmful software in any computer or computer system or computer network, or
(c) intentional harm or attempt to harm the data or data storage of any computer, computer system, or computer network or harms or tries to harm the Programs protected in a computer, computer system, or computer network, or
(d) prevent or attempt to prevent a legal or authorized person from entering any computer, computer system, or computer network in any way, or
(e) intentional creation or attempt to create spam or undesired emails without the permission of the sender or receiver, for the marketing of any product or service, or

(f) illegal Interference to any computer, computer system or Computer network and using these, the commission of an act or attempt to falsely enjoy the service of an individual or transfer of the charge into the account of another.

871. For the commission of such offence, any person, including an organization, shall be liable for imprisonment up to seven years and/or a fine of up to BDT 10,00,000. The scope of this section is very wide as it has included various offences such as cookies, spam, credit card theft, etc. for which various countries have already adopted separate laws or guidelines. Hence, the government needs to frame subsidiary legislation for the successful implementation of this section.

872. It is also an offence to intentionally or knowingly hide, damage or modify the source code used in any computer programme, computer system, or computer network or make an attempt of such activities through another person. However, that source code is to be capable of preservation or maintainable.[827] It may be relevant to share here that the Customs Act, 1969 (Act No. IV of 1969), which was amended in 2001, has also included provisions on the damage and destruction of the 'Customs computer system'.

873. Section 19(1)(a) demands special attention to discuss as it is provided that the collection of any data or data storage, information or part of it from any computer, computer system, or computer network or collection of transferable information or part of it or copy of it stored in the said computer, computer system or computer network is an offence. From a plain reading of this provision where the terms such as 'illegal', 'unauthorised' and 'intention', etc. are absent, it can be said that the compliance to this provision will make the use of computers practically impossible for everyone in an atmosphere when people have been collecting various types of data and information from various computer system available in the internet ecosystem and using external removable devices within an organization or in our daily life. This is even horrendous to share that section 53 of the DSA, 2018 has made this a cognizable and non-bailable offence.

§4. SPAM

874. There is no universally accepted definition of the word 'spam'. It is usually defined as sharing the exhibited four characteristics, i.e., unwanted commercial electronic messages and calls sent in bulk. In 1978, a marketing representative sent the first reported spam email to about 400 people of the US Advanced Research Projects Agency Network (popularly known through its abbreviation as 'ARPANET') containing the marketing information of a new computer.[828] Earlier, people used to receive unsolicited advertisements in the form of, e.g., leaflet inside the newspaper delivered to houses in the morning or in the residential post boxes. Spamming had

827. Section 20, the Digital Security Act, 2018 (Act No. 46 of 2018).

828. Joshua Goodman, David Heckerman & Robert Rounthwaite, *Stopping Spam: What Can Be Done to Stanch the Flood of Junk E-mail Messages?*, 292 Sci. Am., 24–31 (2005).

turned to be an industry since when the internet was made available for the public. While in 2005, more than two-thirds of all emails transmitted over the internet were spam emails;[829] today, it is around 85% of all emails which cost billions of dollars annually by way of productivity loss worldwide. The recent Bangladesh Cyber-threat Landscape, 2020 released by the BGD e-GOV CIRT revealed that spam along with phishing email and ransomware pose the most significant cyber threats in Bangladesh and the country, responsible for 7.1% of the world's spam volume, ranked 29th in the spam sources by country.[830]

875. Several countries in the world have taken legislative measures to regulate spam since the beginning of this century. While some countries enacted special laws in this regard, e.g., the SPAM Act, 2003 (Australia), the Controlling the Assault of Non-Solicited Pornography and Marketing Act, 2003 (US), Unsolicited Electronic Messages Act, 2007 (New Zealand), Spam Control Act, 2007 (Singapore), Canada's Anti-Spam Legislation, 2014 and so on, some countries have been regulating spam through the provisions of the personal data protection (e.g., by way of, *inter alia*, 'do not call' register) or electronic communication laws.

876. Bangladesh has neither enacted any specific law nor personal data protection to regulate spam. Earlier, section 54(1)(h) of the ICT Act, 2006 included provisions that the generation of spam or sending of unwanted emails without the permission of the subscriber for the advertisement of goods and services was an offence for which a person could be punished with imprisonment for ten years or a fine of up to BDT 5,00,000. However, this provision was subsequently repealed by the Digital Security Act, 2018 and a similar provision was included therein section 19(d).

877. This is for sure that the provision on spam under section 54 of the ICT Act, 2006 was not properly implemented and it can safely be doubted about the proper implementation of such provision under the DS A, 2018 also as the netizens and mobile phone users have been receiving unsolicited messages every day from the service providers, along with such auto-generated and pre-recorded calls and messages from many other commercial bodies. In most cases, the service providers contain wide general provisions in the terms and conditions of services and exploit these to send spam. The subscribers, as consumers, in most cases do not read or understand these provisions. Moreover, they are helpless too since they do not have suitable alternatives. Absence of subsidiary legislation under the ICT Act of 2006 specifying the procedural and substantive aspects of spamming could be a reason behind such a scenario.[831] No such subsidiary legislation in this regard has yet been framed under the DSA, 2018.

829. Karim, M.E. & Islam, T.M., *Legally Regulating Spam*, The Daily Star, 13 Feb. 2018, https://www.thedailystar.net/law-our-rights/legally-regulating-spam-1534003.
830. BGD e-GOV CIRT, Bangladesh Cyberthreat Landscape, January–December 2020, Risk Assessment Unit, p. 8.
831. Karim, M.E. & Islam, T.M., *Legally Regulating Spam*, The Daily Star, 13 Feb. 2018, https://www.thedailystar.net/law-our-rights/legally-regulating-spam-1534003.

878. It may be relevant to share here that many countries in the world have enacted specific legislation to regulate spam whereas some countries have incorporated such provisions under the personal data protection law, telecommunication, electronic commerce or multimedia law. These laws contain detailed provisions with strict regulatory requirements to follow by the business community before sending unsolicited messages and provide strict punishments. The government, business communities, especially the e-commerce community, may be reluctant to welcome such moves on the grounds that spam activities assist them in reaching the consumers. While this is true to some extent as they can reach the consumers at a cheaper cost due to the use of ICT services, they should simultaneously appreciate that such activities violate the privacy of the consumers.

879. It may be relevant to share here that the GoBISM, which was developed based on International Standards ISO/IEC 27001:2013 and ISO/IEC 27002:2013, contains some isolated provisions on spam. However, this Manual is intended only for government unclassified systems and information. The government has also formulated the Public EMail Policy, 2018 containing one single reference on spam, for the primary use of all government, semi-government, autonomous, semi-autonomous, and statutory organizations of Bangladesh excluding the national security organizations, law enforcement agencies, financial institutes and Bangladesh missions in abroad. Subsequently, BCC has also formulated Guidelines for Email Account Management, Effective Email Usage & Email Address Format in 2019 containing some provisions on spam emails management. Thus, it is evident that the prime reason to develop these documents is primarily to serve different purposes, i.e., to protect government computer systems and networks. However, a national law on spam regulation aims to protect the consumers. Therefore, the government should actively consider implementing spam-related legal provisions and formulate relevant subsidiary legislation.

880. An analysis of the spam-related laws as available in other parts of the world, some common features of such laws can be identified. These are: prohibition to use misleading email headers, subject line reflecting accurate content of the message, message to be identified as advertisement or promotional, collection of consent before sending a message of commercial nature, option for the receiver of such message to opt-out, sender must have a physical address, information about the collection, process and use of personal data, and inform the receiver about data breaches if any.

§5. IDENTITY THEFT

881. The main substantive criminal law of Bangladesh, i.e., the Penal Code, 1860 (XLV of 1860) contains some provisions on cheating and penalties for this offence. Cheating and cheating by personation are offences under sections 415 and 416 of the Penal Code, 1860 (XLV of 1860) respectively and deserve some discussion. Section 415 provides that someone is said to 'cheat' if he, 'by deceiving any person, fraudulently or dishonestly induces the person so deceived to deliver any property to any person, or to consent that any person shall retain any property, or intentionally induces the person so deceived to do or omit to do anything which he would not do or omit if he were not so deceived, and which act or omission causes or is likely to cause damage or harm to that person in body, mind, reputation or property'. On the other hand, section 416 provides that a person is said to 'cheat by personation' if he cheats by pretending to be some other person, or by knowingly substituting one person for another, or representing that he or any other person is a person other than he or such other person really is. It is further explained that the offence will be committed, and it is immaterial whether the individual personated is a real or imaginary person.

882. The AD discussed the elements of cheating in the case of *Md. Mohasin Ali @ Mohsin v. The State* 8 BLT (AD) 210. According to the AD, for an offence of cheating to be punishable, there are two elements, i.e., deception and dishonest inducement to do or omit to do something. The Court held that 'In such a case the complainant or the informant would have to show not only that he was induced to do or omit to do a certain act but this inducement or omission has caused or was likely to cause him some harm or damage in body, mind, reputation or property and these are presumed to be the four cardinal assets of humanity.'[832]

883. The Supreme Court has also clarified in different instances that to hold someone guilty of the offence of cheating and justify a conviction, the prosecution needs to establish the initial criminal intention of the accused that he intended to deceive the complainant.[833] The court observed on various occasions that the intention of cheating, to be gathered from the facts of the case, its surrounding circumstances and evidence on record. If the fraudulent intent of the accused from the beginning cannot be established, there can be no question of cheating.[834] Besides, this is pertinent to mention here that 'In the absence of *mens rea*, mere breach of contract cannot constitute cheating. Inability to fulfill a promise or contract does not amount to cheating.'[835]

884. Initiatives taken and implemented to promote trust and confidence of the netizens are crucial in order to maximize the benefits of the internet. Mature democracies and developed countries of the world have been treating cheating involving ICT devices both online and offline very seriously to ensure the trust and confidence of the citizens. In the context of Bangladesh, these are still not very seriously considered. As a result, even though there are numerous reports on mobile or online scamming, ATM frauds, etc., the accused remain rather fearless as the limited provisions of the laws are not properly implemented for various reasons, e.g., incompetence of the investigation team due to lack of technical expertise and strengths,

832. *Md. Mohasin Ali @ Mohsin v. The State,* 8 BLT (AD) 210.
833. *Sujit Kumar Rudra & Ors. v. The State,* 8 BLT (HCD) 407; *Alhaj Abul Kashem v. The State,* 15 BLT (HCD) 227.
834. *Mahbubul Alam Gazi v. The State & Anr.,* 8 BLT (HCD) 358; *Sujit Kumar Rudra & Ors. v. The State,* 8 BLT (HCD) 407; *Alhaj Abul Kashem v. The State;* 15 BLT (HCD) 227.
835. *Mahbubul Alam Gazi v. The State & Anr.,* 8 BLT (HCD) 358.

apparent unwillingness of them to understand the seriousness and long term consequences of such offences and lack of proper cooperation from the legal counsels, etc. As a result, even though there are many cases decided and reported on general forms of cheating, not a single case could be located decided by the higher judiciary on cheating involving ICT devices both online and offline.

885. Identity theft or impersonation, in the context of digital devices, is an offence under section 24 of the DSA, 2018. Accordingly, this section provides that 'it is an offence to use any computer, computer program, computer system, computer network, digital device, digital system or digital network intentionally or knowingly:

(a) with the intention to deceive or cheat and bearing of the identity of another person or display of any person's identity as his own, or
(b) intentionally by way of forgery bearing of the identity of a live or dead person as one's own for the following purpose:
   (i) to gain to help to gain some advantage for own or for any other person;
   (ii) to acquire any property or interest in any property;
   (iii) to harm a person by using another person's identity in disguise'.

886. Cybercriminals generally possess sufficient technical knowledge having better technological educational background and, thus, are white-collar criminals. They are capable of using various means and techniques to frustrate the members of the law enforcement agencies so that they fail to establish 'intention' – the most crucial element in identity theft or impersonation offences. This is not a unique problem in the context of Bangladesh; rather most of the countries have been facing this issue, and therefore, they have come up with some guiding documents and manuals.

887. Studies revealed from the state practices of various countries that there is a mixture of legal responses, i.e., some countries have enacted specific statutes on identity theft, whereas some countries utilize the traditional criminal law provisions on fraud, forgery and personal data protection law.[836] While in Bangladesh, the antiquated colonial Penal Code of 1860 and some other special laws, e.g., the DSA, 2018 contain provisions on fraud and forgery, etc., there is no law on personal data or information protection as discussed earlier. Besides, the adequacy of the provisions of the Penal Code can validly be questioned as not a single ATM fraud or scamming case has been reported. In this context, the inclusion of such provision in the DSA, 2018 is very welcoming, though we need to wait for a while to evaluate the effectiveness of this provision. Besides, this will be relevant to see how the law enforcement agencies deal with such offences committed from outside the national jurisdiction of Bangladesh.

836. For example, the US has enacted the Identity Theft and Assumption Deterrence Act of 1998.

888. Realizing the severe consequences of such offence, a special law, i.e., the Identity Theft and Assumption Deterrence Act was enacted in the US in 1998. In 2003, the OECD formulated the Guidelines for Protecting Consumers from Fraudulent and Deceptive Commercial Practices Across Borders containing principles to help the Member States fight fraudulent activities, offline and online to help the consumers. Subsequently, in 2008, OECD released another Policy Guidance on Online Identify Theft. According to the OECD Policy Guidance on Online Identify Theft, 2008, the fraudsters collect personal information of consumers in a number of ways, e.g., dumpster diving (i.e., by collecting receipts thrown in bins), pretexting (i.e., impersonating a legitimate customer with or without the help of an employee inside), shoulder surfing (i.e., looking over the shoulder when someone enters the personal identification number at an ATM), skimming (i.e., collection of encrypted information in the credit card by using various techniques to make duplicate credit card) and business record theft (i.e., stealing of business information personally or with the help of insider(s)).[837] Even though Bangladesh is not a member of OECD, an organization of the industrialized nations, all these options have been reported to be exploited by the criminals in Bangladesh as well.

889. Some of these techniques are not so popular in present times as the fraudsters have lucrative, less risky and more profitable alternatives, i.e., use of software to collect personal information by way of malware, spam, phishing and hacking to commit identity theft offences.[838] Personal data or information is collected by exploiting these techniques; the criminals misuse existing accounts, open new accounts to commit other crimes, or use this information to hide their own identity during the commission of a crime.[839] As this is a global problem, countries have been adopting various initiatives having three aspects: prevention (e.g., use of technological solutions), deterrence (e.g., legal sanctions) and recovery and redress.[840]

890. In 2011, the United Nations Office on Drugs and Crime (UNODC) released a Handbook on Identity-related Crime containing chapters on legal approaches to criminalize identity theft, typology and example of criminalization approaches to identity-related crime, identity-related crime victim issues, best practices on public-private partnerships to prevent economic fraud and identity-related crime, practical guide to international cooperation to combat identity-related crime. As Bangladesh has recently enacted the DSA, 2018 containing provisions on identity theft and in order to implement this provision of the DSA, additional supporting guidelines in the form of, e.g., subsidiary legislation will be required, the policymakers should actively consult these two documents released by OECD and UNODC.

---

837. OECD Policy Guidance on Online Identify Theft, 2008, p. 3.
838. *Ibid.*
839. OECD Policy Guidance on Online Identify Theft, 2008, p. 4.
840. *Ibid.*

§6. Digital or Electronic Fraud and Forgery

891. One of the reasons criminals steal identity online is to commit fraud, and digital devices are used to make forged documents. Therefore, some of the discussion of the preceding section will be relevant here as well. However, digital or electronic fraud can be committed even without the internet, which is apparent from the experience of the US where the Computer Fraud and Abuse Act was enacted in 1986.

892. Digital or electronic fraud and forgery has turned to be a serious concern for the netizens of the present time as organized criminals have been using various innovative techniques to fool ordinary citizens. In Bangladesh, there are regular reports that people have become the victims of various scams and lost a considerable amount. There is some news about the arrest of some of these criminals also though in most of the cases the accused can manage to get out of the court on bail due to some procedural and legal loopholes available and continue the crimes. The government and various stakeholders have taken some initiatives to make people aware of digital or electronic fraud and forgery. Albeit, people are trapped because of, *inter alia*, the lack of awareness, the very organized nature of the crime and criminals and the innovative techniques and technologies used by them.

893. The Penal Code, 1860 (XLV of 1860) has contained various provisions on fraudulent activities and forgery. Nevertheless, digital or electronic fraud is listed as an offence under the DSA, 2018 as well.[841] The law has also included an explanation containing the definition of 'digital or electronic fraud'. According to the explanation to section 22 of the DSA, 2018, 'digital or electric fraud' means to change or delete any information of, or add new information to, or tamper any information of, any computer programme, computer system, computer network, digital device, digital system, digital network or social media by a person, intentionally or knowingly or without permission, and doing so, to diminish the value or utility thereof, or try to get any benefit for himself or any other person, or to cause harm to, or deceive, any other person. From this definition, it is clear that the 'intention' to commit the crime is crucial here. Fraud or forgery can be committed in various ways using the internet and digital devices.

894. Fraud and forgery are related offences, though there is a difference between these two. Where there is an intention to deceive and by means of the deceit to obtain an advantage there is a fraud and if a document is fabricated with such intent, it is a forgery.[842] 'Forgery' means the making of a false document with certain intentions, e.g., to cause damage or injury to a person, or to support any claim or title, to commit fraud.[843] Thus, if an original document is substituted by another fabricated document, or, if a document is created by a fictitious person and not by a genuine

841. Section 22, the Digital Security Act, 2018 (Act No. 46 of 2018).
842. *Jahangir Hossain v. State*, 40 DLR 545.
843. *Amjad Molla v. Syeduzzaman Molla and others*, 46 DLR (AD) 17.

person, it may be called a forgery.[844] It may be relevant to share here that unless there is an element of fraud or intention to cause damage or injury to the public or any person, a fabricated document or part thereof cannot be called a forged document.[845]

895. An aggrieved person, who is a victim of digital or electronic fraud, is entitled to get a similar or reasonable amount of compensation.[846] One of the main limitations of the law here is that the burden to prove the allegation of fraud or forgery is on the person who makes the allegation.[847] Given the socio-economic context of the country, knowledge, education and understanding level of the victims, absence of technology-friendly judicial set up and sophisticated techniques and technologies used by the criminals, etc. this is very often impossible to establish the offence for the victims. It may be relevant to share here that Bangladesh is not the only country facing this due to the presence of these conditions, this is rather a common and general problem faced by every country. Therefore, some developed countries have developed and released some guideline documents.[848] Bangladesh should also consider taking similar approaches.

§7. Criminal Breach of Trust

896. The discussion on the issue of 'criminal breach of trust' is crucial in the context of cybercrimes targeting an organization and the persons related to such organizations as in many cases, the criminals have rapport and understandings with some insider(s). Criminal breach of trust is a punishable offence under section 405 of the Penal Code, 1860 (XLV of 1860), which provides that a person will commit 'criminal breach of trust' if he is in any manner entrusted with property, or with any dominion over property and subsequently misappropriates dishonestly or converts that property to his own use, or dishonestly uses or disposes of that property in violation of any direction of law prescribing the mode in which such trust is to be discharged, or of any legal contract, express or implied, which he has made touching the discharge of such trust, or wilfully suffers any other person so to do. Even though the punishment for criminal breach of trust is imprisonment up to three years or fine or both, the punishment will be higher if such crime is committed by a clerk or servant (imprisonment up to seven years or fine or both),[849] or a public servant, banker, merchant or agent (imprisonment for life or imprisonment up to ten years or fine or both).[850]

---

844. *S.A. Alim v. Dr. Golam Nabi & Another*, 3 BLT (HCD) 1.
845. *Abul Kashem Bhuiyan v. State* 50 DLR 631.
846. Section 37, the Digital Security Act, 2018 (Act No. 46 of 2018).
847. Section 101, the Evidence Act, 1872 (Act No. I of 1872). *Abdullah (Md) and others v. Majibul Huq and others*, 2003, 32 CLC (HCD) [6012] = 56 DLR (2004) 528.
848. For example, the Department of Justice has issued a document titled 'Prosecuting Computer Crimes'. UK has also released Cybercrime-prosecution guidance, https://www.cps.gov.uk/legal-guidance/cybercrime-prosecution-guidance.
849. Section 408, the Penal Code, 1860 (Act No. XLV of 1860).
850. Section 409, the Penal Code, 1860 (Act No. XLV of 1860).

897. It may be relevant to share here that the 'property' can be either moveable or immoveable, tangible or intangible. The existence of the fiduciary relationship, which establishes 'entrustment', is the crux of the provisions in section 405 of the Penal Code on criminal breach of trust.[851] The violation of contract or contractual terms will hold good for such an offence of criminal breach of trust if the condition as to 'entrustment' within the meaning of section 405 is satisfied.[852] Therefore, it will be important to insert relevant provisions in the employees' terms of services contracts. Besides, in such cases, prosecution needs to establish the *mala fide* and criminal intention of the accused as well.[853] Finally, it should be remembered that the criminal breach of trust can result in civil liability too as the law does not preclude a criminal case on the same facts, i.e., the criminal case stands for the offence, while the civil suit is for the realization of money, both can stand together.[854] Thus, a civil suit for recovery of any money misappropriated through a criminal breach of trust can be started side by side in a criminal case.[855]

§8. Sexual Harassment

898. There are provisions on various forms of violence against women under different laws of the land. Harassing women or children through the internet, telephone, cell phone or SMS or any other medium is a punishable offence under section 10(ka) of the *Nari-O-Shisho Nirjaton Daman Ain*, 2000. Besides, transmission or attempt to transmit a false or fabricated, indecent or obscene message with the knowledge is an offence for which an accused can be punished with imprisonment for a term which may extend up to three years, or with fine, or with both.[856] This was also established in the Directives of the HCD in the form of Guidelines delivered in a case relating to the issue of sexual harassment for protecting and safeguarding the rights of the women and girl children at workplaces, educational institutions/universities and other places wherever necessary which has been regularly reported in the media, public and other places.[857] Similar Guidelines were also issued in the case relating to eve-teasing.[858]

899. Even with all these legal provisions, the incidents of sexual harassment have been increasing exponentially, both offline and online as shared earlier.[859] As

851. *Bhaskar Chakraborty v. State*, 59 DLR (2007) 325 = 2006, 35 CLC (HCD) [4022].
852. *Shamsul Alam & others v. AFR Hasan & others*, 40 DLR (1988) 46.
853. *State v. A K M Mohiuddin*, 1996, 25 CLC (HCD) [7094] = 50 DLR (HCD) (1998) 447.
854. *Khondaker Mahatabuddin Ahmed and others v. State*, 49 DLR (AD) 132.
855. *Md. Nazrul Islam v. The State and another*, 1 MLR (1996) (AD) 409.
856. Section 29, the Telegraph Act, 1885 (Act No. XIII of 1885).
857. *Bangladesh National Women Lawyers Association (BNWLA) v. Bangladesh and Others*, 2009, 38 CLC (HCD) [3289] = 29 BLD (HCD) (2009) 415, 14 BLC (HCD)(2009) 694.
858. *Bangladesh National Women Lawyers Association (BNWLA) v. Government of Bangladesh*, 2011, 40 CLC (HCD) [4739] = 31 BLD (HCD) (2011) 324, 18 BLC (HCD) (2013) 290.
859. *See* Part VII, Ch. 1, General Legal Development, §2. Facts and Figures.

a result, the Supreme Court of Bangladesh issued Directives in the form of Guidelines in 2009 in *Bangladesh National Women Lawyers Association (BNWLA) v. Bangladesh and Others*, 2009, 38 CLC (HCD) [3289] = 29 BLD (HCD) (2009) 415, 14 BLC (HCD) (2009):

> 694. Under the Guidelines, Sexual Harassment includes:
>
> a. Unwelcome sexually determined behaviour (whether directly or by implication) as physical contact and advances;
> b. Attempts or efforts to establish physical relation having sexual implication by abuse of administrative, authoritative or professional powers;
> c. Sexually coloured verbal representation;
> d. Demand or request for sexual favours;
> e. Showing pornography;
> f. Sexually coloured remark or gesture;
> g. Indecent gesture, teasing through abusive language, stalking, joking having sexual implication.
> h. Insult through letters, telephone calls, cell phone calls, SMS, pottering, notice, cartoon, writing on the bench, chair, table, notice boards, walls of office, factory, classroom, washroom having sexual implication.
> i. Taking still or video photographs for the purpose of blackmailing and character assassination;
> j. Preventing participation in sports, cultural, organizational and academic activities on the ground of sex and/or for the purpose of sexual harassment;
> k. Making love proposal and exerting pressure or posing threats in case of refusal to love proposal;
> l. Attempt to establish sexual relation by intimidation, deception or false assurance.

900. Such conduct mentioned in clauses (a) to (l) can be humiliating and may constitute a health and safety problem at workplaces or educational institutions; it is discriminatory when the woman has reasonable grounds to believe that her objection would disadvantage her in connection with her education or employment in various ways or when it creates a hostile environment at workplaces or educational institutions.

901. Sexual harassment includes harassment using a cell phone and SMS. It also includes taking still or video photographs for the purpose of blackmailing and character assassination.[860] The government and other stakeholders have been taking some initiatives to reduce the number of such offences. The government has already

---

860. *Bangladesh National Women Lawyers Association (BNWLA) v. Government of Bangladesh*, 2011, 40 CLC (HCD) [4739] = 31 BLD (HCD) (2011) 324 = 18 BLC (HCD) (2013) 290; *British American Tobacco Bangladesh Company Ltd. v. Begum Shamsun Nahar*, 2010, 39 CLC (AD) [8698] = 66 DLR (AD) (2014) 80.

introduced the '333 helpline' service using which information on social problems such as child marriage and sexual harassment can easily be reported.

§9. DEFAMATION

902. Like any other part of the world, the offence of defamation is recognized in Bangladesh also. Article 11 within Part II of the Constitution of Bangladesh, 1972 stipulates that the Republic of Bangladesh shall be a democracy in which fundamental human rights and freedoms and respect for the dignity and worth of the human person, shall be guaranteed. The AD of the Supreme Court found that '[t]hese are not mere empty flowery words. These are the dictates of the Constitution. This Article glorifies the State Policy, emburdening the Republic with the obligations, among others to protect the dignity of its citizens. The dignity of a citizen is no less important than his life or limb. This Article casts a duty upon the State to protect the dignity of its citizens'.[861]

903. Under the same provision of the Constitution, the country is recognized as a democracy in which fundamental human rights and freedoms are guaranteed. Besides, Bangladesh, being an active member of the UN has signed or accessed and ratified the core international human rights instruments. Accordingly, the Constitution has encapsulated widely recognized human rights as enshrined in the core international human rights treaties, including freedom of speech and expression; and freedom of the press. The Human Rights Council of the UN, as has been shared earlier, in 2012 unanimously resolved that ' … the same rights that people have offline must also be protected online, in particular freedom of expression, which is applicable regardless of frontiers and through any media of one's choice, in accordance with articles 19 of the Universal Declaration of Human Rights and the International Covenant on Civil and Political Rights'.[862] This is now recognized by the UN and well-established that the rights people enjoy offline shall be guaranteed online too.

904. It is, nevertheless, relevant to mention here that even though the freedom of speech and expression; and freedom of the press are guaranteed through Article 39 of the Constitution of Bangladesh, these rights are not an absolute right and reasonable legal restriction can be imposed in the interests of the security of State, friendly relations with foreign states, public order, decency or morality, or in relation to contempt of court, defamation or incitement to an offence.

905. The issue of defamation, having both civil and criminal aspects, covers a major part of the discussion on internet regulation and cybercrimes. This is unique in the sense that the respondent or accused often commits this wrong or crime even without realizing the consequences, sometimes out of fun and ignorance without having any intention for financial gain. The DSA, 2018 has specifically stipulated

---

861. *Mohammad Tayeeb and another v. Government of the People's Republic of Bangladesh (Fatwa Judgment),* 2011, 40 CLC (AD) [8867] = 2011, 40 CLC (AD).

862. https://ap.ohchr.org/documents/E/HRC/d_res_dec/A_HRC_20_L13.doc.

in section 29, linking it with the provisions of the Penal Code, that it is an offence to publish any defamatory information in any website or electronic medium.[863]

906. Chapter XXI of the Penal Code, 1860 (sections 499–502) deals with the provisions relating to defamation. Defamation is defined in section 499, which provides that whoever by words either spoken or intended to be read, or by signs, or by visible representations, makes or publishes any imputation concerning any person intending to harm, or knowing or having reason to believe that such imputation will harm, the reputation of such person, is said, except in the cases hereinafter excepted, to defame that person. Few explanations and illustrations are included in this section to make the content of the provision clearer.

907. It is provided that it may amount to defamation to impute anything to a deceased person, if the imputation would harm the reputation of that person if living, and is intended to be hurtful to the feelings of his family or other near relatives.[864] No imputation is said to harm a person's reputation, unless that imputation directly or indirectly, in the estimation of others, lowers the moral or intellectual character of that person, or lowers the character of that person in respect of his caste or of his calling, or lowers the credit of that person, or causes it to be believed that the body of that person is in a loathsome, or in a state generally considered as disgraceful.[865] It may also amount to defamation to make an imputation concerning a company or an association or collection of persons as such.[866] Imputation, in the form of an alternative or expressed, ironically, may amount to defamation.

908. Section 499 has included ten exceptions when any imputation will not be treated as defamation. Accordingly, it is not defamation to:

(a) impute anything which is true concerning any person, if it be for the public good that the imputation should be made or published. Whether or not it is for the public good is a question of fact;
(b) express in good faith any opinion whatever respecting the conduct of a public servant in the discharge of his public functions, or respecting his character, so far as his character appears in that conduct and no further;
(c) express in good faith any opinion whatever respecting the conduct of any person touching any public question, and respecting his character, so far as his character appears in that conduct, and no further;
(d) publish a substantially true report of the proceedings of a Court of Justice, or of the result of any such proceedings;
(e) express in good faith any opinion whatever respecting the merits of any case, civil or criminal, which has been decided by a Court of Justice, or respecting

863. Section 29, the Digital Security Act, 2018 (Act No. 46 of 2018).
864. Explanation 1, s. 499, the Penal Code, 1860 (XLV of 1860).
865. Explanation 4, s. 499, the Penal Code, 1860 (XLV of 1860).
866. Explanation 2, s. 499, the Penal Code, 1860 (XLV of 1860). In *Islami Bank and others v. Dewan Md. Yusuf,* 2002, 31 CLC (HCD) [8003] = 55 DLR (HCD) (2003) 624, it was held that Bank's liability may extend to the tortious law of defamation.

the conduct of any person as a party, witness or agent, in any such case, or respecting the character of such person, as far as his character appears in that conduct, and no further;

(f) express in good faith any opinion respecting the merits of any performance which its author has submitted to the judgment of the public, or respecting the character of the author so far as his character appears in such performance, and no further;

(g) prefer in good faith an accusation against any person to any of those who have lawful authority over that person with respect to the subject matter of the accusation;

(h) make an imputation on the character of another, provided that the imputation be made in good faith for the protection of the interest of the person making it, or of any other person, or for the public good;

(i) convey a caution, in good faith, to one person against another, provided that such caution be intended for the good of the person to whom it is conveyed, or of some person in whom that person is interested, or for the public good.

909. Finally, it is not defamation if a person having over another any authority, either conferred by law or arising out of a lawful contract made with that other, to pass in good faith any censure on the conduct of that other in matters to which such lawful authority relates.[867]

910. To constitute defamation, the words spoken must contain imputation concerning a person intending to harm him in his reputation in the estimation of others.[868] Bringing anything unjust or improper to the notice of the public at large which is earlier published in other newspapers and subsequently published in good faith is not an imputation.[869] Generally, a court shall take cognizance of an offence of defamation only if a complaint is made by some person aggrieved by such offence.[870]

911. The English law of absolute privilege does not apply in Bangladesh regarding statements made by the parties in court proceedings or the statements made by learned Advocates in such proceedings. Therefore, an action would lie for a defamatory statement or utterance made in a judicial proceeding.[871] However, imputation made by a lawyer in the discharge of professional duty on the character of any person in good faith and for the protection of the interest of the person making it or of any other person or for the public good will not constitute an offence of defamation.[872] If a lawyer is called regarding defamatory statements made in the course

867. Seventh exception, s. 499, the Penal Code, 1860 (Act No. XLV of 1860).
868. *A.K.M. Enamul Haque v. Md. Mizanur Rahman and others*, 14 BLD (HCD) 201.
869. *Syed Mohammad Afzal Hossain v. S.M. Salim Idris*, 15 BLD (HCD) 362.
870. Section 198, the Code of Criminal Procedure, 1898 (Act No. V of 1898).
871. *AY Masihuzzaman v. Shah Alam & others*, 1989, 18 CLC (HCD) [5781] = 41 DLR (HCD) (1989) 180.
872. *Sigma Huda v. Ishfaque Samad and others*, 1993, 22 CLC (HCD) [5084] = 45 DLR (HCD) (1993) 129.

of discharging duties as an Advocate, the Court ought to presume that such act was committed in good faith upon instructions of the client and ought to require the party to prove the express malice.[873]

912. With the advancement of ICT and the internet in the country, the number of online newspapers and news portals are mushrooming. In most cases, some people without having the minimum qualifications have been running these so-called online newspapers and news portals. There are allegations that these services are run to spread misinformation and slanderous news. In the view of the Supreme Court of Bangladesh, '[a]lthough freedom of press has been guaranteed under article 39 of the Constitution subject to certain restrictions, a journalist cannot take shelter under the cloak of freedom of press after committing offence of defamation'.[874] However, it is important to share here that, for an aggrieved person, before lodging a complaint about defamation, 'the complainant should send a rejoinder denying the truth of the contents of the publications. If the rejoinder is not published, it can be said that the publication was made without good faith and for public good'.[875]

913. The government was found to be very concerned about the online news portals also and therefore, included a provision in the DSA, 2018. Accordingly, the transmission, publication, etc. of offensive, false or threatening data information is an offence under section 25 of the DSA, 2018. Section 25 (1) of the law provides that it shall be an offence if any person, through any website or any other digital medium, (a) intentionally or knowingly transmits, publishes or propagates any data information which he knows to be offensive, false or threatening in order to annoy, insult, humiliate or malign a person; or (b) publishes or propagates or abets to publish or propagate any information, as a whole or partly, which he knows to be propaganda or false, with an intention to affect the image or reputation of the country, or to spread confusion. Moreover, this is an offence, under section 28 of the DSA, 2018 if any person or group willingly or knowingly publishes or broadcasts or causes to publish or broadcast anything on the website or any electronic format which hurts religious sentiment or values, with an intention to hurt or provoke the religious values or sentiments. The government has simultaneously taken the initiative to bring these news portals under the registration process, even though there are reasons to apprehend that through this measure taken, the government may strictly regulate and control the freedom of the press.

914. With the expansion of internet coverage in the country and the increase of internet subscribers, the number of social media platform users have been increasing significantly. Many of these users have also been spreading misinformation and slanderous news even without realizing that spreading may contain the elements or

---

873. *Ibid.*

874. *Shahadat Chowdhury v. Md. Alaur Rahman*, 1 MLR (1996) (HC) 140; *Shamsul Alam Selim alias Sheikh Selim alias Anik Chowdhury v. State and another*, 2006, 35 CLC (HCD) [8194] = 13 MLR (HCD) (2008) 219.

875. *Shahadat Chowdhury v. Md. Alaur Rahman*, 1 MLR (1996) (HC) 140.

features of propaganda or hurt the religious values of sentiments without verifying the authenticity of the news and thinking about the prospective possible disastrous consequences of this action.

915. It may be relevant to share here that the provisions of sections 25, 28 and 29 of the DSA, 2018 were earlier included in section 57 of ICT Act, 2006, which became a hugely controversial legal provision due to its frequent enthusiast abuse and misuse by the members of the law enforcement agencies to suppress the voice of the opposition party of the government. Besides, the provision of section 57 was found to be 'vague and unclear' as there were no definite guidelines, and as 'section 57 appears to be directly inconsistent with the fundamental rights guaranteed under the constitution … the constitutional validity of the section could be open to challenge'.[876] As a result, the government took initiative to revise the provision of this section and incorporated the revised provisions in three different sections of the DSA, 2018.

916. As the provisions of the previous section 57 of the ICT Act, 2006 were incorporated in the DSA, 2018, it may be pertinent to share that in *Md. Anis Hossain Prodhan alias Anis Hasan Prodhan alias Dollar v. The State, represented by the Deputy Commissioner Lalmonirhat* (Criminal Miscellaneous Case No. 28869/2018), the HCD held that 'the main criteria for constituting an offence under section 57 of the Act is that the fake or obscene information/comments or materials shall have to be published or transmitted for public in general on the website or electronic form, not for any particular individual … mere sending obscene or fake information through SMS from one's cellular phone to another individual's cellular phone cannot be construed as a publication or transmission for the public in general and hence, does not constitute an offence under section 57 of the ICT Act'.

917. The government or the Digital Security Agency has not yet come up with any subsidiary legislation with further explanation and interpretation of these sections. As a result, these sections, along with some other provisions remain at the centre of controversy as these are reported to be abused and misused widely. Besides, the DSA, 2018 further gives immunity to anyone, which may include the members of the law enforcement agencies too, for anything done in the name of action taken in good faith. Section 57 of the DSA, 2018 provides that 'No suit or prosecution or any other legal proceeding shall lie against any employee or person concerned for any damage caused or likely to be caused to any person consequent to anything which is done in good faith under this Act.'

§10. PORNOGRAPHY

918. The Constitution of Bangladesh, as the supreme law of the land, has specially stipulated that it is the duty of the state to adopt effective measures to prevent

876. Justice Kashefa Hussain, *Laws, Special Laws and Effects*, Supreme Court of Bangladesh, Annual Report 2018, pp. 133–136.

prostitution and gambling.[877] Besides, the Constitution guarantees freedom of speech and expression subject to any reasonable restrictions imposed on the grounds of, *inter alia*, decency or morality. In a relatively conservative Muslim-majority country, Bangladesh has been facing the challenges of the wide circulation of pornographic materials. As a result, it has been reported at regular intervals that BTRC blocks sites containing pornographic materials.

919. Issues relating to indent materials are already covered under the Penal Code, 1860.[878] Moreover, transmission or attempt to transmit a false or fabricated, indecent or obscene message with the knowledge is an offence for which an accused can be punished with imprisonment for a term which may extend up to three years, or with fine, or with both.[879] Harassing women or children through the internet, telephone, cell phone or SMS or any other medium is a punishable offence under section 10(ka) of the *Nari-O-Shisho Nirjaton Daman Ain*, 2000. This was also established in the Directives of the HCD in the form of Guidelines delivered in a case relating to the issue of sexual harassment for protecting and safeguarding the rights of the women and girl children at workplaces, educational institutions/universities and other places wherever necessary which has been regularly reported in the media, public and other places.[880] Similar Guidelines were also issued in the case relating to eve-teasing.[881]

920. Even after some provisions available in the domestic legal regime, with the expansion of ICT facilities and availability of the internet, the cybercriminals were circulating indecent and pornographic materials freely. With the provisions of the Penal Code, 1860 (Act No. XLV of 1860), the sale of obscene books through which hardbound pornographic books or obscene acts and songs in the public place could be regulated.[882] It is also considered as an offence to sell, let to hire, distribute, exhibit or circulate to any person under the age of twenty years any obscene

---

877. Article 18(2), the Constitution of the People's Republic of Bangladesh, 1972.
878. For example, ss 292–294, the Penal Code, 1860 (Act No. XLV of 1860).
879. Section 29, the Telegraph Act, 1885 (Act No. XIII of 1885).
880. *Bangladesh National Women Lawyers Association (BNWLA) v. Bangladesh and Others*, 2009, 38 CLC (HCD) [3289] = 29 BLD (HCD) (2009) 415, 14 BLC (HCD)(2009) 694.
881. *Bangladesh National Women Lawyers Association (BNWLA) v. Government of Bangladesh*, 2011, 40 CLC (HCD) [4739] = 31 BLD (HCD) (2011) 324, 18 BLC (HCD) (2013) 290.
882.

> 292. Sale, etc, of obscene books, etc. – Whoever –
>
> (a) sells, lets to hire, distributes, publicly exhibits or in any manner puts into circulation, or for purposes of sale, hire, distribution, public exhibition or circulation, makes, produces or has in his possession any obscene book, pamphlet, paper, drawing, painting, representation or figure or any other obscene object whatsoever, or
> (b) imports, exports or conveys any obscene object for any of the purposes aforesaid, or knowing or having reason to believe that such object will be sold, let to hire, distributed or publicly exhibited or in any manner put into circulation, or
> (c) takes part in or receives profits from any business in the course of which he knows or has reason to believe that any such obscene objects are, for any of the purposes aforesaid, made, produced, purchased, kept, imported, exported, conveyed, publicly exhibited or in any manner put into circulation, or

object.[883] Nonetheless, the problem with these provisions was that the digital version of such materials was not included and the punishments for such offences were very nominal, i.e., imprisonment of three to six months and/or fine. As a result, the members of the law enforcement agencies were facing serious problems in dealing with this menace. Accordingly, the government passed the Pornography Control Act, 2012 (Act No. 9 of 2012) to prevent the degradation of social and moral values.

921. Section 2 of the Law has defined 'pornography' as any indecent dialogue, acting performance, posture, nude or semi-nude dance recorded or captured in the form of cinema, video, audiovisual image, photography, graphics, or any other way, which are displayable and cause sexual arousal without having any artistic or educational value. In this definition, books, magazines, sculptures, cartoons, and leaflets, etc. which are capable of causing sexual arousal are also included. Moreover, the negatives and soft copies of all these are also included in the definition of 'pornography' under this Act.

922. Any camera, computer or parts, CD, VCD, DVD, optical device, magnetic device, mobile phone or parts of it, and any electronic, digital or any technological device used to produce, preserve, capture or display pornography are defined as 'pornographic instruments or tools'. It is prohibited to produce, preserve, market, transport, supply, transact, capture or display pornography.[884]

923. Any softcopy or converted hardcopy, CD, VCD, DVD, computer or any other device or accessories, mobile phone or parts, any other gadget or instrument used for the commission of the offence, any data or memory recorded electronically shall be considered as evidence in the court of law. Moreover, any information preserved by the BTRC or any authorized agency of the government, mobile operator, ISP, the legal VoIP service provider can be collected by the investigating officer and be used as evidence.[885]

(d) advertises or makes known by any means whatsoever that any person is engaged or is ready to engage in any act which is an offence under this section, or that any such obscene object can be procured from or through any person, or

(e) offers or attempts to do any act which is an offence under this section, shall be punished with imprisonment of either description for a term which may extend to three months, or with fine, or with both.

Exception. – This section does not extend to any book, pamphlet, writing, drawing or painting kept or used bona fide for religious purposes or any representation sculptured, engraved, painted or otherwise represented on or in any temple, or on any car used for the conveyance of idols, or kept or used for any religious purpose.

294. Obscene acts and songs.- Whoever, to the annoyance of others, (a) does any obscene act in any public place, or (b) sings, recites or utters any obscene songs, ballad or words, in or near any public place, shall be punished with imprisonment of either description for a term which may extend to three months, or with fine, or with both.

883. Section 293, the Penal Code, 1860 (XLV of 1860).
884. Section 4, the Pornography Control Act, 2012 (Act No. 9 of 2012).
885. Section 6, the Pornography Control Act, 2012 (Act No. 9 of 2012).

924. Any person involved in the production of pornography or creation of pressure to any woman or child to participate in pornography production or to induce any woman, man or child with or without the knowledge to capture a photograph, record video or film shall be liable for imprisonment up to seven years or BDT 2,00,000. Moreover, a person shall be liable for sextortion or harassment and shall be responsible for imprisonment up to five years or BDT 2,00,000. Anyone can be held liable for a similar amount of punishment for the supply or distribution of pornography through the internet or website or mobile phone or any other electronic device.[886] What is the definition of 'supply or distribution' is not clearly mentioned in the law. Anyone can be responsible for creating public nuisance through the exhibition of pornography.

925. The law provides for the highest amount of punishment for child pornography. Thus, the production, distribution, printing and publication of any pornography using any child or the sale, supply or exhibition of child pornography or the advertisement for child pornography is an offence for which an accused may be punished with a maximum of ten years imprisonment and a fine of up to BDT 500,000. Anyone directly involved or assisted in the commission of an offence under this law shall be punished similarly.[887]

926. It may be relevant to share here that the provisions of this law shall not be applicable to murals or sculptures used for religious or artwork purposes.[888] Offences under this law are cognizable and non-bailable.[889] Interestingly, for filing a case, which is ultimately found to be false, blackmailing or harassing in nature, the officer or authority or the complainant shall be liable for punishment, i.e., imprisonment up to two years and a fine of up to BDT 1,00,000.[890]

§11. Cyber Terrorism

927. It is an offence to broadcast any information relating to the activities of the prohibited criminal organizations under section 9(2) of the Anti-Terrorism Act, 2009 (Act No. 16 of 2009). Similarly, the instigation of terrorism is also an offence.[891] Cyber terrorism is also an offence under section 27 of the DSA, 2018. It is provided that- if any person: (a) creates obstruction to make legal access, or makes or causes to make illegal access to any computer or computer network or internet network with an intention to jeopardize the integrity, security and sovereignty of the State and to create a sense of fear or panic in the public or a section of the public; or (b) creates pollution or inserts malware in any digital device which may cause or likely to cause death or serious injury to a person; or (c) affects or damages the supply and service of daily commodity of public or creates adverse effect on any CII; or (d)

886. Section 8, the Pornography Control Act, 2012 (Act No. 9 of 2012).
887. *Ibid.*
888. Section 9, the Pornography Control Act, 2012 (Act No. 9 of 2012).
889. Section 10, the Pornography Control Act, 2012 (Act No. 9 of 2012).
890. Section 13, the Pornography Control Act, 2012 (Act No. 9 of 2012).
891. Section 13, the Anti-Terrorism Act, 2009 (Act No. 16 of 2009).

intentionally or knowingly gains access to, or makes interference with, any computer, computer network, internet network, any protected data information or computer database, or gains access to any such protected data information or computer database which may be used against friendly relations with another foreign country or public order, or may be used for the benefit of any foreign country or any individual or any group, then such person shall be deemed to have committed an offence of cyber terrorism.

928. Cyber terrorism activities may be an organized effort of a group of people. Therefore, it may be relevant to share here the legal provisions on joint liability. Section 34 of the Penal Code, 1860 lays down the principle of joint liability in respect of the commission of a crime which presupposes the existence of common intention and pre-plan. When a crime is committed in furtherance of common intention, each and every such person having taken an active part in the commission of the crime shall be equally liable to the same punishment.[892]

§12. Cyber Espionage

929. The term 'espionage' having its root in French, German and Italian languages simply means 'spy' and can be considered a sub-category of intelligence. The reference to such activities, both as an accepted practice and an act prohibited ethically and morally, can be found in the history of all major capitalizations and religions. Unfortunately, there is no universally accepted definition of the term 'espionage' though the term is generally used to denote the process of obtaining secret military, political, commercial or economic secret information such as plans, activities, capabilities, or resources of competition or enemy by employing spies, secret agents or computer devices and programs, etc.[893]

930. Even though this act of spying has been unofficially recognized and has been being practised by the rules for centuries and the UK enacted the first Official Secrets Act in 1911 containing provisions on spying, etc., the US became the first country that passed the special law on this, i.e., the Espionage Act in 1917 prohibiting the disclosure of national defence-related government and industrial information. The researchers revealed that these two laws of the UK and the US have many similarities.[894]

931. It will be interesting to share here that the then British colonial rulers introduced the concept of protection of government information in this part of the world and enacted the Official Secrets Act, 1923 (Act No. XIX of 1923), which is clearly

892. *State v. Mir Hossain and others*, 10 MLR (2005) (HC) 91.
893. *See*, generally, 1 Lerner, K.L. & Lerner, B.W. (eds), *Encyclopedia of Espionage, Intelligence, and Security* (2004).
894. For a comparison between UK's Official Secrets Act, 1911 and US's Espionage Act, 1917, *see* Katherine Feuer, *Protecting Government Secrets: A Comparison of the Espionage Act and the Official Secrets Act*, 38 BC Int'l & Comp. L. Rev., 91–127 (2015).

derived from the UK's first Official Secrets Act enacted in 1911. The Official Secrets Act, 1923 still in force in Bangladesh containing provisions on military and political espionage.

932. The economic and industrial secrets are very loosely protected, on a very limited and ignorable scale, through the provisions of the Patent and Designs Act, 1911 and the preamble to the Competition Act, 2012. From the reading of these provisions, it can safely be said that these provisions can only be used in instances of *mala fide* disclosure of information. Besides, the law of contract provisions and the Penal Code, 1860 provisions of criminal breach of trust can also be considered if there is a contractual relation and a relation of trust exists between the parties. Nevertheless, all these provisions can only cover a very minor aspect of espionage when the wrongdoer is an insider who is known to the victim, but these provisions cannot be applied in case of spying by an outsider for economic and industrial espionage.

933. In the context of state safety and interest, the Official Secrets Act, 1923 (Act No. XIX of 1923) contains provisions on penalties for spying (section 3) and harbouring spies (section 10), restriction against photographs, sketches, etc., of prohibited and notified areas (section 3a), communications with foreign agents to be evidence of commission of certain offences (section 4) wrongful communication, etc., of information (section 5), unauthorized use of uniforms; falsification of reports, forgery, personation, and false documents (section 6), interfering with officers of the police or members of the armed forces of Bangladesh (section 7), duty of giving information as to commission of offences (section 8) attempts, incitements, etc. (section 9), search warrants (section 11), power to arrest (section 12) restriction on trial of offences (section 13), exclusion of public from proceedings (section 14), offences by companies, etc. (section 15).

934. The concept 'Cyber espionage', often sponsored by the state apparatus, denotes the exploitation of cyberspace to access and collect confidential information having military, political, commercial or economic importance, e.g., trade secrets. Cyber espionage has four constitutive elements, i.e., the (i) non-consensual (ii) copying (iii) of confidential information (iv) that is resident in or transiting through cyberspace.[895] Cyber espionage, an important component of the modern-day state's cybersecurity policy and strategy, is a great concern for the major economies as competitive economies are blamed to hack such secret importation using ICT tools and devices through cyberspace for gains.

935. The DSA, 2018 contains provisions on the offence and punishment for breaching the secrecy of government in section 32. It is provided that it is an offence to commit or abets to commit an offence under the Official Secrets Act, 1923 (Act No. XIX of 1923), shared above, by means of a computer, digital device, computer network, digital network or any other digital means. The DSA, 2018 has not defined 'secrecy of government' and therefore, many apprehend that this provision will limit

895. Buchan, R., *Cyber Espionage and International Law*, 13 (2018).

the scope of investigative journalism, and due to this provision, along with the journalist even the whistle-blowers will also be strictly regulated and cannot report on corruption, irregularities, etc., of the government.

§13. MISCELLANEOUS

936. Even though the relevant laws have included explicit provisions to deal with specific kinds of cybercrimes, the ICT Act, 2006 has incorporated a provision using which the regulators can award fines for the commission of any offences not included in the law. Accordingly, if any person contravenes any rules of this Act for which the provision of penalties has not been fixed separately under the provisions of this Act, or rules and regulations made thereunder, the Controller or any officer of the Government authorized by the Government by special order, as the case may be, can fine the person for breaching the very rule which may extend to BDT 25,000 mentioning reasons in written by administrative order.[896]

937. It is an offence to run any propaganda or campaign through the digital medium against the liberation war of Bangladesh, cognition of liberation war, Father of the Nation, National Anthem or National Flag.[897] This is a very wide and general provision, and there are apprehensions that this provision, especially 'cognition of liberation war', can be used to control the critics of the government. Moreover, the DSA, 2018 has explicitly introduced many new acts as offences. A list of such activities includes unauthorized e-transaction (section 30), deterioration of law and order situation (section 31), invasion of government privacy (section 32), illegal hold and transfer of data and information of any organization (section 33).

938. Fake news or disinformation is a serious problem in Bangladesh in the same way as it is in many other countries. Through this, some people used to spread defamatory news. The country witnessed very shocking incidents happened in different places too including the burning of Buddhist Temple in Ramu, Cox's Bazar, clashes with a religious minority in Nasirnagar, Brahmanbaria and Bhola area recently. Publishing or sending offensive or false information with the intention to annoy, insult, humiliate or denigrate a person or with the intention to tarnish the image of the nation or spread confusion is an offence under the recently enacted DSA, 2018. During the recent general election of 2018, the Election Commission established a body on disinformation. The Bangladesh Police, with the approval of the Ministry of Home Affairs, has taken the initiative to establish a Cybercrime Investigation Bureau to tackle disinformation spread through the internet, especially social media and investigation of cybercrimes. The Ministry of Information has also established a 'Rumour Identification and Removal Centre' to make people aware of rumour through a press release.

---

896. Section 51, the Information and Communication Technology Act, 2006 (Act No. 39 of 2006).
897. Section 21, the Digital Security Act, 2018 (Act No. 46 of 2018).

§14. GOVERNMENT INITIATIVES

939. The government has taken several initiatives to curve the menace of cybercrimes. A Cyber Tribunal, a fast-track court to try cybercrime, was established under section 68 of the ICT Act, 2006 in the Dhaka District and Sessions Judge court premise for the quick disposal and efficient trial of cybercrime cases. However, it has been reported extensively highlighting the inadequacy of such specialized cyber tribunal compared to the number of crimes committed. As a result, the government has recently taken the initiative to set up cyber tribunals in all eight divisional headquarters of the country and judges for these tribunals are also appointed.

940. The government of Bangladesh has established the NMC on 1 January 2008 as per section 97A of the Bangladesh Telecommunication Regulation Act, 2001 as amended in 2006, to provide interception assistance to the law enforcement agencies. Subsequently, on 31 January 2013, NMC was named NTMC, which has started functioning under the Ministry of Home Affairs since February 2014.

941. A Cyber Training Center (CTC) was established in the CID of Bangladesh Police under a project titled 'Enhancing the Cyber Investigation Capability of Bangladesh Police' with the financial assistance of KOICA & designed by Korean cyber experts. With the aims to make a Safe & Secure Digital Bangladesh, CTC has been providing exclusive training on Cybercrime, Cybersecurity, Social Media Monitoring & Digital Forensics.[898]

942. In October 2018, the government-approved Cyber Police Center, upgrading the previous Cyber Crime Unit under the CID to monitor and investigate various crimes such as cyber harassment, cyberstalking & bullying, pornography, especially child pornography via the internet, phishing & spoofing, digital device-based currency and bank fraud, debit & credit card scam, national securities issues on cyberspace, and digital device-based crimes, etc. Earlier, CID established a Digital Forensics Lab in 2011–2012 and this Lab, established with personnel having the training from some of the world's best police forces, is capable to examine all sorts of digital devices such as computers, laptops, mobile phones, tabs, hard disks, pen drives, CD/DVDs, recording devices, digital cameras, VOIP equipment, drones, SIMs, memory sticks, network devices, DVR/NVR (CCTV), etc., seized during the investigation of any case. It was reported that in 2018, this Lab provided cyber forensic expert opinion in almost 1,000 cases involving over 4,000 digital evidence.[899] Besides, metropolitan police departments have also established units responsible for dealing with the investigation of cybercrime and cyber patrolling matters.

898. CTC, Criminal Investigation Department, Bangladesh Police, http://cid.gov.bd/site/content_view/ctc.

899. Digital Forensic Lab, Criminal Investigation Department, Bangladesh Police, http://cid.gov.bd/site/content_view/digital_forensic.

943. The Digital Security Act, 2018, under sections 10 & 11, provide for the establishment of the 'Digital Forensic Lab'. Accordingly, a Forensic Lab was established in 2018 under the BGD e-GOV CERT to conduct a forensic investigation of digital evidence. After an incident occurs, this Lab assists the incident handling unit by providing forensic support on evidence relating to the incident. While doing so, the Lab first detect the evidence, then collect the evidence, after that examine or analyse the evidence and finally, make the documentation and reporting. Any evidence so collected shall be treated as evidence in the trial.[900] This Lab is capable of conducting forensic of computer, mobile, network and is capable of recovering and investigating materials found in a digital device including mobile, PC, Drone or any IoT or computational devices. Capacity building of students and government officials interested in cybersecurity and digital forensics is an important objective of the Lab.

944. In *State v. Oli*, 2019 [Death Reference No. 61 of 2011] Mr Justice Md Ruhul Quddus observed that 'Our Evidence Act has not been amended to deal with the electronic record/document … Mere production of the documents purporting to have been written, printed, signed or generated from an electronic record by a third person is no evidence of its authorship. It is necessary to prove their genuineness, execution and generation.' Moreover, he further observed that 'For the purpose of proving the contents of any electronic record, any procedure for its certification has not yet been introduced. In order to prove an electronic record or signature under the existing law of evidence, it is necessary to stamp its printed version with seal of the company or office and sign it. When it is adduced in evidence in a proceeding of Court, either the person who generates or signs it or in his absence, any other person who is acquainted with the record and signature must come before the Court to prove the contents and his signature thereon.'

945. The Digital Security Rules, 2020 framed under the DSA, 2018 has already incorporated some observations made by Mr Justice Md Ruhul Quddus in the judgment shared in the previous paragraph. Moreover, provisions relating to the manpower, security standards and formalities to be followed by Digital Forensic Lab are also incorporated. Besides, this Digital Security Rules, 2020 have also included important provisions on the forensic analysis of the digital evidence in the Schedule to the Rules and provides that the Digital Forensic Lab shall analyse the digital evidence as a forensic expert. The proper implementation of these provisions has the prospects to improve the situation with regard to digital evidence in the country.

§15. Conclusion

946. The enactment of the DSA, 2018, can be considered as a milestone in dealing with cybercrimes in the Bangladesh context. There were already a few laws, both general and special, and legal provisions which could be used to investigate

900. Section 15, the Digital Security Act, 2018 (Act No. 46 of 2018).

and try various cybercrimes. Nevertheless, those were found inadequate as the elements and definitions of various cybercrimes were not explicitly mentioned. As a result, the criminals were found to be fearless and used to escape their liabilities, though there were instances of abuse of some of these provisions. Accordingly, the government took the initiative to enact this law to facilitate the investigation and trial of various cybercrimes. Unfortunately, there are several criticisms of this law. Some of the provisions of this law may be interpreted as in conflict with the constitutionally guaranteed rights such as the freedom of expression and opinion as encapsulated in Article 39 of the Bangladesh Constitution, 1972. Besides, the scopes of some provisions are very wide and can easily be misused if not supervised properly. As a result, already several cases were filed by the interested corners under these sections, and the higher authorities had to interfere when mass people started to raise their voices using online and other social media platforms. As the law has kept the scope to formulate subsidiary legislation, the government should take the initiative to formulate supporting documents without any delay. While doing so, the stakeholders must be consulted to address many of the concerns. Otherwise, the purpose of enacting this law is going to be frustrating without much doubt.

Chapter 3. Application of Criminal Procedure Law in the Area of ICT

§1. Introduction

947. The substantive provisions of laws are implemented by following the provisions of the procedural laws to ensure rule of law in the administration of justice. The general purpose of any procedural law is to streamline the proper exercise and meaningful implementation of substantive law in its real spirit which is the law above the law. The provisions of the procedural laws help to avoid busybodies or meddlesome interlopers so that the real beneficiaries of laws do not lose in their crowd. Thus, procedural law, instead of hindering or frustrating its real purpose and spirit of law, promotes the substantive right of the people.[901] Any procedural law, unless the legislatures intend otherwise, is retrospective in its operation and a subsequent omission, therefore, by way of amendment of a procedure do not have any consequence in respect of the proceeding already started.[902]

948. The Code of Criminal Procedure, 1898 (Act No. V of 1898), popularly known in its short form as Cr.P.C., is one of the oldest laws in force in Bangladesh. With the last amendment in 2012, this is the main criminal procedural law of the country.[903] The Evidence Act, 1872 (Act No. I of 1872) is the main law on evidence followed in both civil and criminal investigations and trials. Relevant laws on telecommunication and ICT shared and discussed so far in this monograph have included express provisions in this regard that the provisions of Cr. P.C. will be used to investigate, search and seizure, trial and appeal in relation to criminal and other related offences under these laws.[904] Besides, these laws, being special and sectorial

901. *Mohammad Tayeeb and another v. Government of the People's Republic of Bangladesh*, 2011, 40 CLC (AD) [8867] = 4 LNJ AD (2015) 48.
902. *Chowdhury Nasimul Baqui v. Bangladesh Steel and Engineering Corporation& others*, 2000, 29 CLC (AD) [607] = 52 DLR (AD) (2000) 125; *Md. Monsur Ali Sarder & Ors. v. The State*, 18 BLT (HCD) (2010) 13.
903. Section 5 of the Code of Criminal Procedure, 1898 provides that all offences under the Penal Code shall be investigated, inquired into, tried, and otherwise dealt with according to the provisions hereinafter contained. For all offences under any other law, the provisions of this law shall usually be followed unless otherwise specified in those laws as to the manner or place of investigation, inquiry or trial.
904. For example, s. 77 of the Bangladesh Telecommunication Regulation Act, 2001 provides that a Magistrate of the first class or a Metropolitan Magistrate or a court superior to such Magistrate shall be competent to take cognizance of an offence and no court inferior to a Court of Sessions shall be competent to hold the trial of an offence under this Act or regulations. It is further provided that 'where the said court takes cognizance of an offence, it may take all actions in accordance with the Criminal Procedure Code for making the case ready for trial including issuance of summons or warrant arrest for appearance of the accused person in the court'.
   Section 79(1) of the same law provides that '[s]ubject to the provisions of this Act, and the rules and regulations made thereunder, the Criminal Procedure Code shall apply to the investigation of an offence under this Act, trial, appeal and all incidental matters'.
   Under the special laws, e.g., under s. 5 of the Pornography Control Act, 2012, a sub-inspector of police or any officer not below this rank will investigate the offences under that law and follow the provisions of the Code of Criminal Procedure for such investigation to finish it within maximum

law, have also incorporated some procedural provisions to be followed during the investigation, search and seizure, etc., of crimes covered in these laws.

949. It is generally recognized that various aspects of procedural matters, such as investigation, search and seizure, production of evidence and arrest or acquittal, etc., depend on the nature of the crime. Telecommunication and ICT related some substantive crimes are already discussed in the previous Chapter. In order to understand the procedural issues better, the following section will shed focus on the general nature of offences in the Bangladesh context.

§2. OFFENCES IN GENERAL

950. Under Bangladeshi laws, the Penal Code, 1860 (XLV of 1860) is the main substantive criminal law which can be considered as a catalogue of offences and some of which are already discussed in the previous chapter. For the purpose of investigation, search and seizure, trial, etc., of the offences listed in the Penal Code and any other law, e.g., the DSA, 2018, the provisions of the Cr.P.C. apply.[905]

951. For the procedural purpose, it is crucial to understand that the offences are divided into two main categories having different implications. These are: (a) cognizable offence; and (b) non-cognizable offence. When there is any criminal case instituted followed by these offences, they are known as cognizable and non-cognizable cases, respectively. Based on the nature of these offences, the Police officer needs to follow a different procedure. Simply speaking, in case of a 'cognizable offence' or 'cognizable case', a Police officer may, in accordance with the second schedule to Cr. P.C. or under any other relevant law for the time being in force, arrest an accused without warrant.[906] Whereas, in the case of a non-cognizable offence, the police officer, generally, cannot start an investigation and arrest a person accused of an offence without a warrant from a Magistrate.[907] In non-cognizable cases, other than a police officer, an informant can also request the Magistrate for permission and to instruct the police to take cognizance of such offence and to start inquiry or investigation.[908]

952. Cognizable cases, also known as CR cases or Police cases, start by filing a First Information Report (FIR) regarding the commission of the offence to the officer-in-charge of a police station. For example, the provisions of telecommunication services without obtaining the proper licences or necessary permission is

---

seventy-five days. Such police officer, as the investigation officer, shall follow the provisions of the Cr.P.C. to arrest any person involved and search and seize pornographic materials.

905. Section 5, the Code of Criminal Procedure, 1898 (Act No. V of 1898).

906. Section 4(1)(b), the Code of Criminal Procedure, 1898 (Act No. V of 1898).

907. Sections 4(1)(n) & 155, the Code of Criminal Procedure, 1898 (Act No. V of 1898).

908. Section 155, the Code of Criminal Procedure, 1898 (Act No. V of 1898); *Nasiruddin Kazi v. Aleya Khatun alias Fulu*, 1996, 25 CLC (HCD) [7615]=48 DLR (HCD) (1996) 216.

such an offence. On the other hand, a non-cognizable case, also known as a complaint case, is to be instituted in the court of a judicial Magistrate.[909]

953. FIR is an important document in the criminal law procedure; its principal object, from the informant's point of view, is to set the machinery of criminal law into motion and from the view of the investigating agency is to obtain information about the alleged occurrence and to take necessary steps to trace the accused and produce him before the court concern for trial.[910] Nevertheless, the FIR, being the earliest version of the prosecution story, is not a substantive piece of evidence and cannot be used to contradict the evidence of any witness.[911] It can be used for testing the trust of the prosecution story, and only for the purpose of corroborating the statement of the informant under section 157 or contradicting him under section 145 of the Evidence Act thereof.[912]

954. When any police officer-in-charge receives any information relating to a cognizable offence, the officer, after writing down the details of the offence, may, without the order of a Magistrate, investigate the offence.[913] On the other hand, when any police officer in charge receives any information relating to a non-cognizable offence, the officer, after writing down the details of the offence, shall refer the informant to the Magistrate and can only investigate such offence with the order of a Magistrate of the first or second class.[914]

955. It will be relevant to share here that in *Bangladesh & others v. BLAST & others,* 8 SCOB [2016] AD 1, the AD of Bangladesh Supreme Court formulated the following Guidelines for the Magistrates, Judges and Tribunals having the power to take cognizance of an offence:

(a) If a person is produced by the law-enforcing agency with a prayer for his detention in any custody, without producing a copy of the entries in the diary as per section 167(2) of the Code, the Magistrate or the Court, Tribunal, as the case may be, shall release him in accordance with section 169 of the Code on taking a bond from him.
(b) If a law-enforcing officer seeks an arrested person to be shown arrested in a particular case, who is already in custody, such Magistrate or Judge or Tribunal shall not allow such prayer unless the accused/arrestee is produced before him with a copy of the entries in the diary relating to such case and if that the prayer for shown arrested is not well-founded and baseless, he shall reject the prayer.
(c) On the fulfilment of the above conditions, if the investigation of the case cannot be concluded within fifteen days of the detention of the arrested person as required under section 167(2) and if the case is exclusively triable by a court of

909. Section 200, the Code of Criminal Procedure, 1898 (Act No. V of 1898).
910. *Naripokkho & ors. v. Bangladesh & ors.*, 10 SCOB [2018] HCD 140.
911. *State v. Tajul Islam and 8 others*, 1992, 21 CLC (HCD) [7638]=48 DLR (HCD) (1996) 305.
912. *Seraj Miah v. State*, 1997, 26 CLC (HCD) [7251]=49 DLR (HCD) (1997) 192; *State v. Billal Hossain Gazi*, 2004, 33 CLC (HCD) [4558]=56 DLR (2004) 355.
913. Sections 154 & 156(1), the Code of Criminal Procedure, 1898 (Act No. V of 1898).
914. Section 155, the Code of Criminal Procedure, 1898 (Act No. V of 1898).

Sessions or Tribunal, the Magistrate may send such accused person on remand under section 344 of the Code for a term not exceeding fifteen days at a time.

(d) If the Magistrate is satisfied on consideration of the reasons stated in the forwarding letter and the case diary that the accusation or the information is well-founded and that there are materials in the case diary for detaining the person in custody, the Magistrate shall pass an order for further detention in such custody as he deems fit and proper until legislative measure is taken as mentioned above.

(e) The Magistrate shall not make an order of detention of a person in the judicial custody if the police forwarding report discloses that the arrest has been made for the purpose of putting the arrestee in preventive detention.

(f) It shall be the duty of the Magistrate/Tribunal, before whom the accused person is produced, to satisfy that these requirements have been complied with before making any order relating to such accused person under section 167 of the Code.

(g) If the Magistrate has reason to believe that any member of a law-enforcing agency or any officer who has the legal authority to commit a person in confinement has acted contrary to law, the Magistrate shall proceed against such officer under section 220 of the Penal Code.

(h) Whenever a law-enforcing officer takes an accused person in his custody on remand, it is his responsibility to produce such accused person in court upon expiry of the period of remand, and if it is found from the police report or otherwise that the arrested person is dead, the Magistrate shall direct for the examination of the victim by a medical board, and in the event of burial of the victim, he shall direct exhumation of the dead body for fresh medical examination by a medical board, and if the report of the board reveals that the death is homicidal in nature, he shall take cognizance of the offence punishable under section 15 of Hefajate Mrittu (Nibaran) Ain, 2013 against such officer and the officer-in-charge of the respective police station or commanding officer of such officer in whose custody the death of the accused person took place.

(i) If there are materials or information to a Magistrate that a person has been subjected to 'Nirjatan' or died in custody within the meaning of section 2 of the Nirjatan and Hefajate Mrittu (Nibaran) Ain, 2013, shall refer the victim to the nearest doctor in case of 'Nirjatan' and to a medical board in case of death for ascertaining the injury or the cause of death, as the case may be, and if the medical evidence reveals that the person detained has been tortured or died due to torture, the Magistrate shall take cognizance of the offence *suo moto* under section 190(1)(c) of the Code without awaiting the filing of a case under sections 4 and 5 and proceed in accordance with law.

956. For the purpose of understanding the consequences of different substantive offences discussed in this monograph, it is relevant to know that offences are again divided into two categories: bailable offence and non-bailable offence. 'Bailable offence' means an offence shown as bailable in the second schedule to the Cr.P.C., or which is made bailable by any other law for the time being in force, and 'non-bailable offence' means any other offence.[915] In case of bailable offences, an accused or an under trial prisoner is entitled to have bail as a matter of rights. However, the issue is different in the case for a convict as he cannot claim bail as of right rather he needs to rely on the judicially exercised discretion of the court.[916] Whereas, in the case of non-bailable offences, an accused generally cannot claim bail as a matter of right. However, unless for an offence punishable with death or imprisonment for life, an accused may be released on bail to the satisfaction of the court if the trial cannot be concluded with the specified time and the accused is in the custody for a long time.[917] The court can even order a person, arrested or detained for an offence punishable with death or imprisonment for life, if he is of below sixteen years, a woman, sick or infirm person.[918] Generally, an offence which is punishable under any other laws other than the Penal Code, 1860 (Act No. XLV of 1860) is bailable if the punishment for such offence is imprisonment for less than two years or fine only. Finally, some offences listed in the Penal Code, 1860 (XLV of 1860) are compoundable, i.e., the law allows the parties to reach a compromise, and some are non-compoundable.[919]

957. Following the Cr.P.C., section 53 of the DSA, 2018 specifies whether the offences listed in the law are cognizable or non-cognizable and bailable or not. Accordingly, the law provides that the offences such as: illegal access to any CII (section 17), damage of computer, computer system, etc. (section 19), making any kind of propaganda or campaign against liberation war, spirit of liberation war, father of the nation, national anthem or national flag (section 21), digital or electronic forgery (section 22), digital or electronic fraud (section 23), identity fraud or personation (section 24), unauthorized collection, use, etc., of identity information (section 26), cyber terrorism (section 27), publication, broadcast, etc., of information in website or in any electronic format that hurts the religious values or sentiment (section 28), e-transaction without legal authority (section 30), deteriorating law and order (section 31), breaching secrecy of the government (section 32), holding, transferring data information illegally, etc. (section 33), hacking (section 34) are cognizable, i.e., a police office can start the investigation without waiting for the permission of the magistrate and arrest an accused without warrant. These offences are also non-bailable.

Section 53 of the DSA, 2018 further provides that the first time commission of the offences such as: intentional illegal access to a computer, digital device, computer system to commit an offence (section 18(1)(b)), modification of computer source code (section 20), transmission, publication, etc. of offensive, false or threatening data information (section 25), publication, transmission, etc., of defamatory information (section 29) and disclosure of secrecy of the information obtained in course of the investigation (section 47(3)) are non-cognizable, i.e., a police officer

915. Section 4(1)(b), the Code of Criminal Procedure, 1898 (Act No. V of 1898).
916. Section 426, the Code of Criminal Procedure, 1898 (Act No. V of 1898).
917. Sections 339C(4) & 497, the Code of Criminal Procedure, 1898 (Act No. V of 1898).
918. Section 497, the Code of Criminal Procedure, 1898 (Act No. V of 1898).
919. For a list of such offences, *see* section 345, the Code of Criminal Procedure, 1898 (Act No. V of 1898).

can only start the inquiry of these offences after having the permission of the magistrate. Moreover, these offences are bailable too. Finally, under section 18(1)(a) of the DSA, 2018, the offence of intentional illegal access to a computer, digital device, a computer system is non-cognizable, bailable and subject to the permission of the court, compoundable. It is pertinent to mention here that these offences mentioned in this paragraph if committed by a person for the second time or more, shall be cognizable and non-bailable.

§3. Investigation of Offences

958. The nature of the offence, i.e., cognizable or non-cognizable will dictate the investigation of the offence, which includes all the proceedings for the collection of evidence.[920] It has already been shared that apart from the general criminal procedural law, i.e., the Cr.P.C., the special laws, e.g., the DSA, 2018 can also contain provisions on investigation of offence which are more or less based on the provisions of the Cr.P.C.[921]

959. As per the provisions of the Cr.P.C., 'investigation' generally consists of the following steps:

(1) proceeding to the spot;
(2) ascertainment of facts and circumstances of the case;
(3) discovery and the arrest of the suspected offender or offenders; and
(4) collection of evidence relating to the commission of the offence alleged which may consist of:
    (a) the examination of various persons including the accused and the reduction of their statements into writing/if the officer thinks fit;
    (b) the search of places or seizure of things considered necessary for the investigation and to be produced at the trial; and
(5) formation of the opinion as to whether on the materials collected there is a case to place the accused before a court for trial and if so, taking the necessary steps for the same by the filing of a charge sheet under section 173 of the Criminal Procedure Code.[922]

960. The procedure for investigation to be followed by a police officer has been laid down in Chapter XIV (sections 154–176) of the Cr.P.C. Sections 156 and 157 of the Cr.P.C. contain enabling provisions giving power to the officer-in-charge of a police station to hold an investigation in a case involving cognizable offence. The use of the expression 'cognizable case' indicates that there must be a case which

920. Section 4(1)(l), the Code of Criminal Procedure, 1898 (Act No. V of 1898).
921. Section 50 of the Digital Security Act, 2018 (Act No. 46 of 2018) provides that save as anything contrary to the provisions of this Act, the provisions of the Code of Criminal Procedure shall be applicable to the investigation, trial, appeal and all incidental matters related to any offence under this Act.
922. *Mr. Moshanaf Hossain v. State* (1978) 30 DLR (SC) 112.

starts based on credible information received either from a private person or from any intelligence source or agency. Publication of a report in a newspaper about the commission of a cognizable offence against a person is not 'information' within the meaning of section 154 of the Cr.P.C.[923]

961. Chapter VII of the DSA, 2018 while dealing with investigation of offences, provides that for investigation purposes, the provisions of the Cr.P.C. shall be applicable. Besides, the DSA stipulates that if it appears at the beginning of the case or at any stage of investigation that to form an investigation team is necessary for fair investigation, then the Tribunal or the Government may, by order, form a joint investigation team comprising of the investigation agency, the law and order enforcement force and the agency under the control of such authority or agency and on such condition as may be referred to in the order.[924] An investigation officer of such offences needs to complete the investigation within sixty days from the date of getting charge of investigation of an offence and can get an extension of fifteen days with the approval of his controlling officer, another thirty days with the permission of the tribunal and for another reasonable period of time with the approval of the tribunal.[925]

962. The DSA, 2018 authorizes the investigation officer to take assistance from any specialist or any specialized organization while conducting investigation under this Act. Generally, an investigation officer can:

(a) take under his own custody any computer, computer programme, computer system, computer network or any digital device, digital system, digital network or any programme, data information which has been saved in any computer or compact disc or removable drive or by any other means;
(b) take necessary initiatives to collect data information of traffic data from any person or agency;
(c) take such other steps as may be necessary for carrying out the purposes of this Act.[926]

963. During the investigation, the investigation officer may request information from any person, entity or service provider and they are bound to provide the requested information and necessary assistance to the investigation officer.[927] Besides, they need to further maintain the secrecy of information related to the investigation.[928] Moreover, if the Director-General, *suo moto*, or upon an application of the Investigation Officer, believes that it is necessary to preserve any data information saved in a computer for the interest of an investigation, and there is the

---

923. *Mohammod Hossain, Advocate v. Quamrul Islam Siddique, Secretary, Ministry of Housing and Public Works, Bangladesh Secretariat, Dhaka and others*, 2001, 30 CLC (HCD) [3983].
924. Section 39(2), the Digital Security Act, 2018 (Act No. 46 of 2018).
925. Section 40, the Digital Security Act, 2018 (Act No. 46 of 2018).
926. Section 41, the Digital Security Act, 2018 (Act No. 46 of 2018).
927. Section 46, the Digital Security Act, 2018 (Act No. 46 of 2018).
928. Section 47, the Digital Security Act, 2018 (Act No. 46 of 2018).

possibility to damage, destroy or change the data information or to make unavailable, then he may require the person or institution in charge of the computer or computer system to preserve such data information up to 90 days, and with the approval of the tribunal for a period of maximum 180 days in aggregate.[929] However, during the investigation, the legal use of a computer, computer system, computer network or any part cannot be hampered.[930]

§4. Search and Seizure During Investigation

964. The general procedure of search and seizure, which is mandatory to follow in a criminal case, is mentioned in sections 102 and 103 of the Cr.P.C. In simple terms, the law provides that search is to be made in the presence of two or more witnesses who are respectable inhabitants of the locality and a list of all things seized in the course of such search should be prepared and signed by the witnesses.[931] However, when it is required to search a woman, the search shall be made by another woman, with strict regard to decency.[932] Besides, the police must follow Regulation No. 280 of the Bengal Police Regulations.[933] Any search and seizure without strictly following these provisions of the law will be held illegal.[934]

965. It is to be noted that strict non-compliance of section 103 of the Code to search and seizure of illegal substance either from a person or any place will, nevertheless, not render the case unbelievable.[935] Accordingly, if the accused admits of his offence and goods are seized from his possession, then the provisions of sections 103 and 165 Cr.P.C. are of little relevance.[936] A proceeding cannot be quashed depending on the alleged procedural error in the method of collection of evidence to be adduced and used.[937] Recording of a statement of an accused beyond the period of office hours cannot be a plea to hold that the said statement is not true and voluntary. If it is found that the same statement was recorded by the concerned Magistrate having complied with all the provisions of law, then there is no room to say that the said statement is not true and voluntary.[938]

966. The provisions of section 103 Cr.P.C. are designed to create a safeguard against possible chicanery and concoction on the part of the Investigating Officer, and it is obligatory on the officer about to execute a search warrant to call on and

929. Section 44, the Digital Security Act, 2018 (Act No. 46 of 2018).
930. Section 45, the Digital Security Act, 2018 (Act No. 46 of 2018).
931. Section 103, the Code of Criminal Procedure, 1898 (Act No. V of 1898).
932. Section 52, the Code of Criminal Procedure, 1898 (Act No. V of 1898).
933. *Md. Zulfiqure Ali alias Kazal v. The State,* 15 BLD (HCD) 570.
934. *Md. Moklesur Rahman and another v. The State*, 14 BLD (HCD) 126; *Md. Faruque Hossain and 2 others v. The State*, 15 BLD (HCD) 162; *Habibur Rahman alias Jane Alam v. The State*, 15BLD(HCD) 129.
935. *State & ors v. Md. Saiful Islam & ors*, 4 SCOB [2015] HCD 61.
936. *Kamruzzaman alias Babul Sikdar v. The State*, 15BLD(HCD) 486.
937. *Anti-Corruption Commission v. Md. Rezaul Kabir & ors.*, 8 SCOB [2016] AD, 146.
938. *State & ors v. Mufti A. Hannan & ors.*, 9 SCOB[2017]HCD 52.

get two or more respectable inhabitants of the locality to witness the search to ensure that the search is conducted honestly.[939]

967. Sections 42 and 43 of the DSA, 2018 deal with search and seizure by warrant, and search, seizure and arrest without warrant respectively. A police officer, if has reasons to believe that: (a) any offence has been committed or is likely to be committed under this Act; or (b) any computer, computer system, computer network, data information related to an offence committed under this Act, or any evidence thereof has been preserved in any place or to a person, then he may, for reasons of such belief to be recorded in writing, obtain a search warrant upon an application to the Tribunal or the Chief Judicial Magistrate or the Chief Metropolitan Magistrate, as the case may be, and proceed with the following measures, namely: (i) taking possession of the data information of traffic data under the possession of any service provider; (ii) creating obstruction, at any stage of communication, to any telegraph or electronic communication including recipient information and data information of traffic data.[940]

968. The DSA, 2018 further provides that if any police officer has reasons to believe that an offence under this Act has been or is being committed, or is likely to be committed in any place, or any evidence is likely to be lost, destroyed, deleted or altered or made unavailable in any way, then he may, for reasons of such belief to be recorded in writing, proceed with the following measures, namely: (a) to enter and search the place, and if obstructed, to take necessary measures in accordance with the Code of Criminal Procedure; (b) to seize the computer, computer system, computer network, data information or other materials used in committing the offence or any document supportive to prove the offence; (c) to search the body of any person present in the place; (d) to arrest any person present in the place if the person is suspected to have committed or be committing an offence under this Act. After all these, the police officer has to submit a report regarding search to the Tribunal.[941]

§5. Arrest and Detention

969. A police officer may also arrest and detain anyone on the grounds of 'credible information' and 'reasonable suspicion' under section 54 of the Cr.P.C. This provision has been being misused seriously over the years. As a result, the AD of the Supreme Court of Bangladesh shared some observations in *Bangladesh, represented by the Secretary, Ministry of Law, Justice and Parliamentary Affairs and others v. Bangladesh Legal Aid and Services Trust (BLAST)*, 8 SCOB [2016] AD 1. The observations of the SC are equally important and can be considered in dealing with the cases on digital security. The Court found that in clause 'First' of section 54, the expressions 'credible information' and 'reasonable suspicion', are so vague that

939. *Subodh Ranjan and others v. The State*, 13 BLD (HCD) 430.
940. Section 42, the Digital Security Act, 2018 (Act No. 46 of 2018).
941. Section 43, the Digital Security Act, 2018 (Act No. 46 of 2018).

there is a chance for misuse of the power by a police officer, and accordingly, 'a police officer while exercising such power, his satisfaction must be based upon definite facts and materials placed before him and basing upon which the officer must consider for himself before he takes any action. It will not be enough for him to arrest a person under this clause that there is a likelihood of cognizable offence being committed. Before arresting a person out of suspicion, the police officer must carry out an investigation on the basis of the facts and materials placed before him without unnecessary delay. If any police officer produces any suspected person in the exercise of the powers conferred by this clause, the Magistrate is required to be watchful that the police officer has arrested the person following the directions given ... by this [C]ourt'.[942]

970. The AD ruled that 'if the Magistrate finds that the police officer has abused his power, he shall at once release the accused person on bail. In the case of arresting of a female person in the exercise of this power, the police officer shall make all efforts to keep a lady constable present'. The AD observed that 'On the plea of terrorism we cannot give a blank cheque to the law enforcing agencies to transgressing the fundamental rights of the citizens of the country. It should be borne in mind that a terrorist does not lose his fundamental rights even after the commission of terrorist activities and there are laws for the punishment of his crime, but he should not be deprived of his precious rights preserved in the constitution.'[943]

971. In the same decision, the AD of Bangladesh Supreme Court formulated the following Guidelines for the Law Enforcement Agencies to be followed while taking initiatives to arrest an accused:

(i) A member law enforcement officer making the arrest of any person shall prepare a memorandum of arrest immediately after the arrest, and such officer shall obtain the signature of the arrestee with the date and time of arrest in the said memorandum.

(ii) A member law enforcement officer who arrests a person must intimate to the nearest relative of the arrestee and in the absence of his relative, to a friend to be suggested by the arrestee, as soon as practicable but not later than twelve hours of such arrest notifying the time and place of arrest and the place in custody.

(iii) An entry must be made in the diary as to the ground of arrest and name of the person who informed the law-enforcing officer to arrest the person or made the complaint along with his address and shall also disclose the names and particulars of the relative or the friend, as the case may be, to whom information, about the arrest and the particulars of the law-enforcing officer in whose custody the arrestee is staying.

942. *Bangladesh, represented by the Secretary, Ministry of Law, Justice and Parliamentary Affairs and others v. Bangladesh Legal Aid and Services Trust (BLAST)*, 8 SCOB [2016] AD 1.
943. *Ibid.*

(iv) Registration of a case against the arrested person is sine-qua-non for seeking the detention of the arrestee either to the law-enforcing officer's custody or in the judicial custody under section 167(2) of the Code.

(v) No law-enforcing officer shall arrest a person under section 54 of the Code for the purpose of detaining him under section 3 of the Special Powers Act, 1974.

(vi) A law-enforcing officer shall disclose his identity and if demanded, shall show his identity card to the person arrested and to the persons present at the time of the arrest.

(vii) If the law-enforcing officer finds any marks of injury on the person arrested, he shall record the reasons for such injury and shall take the person to the nearest hospital for treatment and shall obtain a certificate from the attending doctor.

(viii) If the person is not arrested from his residence or place of business, the law-enforcing officer shall inform the nearest relation of the person in writing within twelve hours of bringing the arrestee to the police station.

(ix) The law-enforcing officer shall allow the person arrested to consult a lawyer of his choice if he so desires or to meet any of his nearest relations.

(x) When any person is produced before the nearest Magistrate under section 61 of the Code, the law-enforcing officer shall state in his forwarding letter under section 167(1) of the Code as to why the investigation cannot be completed within twenty-four hours, why he considers that the accusation or the information against that person is well-founded. He shall also transmit a copy of the relevant entries in the case diary B.P. Form 38 to the Magistrate.[944]

972. Under the DSA, 2018, a police officer, during the search, if has reasons to believe that an offence under this Act has been or is being committed, can even arrest someone by recording the reasons for such belief in writing.[945]

§6. Trial of Offences

973. It is provided that the Cyber Tribunal as established under section 68 of the ICT Act, 2006 and recognized by the DSA, 2018, can only take the cognizance of any offence under the DSA if and when a police officer makes a report and such tribunal shall only try the offences committed under the DSA, 2018.[946] The DSA, 2018 simultaneously provides that the tribunal shall, while trying an offence under this law, follow the provisions of Chapter XXIII of the Code of Criminal Procedure, 1898 (section 265A–265L) which deals with the trial before the Courts of Sessions subject to being consistent with the provisions of this law.[947] Therefore, it will be relevant to share here these provisions briefly.

944. *Ibid.*
945. Section 43(1)(c), the Digital Security Act, 2018 (Act No. 46 of 2018).
946. Sections 48(1) and 49(1), the Digital Security Act, 2018 (Act No. 46 of 2018).
947. Section 48(2), the Digital Security Act, 2018 (Act No. 46 of 2018).

974. When the accused appears or is brought before the Court in pursuance of section 205C of Cr.P.C., the prosecutor shall open his case by describing the charge brought against the accused and stating by what evidence he proposes to prove the guilt of the accused.[948] If upon consideration of the record of the case and the documents submitted therewith, and after hearing the submissions of the accused and the prosecution in this behalf, the Court considers that there is no sufficient ground for proceeding against the accused, it shall discharge the accused and record the reasons for so doing.[949] However, if after such consideration and hearing, the Court is of the opinion that there is ground for presuming that the accused has committed an offence, it shall frame in writing a charge against the accused, read and explain to the accused and ask he pleads guilty of the offence charged or claims to be tried.[950]

975. If the accused pleads guilty, the Court after recording the plea may, in its discretion, convict him.[951] However, if the accused refuses to plead, or does not plead, or claims to be tried or is not convicted, the Court shall fix a date for the examination of witnesses, and may, on the application of the prosecution, issue any process for compelling the attendance of any witness or the production of any document or other thing.[952]

976. On the date so fixed, the Court will take all such evidence as may be produced in support of the prosecution and may, in its discretion, permit the cross-examination of any witness to be deferred until any other witness or witnesses have been examined or recall any witness for further cross-examination.[953] If, after taking the evidence for the prosecution, examining the accused and hearing the prosecution and the defence on the point, the Court considers that there is no evidence that the accused committed the offence, the Court shall record an order of acquittal.[954]

977. However, if the accused is not so acquitted, he shall be called upon to enter on his defence and adduce any evidence he may have in support thereof. If the accused puts in any written statement, the Court shall file it with the record. If the accused applies for the issue of any process for compelling the attendance of any witness or the production of any document or thing, the Court shall issue such process unless he considers for reasons to be recorded, that such application should be refused claiming it is made for vexation or delay or for defeating the ends of justice.[955]

978. When the examination of the witnesses (if any) for the defence is complete, the prosecutor shall sum up his case, and the accused or his pleader shall be

948. 265B, the Code of Criminal Procedure, 1898 (Act No. V of 1898).
949. 265C, the Code of Criminal Procedure, 1898 (Act No. V of 1898).
950. 265D, the Code of Criminal Procedure, 1898 (Act No. V of 1898).
951. 265E, the Code of Criminal Procedure, 1898 (Act No. V of 1898).
952. 265F, the Code of Criminal Procedure, 1898 (Act No. V of 1898).
953. 265G, the Code of Criminal Procedure, 1898 (Act No. V of 1898).
954. 265H, the Code of Criminal Procedure, 1898 (Act No. V of 1898).
955. 265 I, the Code of Criminal Procedure, 1898 (Act No. V of 1898).

entitled to reply. During this stage, the prosecution may make a submission if there is any law point is raised by the accused side.[956] Finally, after hearing arguments and points of law (if any), the Court shall give a judgment in the case.[957]

979. In a case where a previous conviction is charged, and the accused does not admit that he has been previously convicted as alleged in the charge, the Court may, after it has convicted the said accused, take evidence in respect of the alleged previous conviction, and shall record a finding thereon. However, no such charge shall be read out by the Court nor shall the accused be asked to plead thereto nor shall the previous conviction be referred to by the prosecution or in any evidence adduced by it unless and until the accused has been convicted.[958]

980. An aggrieved person can generally seek relief under the writ jurisdiction of the HCD of the Supreme Court of Bangladesh by filing a writ of mandamus and writ of certiorari under Article 102 of the Constitution. It is to be noted that the HCD, as the writ court, is also a Court of equity where the principles of natural justice, equity and good conscience shall be applied.[959] Nevertheless, where one who seeks equity must come with clean hands. The HCD cannot exercise its writ jurisdiction if the petitioner comes before the court with hands being unclean and dirty.[960] In the case of abuse, the HCD not only can turn down his petition but also penalize him.[961] It should also be considered that the power of the HCD to issue an appropriate writ is discretionary and the HCD in the exercise of its discretion does not ordinarily assist the tardy and the indolent of the acquiescent and lethargic. If there is an inordinate delay on the part of the petitioner in filing a Writ Petition and such delay is not satisfactorily explained, the HCD may decline to intervene and grant relief in the exercise of writ jurisdiction because it is likely to cause confusion and public inconvenience and bring in its train new injustice.[962] Moreover, relief can also be sought by filing criminal revisions against the orders for framing of charge by the Sessions Courts.

§7. Electronic Evidence

981. The Evidence Act, 1872 (Act No. I of 1872), the main law on evidence in Bangladesh, does not contain any specific provision on electronic evidence. However, section 87 of the ICT Act, 2006 provides that in the definition of 'document' in section 3 of the Evidence Act, 1872, the electronically created document will also be included. Besides, in section 58 of the Digital Security Act, 2018, it is explicitly

956. 265J, the Code of Criminal Procedure, 1898 (Act No. V of 1898).
957. *Ibid.*
958. 265L, the Code of Criminal Procedure, 1898 (Act No. V of 1898).
959. *Dr. Moazzem Hossain v. Bangladesh & ors*, 6 SCOB [2016] HCD 34.
960. *Md. Mahbubur Rahman v. Bangladesh & ors*, 10 SCOB [2018] HCD 104.
961. *Khademuzzaman v. Bangladesh & ors.*, 2 SCOB [2015] HCD 62.
962. *Msaharaf Hossain v. Dhaka City Corp. & others*, 2 SCOB [2015] HCD 70.

mentioned that if any forensic evidence is obtained or collected under the provisions of this Act, 2018, this will be treated as evidence in the trial proceedings notwithstanding anything contained in the Evidence Act, 1872. Besides, the status of electronic evidence has already been discussed earlier, and it was shared that the judges have the discretion to consider electronic evidence is admissible in the court of law in Bangladesh.

982. According to section 29 of the Penal Code, 1860 (XLV of 1860), the word 'document' denotes any matter expressed or described upon any substance by means of letters, figures, marks, or by more than one of those means, intended to be used, or which may be used, as evidence of that matter. It is further explained that it is immaterial by what means or upon what substance the letters, figures or marks are formed, or whether the evidence is intended for, or may be used in a Court of Justice, or not. Moreover, the Evidence Act, 1872 (Act No. I of 1872) shall also include the document generated or prepared by electronic machine or technology.

983. Certain domestic laws contain provisions about electronic evidence regarding documents. The list of such laws includes: *Druto Bichar Tribunal Ain*, 2002 (Act No. 28 of 2002) (the Speedy Trial Tribunal Act),[963] *Ain Sringkhola Bighnokari Aporadh Ain*, 2002 (Act No. 11 of 2002) (the Law and Order Violation Offence Act),[964] and the Pornography *Niyontron Ain*, 2012 (Act No. 9 of 2012) (the Pornography Control Act), etc.[965] Besides, the *Oporadh Shomporkito Bishoye Paroshparik Shohayota Ain*, 2012 (Act No. 4 of 2012) (the Mutual Legal Assistance in Criminal Matters Act), helps the foreign countries in investigating e-evidence in Bangladesh and vice versa.[966]

984. From a plain reading of section 16 of the *Druto Bichar Tribunal Ain*, 2002 (Act No. 28 of 2002), it is clear that video cassette or audio cassette or still picture about the occurrence of an offence is admissible in evidence.[967] Regarding mutual assistance in criminal matters, the court or any other competent authority may issue

963. Section 16 of the Act provides that if any police officer or law enforcement member or any other person makes videos or takes pictures or records the conversation or discussion about the commission or preparation or assistance of any crime in a tape record or disc, the video, picture or the tape or the disc shall be admissible as evidence in the speedy trial tribunal. However, the speedy trial tribunal cannot punish any accused solely based on such evidence. Thus, a plain reading of s. 16 of the Druto Bichar Tribunal Ain, 2002, it is clear that video cassette of audio cassette or still picture about the occurrence is admissible as evidence. *See State v. Yeasin Khan Palash*, 2007, 36 CLC (HCD) [8499] = 27 BLD (HCD) (2007) 469.

964. Section 14 of Act provides that if any police officer or law enforcement member or any other person makes videos or takes pictures or records the conversation or discussion about the commission or preparation or assistance of any crime in a tape record or disc, the video, picture or the tape or the disc shall be admissible as evidence in the speedy trial tribunal.

965. Under s. 6(2) of the Act, any softcopy, transformed hardcopy, CD, VCD, DVD, computer or any other device or accessories or part or instruments, any memory or information stored electronically seized during the investigation can be used as evidence in a court of law.

966. Chapter III, the Mutual Legal Assistance in Criminal Matters Act, 2012 (Act No. 4 of 2012).

967. *State v. Yeasin Khan Palash*, 2007, 36 CLC (HCD) [8499] = 27 BLD (HCD) (2007) 469.

an order that the testimony or statement, the identification of a person or thing or any other form of assistance may be provided by the use of video or audio transmission technology.[968]

985. Under Rule 44 of the International Crimes Tribunal Rules of Procedure, 2010, the Tribunal has the discretion to admit any evidence oral or documentary, print or electronic including books, reports and photographs published in newspapers, periodicals, and magazines, films and tape recording and other materials as may be tendered before it and it may exclude any evidence which does not inspire any confidence in it, and admission or non-admission of evidence by the Tribunal is final and cannot be challenged.[969]

986. It is settled principles that where the inference of guilt of an accused is to be drawn from circumstantial evidence only, those circumstances must, in the first place, be cogently established. Further, those circumstances should be of a definite tendency pointing towards the guilt of the accused, and in their totality, must unerringly lead to the conclusion that within all human probability, the offence was committed by the accused excluding any other hypotheses.[970]

987. In *Mrs Khaleda Akhter v. The State* (1985), 5 BLD (HCD) 303, it was held that 'Video cassette is a document within the meaning of the Evidence Act and accordingly is admissible in evidence in judicial proceedings whenever relevant in the like manner as the tape record and its sound and voice.'

988. It will be very timely to share here that in the recently concluded lower court trial in the sensational Nusrat murder case, the Judge used the video testimony of the deceased Nusrat as a dying declaration and used this to reach the conclusion where a total of sixteen accused were awarded death penalty.[971] Moreover, the domestic courts have started to use IMEI as evidence in deciding cases.[972]

989. The recently formulated Digital Security Rules, 2020 contain some provisions on electronic evidence.

---

968. Section 28, the Mutual Legal Assistance in Criminal Matters Act, 2012 (Act No. 4 of 2012).
969. In *Salauddin Qader Chowdhury v. Chief Prosecutor, International Crimes Tribunal, Dhaka, Bangladesh*, 2015, 44 CLC (AD) [9568] = 67 DLR (AD) (2015) 295, it was reported that the Tribunal has discarded some of the evidences on the basis of this provision.
970. *Haji Mahmud Ali Londoni & anr v. State & anr.*, 5 SCOB [2015] AD 102, at p. 107.
971. Mahmud, F., *Nusrat Jahan Rafi Case: Bangladesh Court Due to Deliver Verdict* (24 Oct. 2019), https://www.aljazeera.com/news/2019/10/nusrat-jahan-rafi-case-bangladesh-court-due-deliver-verdict-191023193050731.html.
972. *The State v. Md. Foysal Bin Nayem @ Dip and another* 2017 (2) LNJ 239; *State v. Oli*, 2019 [Death Reference No. 61 of 2011].

§8. BURDEN OF PROOF

990. The fundamental principle of a criminal trial as practised in Bangladesh is that an accused shall be presumed to be innocent until proved guilty and he is not required to adduce any evidence to prove his innocence, and the entire burden of proof of his guilt lies on the prosecution alone.[973] It is always the burden of the prosecution to prove its case beyond reasonable doubts, and this burden never shifts.[974] Moreover, although the law does not require a particular number of witnesses to prove a case, the rule of prudence requires corroboration of a solitary witness.[975]

991. Under Chapter VII (sections 101–114) of the Evidence Act, 1872 (Act No. I of 1872), the prosecution has the burden or responsibility to prove the guilt of the accused beyond all reasonable doubts. Thus, the accused shall be presumed to be innocent until he is found guilty, and the allegation brought against him is proved.[976] The prosecution must prove every link in a chain of evidence as well as every ingredient of the offence beyond reasonable doubts.[977] In a civil proceeding, both parties have a responsibility to prove their respective cases. Although the onus rests upon the plaintiff and to prove his case, the responsibility of the defendant is also there to substantiate his written statement's assertion as per section 103 of the Evidence Act, 1872.[978]

992. Mere knowledge of an accused or his equivocal disclosure about the existence of illegal substance during his police custody shall not expose him to any criminal liability of possessing or controlling that illegal substance.[979] Commission of crime can be proved by circumstantial evidence. Circumstantial evidence is more cogent and convincing than ocular evidence. It is correctly said that witnesses may tell a lie and it is not difficult to procure false tutored and biased witnesses, but it is very difficult to procure circumstantial evidence.[980] Whenever it is noticed that all the mandatory legal formalities in recording the confessional statement are duly observed, and the Magistrate who recorded the confessional statement is satisfied that the confession is voluntary and free from all taint, then, in that case, such confession can be the sole basis of conviction of the confessing accused.[981]

973. *Muslimuddin and others v. The State*, 7 BLD (AD) 1.
974. *Dabir Talukder v. The State* 12 BLD (HCD) 429; *Kawsarun Nessa and another v. The State*, 15 BLD(HCD) 21.
975. *Muslimuddin and others v. The State*, 7 BLD (AD) 1.
976. *Kazi Ibrahim alias Ibrahim Kazi v. The State*, 11 BLD (HCD) 423; *Dabir Talukder v. The State*, 12 BLD (HCD) 429.
977. *Md. Nasir alias Nasir v. The State*, 9 BLD (HCD) 502.
978. *Hayetullah & ors. v. Abdul Khaleque & ors.*, 10 SCOB [2018] HCD 309.
979. *Afangir @ Kulu v. The State*, 7 SCOB [2016] HCD 161.
980. *Md. Forhad Hossain Sheikh v. The State*, 4 SCOB [2015] HCD 102.
981. *State & ors v. Md. Sukur Ali & ors.*, 9 SCOB[2017]HCD 18.

§9. Intention in Crime

993. Like any other crime, the presence of criminal intention or guilty knowledge in the commission of the cybercrime is crucial to hold someone guilty of an offence. It is the responsibility or burden of the prosecution to prove the guilty mind of someone arrested on the charge of crime. Therefore, it will be necessary to have some discussion on 'criminal intention' in the context of Bangladesh. Though section 34 of the Penal Code, 1860 (XLV of 1860) while dealing with the principle of joint liability in respect of the commission of a crime with 'common intention' provides that when a criminal act is done by several persons, in furtherance of the common intention of all, each of such persons is liable for that act in the same manner as if it were done by him alone; the law has not defined the term 'intention'.

994. Intention is a question of fact and has to be gathered from the facts and circumstances of each case. There is no doubt that *mens rea* or criminal intention, which is the mental act of the accused persons, is required to be unearthed before declaring someone guilty of an offence. It is not always possible to prove guilty intention without the help of any evidence, oral or circumstantial, to be adduced by the prosecution during the course of the trial.[982]

995. In the landmark judgment which clarifies that the tenure of life imprisonment as a punishment as included in different penal statutes of Bangladesh mean thirty years, *Ataur Mridha and others v. State*, 2017 (2) LNJ (AD) 35, Surendra Kumar Sinha, CJ observed:

> It is true that intention is a question of fact but where intention is one of the essential elements of the offence, it is always necessary that there should be a definite finding as to whether the necessary guilty intention is or is not present. When a person has caused an injury on a vital organ of the victim the intent of killing can certainly be attributed to him. A person's intention can be gathered from his act, the nature of weapon and the manner of using the weapon. The court on assessment of the evidence comes to the conclusion that the offenders intent the natural consequence of their acts. The presumption that can be arrived at as regards the intention of the offender on consideration of the injury caused, the motive of the offender, the nature of the instrument used, the time and place of attack, the position and condition of the victim, the number of injuries, the causation of the act on the organ of the victim etc.

§10. Bail

996. A discussion on the issue of bail is important in criminal matters, and so it is in cybercrimes. The differences between bailable and non-bailable offences are already highlighted in the previous chapter where it was discussed that in bailable

982. *Moulana Motiur Rahman Nizami and another v. Anti-Corruption Commission and another*, 2011, 40 CLC (HCD) [8242] = 17 BLC (HCD) (2012) 1.

offences, an accused can claim bail as of right and even in non-bailable offences, an accused can be entitled to appeal for bail subject to the presence of some conditions and discretion of the magistrate.

997. It will be relevant to understand that someone or an interested party may file cases against another individual or group of people, and the whole process of investigation and trial may take a considerable amount of time since the courts of law in Bangladesh are overburdened with pending cases while a considerable number of new cases are registered every day. It has already been shared that the fundamental principle of criminal law, i.e., the accused is presumed to be innocent until proved guilty is followed in Bangladesh. Therefore, during this time, the accused person(s) should get the opportunity of getting bail subject to the fulfilment of some conditions imposed by the laws of the land. The Cr.P.C. has contained various provisions in the context of different circumstances on bail and incorporated a completed chapter, i.e., Chapter XXXIX (sections 496–502) on bail.

998. Bail is to set free or liberate a person arrested or imprisoned on taking security for his appearance. The basic conception of the word 'bail' means the release of a person from police custody and delivery unto the hands of a surety who undertakes to produce the accused in Court whenever required to do so.[983] Therefore, a person to be released on bail needs to be in some sort of confinement or custody or otherwise, it is not understood from what confinement or custody he would be released.[984] If there is reasonable ground to believe that an accused is guilty of a non-bailable offence punishable with death or imprisonment for life, then he shall not be released on bail.[985]

§11. Rules for Assessment of Punishment

999. The rules for assessment of punishment are contained in sections 71 and 72 of the Penal Code, 1860 and section 35 of the Cr.P.C. The Penal Code, 1860 provides the substantive law regulating the measure of punishment and does not affect the question of conviction, which relates to the province of the procedure. The court is given the discretion to pass sentences varying with the character of the offender and the circumstances aggravating or mitigating under which the offence is committed. The responsibility for determining the permissible range of sentences in each case remains with the court.[986]

1000. The way it has been interpreted, the word 'life' does not bear its normal linguistic meaning. In other words, a person sentenced to imprisonment for life does not necessarily spend his life in prison, although section 45 of the Penal Code

983. *Crown v. Khushi Md.* (1953) 5 DLR (FC) 143 (150).
984. *Abdus Samad & others v. State*, 1989, 18 CLC (HCD) [6304].
985. *Shaikh Shahidul Islam v. The State*, 13 BLD (AD) 190.
986. *Bangladesh Legal Aid and Services Trust (BLAST) and others v. Bangladesh, represented by the Secretary, Ministry of Home Affairs, Dhaka and others*, 2015, 44 CLC (AD) [9114].

defines 'Life' as the life of a human being unless the contrary appears from the context. The given interpretation has been arrived at with the aid of section 57 of the Penal Code, which provides that in calculating the fraction of terms of punishment, imprisonment for life shall be reckoned as equivalent to rigorous imprisonment for thirty years.[987] This last-mentioned section read with the relevant provision of the Jail Code effectively means that a person sentenced to imprisonment for life will be released after spending a maximum of twenty-two and a half years in prison. Under section 35A of the Code of Criminal Procedure, the period of time spent by the accused in custody during the pendency of the trial would be deducted from his total sentence. Thus, we find that in many serious murder cases, where the trial lasts for many years, the accused who is found guilty and sentenced to imprisonment for life gets released after serving a total of twenty-two years including the period spent in custody during the trial.[988]

§12. Extraterritorial Jurisdiction Issues

1001. In many cases, computer crimes involve attempts from outside Bangladesh. In the absence of any binding or hard international legal instrument on cybercrime and related matters, this is a genuine challenge for the countries to investigate crimes committed outside the country due to the principle of sovereignty and jurisdiction of the states under international law. Moreover, it is also difficult for law enforcement agencies to collect evidence since cybercrimes committed outside the national jurisdiction are organized crimes involving parties from different jurisdictions. Like most of the countries, in case of cybercrimes involving extraterritorial issues, the Bangladesh police generally consider utilizing one of the three available options: (a) use of provisions of the Extradition Act, 1974 (Act No. LVIII of 1974), (b) use of provisions of the Mutual Legal Assistance in Criminal Matters Act, 2012 (Act No. 4 of 2012), and (c) initiate informal police-to-police communications. Moreover, in some serious matters involving national security and interest such as the sensational BB cyberheist case, the government took the assistance of the International Criminal Police Organization.

1002. The Extradition Act, 1974 (Act No. LVIII of 1974) deals with the extradition of fugitive offenders. The government needs to execute a treaty in this regard though the extradition of fugitive offenders can also be done even without a treaty.[989] However, having a treaty in this regard help to foster the process. On the issue of 'reciprocal extradition of offenders' or 'transfer of sentenced persons', Bangladesh has an extradition treaty with only three countries, i.e., (a) Thailand, treaty signed in July 1998, (b) India, treaty signed in January 2013, and (c) the United Arab Emirates, treaty signed in October 2014.

987. *Rokia Begum v. The State*, 4 SCOB [2015] AD 20, at p. 25.
988. *Ibid.*
989. Section 4, the Extradition Act, 1974 (Act No. LVIII of 1974).

1003. Bangladesh has extradition relations with nine states in relation to corruption and money laundering matters. These countries are: Australia, Fiji, India, Malaysia, Papua New Guinea, Samoa, Singapore, Sri Lanka, and Vanuatu. Therefore, if it can be established that cybercrime was committed to committing corruption and money laundering related crimes, then this option can be considered. But the adequate technical soundness and expertise of human resources involved in the investigation process in cybercrimes pose the real challenges. As a result, even though the local newspapers report about some isolated incidents involving corruption and money laundering crimes where this process was followed; it is almost impossible to identify one single incident involving cybercrimes, other than the BB cyberheist, where the government could use this option.

1004. It may be relevant to share here that even in a case where a citizen of a foreign country intends to stay in Bangladesh and if the Government is satisfied that the extradition of such person is called for in order to maintain friendly relations of Bangladesh with foreign States, the Government can on the strength of section 3(i) and section 2(f)(ii) of the Special Powers Act, 1974 extradite such citizen to his own country in absence of any extradition treaty between the Government of Bangladesh and such foreign States.[990] The Government of Bangladesh used this process to extradite Anup Chetia to India in response to the right of India to demand the extradition of Anup Chetia.

1005. The Mutual Legal Assistance in Criminal Matters Act, 2012 (Act No. 4 of 2012) was enacted to make provisions for giving or receiving inter-states assistance in inquiry, prosecution, and judicial proceedings in relation to criminal matters including the matters for freezing and seizing of the proceeds of crime or terrorist property. The law has incorporated a very wide definition of 'criminal matters', which means enquiry, investigation, judicial or other proceedings in respect of the offences falling under the laws of Bangladesh and the requesting State and includes matters, namely: (a) to determine whether any property is proceeds of crime or instrumentalities of crime or terrorist property or is involved in money laundering; (b) a possible confiscation order, whether or not based on any criminal charge; (c) the freezing or seizure of proceeds of crime or instrumentalities of crime or terrorist property.[991]

1006. The law provides that if any request is made by a foreign State for assistance in any inquiry, investigation and in any judicial or other proceedings in respect of committing any offence and if the offence is punishable under the laws of that country, the best mutual assistance about the matter shall be given. It is immaterial if there is an agreement between Bangladesh and any other foreign State regarding mutual assistance in criminal matters or not. However, in the request letter, it shall be certified that if such assistance is asked for by Bangladesh to the requesting State, the State shall also reciprocally give such assistance.[992]

990. *Saiful Islam Dilder v. Govt. of Bangladesh and others*, 18 BLD (HCD) 615.
991. Section 2(1), the Mutual Legal Assistance in Criminal Matters Act, 2012 (Act No. 4 of 2012).
992. Section 8(1), the Mutual Legal Assistance in Criminal Matters Act, 2012 (Act No. 4 of 2012).

1007. In case of mutual assistance, issues such as (a) searching or identifying any person; (b) taking testimony or statements of any person; (c) issuing the process of any foreign court; (d) providing original or certified copies of documents, records and information regarding the relevant matter in which the banking, financial, corporate or commercial records shall also be included; (e) ensuring the availability of the arrested or any other person for giving assistance in any investigation or taking testimony; (f) enquiry and confiscation or arrest; and (g) any kinds of assistance not inconsistent with this Act which the concerned States are mutually agreed upon to provide with shall be included.[993]

1008. Part 5 of the law (sections 28–30) deals with assistance relating to Computer Systems and Computer Data. Accordingly, if any foreign State requests for providing information relating to computer data and traffic data and if the matters relating thereto exist in Bangladesh, the Central Authority may issue an order to any person or organization for storing such data and rendering security.[994] With regard to the production of stored computer data, it is provided that upon request of a foreign State, the court or other competent authority may issue an order to produce, *inter alia*, (a) specific computer data in the possession or control of a person which is stored in a computer system or a computer data storage medium; and (b) subscriber information in the possession or control of a service provider, where such data or information is relevant to the criminal proceeding of the requesting State.[995]

1009. On the issue of search and seizure of computer data, upon request of a foreign State, the court or any other competent authority may issue a search warrant or any other order authorizing a person designated by it to search or otherwise access any computer system or part thereof as well as any computer storage medium in which computer data may be stored. An authorized person shall have the right to: (a) seize or otherwise secure a computer system or part thereof or a computer data storage medium; (b) make a copy of such computer data; (c) maintain the integrity of the relevant stored computer data; and (d) render inaccessible or remove those computer data in the accessed computer system.[996] Similar types of provisions on terrorist activities are also included within the provisions of the Anti-Terrorism Act, 2009 (Act No. 16 of 2009) and the Digital Security Act, 2018.[997]

1010. The scope of the Money Laundering Prevention Act, 2012 (Act No. 5 of 2012) is wide enough to cover money laundering offences that can include cybercrimes too. Under the law, 'money laundering' means, *inter alia*, (a) knowingly moving, converting, or transferring proceeds of crime or property involved in an offence for the following purposes: (i) concealing or disguising the illicit nature, source, location, ownership or control of the proceeds of crime; or (ii) assisting any

993. Section 8(3), the Mutual Legal Assistance in Criminal Matters Act, 2012 (Act No. 4 of 2012).
994. Section 28, the Mutual Legal Assistance in Criminal Matters Act, 2012 (Act No. 4 of 2012).
995. Section 29, the Mutual Legal Assistance in Criminal Matters Act, 2012 (Act No. 4 of 2012).
996. *Ibid.*
997. Section 38, the Anti-Terrorism Act, 2009 (Act No. 16 of 2009); s. 55, the Digital Security Act, 2018 (Act No. 46 of 2018).

person involved in the commission of the predicate offence to evade the legal consequences of such offence, (b) knowingly transferring or remitting the proceeds of crime to a foreign country or remitting or bringing them into Bangladesh from a foreign country with the intention of hiding or disguising its illegal source, and (c) participating in, associating with, conspiring, attempting, abetting, instigate or counsel to commit any offences.[998]

1011. Besides, 'predicate offence' is defined as the offences by committing which within or outside the country, the money or property derived from is laundered or attempt to be laundered. Some of these offences are: (i) counterfeiting deeds and documents; (ii) extortion; (iii) fraud; (iv) forgery; (v) illegal trade in stolen and other goods; (vi) kidnapping, illegal restrain and hostage-taking; (vii) murder, grievous physical injury; (viii) trafficking of women and children; (ix) black marketing; (x) smuggling of domestic and foreign currency; (xi) theft or robbery or dacoity or piracy or hijacking of aircraft; (xii) human trafficking; (xiii) tax-related offences; (xiv) infringement of IPRs; (xv) terrorism or financing in terrorist activities; (xvi) adulteration or the manufacture of goods through infringement of title; (xvii) sexual exploitation; (xviii) organized crime, and participation in organized criminal groups; and (xix) racketeering, etc. All these offences can be committed online and using ICT tools and thus, can be interpreted to be covered within the scope of this law.[999] The commission, abetment or conspiracy to commit these offences is a punishable offence under this law.[1000]

§13. Conclusion

1012. Due to several reasons common to most of the developing countries, Bangladesh could not harness the benefits of ICT in the 1990s and early 2000s. Nevertheless, it is recognized and acknowledged by the globally renowned organization that the country is in the right direction to be a country with very strong economic strength in the years to come. More and more positive stories are being added to the success list of the country. In one of the recent reports of UNCTAD, it was found that the country has set 'exemplary' foundations for a bridge over the digital divide and can be benefitted from an e-commerce boost after laying this foundation.[1001] It can be anticipated that the findings of UNCTAD will surely be revisited after the reporting of the recent shocking instances relating to e-commerce where due to the lack of adequate legal and regulatory frameworks and the improper implementation of the available ones, the consumers of the country had to suffer a lot.

1013. After successfully addressing the UN Millennium Development Goals, Bangladesh has signed the 2030 Agenda for Sustainable Development which has

998. Section 2(v), the Money Laundering Prevention Act, 2012 (Act No. 5 of 2012).
999. Section 2(cc), the Money Laundering Prevention Act, 2012 (Act No. 5 of 2012).
1000. Section 4, the Money Laundering Prevention Act, 2012 (Act No. 5 of 2012).
1001. UNCTAD, Bangladesh: Rapid eTrade Readiness Assessment, 2019.

recognized that the spread of information and communications technology and global interconnectedness has great potential to accelerate human progress, bridge the digital divides and develop knowledge societies. Various predictions by authoritative bodies reiterated that the future of Bangladesh is very prospective and bright. To transform these predictions into reality, there is no alternative to exploit IT and ITES.

1014. After the outbreak of the novel COVID-19 at the beginning of 2020, like most of the countries in the world, the policymakers of Bangladesh also had to initiate the e-judiciary system in the context of lockdown situations to break the chain of infections in the judicial ecosystem. A law titled the Use of Information-Technology by the Courts, 2020 (Act No. 11 of 2020) was enacted in July 2020 in this regard to ensure the use of information technology in the virtual presence of the parties in the trial, judicial inquiry, or hearing of an application or appeal, or the taking of evidence, or arguments, or the delivery of an order or judgment. Accordingly, some selected judicial activities were conducted virtually for some time, and since December 2021, the judiciary decided to back to physical court systems due to various constraints, most notably for the lack of adequate and conducive infrastructure required.

1015. Secured cyberspace is not a matter of one day or time; rather, initiatives need to be taken and to be revised with the passage of time. A political consensus at the national level on important aspects realizing the everlasting effects and consequences of this sector is a must. A comprehensive cyber law regime developed based on international best practices coupled with the scope of mutual cooperation and considering the socio-economic indicators of the country together with updated technological solutions, continuous training of the stakeholders and adoption of regular programs aiming at creating the awareness of mass people can make the dream of the policymakers to turn the country into a developed one come true.

Selected Bibliography

Ananya, R. 'Public Access ICT in Bangladesh'. In *Libraries, Telecentres, Cybercafes and Public Access to ICT: International Comparisons: International Comparisons* Gómez, R. ed., IGI Global, Hershey, Pennsylvania, US, 2011, 249–266.

Asiatic Society of Bangladesh, Banglapedia: National Encyclopaedia of Bangladesh, 2007.

Khondker, B.H. & S. Nowshin. *Developing National Intellectual Property Policy for Bangladesh: An Assessment of National Intellectual Property System* (DRAFT). October 2013, World Intellectual Property Organization.

Bhuiyan, S.H. 'Modernizing Bangladesh Public Administration Through E-governance: Benefits and Challenges'. *Government Information Quarterly* 28, no. 1 (2011): 54–65.

Bhuiyan, S.H. 'Public Sector eService Development in Bangladesh: Status, Prospects and Challenges'. *Electronic Journal of e-Government* 9, no. 1 (2011): 15.

Hasan, S. 'ICT Policies and Their Role in Governance: The Case of Bangladesh'. *Science, Technology and Society* 19, no. 3 (2014): 363–381.

Islam, M.M., H. Rashid & M.G.R. Alam. 'Secure Electronic Payment: Proposed Method for the Growth of E-commerce in Bangladesh'. *Asian Business Review* 5 no. 2 (2015): 89–96.

Islam, M.S. & Å. Grönlund. 'The Bangladesh National Biometric Database: A Transferable Success?'. In *International Conference on Electronic Government and the Information Systems Perspective* Kim Normann Andersen, Enrico Francesconi, Åke Grönlund & Tom M. van Engers eds, Springer, Berlin, Heidelberg, 2010 August, 189–203.

Karim, Md.E. 'Citizen's Right to Privacy: Reflection in the International Instruments and National Laws'. *Bangladesh Journal of Law* 9, nos 1 & 2 (2005): 35–65.

Murphy, G. 'How Legislation Is Drafted and Enacted in Bangladesh'. *Statute Law Review* 27, no. 3 (2006): 133–149.

Kundu, S., et al. 'Cyber Crime Trend in Bangladesh, an Analysis and Ways Out to Combat the Threat'. 2018 20th International Conference on Advanced Communication Technology (ICACT), Chuncheon-si Gangwon-do, Korea (South), 2018, 474–480.

Samarajiva, R. & A. Zainudeen eds. *ICT Infrastructure in Emerging Asia: Policy and Regulatory Roadblocks*. IDRC, New Delhi, 2008.

Selected Bibliography

Siddik, M.N.A., et al. 'Impacts of e-banking on Performance of Banks in a Developing Economy: Empirical Evidence from Bangladesh'. *Journal of Business Economics and Management* 17 no. 6 (2016): 1066–1080.

Yusuf, M.A., A. Quamrul & C. Ken. 'The Mobile Phone Market in Bangladesh: Competition Matters'. *Journal of Asian and African Studies* 45, no. 6 (2010): 610–627.

Index

The numbers here refer to paragraph numbers.

Index

Index

www.ingramcontent.com/pod-product-compliance
Ingram Content Group UK Ltd.
Pitfield, Milton Keynes, MK11 3LW, UK
UKHW020132290926
15471UKWH00003B/437

9 789403 545400